中国数字市场背景下
中西方知名企业的社交媒体营销表现

The social media performance of high profile Chinese and Western companies in the context of Chinese digital market

He Xia | 何　霞　著

西南财经大学出版社
Southwestern University of Finance & Economics Press
中国 · 成都

图书在版编目(CIP)数据

中国数字市场背景下中西方知名企业的社交媒体营销表现=The social media performance of high profile Chinese and Western companies in the context of Chinese digital market/何霞著.—成都:西南财经大学出版社,2021.12
ISBN 978-7-5504-5122-3

Ⅰ.①中… Ⅱ.①何… Ⅲ.①网络营销—研究—中国 Ⅳ.①F724.6

中国版本图书馆 CIP 数据核字(2021)第 210908 号

中国数字市场背景下中西方知名企业的社交媒体营销表现
(The social media performance of high profile Chinese and Western companies in the context of Chinese digital market)
Zhongguo Shuzi Shichang Beijing xia Zhongxifang Zhiming Qiye de Shejiao Meiti Yingxiao Biaoxian
何霞 著

责任编辑:廖韧 李思嘉
责任校对:李琼
封面设计:墨创文化
责任印制:朱曼丽

出版发行	西南财经大学出版社(四川省成都市光华村街 55 号)
网　　址	http://cbs.swufe.edu.cn
电子邮件	bookcj@swufe.edu.cn
邮政编码	610074
电　　话	028-87353785
照　　排	四川胜翔数码印务设计有限公司
印　　刷	四川煤田地质制图印刷厂
成品尺寸	170mm×240mm
印　　张	18.25
字　　数	437 千字
版　　次	2021 年 12 月第 1 版
印　　次	2021 年 12 月第 1 次印刷
书　　号	ISBN 978-7-5504-5122-3
定　　价	98.00 元

Stay Hungry. Stay Foolish.

Steve Jobs

Preliminary notes

It shall be noted hereby that the sections including Section 2. 1 Selection of Chinese social media platforms and Section 3. 1 Context of Chinese social media marketing have been extracted from the previously published paper "Chinese social media strategies: Communication key features from a business perspective" published by He X., & Pedraza-Jiménez R. (2015) in the journal *El Profesional de La Información*, 24(2), 200-210.

Abbreviations

AIDMA	Attention, Interest, Desire, Memory, Action
AISAS	Attention, Interest, Search, Action, Share
API	Application Programming Interface
CNNIC	China Internet Network Information Center
eWOM	Electronic Word-of-Mouth
GT	Grounded Theory
HCA	Hierarchical Cluster Analysis
IA	Information Architecture
ISMAS	Interest, Search, Mouth, Action, Share
KPIs	Key Performance Indicators
O2O	Online-to-Offline & Offline-to-Online
ROI	Return on Investment
SMM	Social Media Marketing

Table of contents

1 INTRODUCTION

1.1 Motivation and the context of the investigation

On one day in autumn of 2011, David, my classmate from a language exchange center, came to my desk and asked me, "Which social media platforms do you use in Spain?" I answered, "Mostly Facebook, Twitter, YouTube and also some Chinese social media tools." David is a business man and exports Spanish products to China. He resumed asking me, "Which Chinese social media tools? I want to promote our products via Chinese social media platforms because I prefer to initiate a social media campaign instead of running advertising on TV. But I know little about Chinese online tools and digital market." He looked very anxious to get the answer. At that moment, one idea flashed through my brain as if a voice was saying, "This will be the research topic that I will do one day." I found that David is just one representative of many Western marketers who have been trying to extend their business into Chinese market. In view of the influence of the popularity of digital marketing, the exploration of China's social media marketing is an important and challenging work for them. In fact, they not only face the unique Chinese social media landscape and sometimes they are "shocked" by the "dazzling" social platforms, but also they need to deal with this kind of question, "How to use properly social media applications with which they are unfamiliar so as to communicate effectively with users in China?"

There is no doubt that social media marketing has become increasingly important to all business. Marketers devote themselves to finding the right way to use social media and to formulate a suitable social media strategy for their brands and services. In an era of the global economy, it is very common that Western companies export their products to Asian market and vice versa. Due to the different cultures, social media platforms and digital consumers, it is difficult for multinational companies to launch an effective social media campaign in overseas markets. In Asian market, China is not only a large potential market, but also a special digital one. The uniqueness of Chinese social media ecosystem such as the localization of social media tools, the fragmentation of each kind of platforms and the diversity of digital users brings Occidental marketers big challenges. What's more, Chinese domestic companies also have to face challenges because they don't have much digital marketing experience, although they know Chinese social media channels better than Western companies①. In this sense, this study can provide some practical recommendations for companies that aim to run social media campaigns in China. Taking into account the motivation and the context of the investigation, the research questions and objectives of this research will be presented next.

1.2 Research questions and objectives

This research focuses on Chinese social media marketing involved by both Chinese and Western companies. Some key elements such as companies, Chinese social media platforms, communicative strategies, and etc. have been considered in this study. The following research questions are raised surrounding these key elements.

1.2.1 Research questions

Research questions are answerable inquiries into specific concerns or issues in line with the research topic. Identifying research questions means that researchers have an idea about what they will study.

In this sense, selecting what kind of companies as research objects has a great impact on the results of this study as different samples usually lead to different results. Different types of companies bear distinct characteristics, namely, the size of the company, industry, market visibility and so on. For example, large-size companies' social media strategies are generally different from those of small-size ones. In line with this consideration, the first research question arises.

---

① In this research, Western companies denotes American companies and European companies.

RQ1: Which companies should be selected in this research? What is the selection criterion?

As mentioned before, this research needs to integrate the selected companies with Chinese social media platforms so as to explore Chinese social media marketing. Therefore, the selected companies are just one part of the research objects. Another part shall be the selected social media channels. The most popular and consolidated Chinese social media platforms can be chosen as the research objects of this research. Thus, the second question comes along:

RQ2: Which Chinese social media platforms should be studied in this research?

In order to explore the performances of all selected companies' social media marketing on each selected platform, an appropriate evaluation system shall be established. Thus, here appears the third question.

RQ3: How to measure/evaluate the performances of all chosen companies' efforts on each selected social media platform? Is it possible to create a systematic measurement framework for this purpose?

In line with the established evaluation system, a series of findings and results can be dug out. It will be helpful to draw some general conclusions and give practical recommendations. Then the fourth question is described below:

RQ4: How to classify all selected companies into different categories/groups? Is it possible to develop several sets of models based on the different performances on the selected platforms?

The fourth research question is an important one that needs to be answered because it involves parts of findings of the research. In addition, RQ4 also contains some derivative questions as follows:

RQ4-1: Which companies are identified as the most failed representatives in line with their social media performance on selected social media platforms?

RQ4-2: Which companies are identified as the most successful representatives in line with their social media performance on selected social media platforms?

RQ4-3: What are the key factors for the success of social media strategies on the selected platforms by analyzing the most successful representatives?

RQ4-4: What are the differences in social media strategies among all the selected companies due to their different geographical attributes (Occident/China)?

RQ4-5: What are the differences in social media strategies among all the selected companies due to their different industries?

1.2.2 Objectives

Research objectives can be clarified after defining a series of research questions. After all, they have a complementary relationship to explain the way in which such a question is going to be answered. The research objectives of this study come along while answering the research questions described above. In this section, general objective is first explained. And then specific objectives are addressed one by one.

General objective

This research focuses on Chinese digital market and aims to measure, evaluate and classify all selected companies' social media performances on the most popular platforms in a semi-macro scale via the establishment of a systematic measurement framework and through cross-case studies so as to identify the most successful representatives and the key factor for their success.

Specific objectives

(1) *Adopting an objective selection patterns including selection criteria and complex filtering steps so as to select a series of companies as research objects of this research. Meanwhile, the most popular Chinese social media are identified.*

With respect to RQ1 and RQ2, both Chinese companies and Western companies with certain selection criterion are selected as the research objects. Meanwhile, some important and popular Chinese social media platforms are identified as the research platforms under the corresponding criteria.

(2) *Proposing and using the evaluation framework from social media strategies perspective to measure all selected companies' performance on the selected platforms.*

In response to RQ3, the assessment framework is built in line with each platform's characteristic and function. In particular, some evaluation rules are common and useful for both platforms.

(3) *Presenting several sets of models to classify all selected companies into different categories in line with their social media performance on the selected platforms.*

Regarding to the answer of RQ4, several sub-objectives are also stated below.

(4) *Identifying the most successful representatives and the most failed representatives among all selected companies.*

(5) *Identifying and recommending key factor for the success of social media strate-*

gies on the selected platforms by analyzing the most successful representatives.

(6) *Demonstrating the differences in social media strategies among all the selected companies from two perspectives: geographical attributes and industries.*

1.3 Structure of the book

This book begins with chapter 1 as a general introduction of research motivations. Research questions and objectives are also presented. This study contains four principle research questions and five derivative questions derived from RQ4. Along with these research questions, research objectives come out including both general and specific objectives.

Chapter 2 presents the research objects. In this chapter, high reputation Occidental and Chinese companies are identified under certain criteria in this research. Meanwhile, this chapter highlights two most popular Chinese social media platforms which form another part of the research objects. In addition, historical roots of Chinese social media and the main social media tools are also addressed in this chapter.

Chapter 3 addresses state of the art and theoretical framework. On one hand, state of the art introduces the context of Chinese social media marketing including the description of Chinese digital consumers' profiles, discussing the predominant uses of Chinese social media marketing such as cross-platforms communication, group buying, and mobile social media marketing by means of several case studies, and the challenges faced by Chinese and multinational companies. In addition, the characteristics of the selected platforms are also presented. On the other hand, theoretical framework including evolution of consumption behavior model from AIDMA (attention, interest, desire, memory, action), AISAS (attention, interest, search, action, share) to ISMAS (interest, search, mouth, action, share), O2O models (online-offline & offline-online), Electronic word-of-mouth (eWOM), and relationship marketing are stated respectively.

Chapter 4 mainly states the research methodologies. This research involves quantitative and qualitative approaches. Case study is firstly introduced with details. And then expert analysis containing grounded theory, key performance indicators (KPIs), information architecture principles are presented respectively. Afterwards, content analysis and statistical analysis methods are stated. It is worth mentioning that the implementation of each research approach in this research has also been explained aiming to resolve relevant questions and to obtain the appropriate objectives.

Chapter 5 and chapter 6 present the results of this research through two case studies. Firstly, the two case study procedures are presented individually in details through a series of analyses with the methodologies described in chapter 4. Of importance, a systematic measurement and classification framework is established to measure and classify the selected companies' social media performance on chosen Chinese social media platforms. Secondly, some interesting results and findings are summarized by analyzing these two case studies. These results have a very important guiding significance for running Chinese social media campaigns.

In the end, the discussion and conclusion are stated in chapter 7. The analysis of cross-case studies is discussed and conducted by combining these two case studies. The corresponding findings have enriched this research because they have answered several derivative questions of RQ4. The conclusions cover not only the results described in two case studies, but also research methodologies and other findings from the rest parts of this research. It is necessary to point out that in this chapter, some useful recommendations and advices are made for marketers to facilitate suitable and effective social media marketing strategies in China. Afterwards, the future work is discussed by considering the limitations of the research.

2 SELECTION OF RESEARCH OBJECTS

The purpose of this chapter is to explore the research objects of this study, and to answer research question RQ1 and RQ2. RQ1: Which companies should be selected in this research? What is the selection criterion? RQ2: Which Chinese social media platforms should be studied in this research?

2.1 Selection of Chinese social media platforms

In this section, the development history of Chinese social media is introduced. And then some main Chinese social media platforms with their Occidental counterparts are stated. Last but not least, the selection of social media platforms as the research objects in line with the certain selection criterion is conducted.

2.1.1 Chinese social media's historical roots

Popular global social media platforms such as Facebook, Twitter, and YouTube dominate the Occidental regions and several Asian countries. But most are inaccessible to the public in China. A brief summary of the history of Chinese social media is of importance to more fully understand the unique and complex Chinese social media landscape.

The first bulletin board system (BBS) was built in 1994 and Chinese netizens quickly began to engage within online forums and communities; one such example was the famous BBS "Xicihutong" (xici.net). At the beginning of the 1990s, computers were luxury products to the ordinary people of China — there were few Internet users.

The real Internet boom in China began with the emergence of instant messaging (IM) with QQ, which was launched by Tencent in 1999. Millions of young people started to chat with friends, or to make new friends, via the QQ platform, which was similar to ICQ (I seek you). BlogChina (blogchina.com), another revolutionary tool, was released in 2002 by founder Fangxingdong. In addition to IMing, Chinese netizens were enthusiastic about blogging, social network sites (SNS), microblogging platforms, and other social media applications. Relevant examples include the social networking service Kaixinwang (kaixin001.com) in 2008; the popular microblogging channel Sina Weibo (d.weibo.com) in 2009; the location-based service (LBS) Jiepang (jiepang.com) and group buying site Meituan (meituan.com) in 2010; and the mobile App WeChat platform (Weixin in China) in 2011.

Nowadays, Chinese digital users normally have several social media accounts and integrate blogging, SNS, microblogging, online photo sharing, and online video sharing. In fact, not only the normal Internet users, but also the professional news websites (for example: *People's Daily*) are accustomed to utilizing local social media applications to meet their needs (Lim, 2014). It shall be kept in mind that almost everyone has a QQ account in China and QQ is linked to Qzone (a social network similar to Facebook). Both QQ and Qzone belong to Tencent holdings. In this way, Qzone bears a significant user base. In general, Chinese social media ecosystem is very special and different from its counterpart of any other country in the world. In fact, these platforms "live" in more complicated competition and quick changing environment. It is normal that every type of social media platform has several "brands" which belong to different companies. All Chinese social media tools are designed and built by local corporations. Therefore, China's social media landscape has the following characteristics: unique, complex, fragmented, and local.

2.1.2 Main social media platforms in China

Currently, social media in China is experiencing impressive growth. It is worth mentioning that Chinese social media applications are not copies of their Western equivalents, but instead they are new creations that have been innovated to meet Chinese netizens' habits and behavior, even if they were initially built based on some functions and characteristics of their Western counterparts (Sullivan, 2014). Today, some Chinese social media innovations are even leading the global trend of social media development. For example, Wechat (similar to WhatsApp) offers multiple features such as voice and text messaging, shaking the handset to look for friends, as well as a social networking function with the name "WeChat Moments". The interesting features of this application have led some experts to consider it better than WhatsApp. Information about this leadership of Chinese platforms can be found even in the Spanish newspaper *El Pais* (Aldama, 2013). As a result, China is becoming one of the most active players in the social media world. Table 2.1 shows main Chinese social media platforms with their Occidental counterparts.

Table 2.1 Main Chinese social media platforms with their Occidental counterparts

Social media types	Chinese social media platforms	Occidental counterparts
Microblog	Sina Weibo	Twitter
Social Network Sites (SNS)	Qzone, WeChat Moments	Facebook
Video Sharing Sites	Youku, Bilibili	YouTube
Photo Sharing Sites	Xiaohongshu	Instagram
Instant Messaging (IM)	QQ, Wechat	Messenger, WhatsApp
Q&A	Zhihu, Baidu Zhidao	Quora
Wikis	Hudong Baike, Baidu Baike	Wikipedia
LBS	Tantan	Tinder

Modified after source: He & Pedraza-Jiménez, 2015.

The landscape of Chinese social media is continuously undergoing fast-paced changes and has become a rich and diverse ecosystem of social media.

2.1.3 The selected social media platforms in this research

In order to answer RQ2 — Which Chinese social media platforms should be studied in this research, **a selection criterion has been defined in this research, i.e., the most popular Chinese social media platforms in business applications.** For this purpose, the following analysis process has been conducted. Firstly, the main Chinese social media types are addressed. Secondly, the top social media platforms of each social media type are stated. Finally, the most popular social media channels in business application are identified as the research objects in this research.

CNNIC (China Internet Network Information Center) published a report entitled *Chinese social media users' behavior research* in July, 2014 (CNNIC, 2014d). According to the report, Instant Messaging, Social Network Sites and Microblog are the main social media types in China (seen in table 2. 2).

Table 2. 2 Coverage rate of the main Chinese social media types

No.	Types of applications	Coverage rate * /%
1	IM	89. 3
2	SNS	61. 7
3	Microblog	43. 6

Source: Chinese social media users' behavior research report published by CNNIC, 2014d.

Notes: * denotes "the percentage of users who used one type of social media applications of the overall users".

Table 2. 2 shows that IM has been the most commonly used by the Chinese Internet users. According to Chinese Internet user's usage behavior and habit, SNS and Microblog are also frequently used by Internet users in China.

Instant Messaging

In line with table 2. 3, the top three popular IM tools are QQ, WeChat and Alitalk in China. It is worth mentioning that QQ and WeChat belong to the same company, Tencent holdings. As mentioned in section 2. 1. 1, QQ drove the real Internet boom in China. What's more, it has gone through a long period of development since it was launched by Tencent in 1999. Based on the two factors noted above, QQ has a huge database and vast users.

Table 2. 3 Penetration rate of IM tools in China

No.	IM tools	Penetration rate/%	Frequent access rate/%
1	QQ	77.8	72. 5
2	WeChat	65. 0	55. 3
3	Alitalk	20. 7	9. 2
4	YY/YY Live	14.8	6.9

Table 2. 3(Continued)

No.	IM tools	Penetration rate/%	Frequent access rate/%
5	Momo	10. 2	4.8

Source: Chinese social media users' behavior research report published by CNNIC, 2014d.

Microblog

As indicated in table 2. 4, the top three microblog platforms are Sina Weibo, Tencent Weibo, and Sohu Weibo. In particular, Sina Weibo is shown to be the most influential microblog platform in China. And many enterprises have been using Sina Weibo to engage with their customers, to do online promotions, and etc.

Table 2. 4 Penetration rate of Microblog in China

No.	Microblog	Penetration rate/%	Frequent access rate/%
1	Sina Weibo	28. 4	21. 7
2	Tencent weibo	27. 2	20. 1
3	Sohu weibo	6. 7	1. 1
4	Netease Weibo	5. 2	0.8

Source: Chinese social media users' behavior research report published by CNNIC, 2014d.

Social Network Sites

It can be seen from table 2. 5 that Qzone has a high penetration rate and frequent access rate which takes advantage of the big users' database of QQ. However, the landscape of SNS in China has undergone great changes in recent years in accordance with two factors: the popularity of smartphones and the development of WeChat application.

Table 2. 5 Penetration rate of SNS in China

No.	SNS	Penetration rate/%	Frequent access rate/%
1	Qzone	57. 3	54. 0
2	Renren.com	16. 4	2. 7
3	Pengyou.com	14.8	1. 1
4	Kaixin001.com	10. 2	0.9
5	Douban.com	9. 3	1. 5

Source: Chinese social media users' behavior research report published by CNNIC, 2014d.

After the smartphone occupying the market, Chinese Internet users prefer mobile phones to access the Internet more than other devices such as desktop, laptop, and tablet in recent years. Up to June of 2016, 92. 5% of Chinese digital users accessed the Internet via mobile phones, which has increased 2. 4% from the end of 2015. On the contrary, the proportion of Chinese Internet users using desktops, laptops and tablets to access the Internet are 64. 6%, 38. 5% and 30. 6% respectively, decreased by 3. 1%, 0. 2% and 0.9% from the end of 2015 respectively (CNNIC, 2016b).

With the rapid development of usage of mobile phones to access the Internet, WeChat, the mobile-oriented social media application, the number of its users has increased significantly. WeChat Moments, as one function of WeChat platform, has been playing an important role of social networking sites and become the most popular SNS in China in line with the report published by CNNIC (2016b) as shown in table 2. 6.

Table 2. 6 Usage rate of typical SNS in China

No.	SNS	Usage rate/%
1	WeChat Moments	78. 7
2	Qzone	67. 4
3	Pengyou.com	13. 1
4	Renren.com	11. 4
5	Douban.com	11. 1

Source: The 38th statistical report on Internet development in China published by CNNIC, 2016b.

In China, social network sites, as an important social media application, not only plays the role of disseminating information, but also plays the role of commerce applications for corporations. In this sense, WeChat Moments is one of the most successful cases. With the help of the huge user database of QQ and due to the fact that WeChat belongs to Tencent holdings, it is very easy to help WeChat users to form an even stronger social relationship chain by interacting with QQ, and thus results in a huge number of WeChat users.

Summary of the most popular social media platforms in China

Based on the previous analyses (shown in table 2. 2-table 2. 6), the popular Chinese social media platforms can be summarized and presented in table 2. 7. QQ and WeChat are the main IM tools. WeChat Moments and Qzone are the most popular SNS in China. It is necessary to point out that WeChat Moments and Qzone are one function of WeChat and QQ respectively and they both belong to the same company — Tencent holdings. Sina Weibo and Tencent Weibo are the most important microblogging platforms in China.

Table 2.7 Popular social media platforms in China

IM tools		SNS		Microblog	
QQ		WeChat Moments		Sina Weibo	
WeChat		Qzone		Tencent Weibo	
Alitalk		Pengyou.com		Sohu Weibo	
YY / YY Live		Renren.com		Netease Weibo	
Momo		Douban.com			
		Kaixin001.com			

In general, QQ, WeChat, and Sina Weibo are the most popular social media platforms in China. QQ and WeChat have different features and product orientation, even though they belong to the same company. QQ has a longer development history than WeChat, the former was born in 1999, and the latter was launched in 2011. QQ is basically designed as a desktop messenger. On the contrary, WeChat is mainly mobile-oriented messenger. QQ has younger users than WeChat, and they use it for chatting with friends. Sullivan (2012) stated that QQ application holds a lot of lower income digital users. WeChat has WeChat Payment and other features for business. What's more, with the rapid development of smartphones, new mobile media through mobile devices have changed greatly individuals' way of living, consuming and socializing, as well as the marketing strategies of enterprises. Under these circumstances, WeChat has now been used by a large number of business enterprises as a marketing channel to reach targeted consumers, sell products, send out newsletters, and etc. Under such a background, WeChat is more popular than QQ in business application. According to the research objective, WeChat is more suitable for the research object in this research.

Therefore, **Sina Weibo and WeChat are selected as the research platforms in this research**, which are deemed to be currently the most popular and important social media channels in China from a business perspective.

2.2 Selection of research companies

In this section, a series of companies with some common characteristics are selected as research objects. Any selection of research behavior should follow certain selection criteria such as the ranking in the field, building some measuring indicators and so on. **In this study, reputation is chosen as the principal criteria to select the relevant companies as the research objects.** The research aims to find some representative Chinese companies and Western companies from different industries which have high reputations in their fields.

As for the definition of reputation, different versions are listed below:

(1) Fombrun and van Riel (1997) defined reputation as "*a collective representation of a firm's past actions and results that describes the firm's ability to deliver valued outcomes to multiple stakeholders*".

(2) Barnett et al. (2006) defined reputation as "*observers' collective judgments of a corporation based on assessments of the financial, social, and environmental impacts attributed to the corporation over time*".

(3) Walker (2010) understood reputation as "*an accumulated opinion about the enterprise, formulated by such a group of stakeholders as: customers, business partners, investors, employees, public administration, local society and total society, on the grounds of perception and evaluation of the various aspects of its activity*".

(4) Lange et al. (2011) considered reputation as a three-pronged conceptualization, which contains the following three key features: ①being known; ②being known for something; ③generalized favorability.

As studied by Decyk (2015), 22% of the total market capitalization of *Standard & Poor's* 500 is represented by reputation's asset value and this strongly proves that reputation is one of the cores of organizational value. Moreover, Szwajca (2016) stated that reputation has been considered as one of the most valuable intangible resources of a company.

Positive reputation can bring strong returns. According to Fombrun and Shanley (1990), enterprises with a high reputation are potentially more competitive than those with a low reputation.

From the point view of sales, positive reputations are the implication of a higher "willingness to pay" by customers, which may thus affect positively the spending and share of wallet, and finally yield purchase intention (Yoon et al., 1993; Graham et al., 2007; Walsh et al., 2012). In addition, as explained by Gatzert and Schmit (2016), a positive corporate reputation can produce positive stakeholders' and customers' behavior.

On the other hand, high reputations are related with positive customer loyalty and word of mouth (Walsh et al., 2009, 2012).

Considering the importance of reputation, many companies believe more and more that it is necessary to assess and measure their reputations in order to compare it with the competitors' reputation (Kitchen et al., 2003). For this purpose, reputation indexes have been the basis for the rankings of the most admired enterprises (Fombrun, 2007).

So which resource can provide the most authoritative reputation indexes of the most worldwide famous companies?

After comparing some database, magazine, websites such as Alexa, Factiva, *FORTUNE* and Nielsen, it can be found that Alexa focuses on websites ranking according to category and country. Nielsen can support many useful reports. Factiva, a useful database, makes the rank in line with their sales or employees or market Cap which means Factiva focuses on finance or revenue. However, as stated before, the selection criterion of this research is reputation not revenue or financial strength of companies.

The magazine *FORTUNE* is best known for fortune global 500, a ranking of companies by revenue which is similar to Factiva. In addition, every year *FORTUNE* releases the Word's Most Admired Companies in line with the selection criteria: innovation, social responsibility, people management, product quality, and etc. which together means corporate reputations. *FORTUNE CHINA*, Chinese version of *FORTUNE* magazine, also does the same work and publishes the Chinese Most Admired Companies every year.

Szwajca (2016) stated that *FORTUNE* magazine is the longest traditional reference of reputation measurement and has been publishing the rankings of the most admired world-wide enterprises since 1983 based on the collected opinions from the executives of the highest management levels and financial analysts. These opinions focus mainly on the following nine enterprise activities: ①innovation; ②long term investment; ③quality of management; ④ social responsibility; ⑤ products / services quality; ⑥people management; ⑦financial soundness; ⑧use of corporate assets; ⑨global competitiveness.

So *FORTUNE* ranking of the Word's Most Admired Companies is appropriate to give a reputation index of the most worldwide famous companies.

2.2.1 High reputation Western companies

FORTUNE published World's Most Admired Companies on February 27th in 2014. There are forty-two American companies in the list among the total fifty companies. Besides, there are five companies from Europe, which are BMW (Germany), Volkswagen (Germany), Nestlé (Switzerland), Unilever (UK) and Accenture (Ireland). The rest three companies are from Asia. They are Singapore Airlines (Singapore), Samsung Electronics (Korea) and Toyota Motor (Japan). Table 2.8 shows the list of the World's Most Admired Companies in 2014 which are initially selected as the representative high reputation Western companies in this research.

Table 2.8 The list of the World's Most Admired Companies in 2014

Ranking	Companies
1	Apple
2	Amazon.com
3	Google
4	Berkshire Hathaway
5	Starbucks
6	Coca-Cola
7	Walt Disney
8	FedEx
9	Southwest Airlines
10	General Electric
11	American Express

Table 2. 8(Continued)

Ranking	Companies
12	Costco Wholesale
13	Nike
14	BMW
15	Procter & Gamble
16	IBM
17	Nordstrom
18	Singapore Airlines
19	Johnson & Johnson
20	Whole Foods Market
21	Samsung Electronics
22	McDonald's
23	3M
24	Microsoft
25	Toyota Motor
26	Boeing
27	Exxon Mobil
28	Wal-Mart Stores
29	Target
30	J.P. Morgan Chase
31	Nestlé
32	UPS
33*	Caterpillar
33*	Goldman Sachs Group
35	Wells Fargo
36	Volkswagen
37	Unilever
38	Facebook
39	Marriott International
40	Home Depot
41	BlackRock

Table 2. 8(Continued)

Ranking	Companies
42	PepsiCo
43	DuPont
44	eBay
45	Accenture
46	Deere
47	Intel
48	Delta Air Lines
49	Cisco System
50	AT&T

Source: *FORTUNE*, 2014.

Notes: * denotes the same ranking.

The selection work cannot be finished in one step. In order to obtain the final list of representative high reputation Western companies, further selection should be made based on the list of the World's Most Admired Companies. Because this study focuses on Chinese social media marketing, all selected representative Western companies should have business in China. Therefore, Berkshire Hathaway, Southwest Airlines, Nordstrom Whole Foods Market, Target, and Home Depot cannot be in the final list because they did not have business in China in the year when this study has already begun to be conducted. In addition, those selected Western companies belonging to the industry of Internet Services and Retailing should be ruled out because in view of the fact that this research is about the commercial application of social media platforms. Companies themselves belong to Internet Services and Retailing sector, to some extent, some of them are social media tools or Internet Service platforms, for example: Facebook. In this sence, some companies such as Amazon.com, Google, Facebook and eBay have been excluded in the final list. What's more, in order to acquire the representative Western companies from the list, Asian companies like Singapore Airlines, Samsung Electronics, and Toyota Motor should not be counted in the final list.

Finally, all selected companies need to use Chinese social media tools in China because this research is based on Chinese social media applications. The Chinese social media platforms used by those selected companies can be obtained through reviewing the official website (Chinese version) of each company, where the presence of different social media tools is shown. In addition, it is necessary to point out that the possibility of change of their social media presences on their official websites depends on whether the official website is updated. In this research, the closing date to access to their official websites (Chinese version) and determine the social media platforms used by each company was 19th of March, 2015. As described in section 2.1.3 WeChat and Sina Weibo are the "darling" platforms for marketers. And it is necessary to find out whether the company has these two platforms' accounts even if they are not shown on its official website.

In general, taking into account the further selection criteria described above, four filtering steps can be summarized as follows:

(1) Step 1: doing business in China.

(2) Step 2: not belonging to the industry of Internet Services and Retailing.

(3) Step 3: non-Asian companies.

(4) Step 4: using Chinese social media in China.

After the first three steps' filtering, thirty-seven companies remain in the list. Taking into account the fourth step's filtering criterion, the social media presence of each company has been revealed by reviewing each company's official website. The results are shown in table 2.9.

Table 2.9 Social media platforms used by Western companies after the first three steps' filtering

No.	Company	Official website	Sina Weibo	WeChat	SNS	Others
1	Apple	https://www.apple.com/cn/	※	※		
2	Starbucks	http://www.starbucks.com.cn/	※	※		
3	Coca-Cola	http://www.coca-cola.com.cn/#/home 与可口可乐共同分享	※	※		
4	Walt Disney	http://www.dol.cn 关注我们 | 收听我们 | 加入小镇粉丝	※	※		

Table 2. 9(Continued)

No.	Company	Official website	Sina Weibo	WeChat	SNS	Others
5	FedEx	http://www.fedex.com/cn/ 关注FedEx	※			
6	General Electric	http://www.ge.com/cn/	※			
7	American Express	http://www.americanexpress.com.cn/ 关注官方微信 关注官方微博	※	※		
8	Costco Wholesale	http://costco.tmall.hk/shop/view_shop.htm				
9	Nike	http://www.nike.com/cn/zh_cn/	※	※		
10	BWM	http://www.bmw.com.cn/cn/zh/index.html	※	※		
11	Procter & Gamble	http://www.pg.com.cn/ RSS订阅	※	※		RSS订阅
12	IBM	http://www.ibm.com/cn/zh/	※	※		
13	Johnson & Johnson	https://www.jnj.com.cn/	※	※		
14	McDonald's	http://www. mcdonalds. com. cn/cn/ch/index.html 关注：微博 微信	※	※		
15	3M	http://solutions. 3m. com. cn/wps/portal/3M/zh_CN/WW2/Country/ 关注我们	※			
16	Microsoft	http://www.microsoft.com/zh-cn/default.aspx 微软@社交媒体	※	※		
17	Boeing	http://www.boeing.cn/ 关注波音中国微博 分享	※			
18	Exxon Mobil	http://www. exxonmobilchemical. com/Chem - Chinese/	※			
19	Wal-Mart Stores	http://www.wal-martchina.com/	※	※		

Table 2.9(Continued)

No.	Company	Official website	Sina Weibo	WeChat	SNS	Others
20	J.P. Morgan Chase	http://www.jpmorganchina.com.cn/pages/jpmorgan/china/cn/home				
21	Nestle	http://www.nestle.com.cn/	※	※		
22	UPS	http://www.ups.com/cn http://madeinchina.ups.cn/	※	※		YOUKU 优酷 LinkedIn
23	Caterpillar	http://www.cat.com/zh_CN.html 社交媒体 卡特彼勒官方微博 - 新浪微博 卡特彼勒官方微博 - 腾讯微博 卡特彼勒官方视频 - 优酷 卡特彼勒官方微信	※	※		YOUKU 优酷
24	Goldman Sachs Group	http://www.goldmansachs.com/worldwide/china/				
25	Wells Fargo	no official website of Chinese version				
26	Volkswagen	http://www.vw.com.cn/zh.html	※	※		
27	Unilever	http://www.unilever.com.cn/	※			
28	Marriott International	http://www.marriott.com.cn/default.mi	※	※		
29	BlackRock	https://www.blackrock.com/cn/home				
30	PepsiCo	http://www.pepsico.com.cn/	※			
31	DuPont	http://www.dupont.cn/ 关注杜邦	※			YOUKU 优酷 LinkedIn
32	Accenture	http://www.accenture.com/cn-zh/Pages/index.aspx 视频 播客 博客	※	※		
33	Deere	http://www.deere.com.cn/zh_CN/regional_home.page	※	※		

Table 2. 9(Continued)

No.	Company	Official website	Sina Weibo	WeChat	SNS	Others
34	Intel	http://www. intel. cn/content/www/cn/zh/homepage.html 	※	※		Intel community
35	Delta Air Lines	http://zh.delta.com/ 				
36	Cisco System	http://www.cisco.com/web/CN/index.html 	※	※		YOUKU 优酷 RSS订阅
37	AT&T	www.ap.att.com/cn http://www.telephones.att.cn/				

Note: ※ denotes that company uses Sina Weibo or WeChat.

As seen in table 2. 9, two companies, Goldman Sachs Group & Delta Air Lines, did not use Chinese social media tools, but utilized Occidental social media such as facebook and twitter in Chinese market; One company Wells Fargo had not a Chinese version of the official website; Four companies, Costco Wholesale, J. P. Morgan Chase, BlackRock and AT&T, did not present any social media platform in their official websites, nor did they use Sina Weibo and WeChat by searching on both platforms for their accounts. Hence, there are thirty companies remaining on the list after the series of filtering work.

Table 2. 10 has summarized social media platforms used by Western companies. It can be seen that very high usage rate of Sina Weibo and WeChat within these companies, i.e., 100% and 73% respectively, indicating also that these two social platforms are the most important and popular ones in China.

Table 2.10 Summary of social media platforms used by Western companies

Platforms							YOUKU 优酷	LinkedIn	RSS订阅	Blog	Community	土豆网	Podcast
Quantity	30	22	4	2	1	5	5	3	3	2	1	1	1
Percentage/%	100	73	13	7	3	17	17	10	10	7	3	3	3

After Step-4 filtering, i.e., the final filtering, thirty Western companies with high reputations have been obtained as the research objects as listed in table 2.11.

Table 2.11 Final list of high reputation Western companies

No.	Ranking	Companies
1	1st	Apple
2	5th	Starbucks
3	6th	Coca-Cola
4	7th	Walt Disney
5	8th	FedEx
6	10th	General Electric
7	11th	American Express
8	13th	Nike
9	14th	BMW
10	15th	Procter & Gamble
11	16th	IBM
12	19th	Johnson & Johnson
13	22nd	McDonald's
14	23rd	3M
15	24th	Microsoft
16	26th	Boeing
17	27th	Exxon Mobil
18	28th	Wal-Mart Stores
19	31st	Nestlé
20	32nd	UPS
21	33rd	Caterpillar
22	36th	Volkswagen
23	37th	Unilever

Table 2. 11 (Continued)

No.	Ranking	Companies
24	39th	Marriott International
25	42nd	PepsiCo
26	43rd	DuPont
27	45th	Accenture
28	46th	Deere
29	47th	Intel
30	49th	Cisco System

It is worth to point out that all of the final selected thirty Western companies have had Sina Weibo accounts when the extraction work was done on March 19th, 2015. However, eight of them have not yet had WeChat official accounts at that moment. Therefore, it is necessary to review and check whether these eight companies have WeChat official accounts before conducting WeChat case study. And it has been proved that these eight companies have created WeChat official accounts before the observation period of WeChat case study in 2016.

2. 2. 2 High reputation Chinese companies

FORTUNE CHINA published "Chinese Most Admired Companies" on September 25th, 2014. There are fifty companies in the list. Table 2. 12 shows the list of the Chinese Most Admired Companies in 2014 which are initially selected as the representative high reputation Chinese companies in this research.

Table 2. 12 The list of the Chinese Most Admired Companies in 2014

Ranking	Companies
1	Alibaba
2	Baidu
3	Huawei
4	Tencent
5	Haier
6	Xiaomi
7	Lenovo

Table 2.12(Continued)

Ranking	Companies
8	Wanda
9	JD
10	Gree
11	BYD
12	SANY
13	China Merchants Bank)
14	Vanke
15	Wahaha
16	Evergrande Group
17	Great Wall Motors
18	Baosteel
19	Midea
20	Tsingtao
21	CRC
22	NetEase
23	TCL
24	KWEICHOW MOUTAI
25	China Mobile
26	Fuyao Group
27	Hisense
28*	Ping An
28*	ZTE
30	STATE GRID Corporation of China
31	COFCO
32	HaiNan Airlines
33	Country Garden
34*	Dongfeng
34*	Saic Motor
36	China Merchants Group)
37	Chery

Table 2. 12(Continued)

Ranking	Companies
38	WangFujing
39	Geely
40	Founder Group
41	New Hope Group
42	YanJing Beer
43	SuNing
44	Fosun
45*	Bailian Group
45*	Yunnan Baiyao
47	CASC
48	Gome
49*	Belle International
49*	Bright Food

Source: *FORTUNE CHINA*, 2014.

Notes: * denotes the same ranking.

Similarly, in order to obtain the final list of representative high reputation Chinese companies, the further filtering procedure need to be followed based on the list of the Chinese Most Admired Companies published by *FORTUNE CHINA* in 2014. Firstly, all selected Chinese companies belonging to the industry of Internet Services and Retailing such as Alibaba, Baidu, Tencent, JD, and NetEase should be ruled out from the list because of the same reason as that for the selection of the Western companies. Secondly, large state-owned enterprises shall also be excluded from the list because they usually get strong financial support from the central government and are not the research objects of this study. Therefore, companies such as China Merchants Bank, Baosteel, CRC, China Mobile, STATE GRID Corporation of China, COFCO, Dongfeng, China Merchants Group, Chery, Founder Group, Bailian Group, and CASC have been taken out from the final list. Finally, all selected companies must use Chinese social media tools in China.

Therefore, taking into account the selection criteria mentioned above, three filtering steps are adopted and described below:

(1) Step 1: not belonging to the industry of Internet Services and Retailing.

(2) Step 2: non-"large state-owned enterprises".

(3) Step 3: using Chinese social media in China.

After the first two steps' filtering, thirty-three companies remain in the list. Similarly, combining with the importance of Sina Weibo and WeChat as mentioned before. Table 2.13 lists the social media applications used by the thirty-three Chinese companies by reviewing their official websites. It is important to note that the closing date of the extraction of the data from these companies' official websites was 19th of March, 2015.

Table 2.13 Social media platforms used by Chinese companies after the first two steps' filtering

No.	Company	Official website	Sina Weibo	WeChat	SNS	Others
1	Huawei	http://www.huawei.com/cn/ 加关注 197.6万	※	※		
2	Haier	http://www.haier.com/cn/	※	※		
3	Xiaomi	http://www.mi.com/index.php? f=xiaomi 关注我们 新浪微博 小米部落 官方微信	※	※		小米部落
4	Lenovo	http://www.lenovo.com.cn/ 成为粉丝 微信服务	※	※		
5	Wanda Group	http://www.chinawanda.com/ 万达集团 QQ 微信 分享到：	※	※		
6	Gree	http://www.gree.com.cn/ 加关注	※	※		
7	BYD	http://www. byd. com. cn/views/home/indexc.htm	※	※		
8	SANY	http://www.sanygroup.com/group/zh-cn/ 官方微博 分享： 在线订阅 移动社交	※	※		RSS订阅

Table 2. 13(Continued)

No.	Company	Official website	Sina Weibo	WeChat	SNS	Others
9	Vanke	http://www.vanke.com/	※	※		
10	Wahaha	http://www.wahaha.com.cn/	※	※		
11	Evergrande Group	http://www.evergrande.com/				
12	Great Wall Motors	http://www.gwm.com.cn/index.html 官方微博 长城汽车	※	※		
13	Midea	http://www.midea.com/cn/	※	※		
14	Tsingtao	http://www.tsingtao.com.cn/index.shtml	※	※		
15	TCL	http://www.tcl.com/ 添加关注：	※	※		
16	KWEICHOW MOUTAI	http://www.moutaichina.com/publish/portal1/ 国酒茅台官微	※	※		
17	Fuyao Group	http://www.fuyaogroup.com/				
18	Hisense	http://www.hisense.com/	※	※		
19	Ping An	http://www.pingan.com/ 官方微博	※	※		
20	ZTE	http://www.zte.com.cn/cn/ 关注我们：	※	※		
21	HaiNan Airlines	http://hnair.travelsky.com/ 海航微博	※	※		
22	Country Garden	http://www.bgy.com.cn/china/index.aspx	※			
23	Saic Motor	http://www. saicgroup. com/chinese/default.shtml 上汽集团官方微博	※			
24	WangFujing	http://www.wfj.com.cn/	※	※		

Table 2. 13 (Continued)

No.	Company	Official website	Sina Weibo	WeChat	SNS	Others
25	Geely	http://www.geely.com/welcome/index.html ›关注吉利	※	※		
26	New Hope Group	http://www.newhopegroup.com/	※	※		
27	YanJing Beer	http://www.yanjing.com.cn/yjqy.html	※	※		
28	SuNing	http://www.suning.cn/	※			
29	Fosun	http://www.fosun.com/	※	※		
30	Yunnanbaiyao	http://www.yunnanbaiyao.com.cn/index 云南白药官方订阅号 newbaiyao	※	※		
31	Gome	http://www.gome.com.cn/	※	※		
32	Belle International	http://www.belleintl.com/				
33	Bright Food	http://www.brightfood.com/cn/index.aspx 官方微博	※	※		

Note: ※ denotes that company uses Sina Weibo or WeChat.

It can be found from table 2. 13 that three companies Evergrande Group, Fuyao Group and Belle International, did not present any social media tool in their official websites, nor did they use Sina Weibo and WeChat by searching on both platforms for their accounts. Therefore, these three companies shall not be put into the final list. So, there are thirty companies remaining on the list after the series of filtering work.

Again, as indicated by table 2. 14, Sina Weibo and WeChat are the most popular social media platforms due to the very high usage rate, i.e., 100% and 90% respectively.

Table 2. 14 Summary of social media platforms used by Chinese companies

Platforms									RSS订阅	Community (小米部落)
Quantity	30	27	2	3	3	1	1	1	1	1
Percentage/%	100	90	7	10	10	3	3	3	3	3

Finally, thirty representative Chinese companies with high reputation are obtained after all three steps' filtering and listed in table 2. 15.

Table 2. 15 Final list of high reputation Chinese companies

No.	Ranking	Companies
1	3rd	Huawei
2	5th	Haier
3	6th	Xiaomi
4	7th	Lenovo
5	8th	Wanda
6	10th	Gree
7	11th	BYD
8	12th	SANY
9	14th	Vanke
10	15th	Wahaha
11	17th	Great Wall Motors
12	19th	Midea
13	20th	Tsingtao
14	23rd	TCL
15	24th	KWEICHOW MOUTAI
16	27th	Hisense
17	28th	Ping An
18	28th	ZTE
19	32nd	HaiNan Airlines
20	33rd	Country Garden
21	34th	Saic Motor
22	38th	WangFujing
23	39th	Geely
24	41st	New Hope Group
25	42nd	YanJing Beer
26	43rd	SuNing
27	44th	Fosun
28	45th	Yunnan Baiyao
29	48th	Gome
30	49th	Bright Food

Similarly as the selected Western companies, the final selected thirty Chinese companies have had Sina Weibo account when the extraction work was done on March 19th, 2015. However, three of them have not yet had WeChat official accounts at this moment. But it has been proved that these three companies have created WeChat official accounts before the observation period of WeChat case study in 2016.

3 STATE OF THE ART AND THEORETICAL FRAMEWORK

The World Wide Web is a great revolution not only for people's daily life, but also for the concept of business environment. Before the birth of the Internet, enterprises used normally traditional media such as television, magazines, and radio to conduct advertising campaigns. With the emerging of new media due to the development of network technology, the marketing models have been changed. Nowadays a new dynamic era of digital engagement has come. Social media as a powerful tool plays a very important role in this campaign. More and more marketers have been using social media channels to do promotion, to build a good relationship with their customers and to improve their brands awareness and market share.

Many scholars have carried out relevant researches in this area. When we talk about social media, we need to mention another relative term — Web 2.0, which was firstly presented in O'Reilly Media Web 2.0 Conferences in 2004 (Graham, 2005). Since then, Web 2.0 has been working as a tool with its strengths for the evolution of social media and thus results in the growing and the boom of social media (Kaplan et al., 2010). Currently, there are various social media definitions; one of the most popular is:

"*Social media is a group of Internet-based applications that build on the ideological and technological foundations of Web* 2.0, *and that allow the creation and exchange of user generated content*." (Kaplan et al., 2010)

In his e-book: *what is social media?*, Mayfield (2008) stated that social media has several features including participation, openness, community, and six types of platforms — social networks, blogs, wikis, podcasts, forums, content communities, and microblogging. Kietzmann et al. (2011) described seven functional blocks of social media: identity, conversations, sharing, presence, relationships, reputation, and groups.

Gupta (2011) forecasted that revenue from advertising, games, and subscriptions from global social media channels would hit $29 billion by 2015; that is more than four times the amount from all of 2010. So, it seems that we are in a new dynamic era of digital engagement and social media plays an important role in this context. More and more companies are using social media applications to collect positive and negative information about their products and services and to engage with their target audience. All these strategies improve their brands' awareness and market share (Abedniya et al., 2010; Culnan et al., 2010; Moran et al., 2010).

Drury (2008) stated that marketing is no longer one-way process; social media brings elements together in a two-way pattern due to the behaviors of exchanging and engaging between companies and consumers. In addition to the popularity in business applications, social media also plays an important role in social movements because it was vital for getting information during the movement (Fernandez-Planells et al., 2014).

With respect to the measurement of social media performance, there is no one-size-fits-all evaluation system to measure all companies' performance. Cvijikj, Spiegler & Michahelles (2013) indicated that the measurement of social media performance is elusive and one method to overcome the challenge is examination of the campaigns launched by the companies and the users' responses to them in the form of assessments.

It's worth pointing out that in the context of globalization the most attractive economies are located in emerging markets. China, as one of the most appealing markets, has been drawing the attention of local and multinational enterprises, especially the latter with a focus on Western corporations in China. According to the report on Internet development in China from China Internet Network Information Center (CNNIC), Chinese Internet users' numbers hit 618 million by the end of December 2013. The Internet penetration rate was 45.8%. In the context of the enterprises these data show that 83.2% of the enterprises used the Internet to conduct official business, 23.5% to perform online sales, and 20.9% to implement marketing and promotion (CNNIC, 2014a).

Social media in the forms of blogs, social network sites, video sharing sites, Wikis, photo sharing sites, and Microblog, has already become an important bridge of communication for consumers and business administrators. Many managers have realized that social media has tremendous influence on online word-of-mouth which is very important for consumers' purchase decision-making (Dellarocas, 2003; Smith et al., 2007; Trusov et al., 2009; Chu et al., 2011). Similarly, the concept of Internet word-of-mouth (IWOM) was introduced by China Investment Corporation (CIC). CIC pointed out that listening to IWOM is very important due to its influence on both information gathering and brands' online reputation (CIC, 2011).

In recent years, some scholars have carried out researches on Chinese social media marketing, in particular, an extensive body of research on the utilization of popular social media channels such as WeChat and Sina Weibo. WeChat (355 million monthly active users) and Sina Weibo (129 million monthly active users) are currently the most popular social media platforms in China (Xu, 2014). Moreover, Liu et al. (2015) stated that WeChat is one of the most popular social media technologies in China. Wang & Cai (2015) mentioned that Sina Weibo has already had a large number of users and a huge amount of message distribution every day.

Zheng, Zhang, and Wang (2014) explored online knowledge sharing based on WeChat channel. Lien & Cao (2014) stated that psychological motivations (entertainment, sociality, and information) can positively affect WeChat users' attitudes and trust which typically affect positive word of mouth. Liu et al. (2015) investigated the use of WeChat groups in enterprise via analyzing the work-related content and the life-related content which have resulted in different consequences. Guillet, Kucukusta & Liu (2015) focused on evaluating social media marketing performance in hotel industry by using the "6Is" (involvement, interaction, intimacy, influence, insights and impact) social media monitoring framework and demonstrated that Sina Weibo and WeChat platforms are used the most by the majority of the hotels.

The following sections will introduce in detail the context of Chinese social media marketing; the characteristics of Sina Weibo and Sina Weibo marketing; the characteristics of WeChat and WeChat marketing.

3.1 Context of Chinese social media marketing

This section describes the actual environments of Chinese social media marketing including Chinese digital consumers' profiles, the dominant use of Chinese social media marketing, and the challenges which both local Chinese enterprises and Western companies have been facing.

3.1.1 Chinese digital consumers

In order to understand better Chinese social media marketing and engage with Chinese digital consumers effectively, it is necessary to explore their users' profiles. Each social media site attracts specific users (Sullivan, 2012), for instance, QQ platform holds a lot of lower income digital consumers via the handsets to get online. Sina Weibo attracts some white-collar employees with higher income and education background.

The number of fans is an important indicator to test whether a social media user has received too much attention. Moreover, contributions to social media development which are composed of original content, forwarding content and comments can show clearly whether a digital account is active. Normally there exist several types of profiles of Chinese digital customers in line with the number of followers and their contributions. Table 3.1 presents a classification of Chinese digital users.

Table 3.1 A classification of Chinese digital consumers

		Followers	
		Less	More
Contributions (Original content, Forwarding content, Comments)	Less	visitors, bystanders	celebrities
	More	content curators, retweeters	web stars, pundits or experts

Source: He & Pedraza-Jiménez, 2015.

3.1.1.1 Celebrities and web stars

Celebrities and Web stars denote super stars and famous persons respectively in cyber space. Normally they have tremendous fans and followers on social media platforms.

Celebrities such as singers, movie stars, writers, sports stars, and etc., are well known to the public because they often appear in TV, magazines, and newspaper as well. Although they contribute limited content, almost every post and tweet they post could be reposted or retweeted by numerous fans. It's of no doubt that they have huge influence on topics they release. Moreover, most of them are key opinion leaders. On the other hand, web stars are normal people before being famous. With their purposes and motivations, some of them conduct some unusual and shocking activities with their backroom team's support and plans. They contribute a lot to online communities' hot topics and enrich the public's leisure life.

3.1.1.2 Pundits or experts

Pundits are highly qualified people who make their commentaries or viewpoints in a specific field in which they are considered an expert. They tend to focus on particular topics and leave some useful advices for netizens. They are also very active within online community and pay more attentions to in-depth discussion. In addition, they have great influence on purchase decision for those Internet users who trust them. In other words, they are the key opinion leaders and the main contributors of word-of-mouth in digital era. Understanding the impact of electronic word-of-mouth is of importance for brands (Kozinets et al., 2010; Trusov et al., 2009). Nowadays, due to the context of the current specific and unique Chinese social culture, ordinary Chinese citizens do not trust the advertising information from large institutions. According to the report of *Blue Book of Social Mentality: Annual Report on Social Mentality of China* (2012-2013), conducted by the Institute of Sociology under the Chinese Academy of Social Sciences, social trust index declines further in China, especially reflecting in the relationship between the authorities and the public such as officials and the public, polices and common people, and medical staff and patients (Wang et al., 2013). Instead, the public prefer word-of-mouth from social media channels and recommendation information released by pundits, friends, and acquaintance.

3.1.1.3 Content curators and retweeters

The scholar Bhargava (2009) considered the content curator as a big job in the future of social media and defined that, "*a content curator is someone who continually finds, groups, organizes and shares the best and most relevant content on a specific issue online*". Content curators are reliable sources in the process of selection and put in extra value along with the process. Moreover, they need to do this work continually. In contrast, simple retweeters are less professional than content curators. But there exist huge amounts of this kind of Internet users in China. They are keen on reposting information, such as text messages, photos, jokes, videos and etc., which they discover from social media channels of celebrities, web stars, or other sources. Although they seldom create original content, simple retweeters are still valuable for brands and services because most of them are active within online communities and maintain large following rates on social media platforms.

3.1.1.4 Visitors

The quiet visitors spend some time daily on viewing online content, such as news, product information, friends' blogs, entertainment, and so on. But they seldom participate in the conversation, discussion, or other type of response. They are not very active and noisy on the Internet. Normally they have their own ideas about products and services after reading relevant online content. However, they may still be influenced by celebrities, pundits or friends who have positive products experience.

3.1.1.5 Bystanders

Bystanders mean spectators who seldom spend time on reading network news and product information. They don't like to follow others, and have the least followers in return. Moreover they rarely participate in online discussions and online activities because they are inactive netizens. They do not release meaningful issues or posting, either. Most of them do not even complete the registration within online community. They have the least influence on brands and services.

Functions of the Chinese digital consumers on social media platforms are summarized in table 3.2.

Table 3.2 Functions of Chinese digital consumers on social media platforms

Profiles	Functions
Celebrities	Huge influence on topics they release. Key opinion leaders
Web stars	Huge influence on topics they release
Pundits or experts	Great influence on purchase decision for their followers. Contributors of electronic word-of-mouth. Key opinion leaders
Content curators	Reliable sources

Table 3. 2(Continued)

Profiles	Functions
Retweeters	Very active. Maintaining large following rates
Visitors	Not very active. Have their own ideas on products
Bystanders	No

Source: He & Pedraza-Jiménez, 2015.

Today, it's essential to understand the Chinese digital generation, which includes those who were born in a peaceful period and grew up in the digital age. The digital generation is a major consumption force and will continue to be in the future. In the book *Understanding China's digital generation — A marketer's guide to understanding young Chinese consumers*, the authors demonstrate that the young digital generation enjoys the online activities of surfing, searching, and shopping (Schultz et al., 2013).

Finally, it is important to mention the income gap between rural and urban areas in China. The imbalance of economic development has led to the existence of different user information behavior between cities and countryside. As noted in the report from CNNIC (2014c), rural users use PCs and tablets to get online less often than urban users. Instead, they use mobile phones to access the Internet more frequently than users in cities. Furthermore, rural users spend five hours less online per week than urban users, and they make fewer e-commerce transactions.

3. 1. 2 Usage of Chinese social media marketing

It is important to be aware of the leading trends of use of social media marketing in China. Only in this way can marketers keep up with the times and run the appropriate online campaign. As stated in the report on Internet development in China (CNNIC, 2014a), online shopping, group buying and mobile social media applications are booming currently in China.

3. 1. 2. 1 The Integration of social media and e-commerce to promote online purchase

E-commerce plays an important role in China's economy. Due to the huge Chinese consumer base and the great online consumption force, Chinese e-commerce is predicted to have sales hitting $420 billion, which is 20 percent higher than the US e-commerce market (Chiu et al., 2012).

Local firms have taken notice of the big opportunity to integrate with e-commerce and sell their products directly online where digital consumers are searching for product information via social media channels. Currently, microblogs are driving a significant amount of traffic for China's e-commerce sites such as Tmall (tmall.com), Jingdong (JD.com), and Taobao (taobao.com). In other words, microblogs are pushing forward the Chinese online consumer with links to these popular e-commerce sites. Microblogs lead netizens to purchase via easy link clicks after exploring the products' quality, price, after-sales service, etc., through two way communications (asking, discussing, opinion exchanging, etc.) on Weibo platforms.

One representative case, from a brand that has had many successful business campaigns via Chinese social media, is from a Xiaomi online sales campaign. Xiaomi is a local brand that launched a smartphone with a media campaign in Beijing in August, 2011. Before and after the smartphone's launch there were numerous hot topics about Xiaomi's reasonable price, clean interface, and nice quality, which were discussed on social media platforms. When Xiaomi opened the online reservation for purchase on September 5th, 2011 via its official website they received more than 300 thousand reservations within 34 hours. The company was forced to close the online booking channel. Xiaomi 1 (the first-generation of Xiaomi smartphone) sales were robust as a result of social media marketing and hunger marketing (Shen, 2012). Xiaomi 2 (the second-generation of Xiaomi smartphone) sales focused on microblogging marketing via direct vending on Sina Weibo platform in December, 2012. Sina Weibo released an advertisement, launched an online sales campaign, and built a booking page on the Weibo platform on December 19th, 2012. Amazingly, Xiaomi sold out of their 50 thousands Mi2 handsets in just five minutes on December 21th, 2012 using Weibo wallet — an online payment system (Chow, 2013). This tremendous effect has been continuing and a large number of comments and retweets have been emerging in Sina Weibo.

3.1.2.2 The boom of group buying

With the inspiration of the great success achieved by group purchase sites like Groupon, various group-buying sites are popular in China such as 55tuan (55tuan.com), Lashou (lashou.com), and Meituan (meituan.com). These group buying sites offer big discounts for a certain quantity of committed pre-orders for items and activities such as travelling, catering, and sports (Jing et al., 2011; Kauffman et al., 2010). This attractive online sales concept has led to a boom in the group purchase market in China. Chinese people prefer online shopping because of the much lower group prices and more convenient express delivery. As noted in the report published by Tuan800. com (group buying navigation website), Chinese group purchase transactions reached \$ 5.94 billion in 2013, which was 67. 7 percent higher than the previous year (Lee, 2014). The popularity of group purchase in China is beyond many Occidental people's imaginations.

Group purchase owes its popularity to attractive low prices — a result of the cooperation between group buying websites and other Chinese social media platforms. It's very easy for netizens to log into the group shopping sites directly via their SNS or microblog accounts. Furthermore, Chinese digital consumers can share information about products or services from group purchase sites and can also look for participants for their deals through social media channels. The following case highlights why group purchase is very appealing and successful in China:

200 Mercedes-Benz Smart cars were offered through group online shopping site Taobao.com on September 9th, 2010. Taobao provided different types of discounts depending on the number of group online buyers. When groupbuying participants reached 50 the price declined to 167 000 yuan (the original price was 176 000 yuan). When 200 participants committed to purchase the price dropped to 135 000 yuan, which meant a 33 percent discount with the group buying power for those digital consumers who committed to purchase a Mercedes-Benz smart car. Finally 205 cars were sold in three and a half hours, which made a new online buying record. It's surprising that the first car was sold after 24 seconds and 55 cars were sold after six minutes (Liang, 2010; CNN, 2010). The cars were sold so fast that it was beyond the company's expectations, because on average Mercedes-Benz sells one Smart car per day in China (CNN, 2010). This online campaign demonstrates that group purchase is popular, not only for low priced products, but also for expensive goods such as cars and home appliances because of the increase in the affluent class in China.

3.1.2.3 The power of mobile social media marketing

At present, handheld devices play an important role in the daily life and also have a profound influence on politics, economy, and culture. With the popularity of smart phones, various mobile phone apps have become the fastest growing part of the social media industry. Kaplan defined mobile social media:

"*as a group of mobile marketing applications that allow the creation and the exchange of user-generated content*" (Kaplan, 2012).

In China, mobile Internet users had reached 500 million by the end of 2013. Among all the Internet users, 81 percent of them used mobile devices to access the Internet, according to the latest report from China Internet Network Information Center (CNNIC, 2014a). In other words, Chinese people prefer mobile devices for surfing the Internet for entertainment and online purchases. As indicated in the report, each day 75.6 percent of users used mobile browsers for webpage browsing, news reading, etc. In addition, mobile maps and mobile e-commerce are becoming increasingly popular in China. In particular, mobile e-commerce has been making great strides in the e-commerce industry, which can partly be attributed to the maturing mobile payment system.

3.1.3 Challenges

It is crucial to run a social media campaign to engage with digital consumers and accelerate brand awareness, which ultimately increases sales in the digital age. However, actual operationalization of engagement, for both local enterprises and multinational enterprises, faces many challenges.

3.1.3.1 Challenges for the local enterprises

Social media is still a relatively new concept for many local firms because it has not gone through a long period of development in China. In the beginning of the Web 2.0 era, most Chinese companies did not realize they would be starting a new marketing campaign and engaging with digital consumers. With the boom of blogs, a few corporations began to build an official corporate blog to enhance their brand awareness and enterprise culture. A thriving social media landscape began to take shape with the launch of microblogging and SNS, capturing millions of Internet users. More and more local enterprises have recognized the benefits of social media marketing and have tried to engage with the existing and new customers via diversified social media platforms. Nevertheless, local companies are still facing some challenges in the process of running social media campaigns. Forrester Research interviewed 24 leading local enterprises with rich social media marketing experience and generated a report in 2013. As this report noted, Chinese companies face mainly four big challenges in the usage of social media for their brands and services (Dink in Forrester, 2013):

(1) Lack of clear social media strategies

Half of the 24 companies considered building an effective social media strategy their biggest challenge. Due to the short history of Chinese social media marketing and few successful cases, they have had to learn through trial and error.

(2) Difficulty to measure social media marketing efforts

Most of the companies took into account increasing brand preference as their primary objective. However, 12 respondents claimed they did not have an effective mechanism to measure the social media marketing outcome.

(3) Understaffing for social media team

Half of 24 local enterprises had a social media team with less than three employees. Understaffing is a common phenomenon for local firms.

(4) Lack of professional consulting from agency

Generally, local enterprises don't employ agencies to deal with issues of originality, traditional media, and social media in the Chinese market. In fact, only 11 firms confirmed they had hired agencies to handle social media marketing.

3.1.3.2 Challenges for the multinational enterprises

Marketers in the Occidental region, America and Europe, have achieved success by using powerful tools such as Facebook, YouTube, Google, and Twitter to run online campaigns in their region. But they face some new challenges when they play the Chinese social media game.

(1) Unfamiliar with local social media platforms

Multinational marketers are confronting an entirely new social media ecosystem and they have to forget the most recognized social media platforms in the West. Instead, they need to know and consider new Chinese platforms with names like Sina Weibo, Tencent QQ, Renren, Kaixin, Youku, etc.

(2) Lack of understanding of Chinese digital consumers

Chinese digital consumers are different from their Western counterparts. Multinational enterprises have to give up the approach they used with the Western digital consumers. So it is necessary for them to understand the Chinese netizens' habits and behavior in order to engage differently with their own target audience.

(3) Difficulty to identify the right platforms

Many multinational enterprises are not clear about how to select the right social media platform for their business because the Chinese social media landscape is more complex and fragmented than its Western counterparts. For instance, Weibo (Twitter-style microblog) comprises Sina Weibo, Tencent Weibo, Sohu Weibo, etc. Each of them attracts a different group of digital consumers. So marketers need to choose the most suitable one to engage with their target audience.

(4) Difficulty to measure social media ROI (return on investment)

According to a social media marketing industry report (2013) from social media examiner, eighty-seven percent of marketers have no idea how to measure their ROI for their social media campaigns. In the last three years this question has become a big problem for marketers (Stelzner, 2013). Multinational companies have even more difficulty in measuring their social media marketing efforts in the complex Chinese social media environment when compared to their domestic environment.

3.2 Characteristics of Sina Weibo and Sina Weibo marketing

Microblog is a shortened version of blogging based on Web 2.0 technology that provides online communication information shared among web users. Twitter, the most popular example of a microblogging, allows its users to write brief text updates of up to 140 characters known as tweets. Tweets are delivered to the author's followers who can comment, like and retweet them. When it comes to the microblog development in China, Chen (2013) defined microblog as broadcasting social media platforms in which users can share real-time information via the "follower" mechanism. eMarketer has published top 15 worldwide social media sites from which it can be found that Facebook is the No.1 worldwide social media platform and Twitter is in the fourth place. Behind Twitter, Sina Weibo is the No.5 social media application in the world (eMarketer, 2013).

3.2.1 Characteristics of Sina Weibo

What is Sina Weibo? It is the most popular Chinese microblogging platform and was launched in 2009 since Twitter was unavailable locally. Not like Twitter, Sina Weibo has removed 140-character limit since January 28th in 2016, which means it enables users to send and read messages of more than 140 characters, although only the first 140 characters will appear on users' feeds. The full text will immediately appear in followers' feeds after clicking "full text" (BBC, 2016). The messages are displayed on a user's profile page and can be viewed by anyone.

Any Sina Weibo user can follow an individual account and read, like, comment or retweet his / her posts, without being followed back. Users can upload videos, images and gifs directly into their posts. Under the influence of the ending of Sina Weibo's 140-character limit, Twitter also updated its 140 character limit policy. And media attachments such as pictures, gifs, videos, polls and quoted Tweets will no longer be counted towards the 140-character limit from September of 2016 (Titcomb, 2016).

In order to support marketing activities, Sina Weibo provides an enterprise edition. The test version of enterprise edition was released on June 13rd, 2011, which provided services such as personalized page display, data analysis, and communication management. In May 2012, Sina Weibo released its formal enterprise edition Version 2.0, which has accelerated the development and application of microblog marketing. According to the corporate report released jointly by Sina and CIC (China Investment Corporation) in February of 2012, up to 130 565 enterprises have registered their Sina Weibo accounts covering a wide range of industries such as food, car, e-commerce, IT, etc. (Zhang et al., 2016).

Figure 3.1 shows an example of BMW enterprise Sina Weibo account. It can be stated from figure 3.1 that the enterprise Sina Weibo account includes a lot of microblogging operating information, e.g., the number of following, follower, and posts; the timeline of the account; and the company information (name, logo, and introduction).

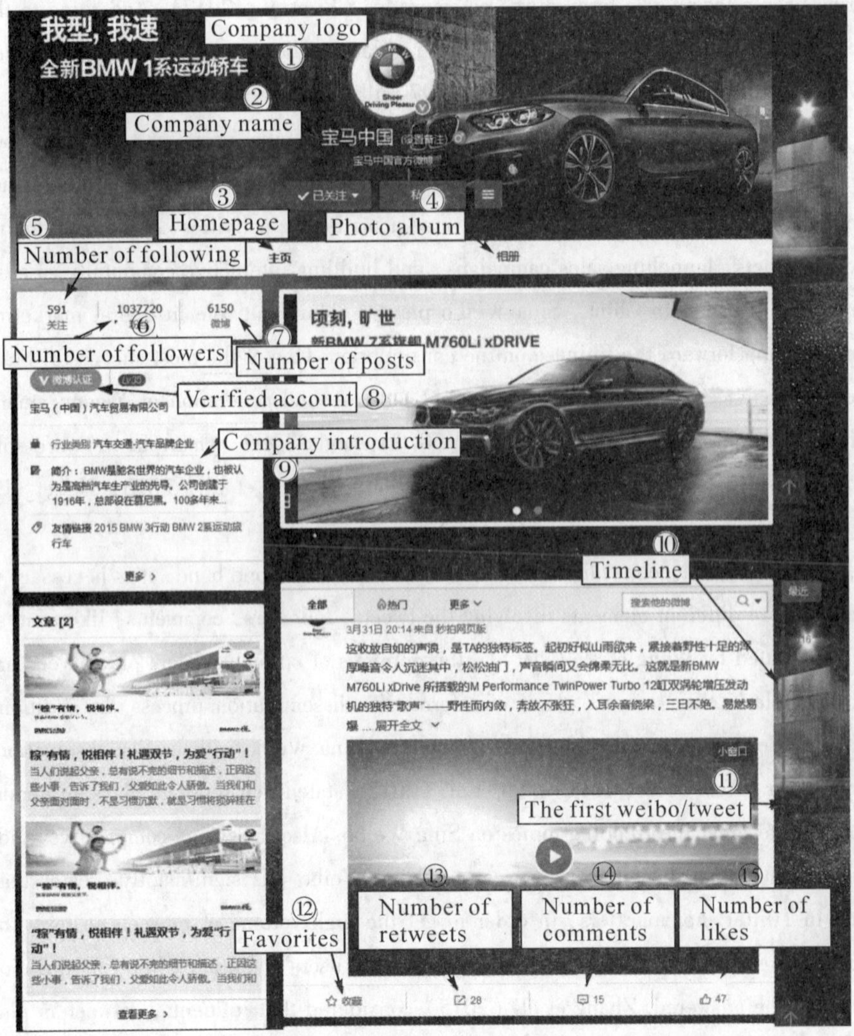

Figure 3.1 Sina Weibo enterprise account display (Example: BMW)

3.2.2 Sina Weibo marketing

As mentioned before, more and more companies have realized the importance of social media marketing. In Web era, microblogging marketing as one of the most popular social media marketing models has become a powerful weapon for market competition and market share among corporations in many countries. In recent years, the rapid development in mobile device has greatly enhanced the popularity of microblogs to bring people together to form online communities (Li et al., 2017). According to the report published by Sina Weibo data center (data.weibo.com), the number of Sina Weibo monthly active users has reached 297 million up to September 30th, 2016.

In consideration of the vast number of Sina Weibo users and its enormous potential commercial opportunities, many companies have registered their official accounts on Sina Weibo to conduct social media marketing activities, e.g., introducing new products, launching sales campaigns, and building interactive community so as to engage with users. In China, Sina Weibo plays a significant role in digital marketing and pushing forward the Chinese online consumption. One of the most successful business campaigns via Sina Weibo is Xiaomi2 (the second-generation of Xiaomi smartphone) online sales campaign in 2012, 50 thousands "Mi2" smartphones were sold out in just five minutes on Sina Weibo platform (Chow et al., 2013; He et al., 2015).

Taking into account microblogging marketing, on the one hand, it is necessary to make use of different elements involving the tweets, followers, comments, likes and so on. As stated by Wang et al. (2014), the opinions of opinion leaders play a very important role in the "share" phase of information dissemination process. In addition, the study of trends in microblogging, comparing Sina Weibo with earlier observations on Twitter (Asur et al., 2011), Yu et al. (2012) stated that retweets plays an important role to creat the trending topics on Sina Weibo. Also, previous comparative study demonstrated that the effect of retweets on Sina Weibo was significantly greater than that in Twitter. For markters, in order to get the high volume of retweets to form the specific trend, what kind of content can attract the users' attention is the first question needs to be answered. Zhang et al. (2015) considered that influential retweeters play an important role in arousing subsequent retweets.

On the other hand, word-of mouth (WOM) mechanism in microblogging marketing has become an effective and crucial channel for companies to promote their products or services. People might be affected while making purchase decisions by the experiences, opinions and comments about a product shared by other netizens. By comparison with offline activities and mass media, the advantages of online WOM of microblogging marketing lie in that they can disseminate messages much more rapidly but with lower costs and higher rates of penetration. For microblogging marketing managers, positive word of mouth is the direction of their pursuit.

Generally speaking, to carry out microblogging marketing, comments, likes, retweets and other elements are the key factors that need to be taken into account. In addition, WOM mechanism and content marketing are also important items that need to be paid attention to.

3.3 Characteristics of WeChat and WeChat marketing

This section introduces firstly the characteristics of WeChat platform and its three types of official accounts, i.e., subscription account, service account and enterprise account; and then describes the current popular WeChat marketing.

3.3.1 Characteristics of WeChat

WeChat, a popular social media application developed by Tencent Holdings in China, was launched in January 2011. For a lot of Internet users, WeChat is considered as the western social media WhatsApp's counterpart in line with their respective functions. However, nowadays WeChat encompasses more new features than WhatsApp, which is the reason WeChat attracts a large number of users. The main features of WeChat are described below:

(1) Instant Messaging

IM is the basic function of WeChat, which includes text messaging, hold-to-talk voice messaging, video chat, voice calling, broadcast (one-to-many) messaging, and video conferencing. A lot of people use text messaging and voice messaging to communicate with their friends in China.

(2) WeChat Moments

WeChat Moments is its social network function which supports users to share photographs, videos, articles, and music within their friends circle. WeChat Moment also provides "comment" and "like" functions.

(3) WeChat Payment

WeChat Payment, a digital wallet service, allows users to do mobile transactions such as mobile payments and sending money between contacts via TenPay (a version of PayPal). WeChat released a new function for distributing virtual red envelopes inside with money in 2014. The new feature allows users to send money to friends as gifts and becomes more and more popular because exchanging red envelopes of money is a traditional Chinese etiquette among friends and family members during holidays.

(4) QR Code

WeChat provides a standard QR code reader. It comes along a lot of convenience for its users. Every WeChat account has a QR code. Users not only can scan a friend's QR code and send a greeting in WeChat, but also can scan the QR code to log into Web WeChat. Under the influence of QR popularity, many business cards are designed with a QR code in China which is integrated with rich information and easily scanned into the WeChat app.

(5) Games

WeChat offers lots of different types of games directly inside the App itself which is called the game center. Users can download them and play them in their leisure time. For young gamers, they can play the games solo or with their WeChat friends depends on their needs.

Nowadays, WeChat users can do many things which are relevant to daily life in China. For example, users can order food, buy goods, read the news, and even book a doctor appointment.

Then, let's talk about three types of official accounts.

It is worthy to point out that official accounts are different from normal accounts. WeChat official accounts can broadcast information to their fans. Meanwhile, the followers can discuss with the official account owners or leave the message for them, even retweet the broadcast information from official accounts in their own WeChat moments. Official accounts are used by many companies integrated with social media marketing strategies in China. There are three types of official accounts: subscription account, service account and enterprise account.

(1) Subscription account

According to Tencent Holdings design, WeChat subscription account which enables subscription account owners to push feeds to subscribers, interact with subscribers. **Account manager can push messages to followers once a day, although the messages are not shown in the user's session list, they are folded into a folder in that containing all the subscription accounts.** If a follower wants to read the information from a specific company, he or she firstly needs to click the folder and find the company's subscription account to read the relevant information.

According to every company's social media strategy, some companies need to push too much information to followers frequently; subscription account is the best choice.

(2) Service account

Service account provides more APIs (Application Programming Interface) than subscription account and then companies can build its own application with their needs to realize more service functions to followers. Compared to subscription account, **WeChat service account offers more business service**, advanced functionality that can be integrated into service accounts, and user management capabilities, **but less push notification: four times per month. It is necessary to point out that the messages are shown in the user's session list. That means users can receive and read the information directly when they open the WeChat app.** The percentage of information reaching to followers is higher than subscription accounts in some way.

In general, service accounts are suitable for enterprises and organizations that pay more attention to business service function.

(3) Enterprise account

Enterprise account, also called corporate account, are very different from subscription account and service account which these two types of account are designed for marketing outside of the corporate. However, **enterprise account is addressed for a company's internal management** such as private group chat, task arrangement, coordination between departments, and so on. One highlight of enterprise accounts is users have to go through authentication process before he or she becoming a follower which ensures that the company's internal network security. In the future more and more new features will be developed due to corporate accounts' growing popularity among many companies.

There is no doubt that enterprise accounts are not fit for marketing outside of a company in line with its features.

3.3.2 WeChat marketing

As stated previously, WeChat has been becoming a more and more important marketing channel to reach target consumers in Chinese market. Business information or contents can be disseminated quickly, conveniently, interactively, and cost-efficiently via WeChat application. During this process, a new Internet marketing method called WeChat marketing has arisen gradually. Zhang (2015) stated that Wechat marketing is a mixed product by combining market economy and network economy. Currently a lot of enterprises have been using WeChat to spread company cultures, to promote products or services, to collect market information, to interact with consumers, and consequently increase their brand influence at low cost.

With respect to WeChat marketing, the selection of the suitable type of official accounts is the core point for many corporations. Or, in other words, companies need to choose subscription account or service account depends on their needs and social media marketing strategies. After registering WeChat official account, companies need to increase the positive exposure, to attract users to follow their accounts and maintain their interest via the appropriate WeChat marketing campaigns.

Normally WeChat users may become a fan of an official WeChat account through a search or through scanning a QR code depends on their needs. Once the user has become a follower of a specific WeChat account, he or she can receive the push notification sent by the official account administrator. However, the messages might not be welcomed and the fans may choose to quit or refuse to receive push notifications from an official WeChat account. Therefore, how to maintain the user's interest is a challenge that the managers need to face when they conduct WeChat marketing.

Moreover, some scholars have carried out the research on WeChat marketing from different angles. Lien & Cao (2014) investigated the WeChat users' motivations (entertainment, sociality, and information), attitudes, trust, and their behavior and found that users' motivation and trust positively influence their attitudes and leading to positive word-of-mouth. Min (2014) performed research on the enterprise WeChat marketing strategies from four angles which are channel, need, relationship and value based on the SICAS (Sense, Interest & Interactive, Connect & Communication, Action, and Share) Model. Du (2015) conducted an analysis on university students' attitudes towards understanding of WeChat marketing and found that WeChat has generally been accepted by students as a commercial channel.

In general, the selection of the suitable type of WeChat official account is a key move before conducting WeChat marketing. In addition, the adoption of appropriate WeChat marketing strategies is practical measures so as to maintain users' interest.

3.4 Related theoretical framework in the context of social media

In the context of social media, some theoretical frameworks that differ from those of traditional media environment have emerged and have been discussed by scholars. Although these theoretical frameworks have not been implemented directly in this research, it has been considered convenient to introduce them in this research because of the relevance of this study to other researches that involve the investigation of social media. This section states several relevant typical theoretical frameworks under the influence of social media.

3.4.1 Evolution of consumption behavior model from AIDMA, AISAS to ISMAS

With the evolution of the media, consumers' consumption behavior has also been changed. Or, in other words, the consumption behavior pattern of the mass media age is different from that of the social media environment.

AIDMA (Attention, Interest, Desire, Memory, and Action) is a consumers' psychological process model and was first advocated by Roland Hall, an American economist, around 1920 (Sugiyama et al., 2011).

This model demonstrates the five psychological phases of consumers from being aware of a product to buying it. Firstly, the corporations use the mass media to disseminate the information of their products or services to attract the consumers' attention. Secondly, consumers could become interested in these products or services. Thirdly, consumers show the desire of buying the products which would be committed to lead to the fourth step: leaving a memory. Finally, consumers take the action: buying. AIDMA model can interpret the consumption behavior in the context of traditional mass media; meanwhile, this model emphasizes the benefits of sellers.

However, with the rapid development of information technologies in the past decades, consumers' consumption behavior has changed significantly due to the formation of the online interactivity between consumers and sellers. Under such a circumstance, AIDMA model's limitations have been revealed because it cannot meet the demands of market in the era of new media.

In order to meet the new challenge induced by the Internet revolution, the international 4A advertising agency DENTSU created a new consumers' consumption behavior model, namely, AISAS (Attention, Interest, Search, Action, and Share) model in 2004 (Sugiyama et al., 2011).

The first two stages of AISAS model are the same as those of AIDMA model. Whereas AISAS model puts emphasis on two typical Internet users' behavior patterns: search and share. Firstly, the search engine technology provides the chances for consumers to obtain actively the relevant information that they want through a simple search operation. Hence this changes the process of purchase decision-making. In the AISAS model, consumers can search product information through the Internet, make comparisons among similar products and finally make the decision to buy or not to buy the product or service. After buying products, consumers are capable of commenting and sharing information with other consumers so as to provide them a decision-making reference.

Based on AISAS model, many enterprises have adjusted their marketing strategies in order to strengthen the online interaction and information sharing with users aiming to enhance their brand awareness and attract more potential consumers. Wang et al. (2014) stated that Sina Weibo users' behavior matches the exact phases of AISAS model.

Last few years, new technologies such as 5G network and mobile payment have been developed very quickly. Especially in China, these new technologies are very popular. Under the influence of mobile media, consumers' behaviors and habits have also been changed. As a result, a new consumption model is needed to improve the AISAS model in line with the changes of digital users' life style. For this purpose, Liu & Chen (2013) raised an improved model, i.e., ISMAS (Interest, Search, Mouth, Action, and Share) based on AISAS model to meet the necessity in mobile media era by defining new consumption trends under the new social media environment.

Nowadays consumers live in the era of information explosion; the diversity of products and services has dispersed greatly their attention. In this sense, consumers can search relevant information according to their own interests but by referring to the WOM (word-of-mouth) of the products or services. After searching information and understanding word-of-mouth, consumers will eventually make the decision to buy or not to buy it. After completing purchases, consumers can share the buying experience and comments on the product through different social media channels.

Figure 3.2 expresses the evolution of consumption behavior model: from AIDMA, AISAS to ISMAS.

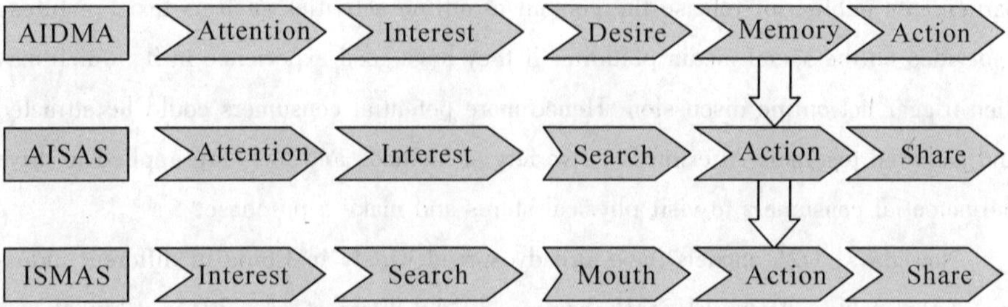

Figure 3.2 Evolution of consumption behavior model

3.4.2 O2O models

With the Internet playing a greater role in people's day life, the terms of "online" and "offline" has been becoming increasingly popular in many fields, especially in the e-commerce sector. In this study, O2O models refer to online-to-offline model and offline-to-online model. These two models have integrated many different online and offline channels such as online forum, online shopping, online community, retail stores, delivery service and etc.

On one hand, companies can acquire better sales performance and more profits from both online and offline channels. On the other hand, consumers can also get lots of benefits such as lower prices and better service by using online and offline tools.

Ahn, Ryu, and Han (2004) investigated the user acceptance of Internet shopping malls and found that both online features (system quality, information quality, and service quality) and offline features (product quality and delivery service) have greater influence on the usefulness, attitude, and intention to use than either online or offline features separately.

Online-to-offline model, as a business strategy, identifies potential customers from online channels such as through Sina Weibo, WeChat, and emails, and then draws them to offline spaces, e.g., physical stores to buy a product by using the appropriate approaches and strategies. In the Occidental region, Uber is a well-known case of using online-to-offline model. In China, a few technology trends such as online payment, voice-based apps, QR codes, and location-based apps have fueled the vast usage of online-to-offline model.

Regarding offline-to-online model, enterprises design and plan at first offline activities in order to attract consumers to participate in online conversation. Normally the participants publish or release the content of offline activities such as text, pictures, and video on the social media platforms if they have good experience in it, which may then trigger hot online discussion. Hence more potential consumers could be attracted and gathered together. Afterwards, a variety of methods and tools are applied to drive the potential consumers to visit physical stores and make a purchase.

Nowadays, O2O models have already spread widely in China in different industries (Du et al., 2014; EU SME centre, 2014; Weng et al., 2015; Chiu et al., 2016). In fact, O2O models have been applied in many fields including politics, communications, public affairs, social movements. Especially in the commercial field, more and more corporations have integrated O2O models into their marketing strategies to increase market share, to improve their brand awareness, and to gain greater success in the highly competitive business environment (Tsai et al., 2013; Xia et al., 2014; Shen, 2015; Ma, 2017). Meanwhile, social media as online tool plays an important role in the O2O models. With the help of social media, companies can not only engage with their audience, but also identify the potential consumers so as to increase revenue.

3.4.3 Electronic word-of-mouth (eWOM)

The importance of word of mouth (WOM) has been well known for marketers because WOM represents consumers' behavior of information exchanging about the products and services and plays a critical role in changing consumers' purchase decision and attitudes towards brands, products and services. With the emergence of Internet, WOM exists also in online media except the traditional offline communities and belongs to electronic word-of-mouth (eWOM). Hennig-Thurau et al. (2004) defined eWOM as "*any positive or negative statement made by potential, actual, or former customers about a product or company, which is made available to a multitude of people and institutions via the Internet*". In China, the institute CIC proposed the similar concept Internet Word of Mouth in 2011. Based on eWOM has a great influence on brands and services, it is very helpful for marketers to listen to eWOM especially when potential digital customers share and exchange their viewpoints on products, brand, and services online.

eWOM includes two types of information, i.e., positive one and negative one. The latter has a negative impact on the company's reputation and social promotion. Ma et al. (2008) developed a simple example of how to defend against negative information due to the effects of power-law distribution property of social networks. As for managers, not only face the negative word of mouth, but also learn from them, and then try their best to transform some negative eWOM to positive eWOM by adjusting the social media strategies.

On one hand, marketers consider that eWOM marketing is one of the most effective and cheapest patterns of advertising within online communities. On the other hand, online shopping buyers are inclined to believe eWOM and can obtain the relevant product information from other netizens' recommendations and experiences (He et al., 2015). EWOM is a new channel for both enterprises and consumers to meet their own requirements during trading process. In this sense, social media provides the essential platform for them.

3.4.4 Relationship marketing

From the philosophy of relationship marketing, it was defined as "*attracting, maintaining and enhancing customer relationships*" (Berry, 1983; Percy et al., 2010). In the same year, Gummesson (1983) presented the concept of relationship marketing in a conference. Since then, some definitions about relationship marketing came along. The Grönroos's definition is of representative and is given below:

"*Relationship marketing is to identify and establish, maintain, and enhance relationships with customers and other stakeholders, at a profit, so that the objectives of all parties involved are met; and this is done by a mutual exchange and fulfillment of promises.*" (Grönroos, 1991; Yang et al., 2007)

The key point of relationship marketing is relations. In the era without network, the most important maintenance of relationship between enterprises and customers is through traditional media and offline activities. However, with the advent of Internet, the relationship-type marketing strategy (Grönroos, 1994) has been discussed by scholars and market practitioners.

Nowadays, due to the rapid development of social media, the relationship maintenance between the companies and the consumers has changed greatly and evolved quickly. The relationship modes among online users are different depending on different social media platforms. For example, WeChat, a popular mobile-oriented social media platform, has the feature of strong ties between its users. Or, in other words, most of WeChat users' contact lists are their acquaintances or friends. What's more, a variety of information sharing such as job recruitment information and shopping experience is always released on their WeChat Moment. In such an acquaintance circle, this kind of information sharing is more credible and persuasive. Once the company's products get one of its WeChat users' approvals due to her or his pleasant product experience, it will be quite possible for the company to acquire more users under the driving through positive eWOM within user's friends circles. Whereas, compared with WeChat application, the connection between users for Sina Weibo is weaker than that of WeChat. Therefore, enterprises need to establish different relationship marketing methods in line with different social media platforms. The main idea is to create customer loyalty so that a stable, win-win and long-term relationship can be established and enhanced.

4 METHODOLOGY

The purpose of this chapter is to present the methodologies for this research. Quantitative and qualitative approaches are used in this study.

In general, there are four main types of qualitative research: phenomenology, ethnography, case study and grounded theory. Two of them are applied to this research, namely, case study and grounded theory. Case study, an in-depth description and analysis of one or more "cases", has formed fundamentally the research core in this research. Grounded theory, an inductive method to develop theory by using raw data, was adopted in the whole process of case studies in this research.

In this research, two case studies were designed and conducted in line with the social media platforms Sina Weibo & WeChat to evaluate the performances of purposely selected Chinese and Western companies. Moreover, several qualitative and quantitative approaches have been applied to analyze these two cases in this study. Specifically, key performance indicators (KPIs), information architecture principles, content analysis, and statistical analyses have been cooperated to explore profoundly the collected data from two principal case studies so as to acquire the relevant results. In this chapter, all methodologies have been introduced respectively, and then their implementations in this research have been explained as well.

During the process of performing both case study analyses, KPIs were identified based on the preliminary analyses on the features of the two social media platforms. As for the data collection, the research data was schemed to be gathered in line with the observation timeline for both cases. Afterwards, the relevant database was established in which quantitative indicators were analyzed in a statistical analysis way by adopting direct mathematical formula integrating KPIs contributions and by using a statistical software SPSS (Statistical Package for the Social Scientists) to perform:

- Descriptive statistics analyses with results expressed through frequencies tables & charts, in which the corresponding statistical information can be summarized to explore the KPI trend, coding element evolution, and etc.
- Cluster analysis to reveal natural groupings or clusters within the collected data, in which the different performance characteristics of each group can be dug out and deducted.

With the integration of the qualitative and quantitative analyses, a systematic evaluation and classification system was created to evaluate the performances of all selected companies on the two social media platforms.

In addition, within-group & cross-case comparisons were made between both Western and Chinese companies to explore further findings and make conclusions. All the relevant details will be described in the following sections.

4.1 Case study

This section begins by describing the definition of case study. And then case study design, data collection, analysis and interpretation are introduced. Finally, the application of case study in this research is presented.

4.1.1 Definition of case study

Case study is the study of a phenomenon, i.e., case, and case study method indicates the method used to study the case (Ruzzen, 2014; Yin, 1984). There have been some different versions regarding the definition of case study (Fry et al., 1999; Robson, 1997; Hussey et al., 1997; Creswell, 2009). Here a representative version is referred below:

"*Case studies are a strategy of inquiry in which the research explores in depth a program, event, activity, process, or more individuals. Cases are bounded by time and activity and researchers collect detailed information using a variety of data collection procedures over a sustained period of time.*" (Creswell, 2009)

Case study has been considered as a robust research method (Zainal, 2007). One of its advantages is that it allows the exploration and understanding of complex phenomena. Moreover, as explained by Tellis (1997), case study helps find out both the process and outcome of a phenomenon through observations and analysis of all collected quantitative and qualitative data.

Case study has been recognized and widely adopted in many social science studies and it has been becoming more and more prominent in social sciences (Grassel et al., 2006; Zainal, 2007; Ruzzene, 2014; Pérez-Altable, 2016).

4.1.2 Design of case study

As pointed out by Zainal (2007), careful case study design shall be made to assure that the case study is feasible to obtain data from the research subjects, suitable for the research question, and related to some certain theoretical framework (Tellis, 1997). In addition, with an appropriate case study design, scientific conventions used in social sciences and a set of procedures with proper application can be followed. Moreover, case study design defines also the systematical recording and archiving method of the main sources of data.

According to Yazan (2015), case study design includes mainly the following five components: ①study questions; ②propositions; ③analysis units; ④data linking logic to the propositions; ⑤criteria to interpret study findings.

Either a single-case or multiple-case design can be adopted by researchers depending on the issue in question. In particular, as stated by Campbell (1975), with proper techniques, multiple-case design may support and enhance the preliminary results.

The selection of cases depends mainly on the research objectives. Mann (2006a; 2006b) has summarized the category of case study including descriptive, critical instance, exploratory and cumulative case studies.

4.1.3 Data collection, analysis, and interpretation in case study

4.1.3.1 Data collection in case study

Hox and Boeije (2005) mentioned primary data (gathered by researchers) and secondary data (existing data available from other sources).

Various data collection methods are available for case study including the use of the questionnaire, interviews and observations, and gathering of documentation. Powell (1997) discussed data collection techniques and identified three methods: questionnaire, interview and observation. Yin (1994; 2002; 2009) suggested researchers make use of data sources such as documentation, interviews, archival records and observations.

In particular, observation is a basic and useful technique which has been utilized generally in case studies. According to Bernard (1988), "*observation usually means the researcher's act to find out what people do*". From the point view of marketing, observation method can help understand marketing aspects such as consumers' attitudes and behaviors to specific products or services, how customers make the buying decisions, and how companies respond to the customer's inquires or concerns.

4.1.3.2 Data analysis in case study

Both qualitative and quantitative analyses can be applied in case study. On one hand, some researchers have presented qualitative analyses as part of a case study (Yin, 1994; Miles et al., 1994; Hussey et al., 1997; Leedy et al., 2001; Patton, 2002). Table 4.1 lists a number of techniques in qualitative analyses, which have been adopted by some researchers (Rein et al., 1977; Gherardi et al., 1987; Bernard, 1988; Carney, 1990; Miles et al., 1994; Yin, 2009; Baškarada, 2014).

Table 4.1 Summary of qualitative analysis techniques in case study

Qualitative analysis techniques in case study	Description
Chronology	Illustrating and organizing data by date
Matrices	Explaining the interrelationship between identified factors
Coding	Generalizing data and creating structured database
Clustering	Identifying groups / clusters as per specific characteristics
Expert analysis	A technique that involves a heuristic process
Content analysis	Make valid inferences by explaining various aspects of the content
Cross-case analysis	Making comparisons among multiple cases so as to obtain more general common findings
Explanation building	A type of pattern matching technique to analyze the case study data by building an explanation about the case
Time-series analysis	A type of pattern matching technique involving possibly statistical analysis method
Constant comparative method	For the creation of theories that are grounded in the data

Sources: Rein et al., 1977; Gherardi et al., 1987; Bernard, 1988; Carney, 1990; Miles et al., 1994; Yin, 2009; Baškarada, 2014.

On the other hand, quantitative analysis has also been widely utilized in case studies. Especially, the combination of both quantitative and qualitative analyses in case study may help a lot to explore more profoundly cases under investigation (Tellis, 1997). One of the most popular quantitative analysis techniques is statistical analysis tool.

Moreover, if the study involves multiple cases, cross-case analysis may also be carried out once the analysis of individual cases is completed.

4.1.3.3 Interpretation of data analysis in case study

After completing all the previous work, the final step is to present the findings and conclusions through a procedure that can best describe and interpret the results of data analysis. The relevant skills comprise chronological description, descriptions developed and derived from secondary data, tabular and graphic presentation summarizing key features of each case.

While involving multiple cases, researchers may consider describing cases separately or, alternatively, in the form of a cross-case analysis. Barratt et al. (2011) pointed out that case studies involving both within-case and cross-case analyses have been found to be effective in setting up theoretical frameworks.

4.1.4 Procedure of case study

Baškarada (2014) presented case study guidelines based on the universally accepted six-stage case study process developed by Yin (2009) as presented in figure 4.1 and table 4.2.

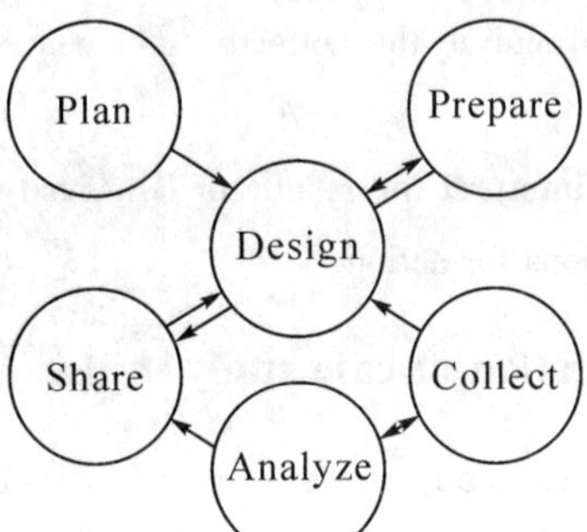

Figure 4.1 Case study process

(Source: Yin, 2009.)

Table 4.2 Case study process

No.	Process	Description
1	Plan	Identifying research questions
2	Design	Defining analysis units, selecting cases, developing theory/propositions, clarifying research issue/topic, making case study design, and developing appropriate procedures for data analysis
3	Prepare	Developing skills and training for a specific case study, setting up a case study protocol, making data collection scheme, conducting a pilot case, and etc.
4	Collect	Using multiple data sources, collecting data, performing data preprocessing and creating a case study database
5	Analyze	Analyzing collected data with proper techniques
6	Share	Defining the audience, releasing textual and visual materials, displaying enough information for the audience to make their own decisions / conclusions, and reviewing and re-writing until done well

Source: Yin, 2009; Baškarada, 2014.

By integrating the mentioned processes into the specific context of this research, the case study process for this research can be adapted and modified as follows:

(1) Plan: to define research questions.

(2) Design: case selection & case study categorization in view of the research objectives.

(3) Preparation: to develop a case study protocol and data collection scheme; to determine data analysis techniques.

(4) Data collection: to collect data as planed and designed.

(5) Data Analysis: to analyze the collected data via defined data analysis techniques.

(6) Interpretation: to interpret the results of data analysis, to report the findings and to make recommendations for action.

4.1.5 Implementation of case study in this research

The aforementioned case study process has been implemented in this research with details explained in the following sections.

In this research, "cases" being studied are two popular Chinese social media platforms Sina Weibo and WeChat with the research objectives to evaluate the performance of thirty Chinese companies and thirty Western companies on each platform, and aiming to provide empirical evidence to explore Chinese social media marketing strategies based on the two most important Chinese social media applications. The reason to select these two platforms has been explained in section 2. 1.

4. 1. 5. 1 Plan

This research involves two case studies (Sina Weibo case study and WeChat case study), which aims to answer the main research questions RQ3 and RQ4 defined in section 1. 2. 1 and listed in table 4. 3.

Table 4. 3 Description of the main research questions

Research Question No.		Description
RQ3		How to measure/evaluate the performances of all chosen companies' efforts on each selected social media platform? Is it possible to create a systematic measurement framework for this purpose?
RQ4		How to classify all selected companies into different categories/groups? Is it possible to develop several sets of models based on the different performances on the selected platforms?
Derivative Questions	RQ4-1	Which companies are identified as the most failed representatives in line with their social media performance on both selected social media platforms?
	RQ4-2	Which companies are identified as the most successful representatives in line with their social media performance on both selected social media platforms?
	RQ4-3	What are the key factors for the success of social media strategies on the selected platforms by analyzing the most successful representatives?
	RQ4-4	What are the differences in social media strategies among all the selected companies due to their different geographical attributes (Occident/China)?
	RQ4-5	What are the differences in social media strategies among all the selected companies due to their different industries?

4. 1. 5. 2 Design

Sina Weibo case study aims to evaluate and measure the microblogging marketing performance of the high-reputation Chinese and Western companies through the analysis of data collected over an observation period. In WeChat case study, the similar research purpose is achieved through the corresponding research steps. According to the research objective, the selection of sixty Sina Weibo enterprise accounts and sixty WeChat official accounts can be conduted in "design" phase.

(1) Selection of Sina Weibo enterprise accounts

It is worthy to point out that the fragmentation of Sina Weibo enterprise accounts is normal, which means that many companies own several Sina Weibo accounts. For example, the British company "Unilever" possesses three Sina Weibo accounts, i.e., campus recruitment, social recruitment and the general account respectively. The Chinese company "Haier" owns more than six Sina Weibo accounts such as Haier refrigerator, Haier TV, Haier washing machine, Haier water heater, Haier air conditioner and Haier kitchen appliance. In this research, only one Sina Weibo account from each company is selected as a research object.

In cases that one company has several Sina Weibo accounts, only the account which covers the general information could be selected as the research object. Accoding to figure 4.2, normally the selected Sina Weibo official account includes the following elements: company logo, account name, verified or non-verified account, and account owner.

Figure 4.2 A selected Sina Weibo account display (Example: PepsiCo)

In this way, a total of sixty Sina Weibo accounts have been obtained in this study and shown in figure 4.3 and figure 4.4.

Figure 4.3 lists the thirty Western companies' Sina Weibo accounts with elements described above used in this research.

Figure 4.4 lists the thirty Chinese companies' Sina Weibo accounts with elements described above used in this research.

Figure 4. 3 List of Western companies' Sina Weibo accounts used in this research

Figure 4.4 List of Chinese companies' Sina Weibo accounts used in this research

(2) Selection of WeChat official accounts

As stated before, the fragmentation of Sina Weibo enterprise accounts is very common. WeChat official accounts have the similar situation. Many companies have more than one WeChat official account depending on the needs of their products or services. For example, the Chinese corporate "Haier" owns several WeChat official accounts such as Haier refrigerator, Haier air conditioning, Haier washing machine and so on. In this research, only one WeChat official account from each company is selected as a research object. This selected official account represents the company's general information.

Table 4.4 lists the basic information of the selected sixty WeChat official accounts for both Western and Chinese companies.

Table 4.4 Basic information of the selected WeChat official accounts for all companies

Company	WeChat name/WeChat ID	Industry	Account type	Verified account
Apple	iPhone 中文网/apple4cn	Computers	Subscription	By Sina Weibo
Starbucks	星巴克中国/xingbakezhongguo	Food Services	Service	By Tencent
McDonald's	麦当劳/mcdonalds888	Food Services	Service	By Tencent
Coca-Cola	可口可乐中国/coke1886	Beverages	Subscription	By Tencent
Walt Disney	迪士尼中国/disney_china	Entertainment	Subscription	By Tencent
FedEx	FedEx 中国/FedEx_China	Delivery	Service	By Tencent
UPS	UPS 中国动态/UPS_China_News	Delivery	Subscription	No
General Electric	GE 中国/GEandME	Electronics	Subscription	By Tencent
American Express	美国运通/AmexChina	Consumer credit card and Related Services	Subscription	By Tencent
Nike	NIKE/nikejdi	Apparel	Service	By Tencent
BMW	宝马中国/BMW_Official_Wechat	Motor Vehicles	Subscription	By Tencent
Volkswagen	VWLive 大众共线/dzqczg	Motor Vehicles	Subscription	By Tencent
Procter & Gamble	宝洁中国/pgchina1988	Soaps & Cosmetics	Subscription	By Tencent
IBM	IBM 中国/IBMGCG	Information Technology Services	Subscription	By Tencent
Accenture	埃森哲中国/accenture_china	Information Technology Services	Subscription	By Tencent
Johnson & Johnson	强生中国/JNJ_YAES	Pharmaceuticals	Subscription	No
3M	3M 中国区/mmm_china	Medical Products and Equipment	Subscription	By Sina Weibo
Microsoft	微软科技/mstech2014	Computer Software	Subscription	By Tencent
Boeing	波音中国/boeingairplanes	Aerospace and Defense	Subscription	By Tencent
Exxon Mobil	埃克森美孚中国/ExxonMobil-China	Petroleum Refining	Subscription	By Tencent
Wal-Mart Stores	沃尔玛/Walmart_Hyper	General Merchandisers	Service	By Tencent
Nestle S.A.	雀巢中国/NestleCN	Consumer Food Products	Subscription	By Tencent
Unilever	联合利华 U 关注/unileverofficial	Consumer Food Products	Subscription	By Tencent
PepsiCo	百事中国/BAISHIPEPSICO	Consumer Food Products	Service	By Tencent
Caterpillar	卡特皮勒中国/caterpillarinchina	Construction and Farm Machinery	Subscription	By Tencent
Deere	约翰迪尔/JohnDeereChina	Construction and Farm Machinery	Service	By Tencent
Marriott International	万豪礼赏/ marriottgroup	Hotel/Casino/Resorts	Service	By Tencent
DuPont	杜邦特能壁纸	Chemicals	Service	By Tencent
Intel	英特尔中国/intel-china	Semiconductors	Service	By Tencent
Cisco System	思科联天下/ciscowechat	Network and other Communication Equipment	Subscription	By Tencent
Huawei	华为/huaweicorp	Telecom manufacturing and services	Subscription	By Tencent
ZTE	中兴通讯/ZTEInChina	Telecom manufacturing and services	Subscription	By Tencent
Haier	海尔家电/Haier_jiadian	Electronics / Electrical Appliances	Service	By Tencent
Xiaomi	小米手机/xmsj816	Electronics / Electrical Appliances	Service	By Tencent
Lenovo	联想/lenovo1984	Electronics / Electrical Appliances	Service	By Tencent
Gree	格力电器/glfwh1991	Electronics / Electrical Appliances	Service	By Tencent

Table 4.4(Continued)

Company	WeChat name/WeChat ID	Industry	Account type	Verified account
Midea	美的会员/mideafw	Electronics / Electrical Appliances	Service	By Tencent
TCL	TCL 铁粉社区/tcltiefen	Electronics / Electrical Appliances	Subscription	By Tencent
Hisense	海信/hisense1969	Electronics / Electrical Appliances	Service	By Tencent
BYD	比亚迪汽车/byd-auto	Motor Vehicles / Motor Vehicles Parts	Subscription	By Tencent
Great Wall Motors	长城汽车/greatwallmotor	Motor Vehicles / Motor Vehicles Parts	Subscription	By Tencent
Saic Motor	上汽集团/SAIC_MOTOR_	Motor Vehicles / Motor Vehicles Parts	Service	By Tencent
Geely	吉利控股集团/jilikonggujituan	Motor Vehicles / Motor Vehicles Parts	Subscription	By Tencent
Wahaha	娃哈哈/YourWahaha	Food / Beverage	Service	By Tencent
Tsingtao	青岛啤酒/Tsingtao_Since1903	Food / Beverage	Subscription	By Tencent
Kweichow Moutai	国酒茅台/maotaiguojiu	Food / Beverage	Subscription	By Tencent
YanJing Beer	燕京啤酒/yanjing_beer_group	Food / Beverage	Service	By Tencent
Bright Food	光明食品集团/brightfoodgroup	Food / Beverage	Subscription	By Tencent
HaiNan Airlines	海南航空/Hnairlines	Airlines	Service	By Tencent
Yunnan Baiyao	云南白药/newbaiyao	Pharmaceuticals	Subscription	By Tencent
Ping An	中国平安/zhongguopingan_95511	Insurance	Subscription	By Tencent
WangFujing	王府井集团/wfjbh1955	Wholesale / Retail / Distribution	Service	By Tencent
SuNing	苏宁/suning265	Wholesale / Retail / Distribution	Subscription	By Sina weibo
Gome	国美在线/gome1314	Wholesale / Retail / Distribution	Service	By Tencent
Wanda	万达集团/guojiwanda	Real Estate	Subscription	By Tencent
Vanke	万科周刊/vankeweekly	Real Estate	Subscription	By Tencent
Country Garden	碧桂园/bgydream	Real Estate	Subscription	By Tencent
SANY	三一重工/sanyibox	Manufacturing	Subscription	By Tencent
New Hope Group	新希望集团/newhopewindows	Diversification	Subscription	By Tencent
Fosun	复星/fuxing_2014	Diversification	Service	By Tencent

Western and Chinese companies' WeChat official accounts are shown in table 4.4. Every official account has its WeChat Name and WeChat ID. Meanwhile, this table also reflects each company's industry. As mentioned before, there are three types of official accounts: subscription account, service account and enterprise account. Since enterprise account is addressed for a company's internal management, it is normal that subscription account and service account are used for marketing by companies. What is verified account? WeChat verified official account can not only intend to make followers believe that they are dealing with a reliable account, but also provide more advanced APIs and full access of advanced WeChat platform functions such as payments, users' location, third-party apps, and so on. Generally speaking, one company chooses to verify WeChat official account after registering it aiming to guarantee the truth and security of official account information on the WeChat official account admin platform and to obtain more advanced features. As can be seen from table 4.4, only two companis' (UPS and Johnson & Johnson) WeChat official accounts have not been verified until November 4th, 2016 (the closing date of these accounts were observed for their interface & menu analysis). Meanwhile, fifty-five WeChat official accounts have been verified by Tencent Company which means that they are verified by WeChat official account admin platform because WeChat belongs to Tencent Holdings Limited. The rest three WeChat official accounts are verified by Sina Weibo.

4.1.5.3 Prepare

The research data collection on Sina Weibo case study was schemed to be done in a four-week observation period (from June 1st to 28th of 2015). In WeChat case study, two observation periods have been set in line with the specific characteristics of WeChat official account. One is for the interface & menu analyses of the WeChat accounts of all Chinese and Western companies. Another one is built to investigate the marketing of push notification of all selected companies. The observation and data collection period for the analysis of WeChat push notification marketing is one month (from November 1st to November 30th of 2016). And the observation timeline of interface & menu analyses of the WeChat accounts was from October 21st to November 4th of 2016.

The research on Sina Weibo case mainly adopts content analysis, cluster analysis, and expert analysis including approaches from grounded theory and KPIs concept.

For the WeChat case study, new research approach has been adopted in it although some similar methods applied in Sina Weibo case study have also been used in WeChat case.

4.1.5.4 Data collection

Both qualitative (text, graphics, etc.) and quantitative data (numerical records such as numbers of posts, retweets, and likes) have been recorded purposely for the two cases in line with the observation period. In general, the data are mainly the first-hand data in this research.

After data checking, logging, inputting into computer, categorizing, transforming, coding, sorting, and etc., structured databases was established in text, graphics, excel and SPSS statistical formats.

In this research, data coding depends on the general attributes of cases. Therefore, for Sina Weibo and WeChat cases, the data coding process shall be different and customized respectively. However, some general data coding for both cases can be made as shown in table 4. 5 & table 4. 6 which are basic parts of coding process based on categories such as country region and industry.

Table 4. 5 Data coding as per country region

No.	Attribute / Category	Coding
1	Country region	Western: 0; Chinese: 1

Table 4. 6 Data coding as per industry

Industry coding	Industry description
1	Food
2	IT
3	Entertainment
4	Delivery
5	Electronics
6	Consumer Credit Card
7	Hotel
8	Apparel
9	Motor
10	Chemicals
11	Medicals
12	Aerospace
13	Petroleum Refining
14	Wholesale / Retail / Distribution
15	Construction and Farm Machinery
16	Airlines
17	Insurance
18	Diversification
19	Real Estate

4.1.5.5 Data analysis

The databases were then analyzed by using different techniques such as expert analysis approach, content analysis method and statistical method. These techniques are presented in the following sections 4.2, 4.3 and 4.4.

4.1.5.6 Interpretation

The two case studies were interpreted and described separately. During the process of interpretation, tabular and graphic presentation manners and other statistical tool have been utilized. Meanwhile, the comparative interpretation has also been made.

4.2 Expert analysis

Expert analysis in this research includes approaches from grounded theory, KPIs concept, and Information architecture principles, which are described individually in the following parts.

4.2.1 Grounded theory

The Grounded Theory (GT) was firstly developed by Glaser and Strauss (1967). It is considered as a way of thinking about and conceptualizing data. Glaser and Strauss (1967) emphasized that the grounded theory approach is different from the traditional research model because it enables researchers to establish theories through data analysis under flexible guidelines. GT approach has become a general qualitative research methodology.

According to Creswell (2009), *grounded theory is "a qualitative strategy of inquiry in which the researcher derives a general, abstract theory of process, action, or interaction grounded in the views of participants in a study"*.

As pointed out by Glaser & Strauss (1967), grounded theory is the study of a concept aiming mainly to conceptualize an issue via empirical research. The nature of grounded theory method is to build a theory in a systematic way from the original data. It bears two goals: ①to formulate hypotheses based on conceptual ideas; ②to comprehend the main concern and figure out the way to resolve it.

The development of grounded theory involves mainly the following stages and branches:

(1) Starting stage: represented as Glaser's approach (Glaser et al., 1967).

(2) Intermediate stage: denoted by Strauss and Corbin's approach (Strauss, 1987; Strauss et al., 1990).

(3) Modern stage: recognized as constructivist grounded theory (Byrant, 2002; Charmaz, 2000; Charmaz, 2006; Charmaz, 2008; Charmaz, 2009; Mills et al., 2006; Thornberg et al., 2012; Alemu et al., 2015).

Grounded theory is not restricted to particular disciplines. As a matter of fact, grounded theory focuses more on the procedure and not on the discipline. Grounded theory has been found useful in many research areas such as psychology, sociology, public health, business, information technology, nursing, sociology, and etc.

4.2.1.1 Implementation of grounded theory in this research

In this research, the grounded theory has been implemented into case studies (Sina Weibo & WeChat). To some extent, the whole process of each case study is the embodiment of the application of grounded theory.

In this research, analyzing the two social media platforms themselves is the first step because grounded theory begins with the original data and demands empirical facts as a start-up basis.

Figure 4.5 and figure 4.6 present the flow charts of the grounded theory applied to the two case studies in this research.

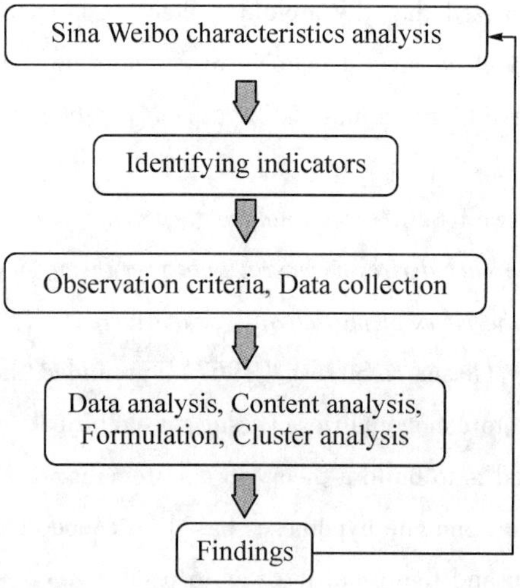

Figure 4.5 Flow chart of the grounded theory applied to Sina Weibo case

As shown in figure 4. 5, during the process of applying grounded theory to Sina Weibo case study, the platform itself and its features were analyzed in the first step; the quantitative and qualitative indicators have been extracted from the original material. And then a lot of data can be obtained in line with the observation period. After reviewing on these data, ideas, concept, and element can become apparent. The relevant methods were applied to analyze these data such as descriptive statistical analysis, formulation, and cluster analysis. With deeper analysis, the findings were becoming clearer and clearer. During the analysis process, tracing back to the previous steps may be happened ever and again. The final outcome can be obtained with the repeated data mining and analysis.

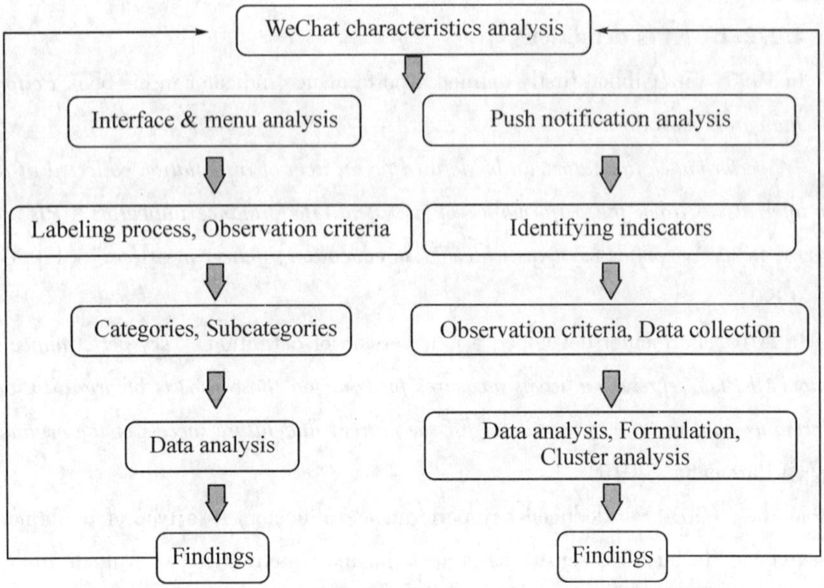

Figure 4. 6 Flow chart of the grounded theory applied to WeChat case

According to figure 4. 6, as for WeChat case study, focusing on the platform itself and its characteristics analysis was very vital work. Based on the previous work, two research lines were extended in their way. One research line was similar to the Sina Weibo case, a series of indicators were extracted from the original material so as to get abundant data combination with the observation period. And then reviewing on these data, deeper analysis, data processing, etc., were developed. Afterwards, the findings of this research line can be obtained. Another research line focused on the interface & menu analysis of all WeChat official accounts. Labeling process was applied to acquire the categories and subcategories after reviewing, analyzing, and summarizing all WeChat fficial accounts' menu settings. And then the relevant data analysis was conducted in line with the research objectives. With the further analysis and deeper digging, the findings of this research line can be obtained.

4.2.2 KPIs concept

This section introduces KPIs definition and its application in the different fields. Especially, the application of KPIs in social media has been addressed with datails. Finally, the implementation of KPIs in the Sina Weibo and WeChat case studies are explained.

4.2.2.1 KPIs definition

In 1990, Fitz-Gibbon firstly defined a performance indicator in his book *Performance Indicators* as follows:

"*A performance indicator can be defined as an item of information collected at regular intervals to track the performance of a system. Performance indicators (PIs) are collected in many complex systems which, like education, deliver a service.*" (Fitz-Gibbon, 1990)

In 2010, Parmenter developed a new version of definition, "*key performance indicators (KPIs) represent a set of measures focusing on those aspects of organizational performance that are the most critical for the current and future success of the organization*". (Parmenter, 2010)

Mathew (2014) introduced key performance indicators as a type of performance measurement. In business sense, KPIs are a business metric used to evaluate the crucial factors contributing to the success of an organization. Sawang (2011) stated that KPIs are helpful for an organization to define and measure the progress toward organizational objectives. Cox et al. (2003) considered KPIs as quantifiable measurements to examine the improvement in triggered activities that are crucial to the success of a business.

4.2.2.2 KPIs applications

There have been wide applications of key performance indicators which are suitable to each type of organization such as marketing and sales, social media, manufacturing, IT operations, health, environments, government, and etc. For example,

Sawang (2011) adopted KPIs from the perspective of sales to explore the relationship between the perceived importance and the actual use of key performance indicators from manufacturing and non-manufacturing industries.

Tested Digital Expert Ltd (2015) suggested some general KPIs (as given in table 4.7) to be implemented in four different digital marketing sectors, sales, marketing, social media, and SEO search engine optimization, to acquire more insights about follower bases.

Table 4.7 General KPIs in the fields of Sales, Marketing, Social Media and SEO

Sales KPIs	Marketing KPIs	Social Media KPIs	SEO KPIs
Sales Growth	Return on Investment (ROI)	Key Social Metrics	Keyword Opportunity
Sales Opportunities	Incremental Sales	Social Followers vs. Target	Keyword Click Through Rate
Product Performance	Traffic Sources	Social Interactions	Search Traffic Performance
Sales Target	Purchase Funnel	Social Events	Keyword Ranking
Average Purchase Value	Goal Completion Rate	Social Traffic & Conversions	Domain Authority
Sales by Contact Method	Keyword Performance	Social Visits & Leads	
Sales Bookings	End Action Rate	New Followers	
Constant comparative method (CCM)	Cost Per Lead		
Quote to Close Ratio	Email Marketing Engagement		
Sales Per Rep	Social Interactions		

Source: Tested Digital Expert Ltd, 2015.

KPIs concept has been adopted very frequently in social media, especially with the booming emergence of social media marketing applied in different industries and different regions. For instance, Podobnik (2013) presented a good example of integrating KPIs from the flagship social media marketing (SMM) platform Facebook in a case study of five largest Premier League brands. The general consideration and procedure related to KPIs have been expressed as well. As stated by Strutta (2015), like other marketing approaches, SMM needs to be managed with a strategy in spite of its inherent advantages. It is of importance to identify proper KPIs to monitor and understand the effectiveness of the relevant social marketing tactics.

In particular, it is very important to measure the Reach and Engagement in order to achieve social media success. Mishra (2013) presented a general view about social media measurement on the basis of KPIs. And Ramachandran (2015) introduced the basic principles of Reach and Engagement.

(1) Reach

Ramachandran (2015) defined Reach as "*a measure of the range of influence of any content — it is the measurement of how content is spread across various social media channels*".

As per Mishra (2013), the overall reach is related with fans on social media platforms such as Facebook, Twitter, YouTube, Slideshare and LinkedIn. It can provide general initial information about how the published information or data reaches out to the audience. Reach can be used to denote the engagement rate metric.

(2) Engagement

According to Ramachandran (2015), Engagement denotes a kind of measurement on the actions such as comments, likes, retweets, mentions, favorites, clicks, views and etc. engaged by users on the posts. Engagement has become a critical element to formulate a successful social media marketing strategy.

Mishra (2013) listed the metrics to measure engagement as: post likes, post comments, post shares, photo views, video plays, replies, mentions, retweets, clicks on links, and file downloads.

Caylor (2015) posted an article about social media KPIs on Caylor Solutions Web Blog, where he summarized the popular KPIs on some representative Western social media platforms such as Facebook, Twitter, Instagram, LinkedIn, YouTube and Pinterest (as seen in table 4.8).

Table 4.8 Popular KPIs on representative Western social media platforms

Facebook	Twitter	Instagram	LinkedIn	YouTube	Pinterest
Reach: the number of users and posts	Followers	Click-Through Rate	Engagement Rates	Overall Views	Website Pins
Engaged Users	User Engagement	Engaged Rates	Click-Through Rate	Viewer Duration	Audience Reach

Table 4. 8(Continued)

Facebook	Twitter	Instagram	LinkedIn	YouTube	Pinterest
Click-Through Rate for External Links	Click-Through Rate	Opportunities to Engage with User-Generated Content	Followers to Company Page or Members in Group	Views in Relation to Subscribers	Repinned Content
New Likes		Click-Through Rate	University Page Metrics	Views in Relation to User Interactions	Clicked Content/Click-Through Rate
Negative Feedback				Click-Through Rate	
				Subscribers	

Source: Caylor, 2015.

4. 2. 2. 3 Implementation KPIs in this research

In this research, KPIs have been implemented in both case studies of Sina Weibo & WeChat. The detailed explanations are described in the following parts.

(1) Sina Weibo Case

① Identification of KPIs on Sina Weibo platform

Social media metrics and key performance indicators are values used by digital marketing managers to measure the effectiveness of social media campaigns. Identifying the appropriate key performance indicators is the most important task before conducting the measurement for all campaigns. It is worth mentioning that it is not just outlining a handful of key performance indicators, but meeting some suitable KPIs in line with the characteristics of the specific platform during the process of identification of KPIs.

Both qualitative and quantitative KPIs have been identified for Sina Weibo case based on the features of this platform and data available on Sina Weibo official accounts. Meanwhile, a four-week observation period has been set to observe these indicators and obtain the relevant data. The purpose of the identification of KPIs is to conduct two dimensional analyses (a detailed explanation referred to section 5. 3) in Sina Weibo case study.

According to the description in section 3. 2. 1, the third party can obtain the number of followers, the number of following, the number of posts, and the number of comments and likes of each post, and etc. through reviewing each company's Sina Weibo official account. During the process of identifying KPIs, the combination of quantitative indicators and qualitative indicators has been considered. Quantitative indicators can be presented with a number, whereas qualitative indicators cannot be presented as a number, but can be presented as other formats such as text and picture. First of all, the quantitative indicators are identified and described below.

Quantitative KPIs include:

A. Change of follower number;

B. Change of following number;

C. Number of posts;

D. Sum of retweets;

E. Sum of comments;

F. Sum of likes.

It is necessary to clarify that "change of follower number" and "change of following number" are to observe whether the number of follower or following per week has increased or decreased. "Number of posts" means how many posts have been released by company per week. In addition, "Sum of comments" "sum of retweets" and "sum of likes" denote the total number of comments, retweets and likes of all posts every week.

Figure 4.7 and figure 4.8 show some examples to help understand how these quantitative key performance indicators work.

Figure 4.7 The number of following & follower shown in the third week (Example: BMW)

Figure 4.8　The number of following & follower shown in the fourth week (Example: BMW)

By comparing two figures (figure 4.7 and figure 4.8), some indicators can be calculated such as "*change of follower number*" = 942 642 − 939 395 = 3 247 and "*change of following number*" = 575 − 575 = 0 during the observation period from the third week to the fourth week.

Once the quantitative indicators have been explained, the qualitative indicators are presented behind that. In line with the description in section 3.2.1, only the number of retweets, comments, and likes of each post can be acquired by the authors. Hence, each company can generate the following three types of posts, namely, one post which has been retweeted the most; one post which has got the most comments; one post which has got the most likes within an observation unit, i.e., one week. These three types of posts represent successful content marketing. Therefore, it is necessary to analyze the content features of these posts. Based on the analysis and consideration described above, the qualitative indicators are identified and summarized below.

Qualitative KPIs include:

A. Top-one post which has been retweeted the most;

B. Top-one post which has got the most comments;

C. Top-one post which has got the most likes.

It is important to note that the following three factors have been considered to investigate the content features of all top-one posts:

A. The best day to publish it: identification of the best day to publish it within a week so as to achieve the best return.

B. The format of the post: pictures, text, video, etc.

C. Content relevance: Is the content of the post related to the company information? It is important to note that content relevance denotes whether the content of the post is related to any information of company such as company news, products, services, the company's LOGO, and so on. **Strictly speaking, mentioning of any information about the company means the content of the post is related to company information.**

Figure 4.9 displays an example of top-one post from Coca-Cola's official Sina Weibo account. The translation of the text content of this post is as: "*May you have a child-like smile every day, sharing happiness, keeping childlike innocence.*" The post was followed sequentially with number "19" "7" and "20" which denote respectively retweet, comments and likes.

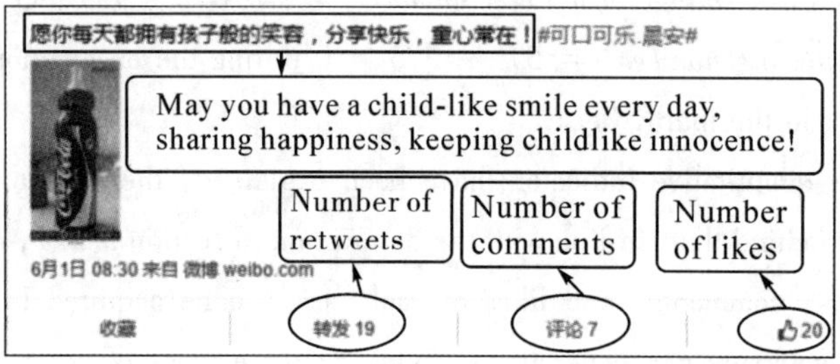

Figure 4.9 An example of top-one post from Coca-Cola's Sina Weibo account

During the first week of observation period, this post was ranked number one among all posts because it has got the biggest number of retweets, comments, and likes in the same week. In order to study this post, three factors mentioned above are taken into account:

A. This post **was published on Monday;**

B. The **format** of this post: **picture + text;**

C. **Is the content** of the post **related to the company information? Yes.** Because the company logo *Coca-cola* appears in the picture in spite of the text content of the post has nothing to do with the company information. To some extent, this is an advertising campaign.

② Observation criteria

This section describes the general observation criteria and data collection scheme in Sina Weibo case study.

Observation period setting

Observation criteria involve not only the observation period setting, but also the observation behavior in line with the research objects. In this research, four weeks' observation period has been adopted to observe both Chinese and Western companies' microblogging marketing performance on Sina Weibo platform by combining the KPIs.

In this research, observation period is from June 1st to June 28th of 2015 including four weeks. This can be seen clearly in table 4. 9.

Table 4. 9 Observation period setting for Sina Weibo case study

Classification	The first week	The second week	The third week	The fourth week
Period	June 1st to June 7th	June 8th to June 14th	June 15th to June 21st	June 22nd to June 28th

The way to collect data with KPIs

In Sina Weibo case study, PC has been chosen as the equipment to collect data from Sina Weibo platform due to its convenience although other terminals, e. g., mobile phone with Sina Weibo App are also available, but normally more onerous.

In general, two types of data have been collected. One is qualitative data and another one is quantitative data. This conforms also to the quantitative and qualitative KPIs. In addition, the collected data is type of primary and original data.

How to collect quantitative data

This section describes how to collect the original data in terms of quantitative indicators. In this research, the first week to be observed was from June 1st to June 7th of 2015, the data collection for the first week was carried out during the second observation week. It is important to note that the closing date for the original reference number of "change of follower number" and "change of following number" for the first week was May 31st of 2015. As shown in table 4. 10, the original reference number of "change of follower number" for the first week is 539 984. In this way, quantitative data has been acquired for all selected companies during the observation period. McDonald is taken as an example to present the quantitative data collection in terms of quantitative indicators as shown in table 4. 10.

Table 4.10 Quantitative data collection (Example: McDonald's)

Key Performance Indicator	1st week	2nd week	3rd week	4th week
Change of follower number	+ 67 042 (539 984/607 026)	+2 628 (607 026/609 654)	+448 (609 654/610 102)	+4 693 (610 102/614 795)
Change of following number	+3 (52/55)	+2 (55/57)	+3 (57/60)	+2 (60/62)
Number of posts	33	34	48	35
Sum of retweets	22 568	8 676	12 519	7 125
Sum of comments	9 408	3 648	5 468	3 978
Sum of likes	30 837	8 487	8 565	5 375

As per table 4.10, the following information on McDonald's Sina Weibo account can be acquired: the evolution of fans; the number of posts; the number of retweets, comments and likes.

How to collect qualitative data

This section explains how to collect qualitative data in terms of qualitative indicators. The method of collecting qualitative data is the same as that of quantitative data collection.

Figure 4.10 shows qualitative data collection for McDonald's during the observation period. Each type of top-one post has the exact number of retweets/comments/likes. Besides, the format of each post has been stated. What's more, whether the content of the post is related to the company information is presented by the answer "Yes" or "No". Specifically, "Yes" means that there exists content relevance, "No" means that there does not exist content relevance.

Once the implementation of KPIs in Sina Weibo case study has been explained, the application of KPIs in WeChat case study is presented in the following parts.

(2) WeChat Case

Similarly as described in Sina Weibo case, the identification of key performance indicators is vital for the analysis of WeChat case. The purpose of the identification of KPIs is to conduct two dimensional analyses (a detailed explanation referred to section 6.2.3) in WeChat case study.

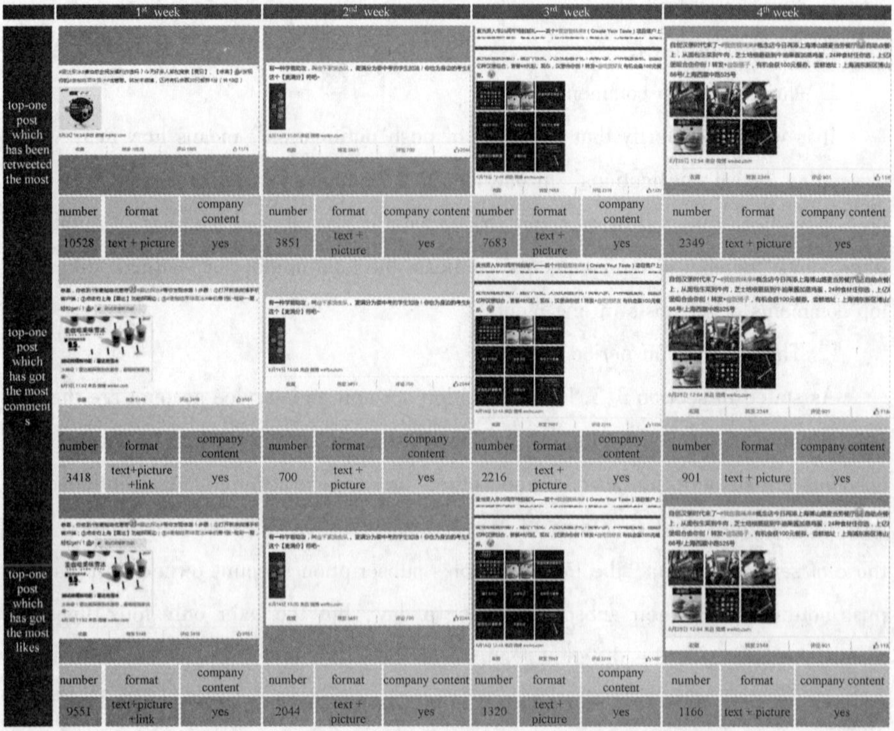

Figure 4.10 Qualitative data collection (Example: McDonald's)

As same as Sina Weibo case study, the suitable KPIs have been identified for WeChat case based on the features of this platform and data available on WeChat official accounts. Meanwhile, one-month observation period has been set to observe these indicators and obtain the relevant data. It is necessary to point out that limited data such as the number of push notification, the number of posts, the number of reading, and the number of top comments (up to the top 100 comments) can be obtained by the third party (the explanation referred to chapter 6). As a matter of fact, some important indicators, e.g., number of followers cannot be acquired by the third party. Based on the analysis and consideration described above, WeChat key performance indicators are presented blow.

① WeChat KPIs

WeChat KPIs include:

A. Number of push notification;

B. Number of posts;

C. Number of readings;

D. Number of likes;

E. Number of top comments.

It is worthy to clarify that "number of push notification" means how many times of sending "push notifications" in one month. "Number of posts" refers to how many posts have been released by company in one month. "Number of readings" "number of likes" and "number of top comments" indicate the total number of readings, likes and top comments of all posts in one month.

② The observation period

As stated in section 3. 3. 1, subscription account and service account are the typical official accounts for conducting WeChat marketing. In this research, some selected accounts are subscription accounts and others are service accounts. As mentioned before, the features and functions of WeChat subscription account are different from those of service account, the former enables subscription account owners to broadcast push notification to their subscribers once a day, but the later only four times per month. According to the different features of these two types of WeChat official accounts, the data collection is conducted in one month that is reasonable for both types of accounts. **Based on the consideration, the observation period was determined to be one month from November 1st 2016 to November 30th 2016.**

It is clear that there are totally five weeks: the first week includes six days (from November 1st to November 6th); the second week includes seven days (from November 7th to November 13th); the third week includes seven days (from November 14th to November 20th); the fourth week includes seven days (from November 21st to November 27th); the fifth week includes three days (from November 28th to November 30th). The corresponding data collection has been conducted in accordance with KPIs during the observation period.

4. 2. 3 Information architecture

This section introduces the definition and application of IA (information architecture). Moreover, the implementation of IA in WeChat case study has also been presented.

4. 2. 3. 1 IA definition

A representative definition of IA was proposed by Rosenfeld, Morville & Arango

(2015) and described below:

"*Information architecture (IA) is a design discipline that is focused on making information findable and understandable. Because of this, it is uniquely well suited to address these challenges. IA allows us to think about problems through two important perspectives: that information products and services are perceived by people as places made of language, and that these information environments can be organized for optimum findability and understandability.*"

Moreover, Rosenfeld, Morville & Arango (2015) clarified IA in line with the following four points:

① The structural design of shared information environments;

② The synthesis of organization, labeling, search, and navigation systems within digital, physical, and cross-channel ecosystem;

③ The art and science of shaping information products and experiences to support usability, findability, and understanding;

④ An emerging discipline and community of practice focused on bringing principles of design and architecture to the digital landscape.

According to Rosenfeld, Morville & Arango (2015), three circles (context, content and users) are involved in IA (shown in figure 4.11).

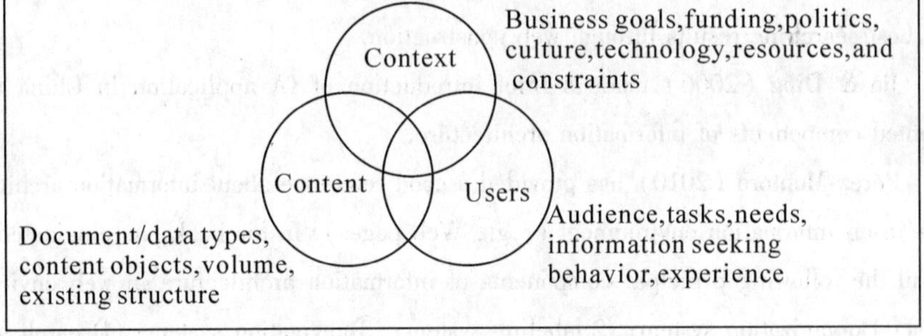

Figure 4.11 Three circles of IA

(Source: Rosenfeld et al., 2015)

(1) Context

The term "context" refers to factors such as business goals, funding, resources, technology, culture, politics and constraints. According to Spencer (2010), the context mainly contains the following areas: ①goals; ②design; ③technology; ④stakeholders; ⑤culture.

(2) Content

The term "content" represents generally document/data type, content objects, volume and existing structure. It comprises documents, scheme, applications, services and metadata (Kaario et al., 2008).

(3) Users

The term "users" indicates that it is important to comprehend users' information seeking behaviors in line with their needs. It contains some core elements such as audience, information seeking behavior and experience.

4.2.3.2 IA applications

Originally, IA principles was applied in the architecture of text information (Wurman, 1997) and then extended to information and library science.

With the rapid development of the Internet, network information has been growing explosively and information architecture has been adopted to deal with massive information under information-rich environments such as the World Wide Web, mobile application design and development, graphic and information design, and etc. (Rosenfeld et al., 2015; Resmini et al., 2009).

According to McNay (2003), when it comes to web, IA involves mainly two tasks: ①organization of a website's content into categories; ②creation of an interface to support categories. In this sense, the goal of information architecture is to achieve the best searching results through web construction.

Jia & Ding (2006) made a brief introduction of IA application in China and counted components of information architecture.

Pérez-Montoro (2010) has provided a good reference about information architecture in an information environment (e.g., Web pages). In his book, he elucidated in detail the following principal components of information architecture in web environment: ①organization system; ②labeling system; ③navigation system; ④search system; ⑤controlled vocabularies.

IA has also been applied to social media and user interface (UI) design. Moore (2014) presented a social media case study on building an event on Twitter by adopting information architecture.

Liu et al. (2015) put forward a method of invisible grid management of information architecture of UI design. In their study, information architecture principles were used to design web & mobile App (WeChat) interface layout for business targets.

4.2.3.3 Implementation of IA in this research

In this study, information architecture principles have been adopted in the WeChat official accounts' interface & menu analysis. Sixty high reputation companies' WeChat official accounts' interface and menus have been reviewed and analyzed in line with the observation period from October 21st of 2016 to November 4th of 2016.

In order to organize all information into different categories and subcategories, the labeling process has been conducted. Finally, six types of categories and forty subcategories have been obtained. The detailed explanation of the implementation of IA in this research has been stated in section 6.1.

4.3 Content analysis

The section introduces the definition and applications of content analysis. And then the implementation of content analysis in this research has also been stated.

4.3.1 Definition of content analysis

Berelson (1952) firstly defined content analysis as "*a research technique for the objective, systematic and quantitative description of the manifest content of communication*". Holsti (1969) stated that content analysis is "*any technique for making inferences by objectively and systematically identifying specified characteristics of messages*". Wright (1986) claimed "*it is a research technique for the systematic classification; it may involve quantitative or qualitative approaches, or both*". Neuman (1997) described content analysis as "*a technique for gathering and analyzing the content of text*". Krippendorff (2004) presented that "*content analysis is a research technique for making replicable and valid inference from texts (or other meaningful matter) to the contexts of their use*". Baran (2002) stated that content analysis is a social science methodology concerned with the objective, systematic, and quantitative description of the content of communication.

According to Lai & To (2015) and Snelson (2016), content analysis techniques can also be divided into 3 types: ①qualitative; ②quantitative; ③mixed. Snelson (2016) stated that content analysis can be conducted with qualitative or quantitative methods, and also probably the combination of both methods.

4.3.1.1 Qualitative content analysis methodology

According to Macnamara (2005), qualitative content analysis examines the relationship between the text and its likely audience meaning and also determines the likely meaning of texts to audiences. It considers not only the text, but also audience, media and contextual factors. Sellson (2016) regarded qualitative content analysis as a descriptive research method involving development of a coding frame and qualitative coding of data, which has been applied by Schreier (2012).

4.3.1.2 Quantitative content analysis methodology

As for quantitative content analysis, the data collected based on media content is presented in number format and analyzed in mathematical, statistical or any other quantitative manners.

4.3.1.3 Mixed methodology

Macnamara (2005) discussed that the combination of both qualitative and quantitative methods seems to be the ideal approach. On one hand, quantitative content analysis can conform to the scientific method and yield reliable findings. On the other hand, qualitative analysis of texts helps understand deeper meanings and likely interpretations by audiences.

4.3.2 Application fields of content analysis

Content analysis methodology has been used in advertising, communication and journalism to analyze mass media content and to study cultural values in traditional media (Cutler et al., 1992; Albers-Miller et al., 1996; Rafaeli et al., 1997; Ju-Pak, 1999; Singh et al., 2004).

Furthermore, content analysis method has also been widely used in sales and marketing to understand the characteristics and behavior of the target market.

With the advent of new media, it has been increasingly applied to a wide range of disciplines related to new media, especially social media.

The booming of Web 2.0 has driven content analysis method become a dominant analytic approach in the studies of social media content such as Facebook posts, Twitter posts and YouTube videos. For example, Cohen and Duchan (2012) conducted a qualitative analysis of the content of Twitter posts submitted by teenage students in their study of the role of Twitter in the teaching and learning process. Chen (2013) coded the content of YouTube videos of people interviewed as part of a qualitative research study of personal branding.

In particular, Ma (2013) made a cross-cultural content analysis to compare microblogging contents on Twitter in the US and Weibo in China. And Liang (2015) performed both quantitative and qualitative content analyses on Sina Weibo posts to discover how Chinese international students use Sina Weibo to seek health related information. As mentioned by Liang (2015), the content analysis of Sina Weibo users' posts/retweets, language usage, and types of interaction messages shared with each other helps discern how Sina Weibo facilitates to create a virtual community.

Recently, Balslery (2016) presented an interesting content analysis to examine how politicians such as Donald Trump have been using social media platforms, e.g., Twitter, to reach voters in the 2016 presidential race.

4.3.3 Implementation of content analysis in this research

This section states the content analysis used in Sina Weibo case study to analyze the top-one posts from all selected companies' Sina Weibo official accounts.

In Sina Weibo case study, every week three types of top-one post (top-one post which has been retweeted the most; top-one post which has got the most comments; and top-one post which has got the most likes) have been identified and represented as the most successful content marketing. There are three factors to explore their content features which are "*the best day to publish it*" (exploring which day to publish it), "*format*" (text, picture, video, etc.), and "*content relevance*" (whether the content of the post is related to the company's news, advertising, activity, products, services, etc.).

The distinctive characteristic of top-one posts is they have got bigger number than other posts within the same week's timeline. Or, in other words, users have paid more attention and interests on these top-one posts. In this sense, a better engagement with users has been achieved by these posts with big number of retweets/comments/likes. So it is necessary to analyze all top-one posts in line with the three factors described above. Figure 4.12 shows an example of top-one post from company BYD. Trying to find out the reasons of being the top-one post can help understand why it has attracted its followers.

Figure 4. 12　An example of top-one post from BYD's Sina Weibo account

The translation of the content of this post in figure 4. 12 is given below:

"*Opening match of CRC (China Rally Championship) will be held today, Netizens express great interest in it. Learning some relevant knowledge and skills could be helpful to communicate with others. Today, another question needs you to answer it. Please remember that giving your answer meanwhile retweeting this post plus hashtags # Qin war CRC# and #return of the king#, @ BYD and three friends of yours after following @ BYD official account and #Qin war CRC#topic. In line with the rules described above, five lucky draw towards to all of participants in the activity will be generated every day. The closing date of this activity is June 3rd, and a Grand Prize will be drawn among the participants who have given the right answer! Move up!*"

This post was published by company BYD on June 1st, 2015. During the first week's (from June 1st to June 7th) observation period, this post has not only been identified as the top-one post which has got the most comments with the big number "5 610", but also as the top-one post which has been retweeted the most because it has been retweeted 9 798 times by other users.

This post was published on Monday. In addition, from the perspective of format applications, text plus picture have been adopt in this post. It is consistent with the idea that the picture is easier to attract the audience's attention in the era of the picture reading.

After analyzing the content of this post, it is clear that followers had the chance to win an award if they answered the question and retweeted this post in accordance with the rules described above. Or, in other words, followers needed to complete two things so as to participate in luck draw every day. Specifically, they had to answer this question and left one comment; and they needed to retweet this post. These two things can explain why the post has acquired the big number of retweets and comments. Based on the analysis mentioned above, it can be stated that creating the users' benefit-oriented content can help acquire easily high attention from users.

4.4 Statistical method

As elucidated previously, data analysis via quantitative method could help the profound digging of collected data from case studies. And one of the most popular quantitative analysis methods to perform data analysis is statistical analysis approach. This section describes this methodology and its application in this research.

Normally there are two categories of statistical analysis methods: ①descriptive statistical method; ②inferential statistical method.

4.4.1 Descriptive statistical method

This method is used to present the basic characteristics of the gathered data in a research by summarizing the simple statistical information such as frequency distribution, the mean, sample size, standard deviation, standard error, the maximum, the minimum, range, statistical significance, and etc. Both tabular and graphical forms can be utilized in this method to show the data analysis results.

4.4.2 Inferential statistical method

Compared with descriptive statistical method, inferential statistical method is not direct, but more advanced aiming to explore further information from the collected data which cannot be easily figured out by direct simple statistical analysis. This method comprises advanced statistical analyses such as cluster analysis, factor analysis, regression, testing, fitting, and etc. In this study, cluster analysis is an important technique and will be described in the following section.

Similarly, the analysis results can be expressed in both tabular and visual manners. In this study, both manners have been used. With this method, more general findings may be detected.

As stated by some researchers (Abonyi et al., 2007; Romesburg, 2004), cluster analysis is a type of techniques and a multivariate method that is used for data mining in order to classify objects/subjects/cases based on measured variables into different groups (called clusters). No prior information about the cluster membership is needed in cluster analysis.

The principal process of cluster analysis includes: ①problem formulation; ②selection of distance measurement method; ③clustering procedure selection; ④determination of cluster number; ⑤interpretation of cluster profile.

In general, in line with different clustering methods or measurement references during this process, there are three types of cluster analyses: ①hierarchical cluster analysis; ②non hierarchical cluster analysis; ③two-step cluster analysis.

Hierarchical cluster analysis (HCA) is an exploratory technique to detect natural clusters based on a database and is suitable for cases or variables with less than a few hundred of objects. In a hierarchical cluster, a tree structure is developed for cluster grouping via one of the two typical procedures: ①agglomerative method; ②divisive method.

The non-hierarchical cluster analysis is also called k-means cluster analysis procedure which is suitable for continuous data and needs to specify the number of clusters in advance. K-means cluster analysis is most useful while classifying a large number of cases or variables.

The two-step procedure automatically selects the optimal number of clusters.

In this research, hierarchical cluster analysis with agglomerative method has been adopted. In practice, agglomerative methods are used more often than divisive ones.

4.4.3 Statistical analysis tool

There exist many types of statistical software. One of them, which has been widely used for statistical analysis in social science and marketing, is SPSS software — a data management and statistical analysis tool with very versatile data processing capabilities.

SPSS can handle large amounts of data and perform a comprehensive statistical analysis with results expressed in tables and graphs.

The main functions of SPSS include:

(1) Flexible and robust data pre-posting and transforming.

(2) Descriptive statistics: frequencies, descriptive, explore, cross tables, descriptive ratio statistics, and etc.

(3) Bivariate statistics: means, t-test, ANOVA, correlation, nonparametric tests, etc.

(4) Model prediction: linear regression, curve estimation, weight estimation, etc.

(5) Cluster/group identification: factor analysis, cluster analysis (hierarchical, k-means, and two-step), discriminant analysis, etc.

With regards to the SPSS software interface, tutorial, manuals, and etc. refer to the online IBM SPSS Statistics Documentation with the following Internet link: http://www-01.ibm.com/support/docview.wss? uid=swg27038407#en.

Cluster analysis method has been used widely in many fields including marketing and social media.

4.4.4 Implementation of statistical method in this research

In this study, statistical analyses via SPSS mainly contain descriptive statistics analysis and hierarchical cluster analysis.

The basic procedure to conduct HCA includes data processing, data transforming, clustering, and optimal cluster determination.

4.4.4.1 Data transforming

It is a common practice in statistical analyses to normalize the original data in order to eliminate the data diversity or with large differential magnitudes and so as to obtain relatively uniform data structure. In SPSS, the following normalization methods are available:

①Z scores;

②Range −1 to 1;

③Range 0 to 1;

④Maximum magnitude of 1;

⑤Mean of 1;

⑥Standard deviation of 1.

In this research, "Range 0 to 1" method has been adopted especially when the magnitude of the dataset is diverse. In this situation, it is necessary to reduce the dataset to a common denominator in order to make the data comparable (Borgatti, 2002). One way to get around this different scale issues is to normalize the original data by scaling between 0 and 1 as given below:

$$X_i = \frac{X_i - X_{min}}{X_{max} - X_{min}}$$

where

X_{min} = the minimum value for variable X

X_{max} = the maximum value for variable X

4.4.4.2 Database creation

Database has been set up after data categorizing and data coding. Its form can be ASCII file (*.dat), excel, and etc.

Excel format has been adopted in this research to create the database. This excel format database was imported into the statistical analysis software — SPSS via Open Database option within the "File" menu (referred to the online IBM SPSS Statistics Documentation, http://www-01.ibm.com/support/docview.wss? uid=swg27038407#en).

Once the methodologies for this research have been explained, the following chapters present the results that have been obtained in this study. Specifically, the results are grounded in two case studies. Chapter 5 collects the results of the Sina Weibo case study. Chapter 6 presents the results of the WeChat analysis. The general discussion of the results of both case studies is presented in chapter 7.

5 SINA WEIBO CASE STUDY AND RESULTS

This chapter presents Sina Weibo case study and its results with the purpose to measure all selected companies' social media performance on Sina Weibo platform. Specifically, the results refer to the following aspects:

- social relationship among all companies in view of "following" and "followers";
- the history of usage of Sina Weibo marketing of all companies;
- the content features of the important tweets;
- a systematic measurement and classification framework built to measure all companies' performance on Sina Weibo channel.

Moreover, the corresponding methods presented in chapter 4 such as KPIs concept, content analysis, descriptive statistical analysis, and cluster analysis have been adopted in Sina Weibo case study.

5.1 Exploring social relationship among all companies

This section presents the exploration of the social relationship among all selected companies from the respective of "following" and "follower".

Small social circle has been formed among all companies on Sina Weibo channel. It is very interesting to clarify the relationship of their "following" and "followers" only between themselves. Table 5.1 reveals the "social relationships" in terms of "following" and "followers" among all companies on Sina Weibo. It is necessary to note that the last access to all companies' Sina Weibo accounts so as to acquire the list of followers and followings was on May 28th of 2015. As shown in table 5. 1, each company's followings and followers have been listed one by one inside this small social circle.

Table 5. 1 Exploration of social relationship in view of followings and followers

Company	Following	Follower
Apple	Intel	TCL
Starbucks		Nike, GE, Lenovo, Kweichow Moutai, Midea
McDonald's	Coca-Cola	Coca-Cola, Kweichow Moutai, GE, Pingan
Coca-Cola	McDonald's, GE	McDonald's, GE, Wahaha
Walt Disney		Wangfujing
FedEx	Boeing	Boeing
UPS		
General Electric	Fosun, HaiNan Airlines, Sany, Accenture, Boeing, McDonald's, P&G, Coca-Cola, Starbucks	Saic Motor, Sany, Coca-Cola, Fosun, Microsoft, Accenture, Boeing,
American Express		
Nike	Starbucks	
BMW	HaiNan Airlines	HaiNan Airlines, Saic Motor, Fosun, Volkswagen, Wahaha, Geely, Midea
Volkswagen	BMW	
Procter & Gamble		Fosun, GE, Wahaha, Wal-Mart Stores, Midea
IBM	Haier, Intel, Microsoft, SuNing	Intel, SuNing
Accenture	GE	GE
Johnson & Johnson		
3M		
Microsoft	Lenovo, Intel, Boeing, GE,	Intel, IBM, Gome, Lenovo, Boeing
Boeing	HaiNan Airlines, Microsoft, GE, FedEx	HaiNan Airlines, Microsoft, GE, FedEx
Exxon Mobil		
Wal-Mart Stores	Gree, PepsiCo, Unilever, P&G,	Wahaha
Nestlé S.A.	Lenovo, Xiaomi, Intel	Lenovo, Intel, Xiaomi

Table 5.1 (Continued)

Company	Following	Follower
Unilever	Tsingtao	Wal-Mart Stores, Midea
PepsiCo		Wal-Mart Stores, Wahaha
Caterpillar		Deere
Deere	Caterpillar	
Marriott International		
DuPont	BYD	
Intel	Gome, ZTE, Lenovo, Nestlé S.A. Microsoft, IBM	ZTE, Lenovo, Nestlé S.A. TCL, Gome, Microsoft, IBM
Cisco System		
Huawei		Fosun
ZTE	Intel	Intel
Haier		Midea, IBM, TCL
Xiaomi	Nestlé S.A.	Nestlé S.A., Fosun, Wahaha
Lenovo	Intel, Microsft, Starbucks, Nestlé S.A.,	Saic Motor, Fosun, Nestlé S.A., Intel, Gome, Microsoft, TCL, Wahaha
Gree	Midea	Gome, Wal-Mart Stores, Midea
Midea	Gome, Pingan, Gree, Haier, Unilever, P&G, BMW, Starbucks	Gree
TCL	Gome, Lenovo, Haier, Intel, Apple	Fosun
Hisense	Gome	
BYD		Saic Motor, Geely, DuPont
Great Wall Motors		Geely
Saic Motor	Bright Food, Geely, BYD, Lenovo, BMW, GE	Bright Food
Geely	Fosun, Great Wall Motors, BYD, BMW	Saic Motor, Fosun
Wahaha	Xiaomi, Lenovo, PepsiCo, Wal-Mart Stores, P&G, BMW, Coca-Cola	
Tsingtao	YanJing Beer,	Unilever
Kweichow Moutai	Gome, McDonald's, Starbucks	
YanJing Beer		Tsingtao

Table 5.1(Continued)

Company	Following	Follower
Bright Food	Fosun, Saic Motor	Fosun, Saic Motor
HaiNan Airlines	Gome, Boeing, BMW	Gome, Boeing, BMW, GE
Yunnan Baiyao		
Ping An	McDonald's	Midea
WangFujing	Walt Disney	
SuNing	Midea, Hisense, TCL, Lenovo, Haier, Intel, Microsoft, IBM	Midea, IBM, Fosun, Microsoft, Lenovo, Haier, Hisense, TCL
Gome	HaiNan Airlines, Gree, Lenovo, Intel, Microsoft	Midea, HaiNan Airlines, Intel, Kweichow Moutai, Hisense, TCL
Wanda		
Vanke		
Country Garden		
SANY	GE	GE
New Hope Group		
Fosun	Xiaomi, Bright Food, Geely, TCL, Lenovo, Huawei, P&G, BMW, GE	Bright Food, Geely, GE

According to table 5.1, it can be seen that some companies were very active in this small social circle such as General Electric which was the fan of nine companies (Fosun, HaiNan Airlines, Sany, Accenture, Boeing, McDonald's, P&G, Coca-Cola, and Starbucks). Meanwhile, it had seven followers (Saic Motor, Sany, Coca-Cola, Fosun, Microsoft, Accenture, and Boeing) in this online community. Chinese company SuNing was another active example. It followed eight companies (Midea, Hisense, TCL, Lenovo, Haier, Intel, Microsoft, and IBM). At the same time, it had eight fans (Midea, IBM, Fosun, Microsoft, Lenovo, Haier, Hisense, and TCL) inside this small social circle.

However, some companies did not build "social relationship" in this community, e.g., UPS, American Express, Johnson & Johnson, 3M, Exxon Mobil, Marriott International, Cisco System, Yunnan Baiyao, Wanda, Vanke, Country Garden, and New Hope Group. This implies that these companies did not pay attention to build connection with the rest companies within this circle. In other words, neither they were fans of any company, nor they had any followers from the community.

Moreover, there seems to be more relationships built in the same or similar industry. For example, McDonald's and Coca-Cola which were mutual fans of each other. IBM preferred to follow companies from its similar industry such as Intel and Microsoft.

Besides, it is necessary to explore in this small social circle whether there exists region difference in view of the followings and followers. As described in table 5.2, it seems that thirty Western companies preferred to follow companies from Western region rather than Chinese companies although their followers did not have a geographical difference in this community.

Table 5.2 Exploration of the region differences in view of followings & followers

30 Western companies				30 Chinese companies			
Following		Follower		Following		Follower	
Western companies	Chinese companies	Western companies	Chinese companies	Western companies	Chinese companies	Western companies	Chinese companies
30	16	29	32	33	39	17	38

Similarly, region difference did also exist in thirty Chinese companies' followings and followers, which had larger number from domestic Chinese companies than Occidental ones. In this sense, stronger links have been established within those companies from the same region in this small community which integrated Chinese and Western companies on Sina Weibo platform. That is to say, Western and Chinese companies have established respectively a relatively closer relationship than the cross-regional connections.

Furthermore, it is worth exploring the relationship among companies that pay attention to each other, i.e., company A is a fan of company B, and company B is also a follower of company A. They are mutual fans. Figure 5.1 shows the relationship map among these companies.

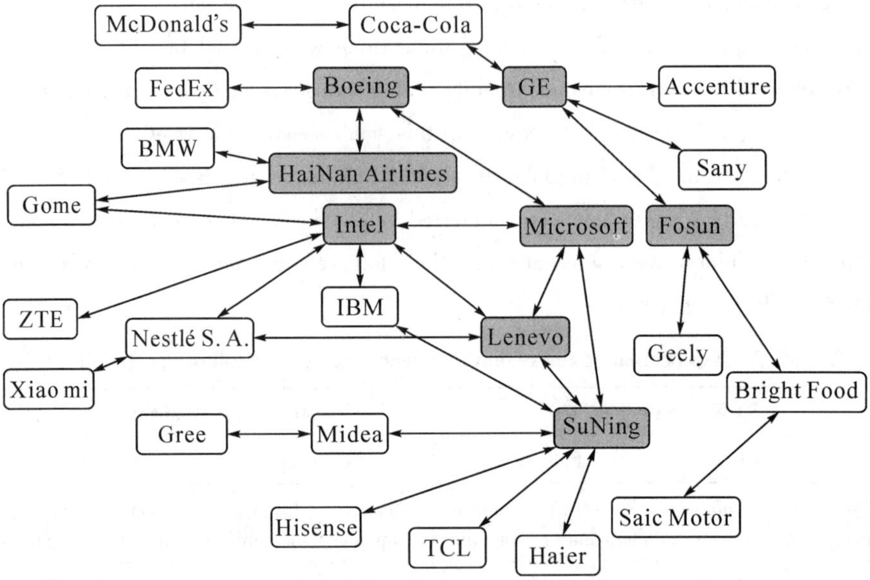

Figure 5. 1 The relationship map among companies which were mutual fans

The relationship map is made up of twenty-seven companies, with some important nodes labeled in gray color which are helpful to connect to all companies in this map. The eight important nodes in gray color denote the following companies: Boeing, HaiNan Airlines, Intel, GE, Microsoft, Fosun, Lenovo and SuNing, each of which has at least three companies of mutual concern involving both Western and Chinese companies. Figure 5. 1 also reveals that it is more likely for companies to follow companies from the same or similar industry sectors. For instance, there are some groups of mutual fans such as Intel & Microsoft, Lenovo & Microsoft, Intel & Lenovo, and so on.

Generally speaking, **stronger links or closer relationships have been established within companies from the same region than those cross-regional connections** inside this small social circle. At the same time, companies have shown some preferences when they decide which companies to follow. Normally **they prefer to follow companies from their own or similar industries.**

5.2 The history of usage of Sina Weibo from 2009 to 2014

This section aims to explore the results of the history of usage of Sina Weibo among all selected companies from 2009 to 2014.

Firstly, this section demonstrates the first usage of Sina Weibo channel for microblogging marketing by these companies since Sina Weibo's birth in 2009. Or, in other words, this section explores when these companies started microblogging marketing journey.

Moreover, two types of primary data have been collected. One part is the specific date of first usage of Sina Weibo platform for all companies. Another part is annual statistic "number of original posts vs. number of retweets" of all companies' Sina Weibo official accounts from 2009 to 2014. These data have been collected respectively for the thirty Western companies and the thirty Chinese companies. Based on these data, the evolution of "number of original posts vs. number of retweets" regarding the sixty companies' Sina Weibo official accounts from 2009 to 2014 has been explored.

5.2.1 The first usage of Sina Weibo

From the homepage of each company's Sina Weibo account, the specific date of first post publishing can be obtained. This indicates when each company started being involved in Sina Weibo marketing.

Table 5.3 reveals when all selected reputation Western companies started to use Sina Weibo. Since then, these companies have embarked on a long microblogging marketing trip.

Table 5.3 The dates of first post publishing on Sina Weibo (Western companies)

No.	Company name	The date of first post
1	Apple	14/12/2010
2	Starbucks	14/05/2010
3	McDonald's	08/04/2011
4	Coca-Cola	11/10/2010

Table 5.3(Continued)

No.	Company name	The date of first post
5	Walt Disney	25/11/2010
6	FedEx	05/07/2010
7	UPS	20/09/2010
8	General Electric	××/12/2010
9	American Express	27/04/2012
10	Nike	06/07/2011
11	BMW	23/02/2010
12	Volkswagen	05/11/2012
13	Procter & Gamble	22/06/2010
14	IBM	31/01/2011
15	Accenture	09/07/2012
16	Johnson & Johnson	27/08/2012
17	3M	18/03/2011
18	Microsoft	23/09/2011
19	Boeing	23/05/2011
20	Exxon Mobil	09/03/2014
21	Wal-Mart Stores	08/11/2012
22	Nestlé S.A.	12/08/2011
23	Unilever	04/01/2011
24	PepsiCo	19/07/2010
25	Caterpillar	15/11/2011
26	Deere	10/04/2011
27	Marriott International	22/10/2012
28	DuPont	01/12/2009
29	Intel	19/03/2012
30	Cisco System	04/01/2012

After further analysis of table 5.3, the number of Western companies' newly-present on Sina Weibo platform per year is revealed and listed in table 5.4.

Table 5.4 The number of Western companies newly-present on Sina Weibo per year (2009-2014)

Year	2009	2010	2011	2012	2013	2014
No. of Companies newly-present	1	10	10	8	0	1

Table 5. 4 shows that only one Western company started to use Sina Weibo in the year of the birth of Sina Weibo, i.e., 2009. However, in the next three years, there has been a significant growth in the usage of Sina Weibo among thirty Western companies.

It is interesting to see from table 5. 3 that an Western company DuPont is the first company registering its Sina Weibo's enterprise account and beginning relevant activities within all Western companies.

In 2010, much more Western companies (total 10) have had Sina Weibo's enterprise accounts and began to run related activities. In 2011, the number of Western companies which started microblogging marketing on Sina Weibo platform doubled. By 2012, nearly all Western companies involved in Sina Weibo marketing through their Sina Weibo's enterprise accounts. Till 2014, all the selected thirty Western companies have created Sina Weibo's enterprise accounts and have had relevant activities on these accounts.

As for the Chinese companies, the dates of first post publishing on their Sina Weibo accounts are presented in table 5. 5.

Table 5.5 The dates of first post publishing on Sina Weibo (Chinese companies)

No.	Company name	The date of first post
1	Huawei	28/12/2011
2	ZTE	22/12/2010
3	Haier	13/04/2010
4	Xiaomi	19/07/2010
5	Lenovo	15/07/2011
6	Gree	27/09/2010
7	Midea	11/05/2010
8	TCL	10/06/2011
9	Hisense	29/10/2010

Table 5. 5(Continued)

No.	Company name	The date of first post
10	BYD	24/05/2010
11	Great Wall Motors	06/11/2009
12	Saic Motor	17/04/2012
13	Geely	21/06/2011
14	Wahaha	02/05/2013
15	Tsingtao	26/01/2011
16	Kweichow Moutai	19/01/2013
17	YanJing Beer	11/04/2013
18	Bright Food	21/06/2012
19	HaiNan Airlines	20/05/2010
20	Yunnan Baiyao	16/10/2012
21	Ping An	10/10/2009
22	WangFujing	25/04/2011
23	SuNing	02/11/2010
24	Gome	07/01/2011
25	Wanda	30/08/2013
26	Vanke	25/10/2010
27	Country Garden	13/05/2011
28	SANY	07/07/2011
29	New Hope Group	21/04/2010
30	Fosun	29/06/2011

In order to get the number of companies that began to carry out microblogging activities per year, the further analysis of table 5. 5 has been conducted and the findings are shown in table 5. 6.

Table 5. 6 The number of Chinese companies newly-present on Sina Weibo per year (2009-2014)

Year	2009	2010	2011	2012	2013	2014
No. of Companies newly-present	2	11	10	3	4	0

It can be seen from table 5. 6 that only two Chinese companies started to register Sina Weibo account in 2009. But the number of companies newly-present on Sina

Weibo platform in 2010 and 2011 reached eleven and ten respectively.

The two Chinese companies (Great Wall Motors and Ping An) were first movers to register their Sina Weibo's enterprise accounts and ran microblogging marketing in 2009. Afterwards, there were eleven companies joining this big family on Sina Weibo channel in 2010. In particular, five companies (Haier, Gree, BYD, Great Wall Motors and Ping An) were quite active on Sina Weibo platform because they were keen on both behaviors of producing the original tweets and forwarding posts in 2010. By 2011, a total of twenty-three Chinese companies involved in Sina Weibo marketing with ten companies joining newly into the big family. It is noticeable that almost all companies were more active than the previous year. In addition, four Chinese companies (Wahaha, Kweichow Moutai, YanJing Beer and Wanda) began to use Sina Weibo channel for their digital marketing in 2013. It is relatively late for these four companies to realize the importance of microblogging marketing and to develop relevant activities.

In general, **the selected sixty high reputation companies were gradually involved in microblogging marketing on Sina Weibo platform from 2009 to 2014. Both Chinese and Western companies grew significantly from 2010 to 2012.** This indicates that Sina Weibo platform has become more and more popular no matter how these companies behave on it. Their efforts on Sina Weibo platform can be reflected by their original posts and retweets. The next part aims to explore the evolution of number of original posts vs. number of retweets of these companies from 2009 to 2014.

5.2.2 Evolution of "No. of original posts vs. No. of retweets" for Western companies

In order to explore the trend of original tweets and retweets for both Western and Chinese companies from 2009 to 2014, the corresponding evolution figures have been drawn and displayed as follows:

5.2.2.1 Evolution of number of original posts (Western companies)

Figure 5.2 shows the evolution of number of original posts based on the data collected from 2009 to 2014.

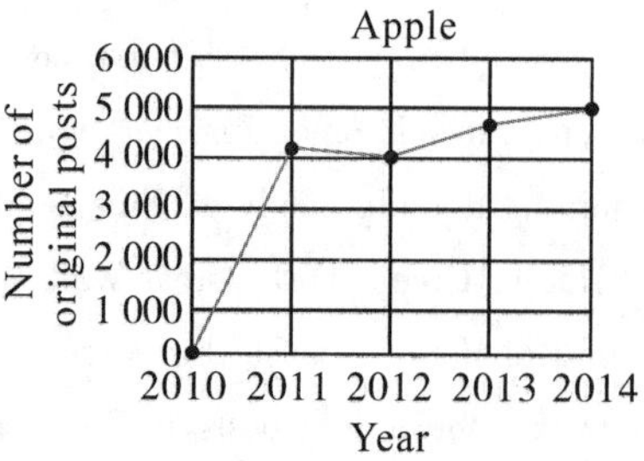
Apple
Number of original posts
6 000
5 000
4 000
3 000
2 000
1 000
0
2010 2011 2012 2013 2014
Year

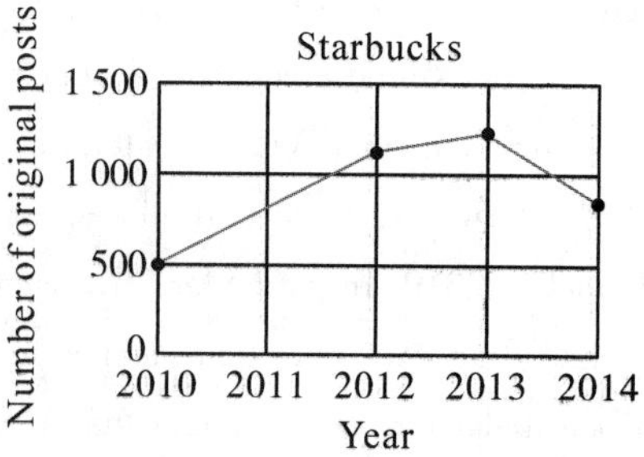
Starbucks
Number of original posts
1 500
1 000
500
0
2010 2011 2012 2013 2014
Year

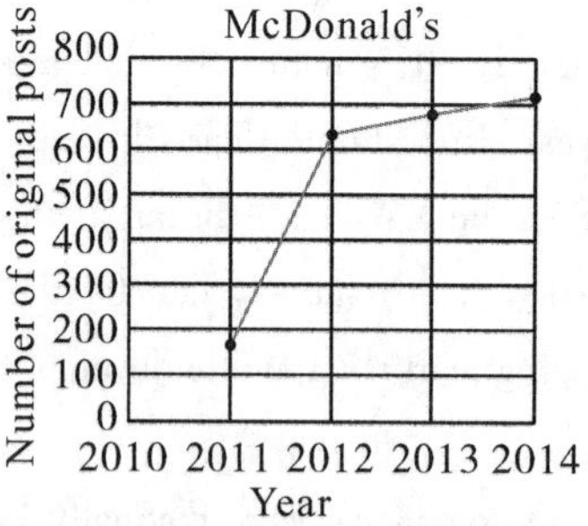
McDonald's
Number of original posts
800
700
600
500
400
300
200
100
0
2010 2011 2012 2013 2014
Year

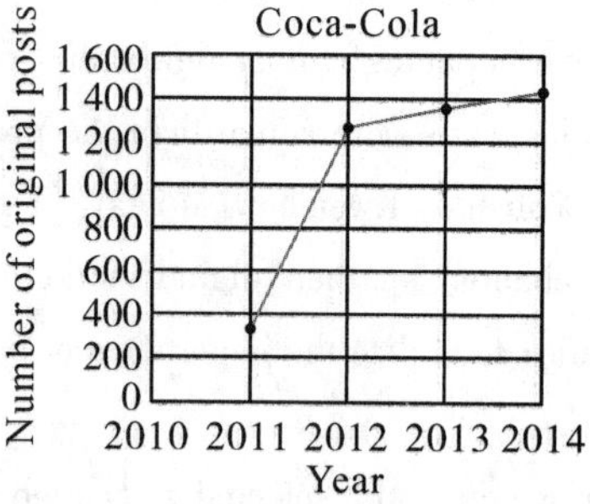
Coca-Cola
Number of original posts
1 600
1 400
1 200
1 000
800
600
400
200
0
2010 2011 2012 2013 2014
Year

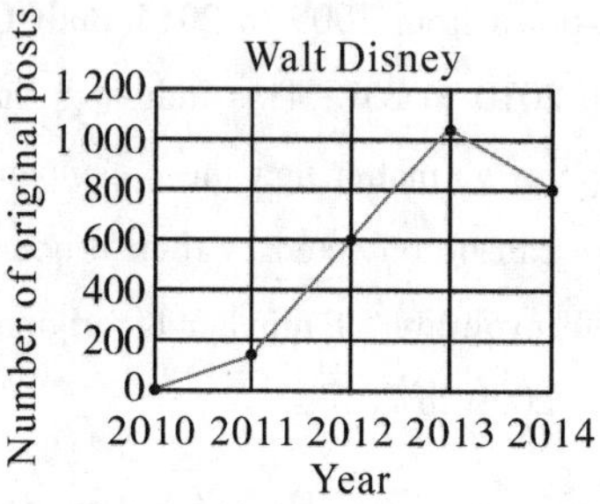
Walt Disney
Number of original posts
1 200
1 000
800
600
400
200
0
2010 2011 2012 2013 2014
Year

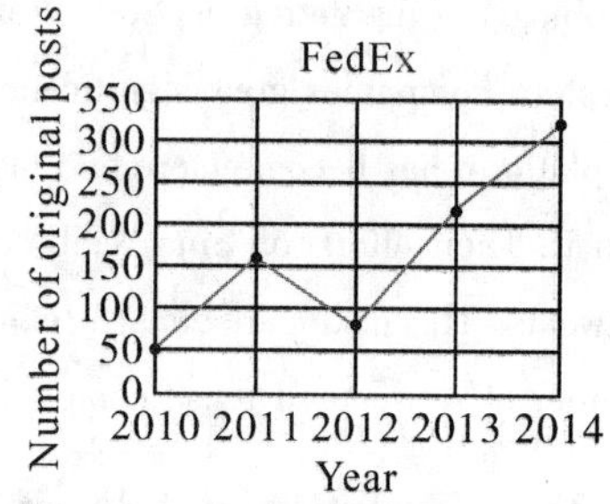
FedEx
Number of original posts
350
300
250
200
150
100
50
0
2010 2011 2012 2013 2014
Year

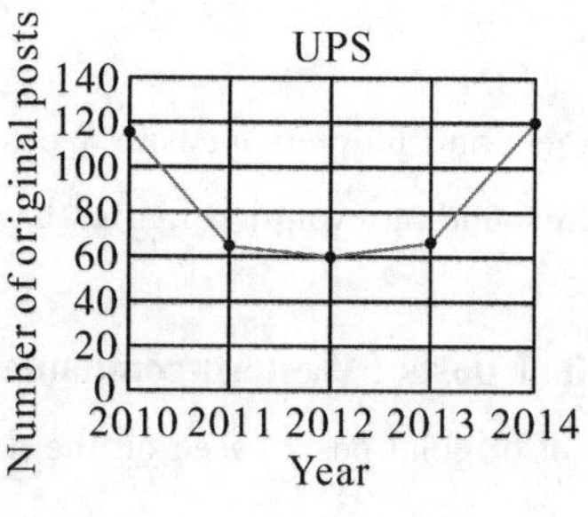
UPS
Number of original posts
140
120
100
80
60
40
20
0
2010 2011 2012 2013 2014
Year

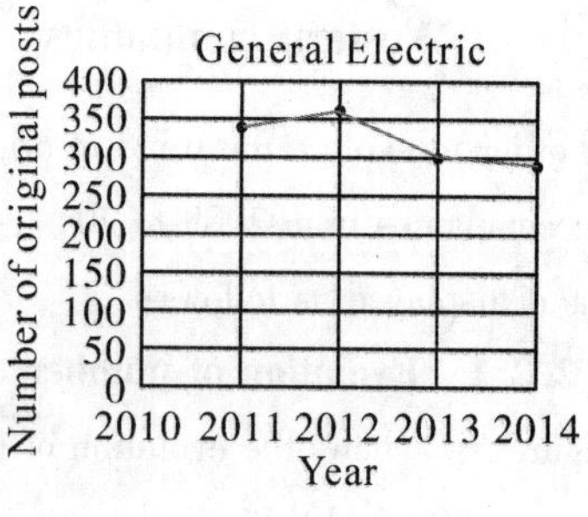
General Electric
Number of original posts
400
350
300
250
200
150
100
50
0
2010 2011 2012 2013 2014
Year

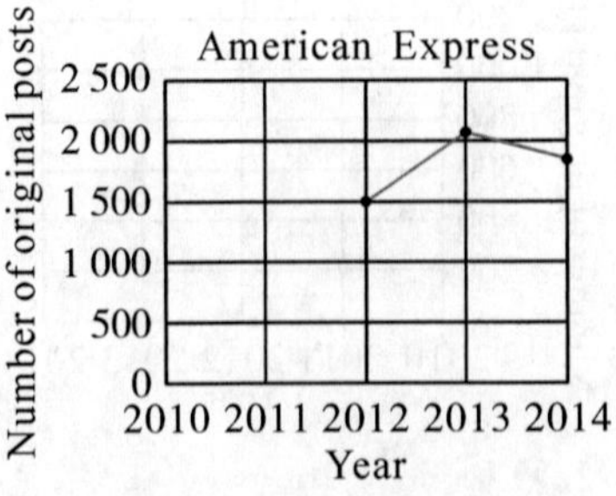
American Express
Number of original posts
2 500
2 000
1 500
1 000
500
0
2010 2011 2012 2013 2014
Year

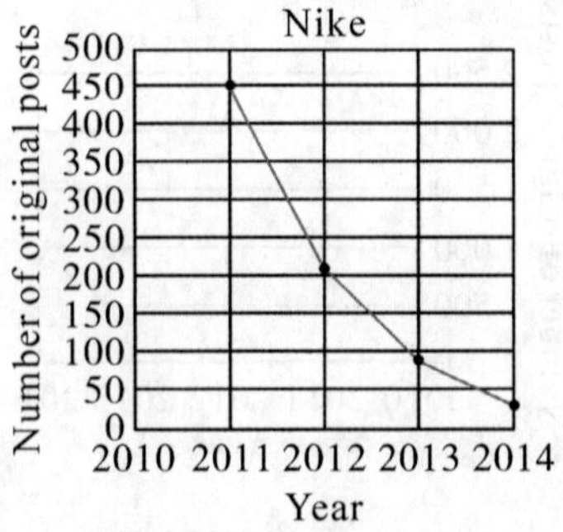
Nike
Number of original posts
500
450
400
350
300
250
200
150
100
50
0
2010 2011 2012 2013 2014
Year

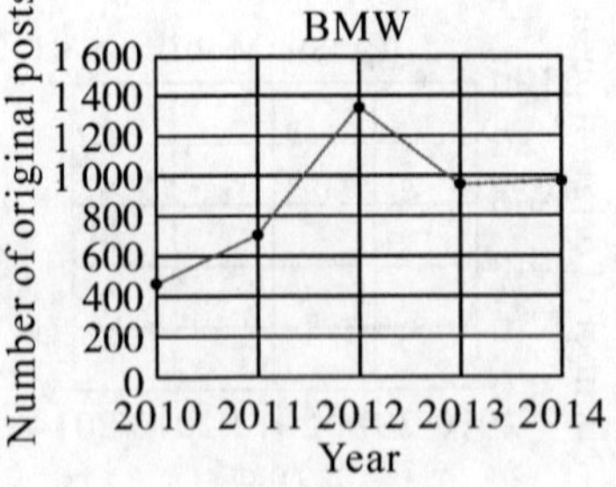
BMW
Number of original posts
1 600
1 400
1 200
1 000
800
600
400
200
0
2010 2011 2012 2013 2014
Year

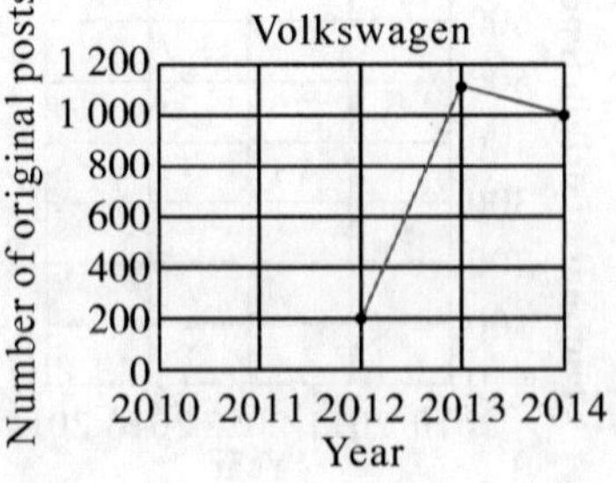
Volkswagen
Number of original posts
1 200
1 000
800
600
400
200
0
2010 2011 2012 2013 2014
Year

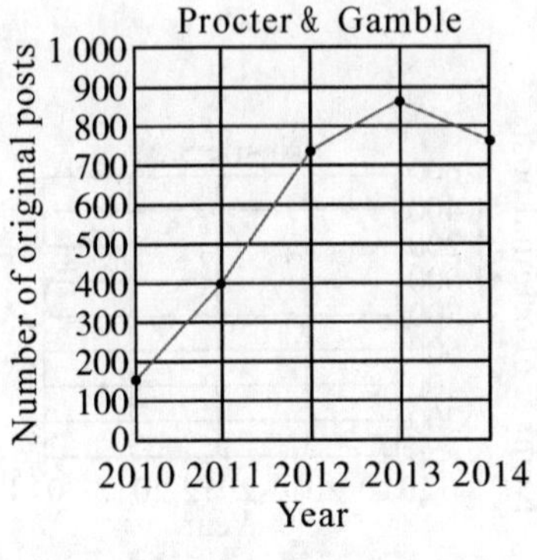
Procter & Gamble
Number of original posts
1 000
900
800
700
600
500
400
300
200
100
0
2010 2011 2012 2013 2014
Year

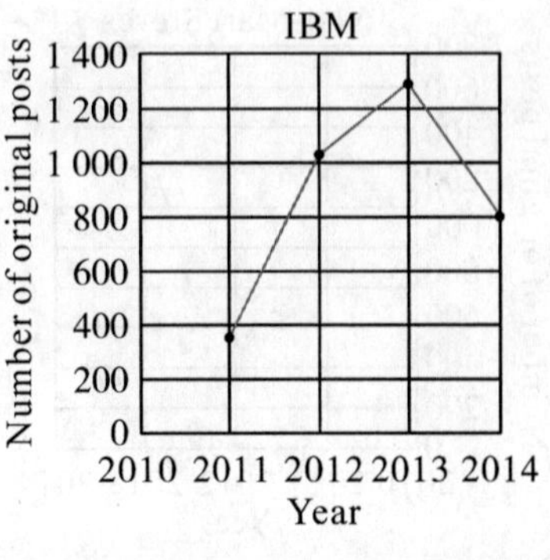
IBM
Number of original posts
1 400
1 200
1 000
800
600
400
200
0
2010 2011 2012 2013 2014
Year

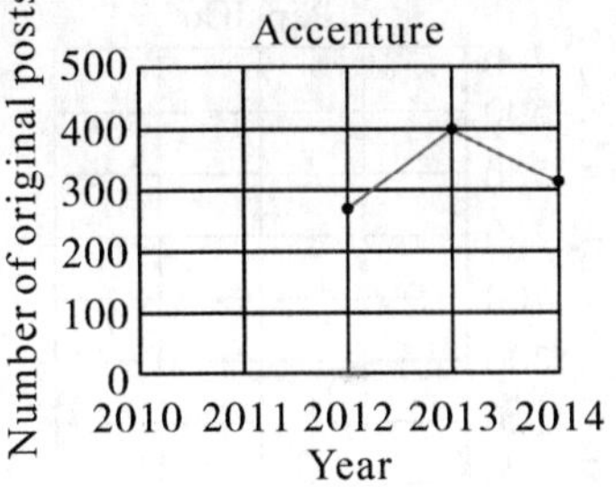
Accenture
Number of original posts
500
400
300
200
100
0
2010 2011 2012 2013 2014
Year

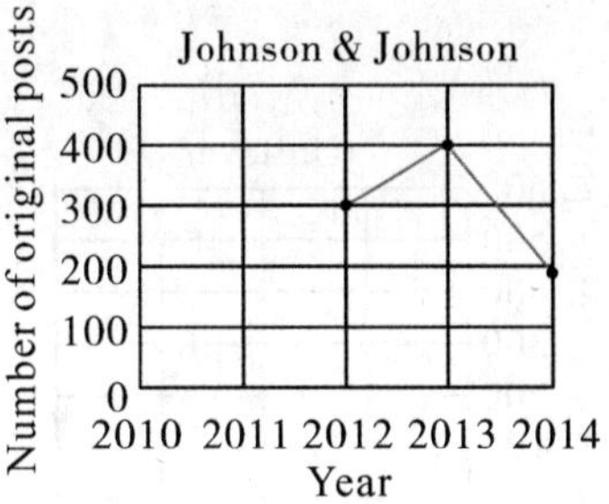
Johnson & Johnson
Number of original posts
500
400
300
200
100
0
2010 2011 2012 2013 2014
Year

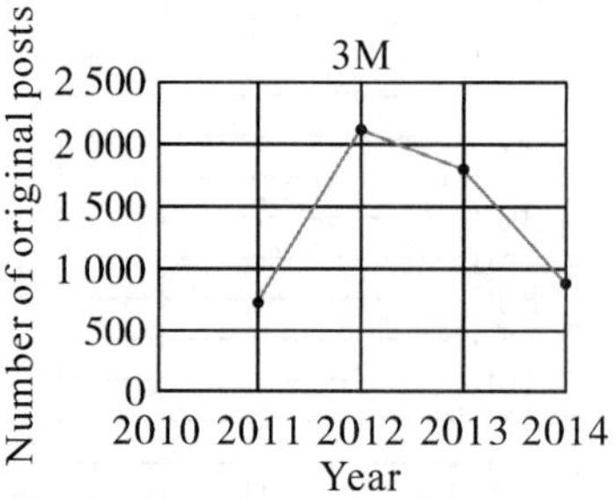
3M
Number of original posts
2 500
2 000
1 500
1 000
500
0
2010 2011 2012 2013 2014
Year

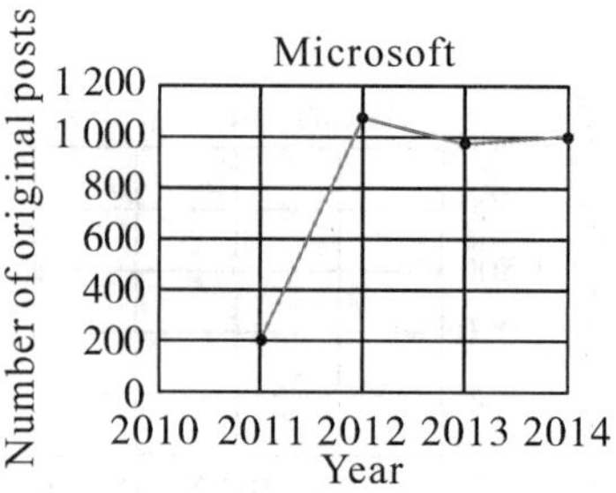
Microsoft
Number of original posts
1 200
1 000
800
600
400
200
0
2010 2011 2012 2013 2014
Year

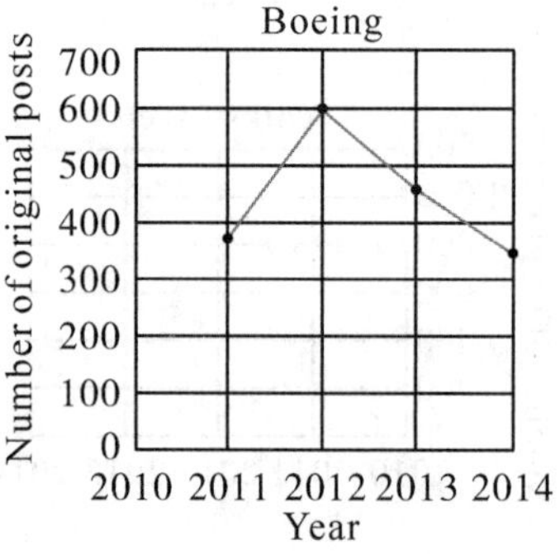
Boeing
Number of original posts
700
600
500
400
300
200
100
0
2010 2011 2012 2013 2014
Year

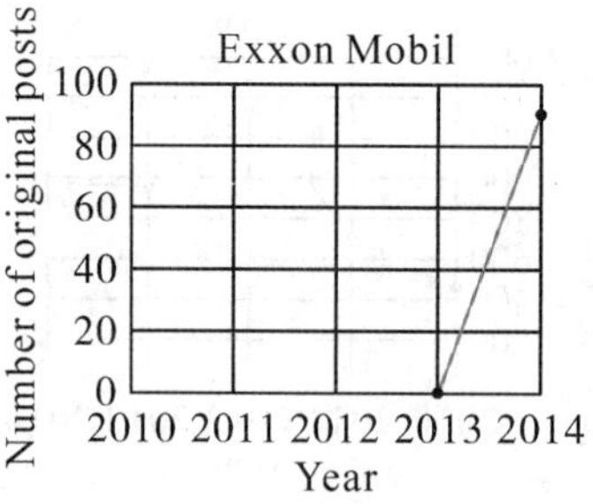
Exxon Mobil
Number of original posts
100
80
60
40
20
0
2010 2011 2012 2013 2014
Year

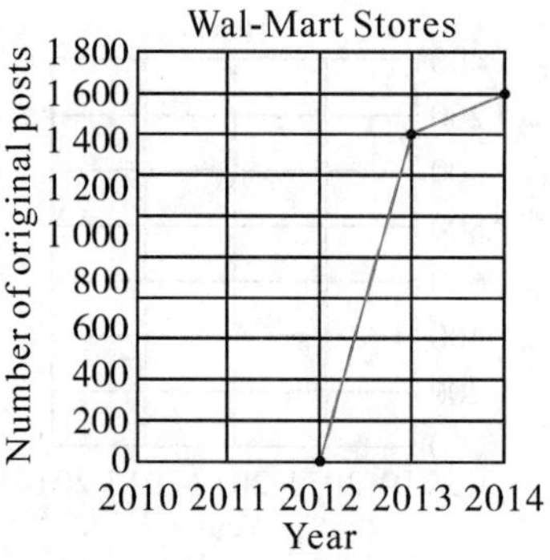
Wal-Mart Stores
Number of original posts
1 800
1 600
1 400
1 200
1 000
800
600
400
200
0
2010 2011 2012 2013 2014
Year

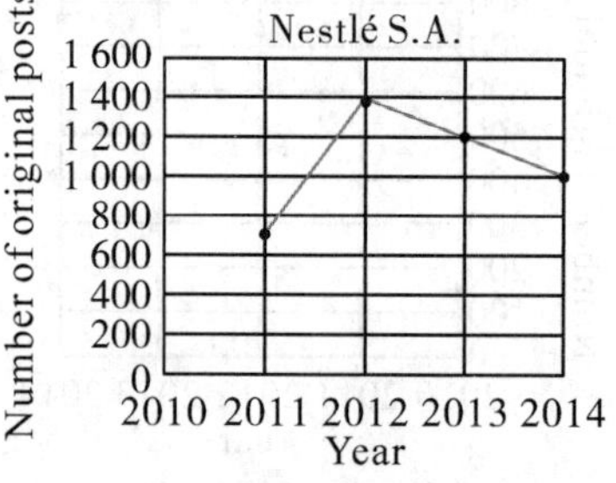
Nestlé S.A.
Number of original posts
1 600
1 400
1 200
1 000
800
600
400
200
0
2010 2011 2012 2013 2014
Year

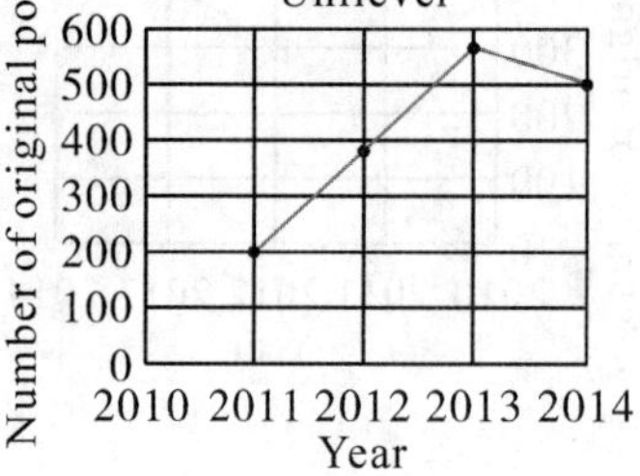
Unilever
Number of original posts
600
500
400
300
200
100
0
2010 2011 2012 2013 2014
Year

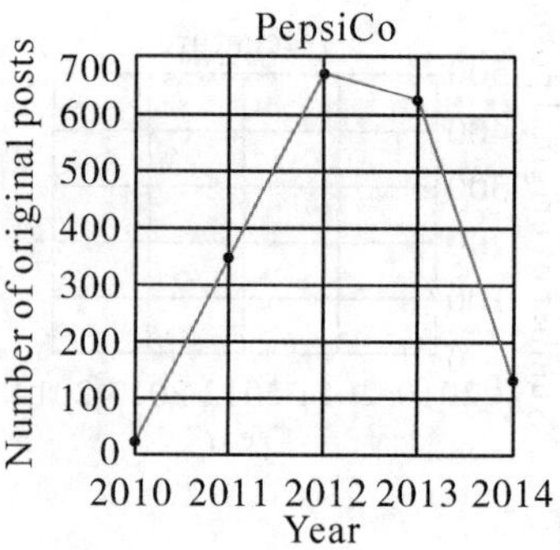
PepsiCo
Number of original posts
700
600
500
400
300
200
100
0
2010 2011 2012 2013 2014
Year

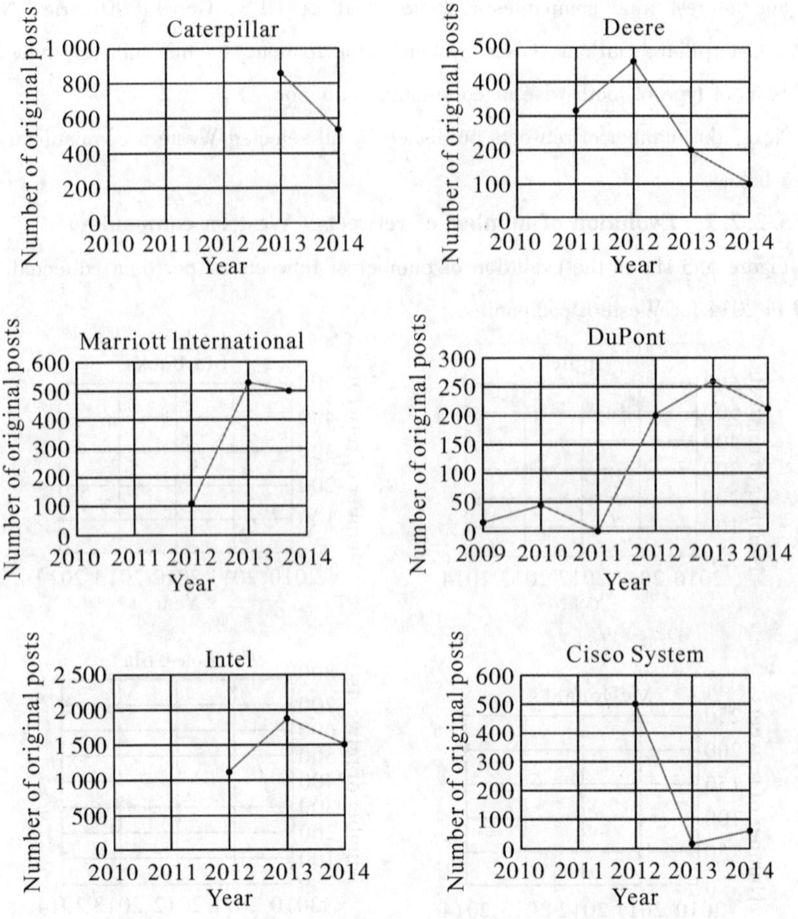

Figure 5. 2 The evolution of number of original posts

(Western companies)

According to figure 5. 2, there is not a general tendency **with respect to the evolution of number of original posts** from 2009 to 2014. Nevertheless, **a decreasing tendency is detected in most of companies (total 21) between 2013 and 2014.**

For seventeen companies (Starbucks, Coca-Cola, Walt Disney, American Express, Volkswagen, Procter & Gamble, IBM, Accenture, Johnson & Johnson, 3M, Microsoft, Boeing, Nestlé S.A., Unilever, PepsiCo, Deere, Intel), this number increases initially and then decreases slightly or to some degree.

For four companies (McDonald's, Exxon Mobil, Wal-Mart Stores, Marriott International), this number keeps increasing from 2009 to 2014.

For the rest nine companies (Apple, FedEx, UPS, General Electric, Nike, BMW, Caterpillar, DuPont, Cisco System), the tendency of this number from 2009 to 2014 is of type of tooth-wise or continuous reduction.

Next, the number of retweets published by all selected Western companies is analyzed below.

5.2.2.2 Evolution of number of retweets (Western companies)

Figure 5.3 shows the evolution of number of retweets as per data collected from 2009 to 2014 for Western companies.

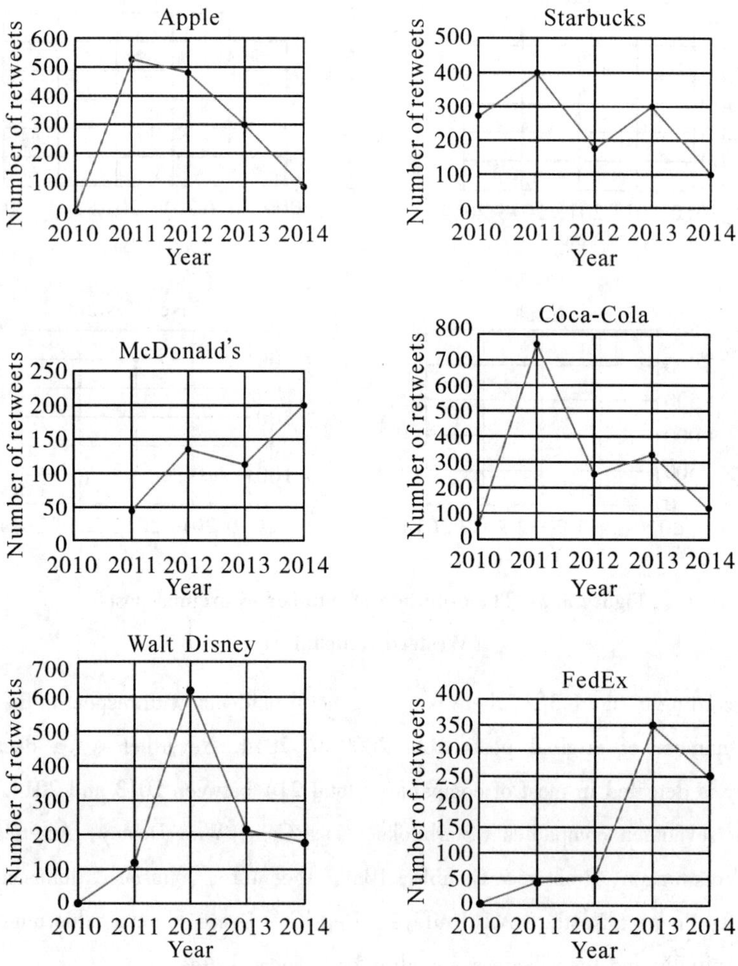

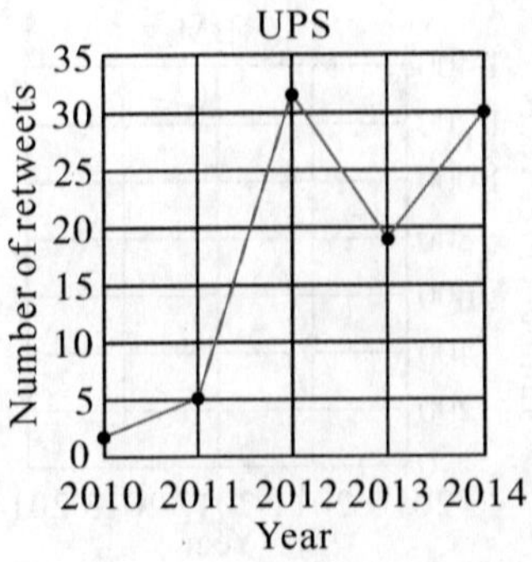
UPS
Number of retweets
35
30
25
20
15
10
5
0
2010 2011 2012 2013 2014
Year

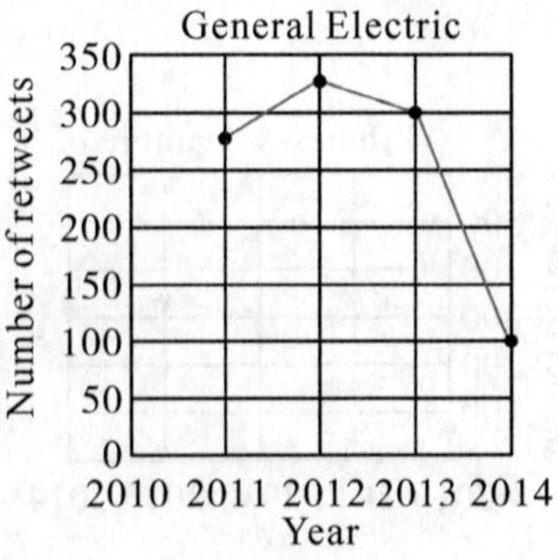
General Electric
Number of retweets
350
300
250
200
150
100
50
0
2010 2011 2012 2013 2014
Year

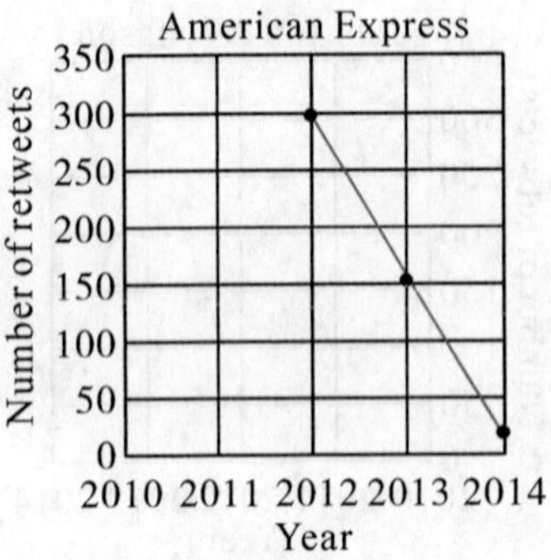
American Express
Number of retweets
350
300
250
200
150
100
50
0
2010 2011 2012 2013 2014
Year

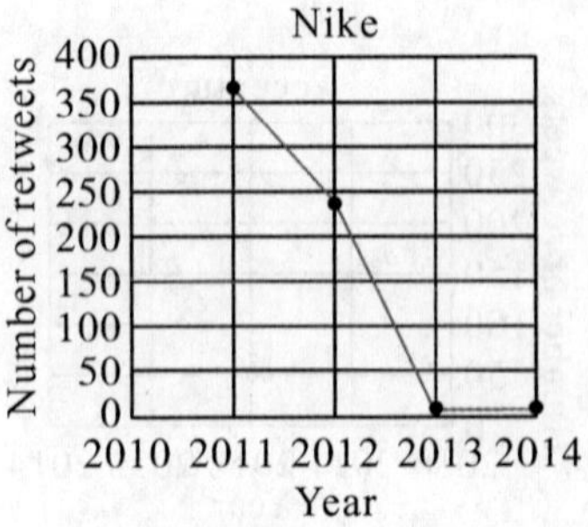
Nike
Number of retweets
400
350
300
250
200
150
100
50
0
2010 2011 2012 2013 2014
Year

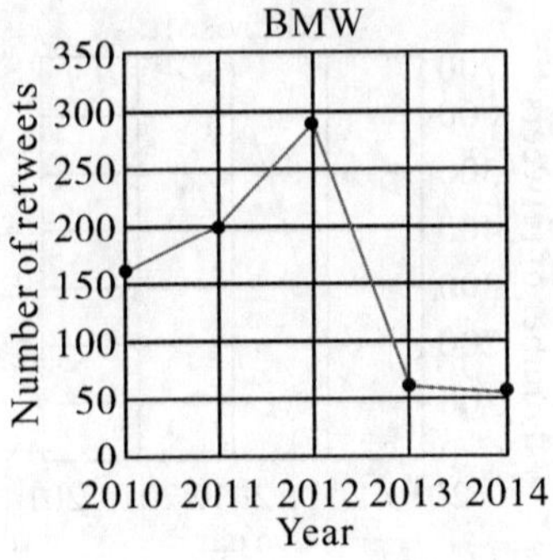
BMW
Number of retweets
350
300
250
200
150
100
50
0
2010 2011 2012 2013 2014
Year

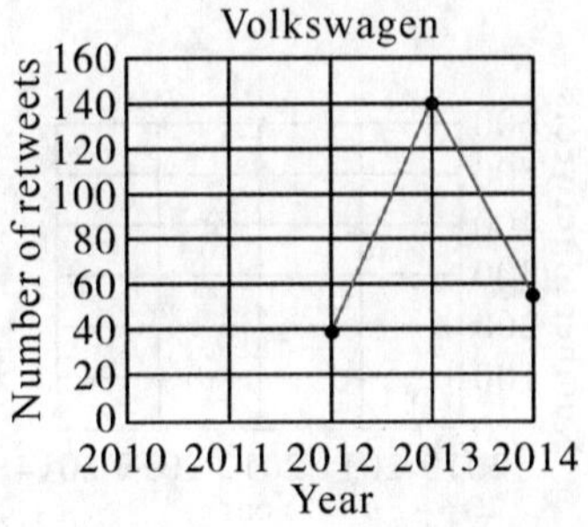
Volkswagen
Number of retweets
160
140
120
100
80
60
40
20
0
2010 2011 2012 2013 2014
Year

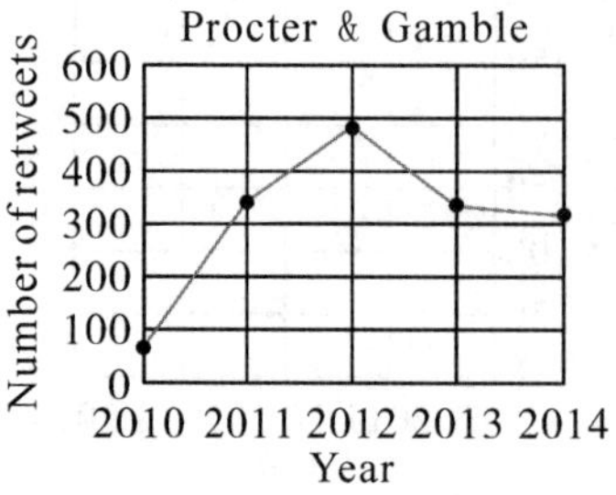
Procter & Gamble
Number of retweets
600
500
400
300
200
100
0
2010 2011 2012 2013 2014
Year

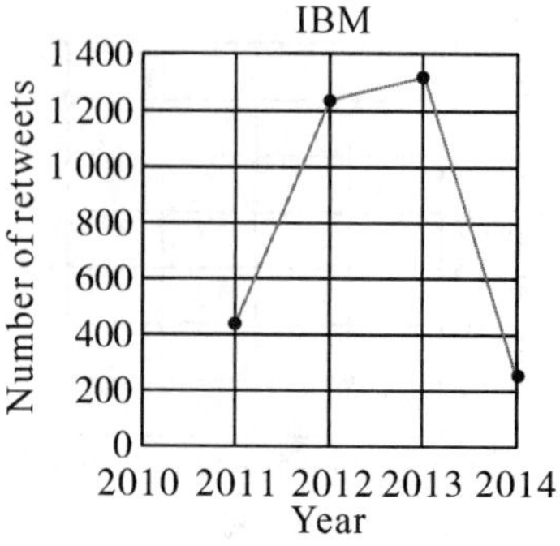
IBM
Number of retweets
1 400
1 200
1 000
800
600
400
200
0
2010 2011 2012 2013 2014
Year

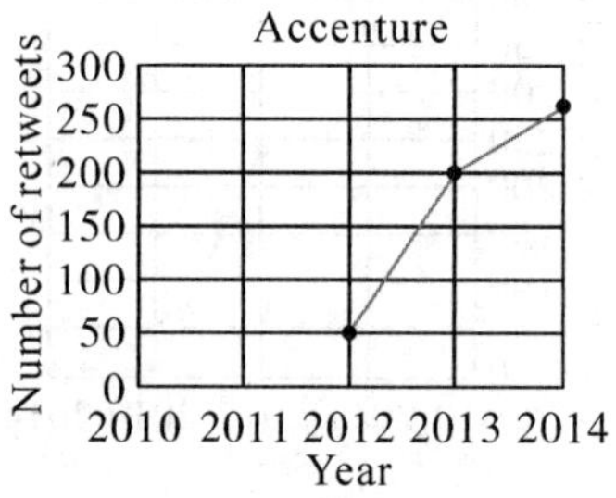
Accenture
Number of retweets
300
250
200
150
100
50
0
2010 2011 2012 2013 2014
Year

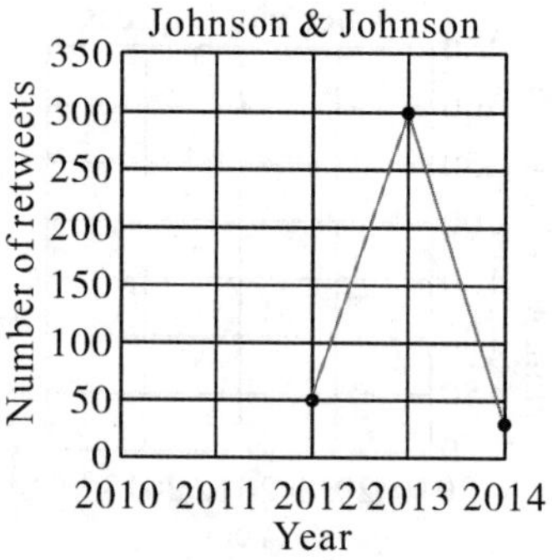
Johnson & Johnson
Number of retweets
350
300
250
200
150
100
50
0
2010 2011 2012 2013 2014
Year

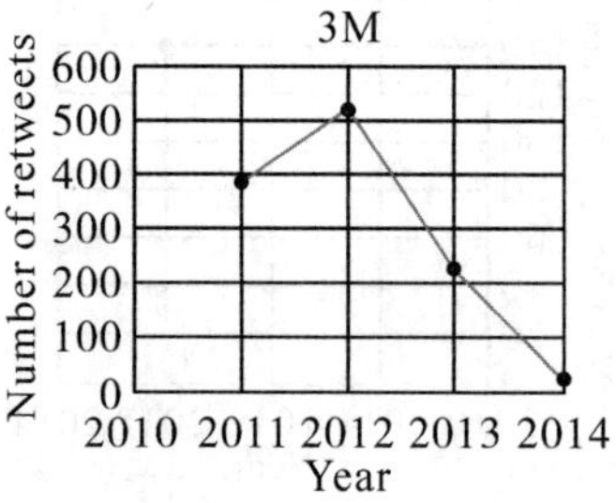
3M
Number of retweets
600
500
400
300
200
100
0
2010 2011 2012 2013 2014
Year

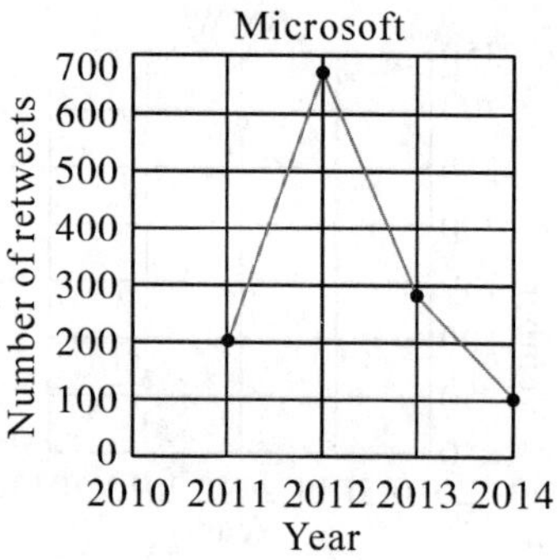
Microsoft
Number of retweets
700
600
500
400
300
200
100
0
2010 2011 2012 2013 2014
Year

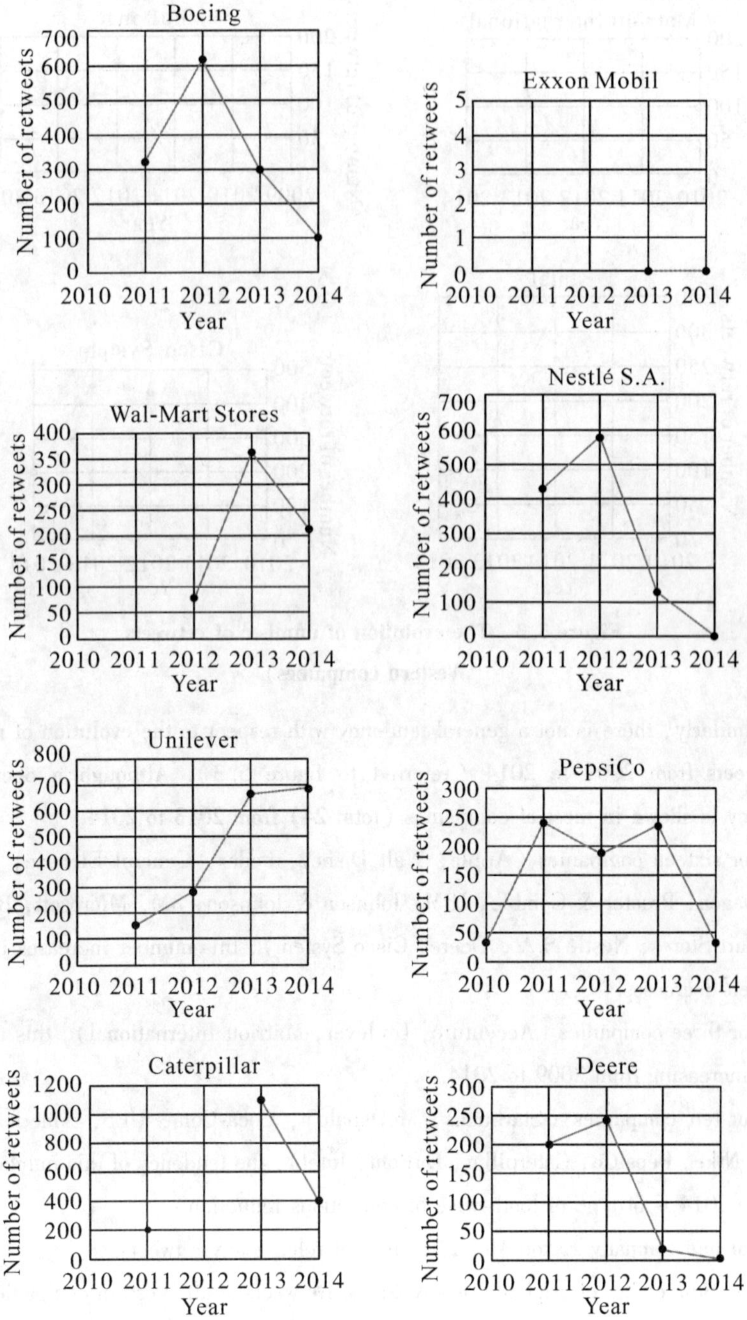
Boeing
Exxon Mobil
Wal-Mart Stores
Nestlé S.A.
Unilever
PepsiCo
Caterpillar
Deere
Number of retweets
Year
2010 2011 2012 2013 2014

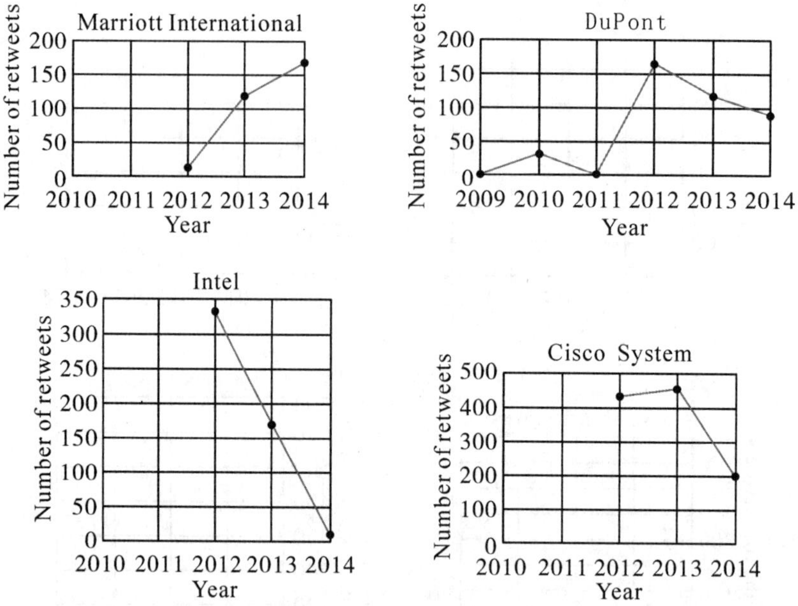

Figure 5.3 The evolution of number of retweets (Western companies)

Similarly, there is not a general tendency **with respect to the evolution of number of retweets** from 2009 to 2014 (referred to figure 5.3). Although **a decreasing tendency is shown in most of companies (total 24) from 2013 to 2014.**

For sixteen companies (Apple, Walt Disney, Fedex, General Electric, BMW, Volkswagen, Procter & Gamble, IBM, Johnson & Johnson, 3M, Microsoft, Boeing, Wal-Mart Stores, Nestlé S.A., Deere, Cisco System), this number increases initially and then decreases.

For three companies (Accenture, Unilever, Marriott International), this number keeps increasing from 2009 to 2014.

For ten companies (Starbucks, McDonald's, Coca-Cola, UPS, American Express, Nike, PepsiCo, Caterpillar, DuPont, Intel), the tendency of this number from 2009 to 2014 is of type of tooth-wise or continuous reduction.

For one company Exxon Mobil, it did not release any retweets.

The Sum of No. of original posts & No. of Retweets of all Western companies from 2009 to 2014 can be summarized in table 5.7.

Table 5.7 Evolution of sum of No. of original posts & No. of retweets of Western companies

Year	Sum of No. of original posts (thirty Western companies)	Sum of No. of retweets (thirty Western companies)
2009	20	2
2010	1 549	656
2011	11 376	5 543
2012	22 318	8 922
2013	27 607	8 700
2014	23 243	4 318
	Total:86 113	Total:28 141
	Percentage:75.37%	Percentage:24.63%

It can be derived from table 5.7 & figure 5.4 that **Western companies published more their own original content (75.37%) than the retweets (24.63%).** Moreover, the microblogging activities of Western companies increased very slowly from 2009 to 2010, then grew rapidly from 2010 to 2013, and afterwards decreased slightly from 2013 to 2014. This general tendency is consistent with the evolution of usage rate of Microblog in China as shown in table 5.8 and figure 5.5, which are extracted from the reports published by CNNIC (2011a; 2011b; 2012a; 2012b; 2013a; 2013b; 2014a; 2014b; 2015a; 2015b; 2016a; 2016b; 2017) from 2011 to 2017. It can be noted that there has been a usage rate reduction, i.e., loss of users since the middle of 2013.

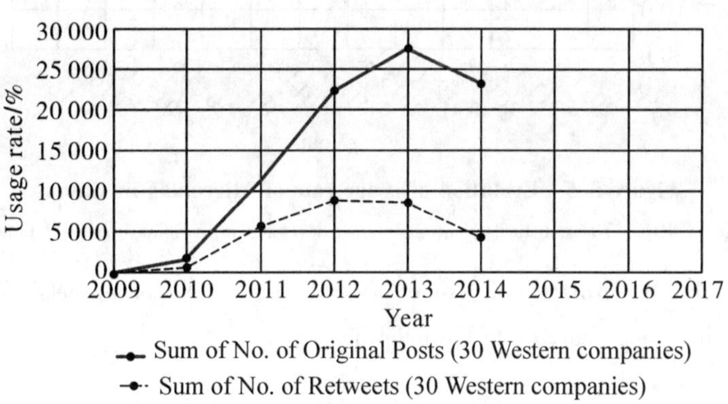

Figure 5.4 Evolution of sum of No. of original posts & No. of retweets of Western companies

Table 5.8 Usage rate of Microblog in China

Year	Usage rate of Microblog in China/%
2009	–
2010. 12	13. 8
2011. 6	40. 2
2011. 12	48. 7
2012. 6	50. 9
2012. 12	54. 7
2013. 6	56. 0
2013. 12	45. 5
2014. 6	43. 6
2014. 12	38. 4
2015. 6	30. 6
2015. 12	33. 5
2016. 6	34. 0
2016. 12	37. 1

Source: CNNIC, The statistical report on Internet development in China from 2011 to 2017.

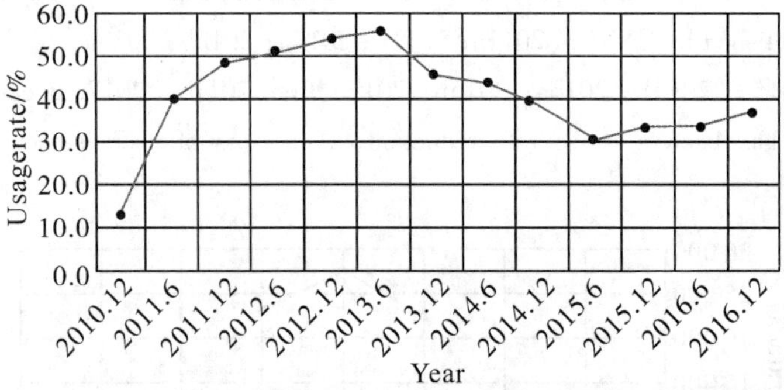

Figure 5.5 Evolution of usage rate of Microblog in China

(Source: CNNIC, The statistical report on Internet development in China from 2011 to 2017.)

Similarly, the evolution of "No. of original posts vs. No. of retweets" for Chinese companies has been analyzed in the following parts.

5.2.3 Evolution of "No. of original posts vs. No. of retweets" for Chinese companies

5.2.3.1 Evolution of number of original posts (Chinese companies)

Figure 5.6 shows the evolution of number of original post based on the data collected from 2009 to 2014 for Chinese companies.

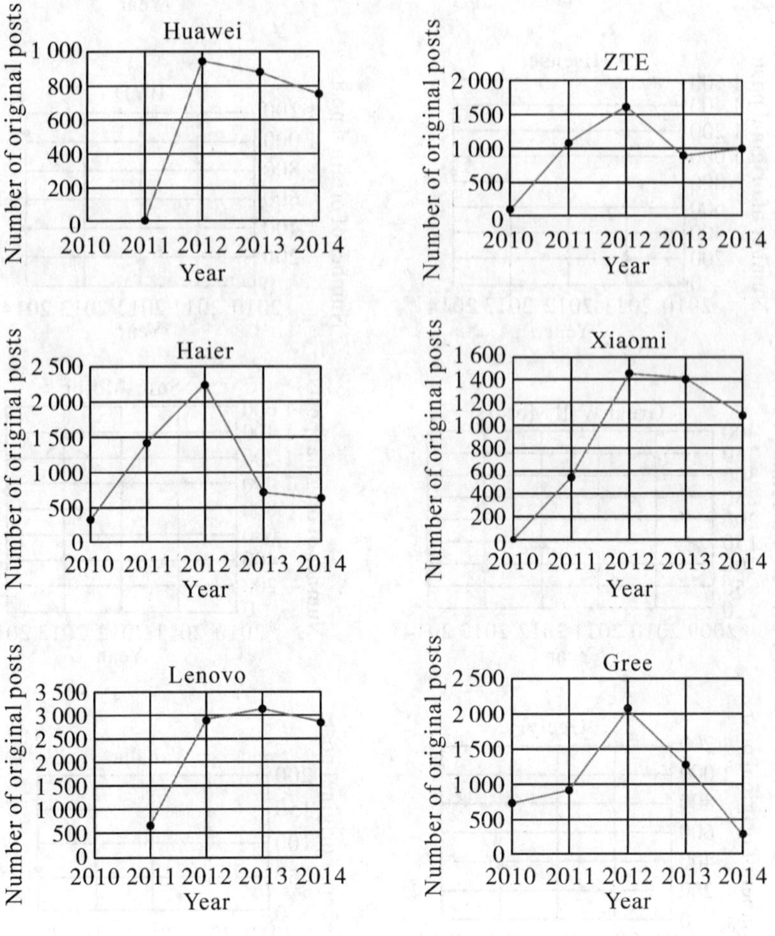

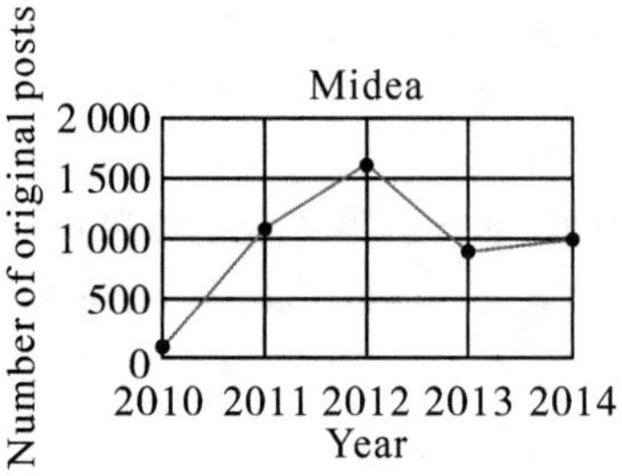
Midea
Number of original posts
2 000
1 500
1 000
500
0
2010 2011 2012 2013 2014
Year

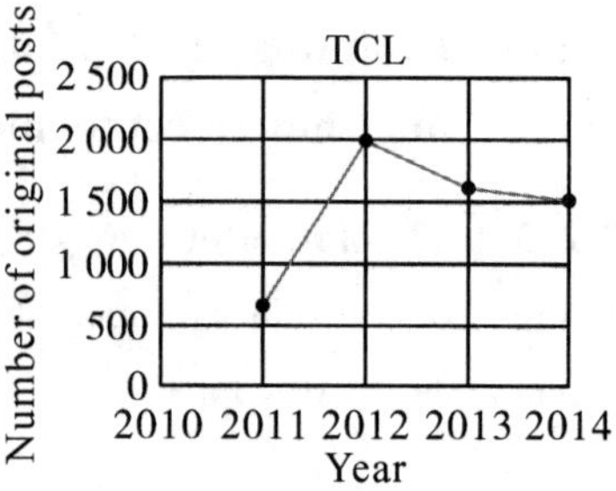
TCL
Number of original posts
2 500
2 000
1 500
1 000
500
0
2010 2011 2012 2013 2014
Year

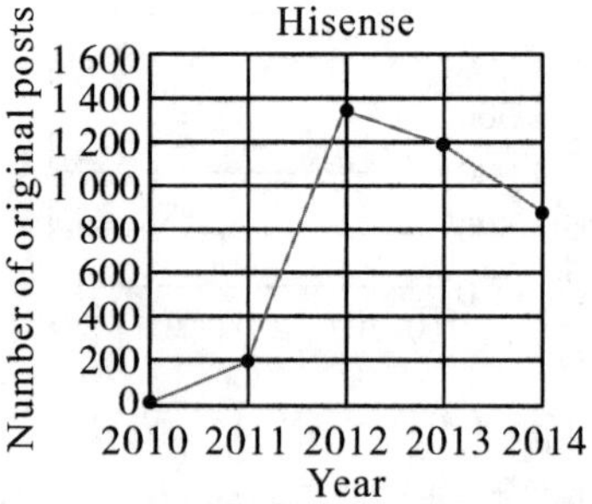
Hisense
Number of original posts
1 600
1 400
1 200
1 000
800
600
400
200
0
2010 2011 2012 2013 2014
Year

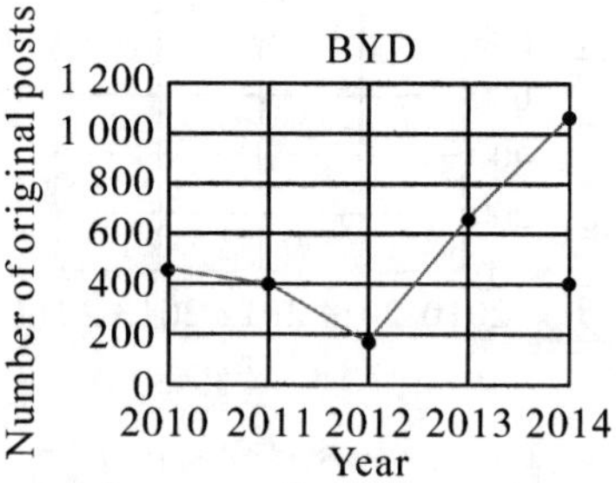
BYD
Number of original posts
1 200
1 000
800
600
400
200
0
2010 2011 2012 2013 2014
Year

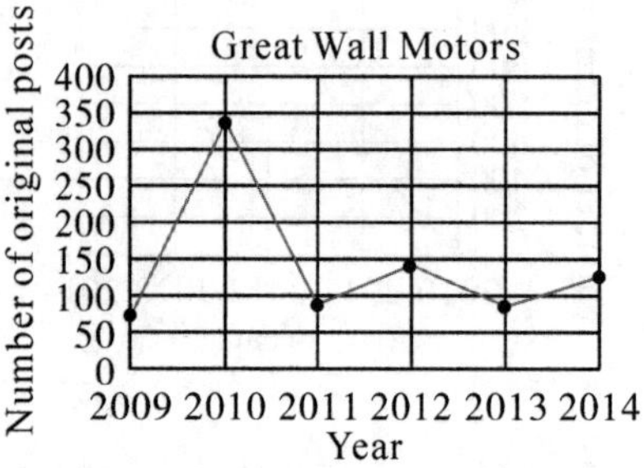
Great Wall Motors
Number of original posts
400
350
300
250
200
150
100
50
0
2009 2010 2011 2012 2013 2014
Year

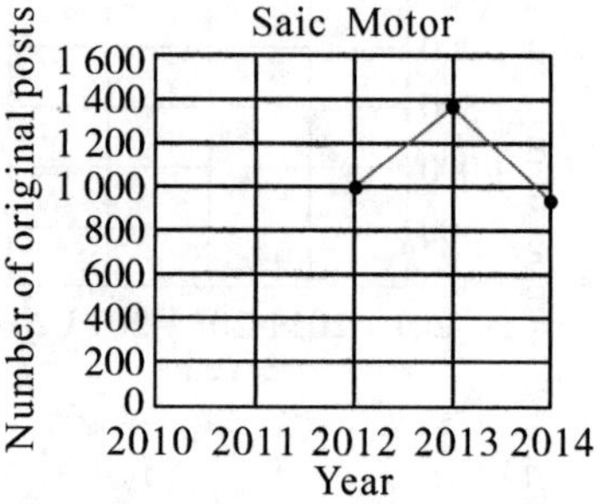
Saic Motor
Number of original posts
1 600
1 400
1 200
1 000
800
600
400
200
0
2010 2011 2012 2013 2014
Year

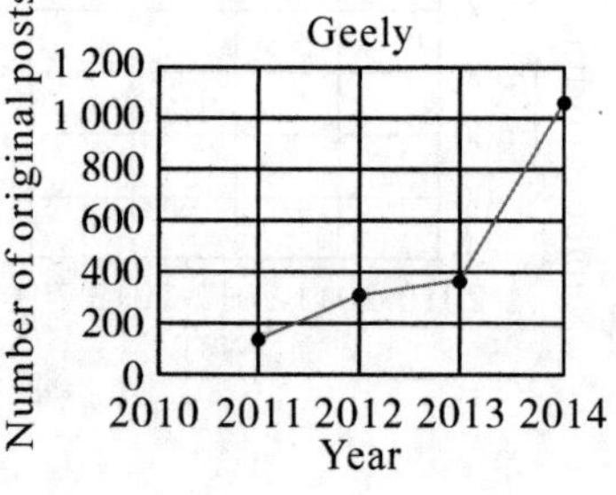
Geely
Number of original posts
1 200
1 000
800
600
400
200
0
2010 2011 2012 2013 2014
Year

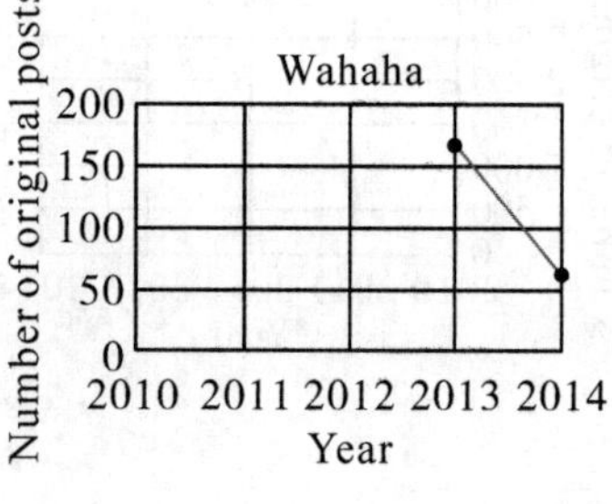
Wahaha
Number of original posts
200
150
100
50
0
2010 2011 2012 2013 2014
Year

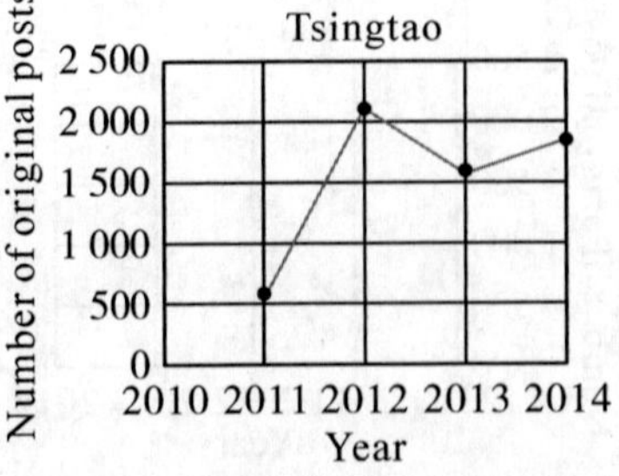
Tsingtao
Number of original posts
2 500
2 000
1 500
1 000
500
0
2010 2011 2012 2013 2014
Year

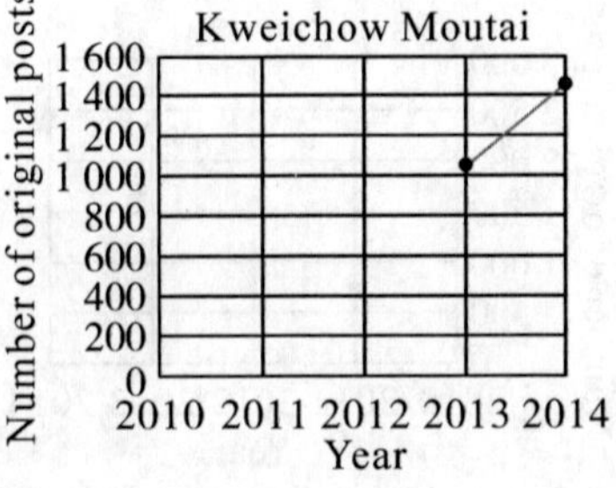
Kweichow Moutai
Number of original posts
1 600
1 400
1 200
1 000
800
600
400
200
0
2010 2011 2012 2013 2014
Year

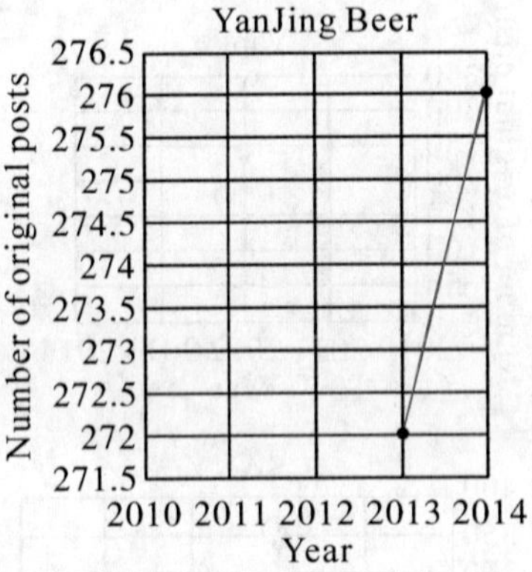
YanJing Beer
Number of original posts
276.5
276
275.5
275
274.5
274
273.5
273
272.5
272
271.5
2010 2011 2012 2013 2014
Year

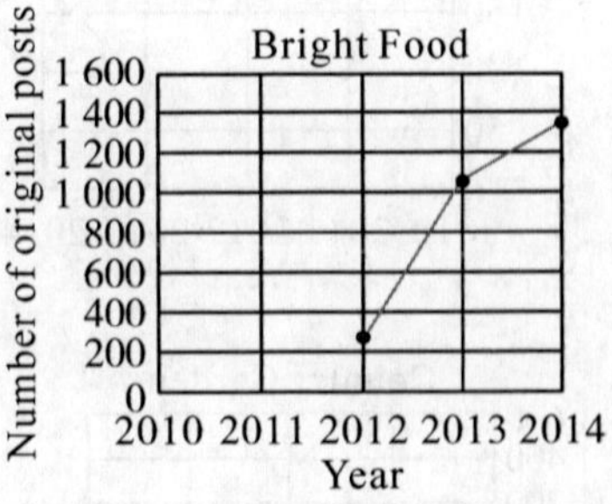
Bright Food
Number of original posts
1 600
1 400
1 200
1 000
800
600
400
200
0
2010 2011 2012 2013 2014
Year

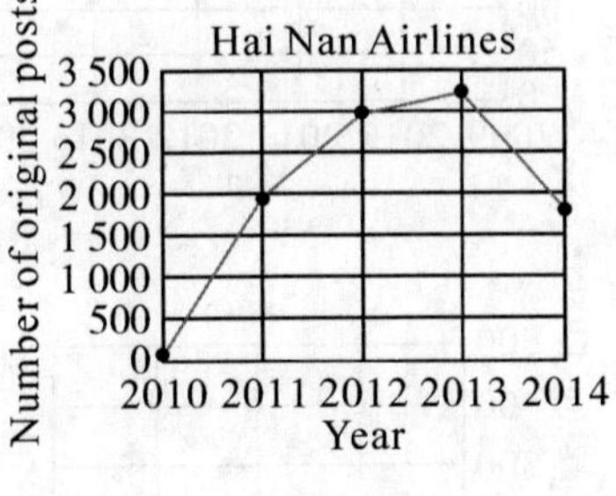
Hai Nan Airlines
Number of original posts
3 500
3 000
2 500
2 000
1 500
1 000
500
0
2010 2011 2012 2013 2014
Year

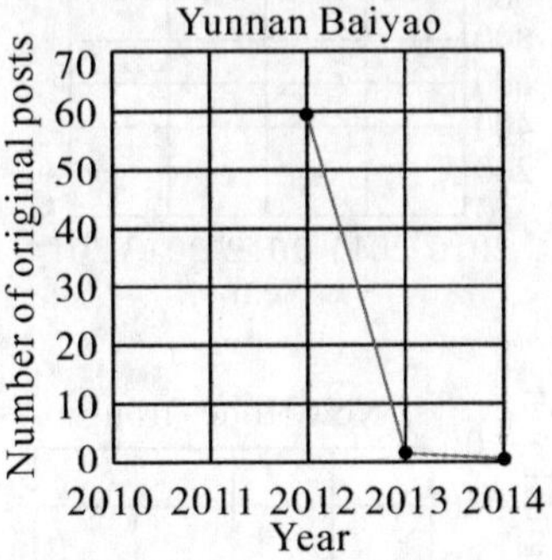
Yunnan Baiyao
Number of original posts
70
60
50
40
30
20
10
0
2010 2011 2012 2013 2014
Year

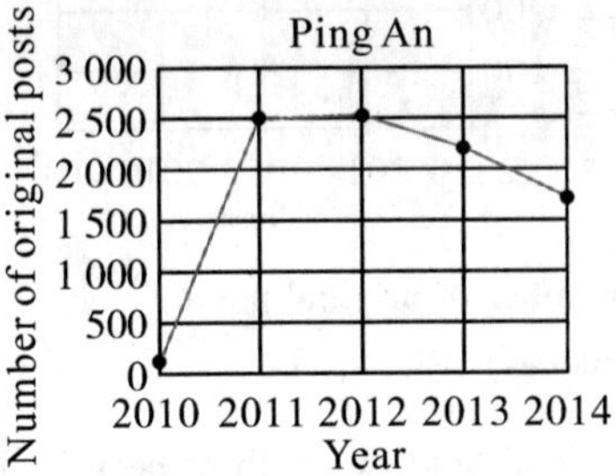
Ping An
Number of original posts
3 000
2 500
2 000
1 500
1 000
500
0
2010 2011 2012 2013 2014
Year

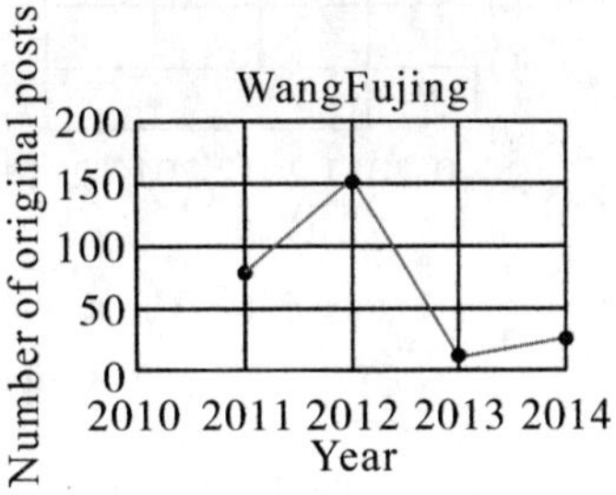
WangFujing
Number of original posts
200
150
100
50
0
2010 2011 2012 2013 2014
Year

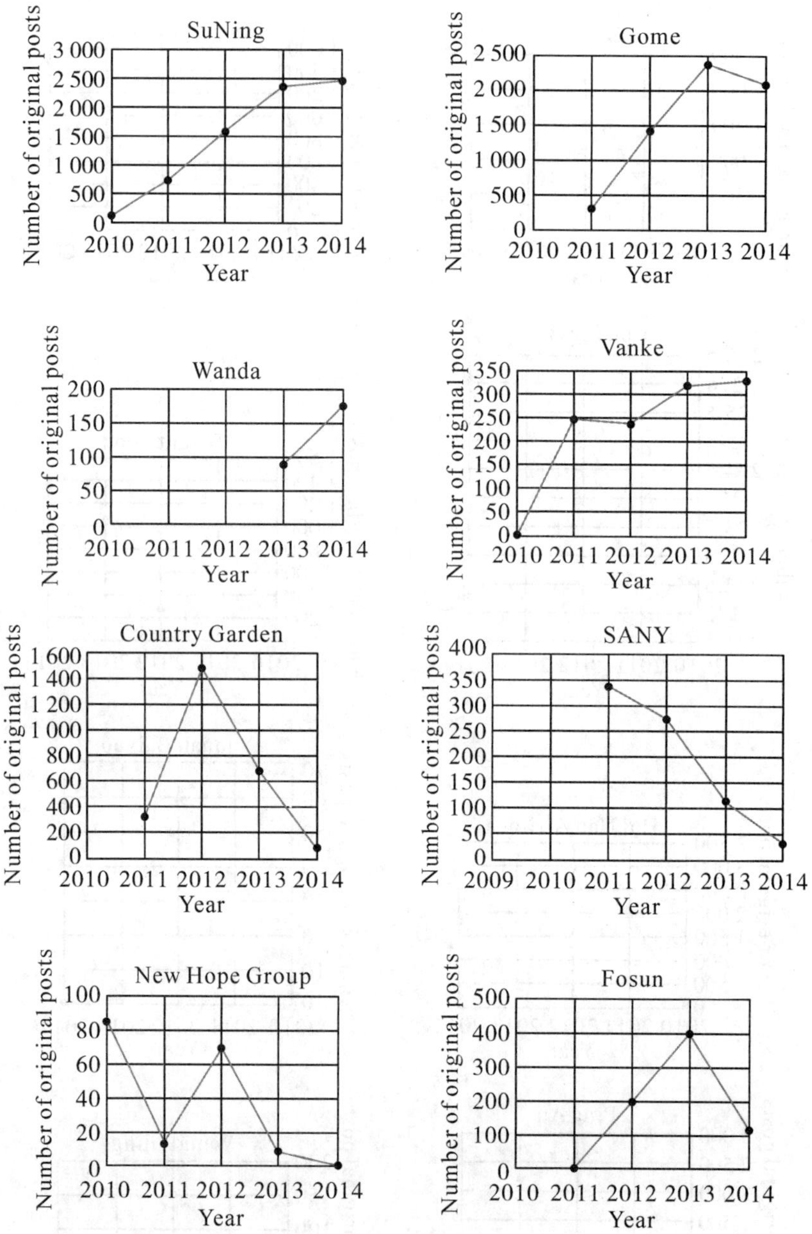

Figure 5.6 The evolution of number of original posts (Chinese companies)

According to Figure 5.6, there is not a general tendency **with respect to the evolution of number of original posts** from 2009 to 2014. Nevertheless, **a decreasing tend-**

ency is demonstrated in most of companies (total 18) between 2013 and 2014.

For fourteen companies (Huawei, Haier, Xiaomi, Lenovo, Gree, Midea, TCL, Hisense, Saic Motor, HaiNan Airlines, Ping An, Gome, Country Garden, Fosun), this number increases initially and then decreases slightly or to some degree.

For six companies (Geely, Kweichow Moutai, Yanjing Beer, Bright Food, Su-Ning, Wanda), this number keeps increasing from 2009 to 2014.

For nine companies (ZTE, GreatWall Motors, Wahaha, Tsingtao, Yunnan Baiyao, WangFujing, SANY, New Hope Group, Vanke), the tendency of this number from 2009 to 2014 is of type of tooth-wise or continuous reduction.

For one company BYD, this number decreases initially and then increases significantly.

5.2.3.2 Evolution of number of retweets (Chinese companies)

Figure 5.7 shows the evolution of number of retweets of selected Chinese companies as per data collected from 2009 to 2014.

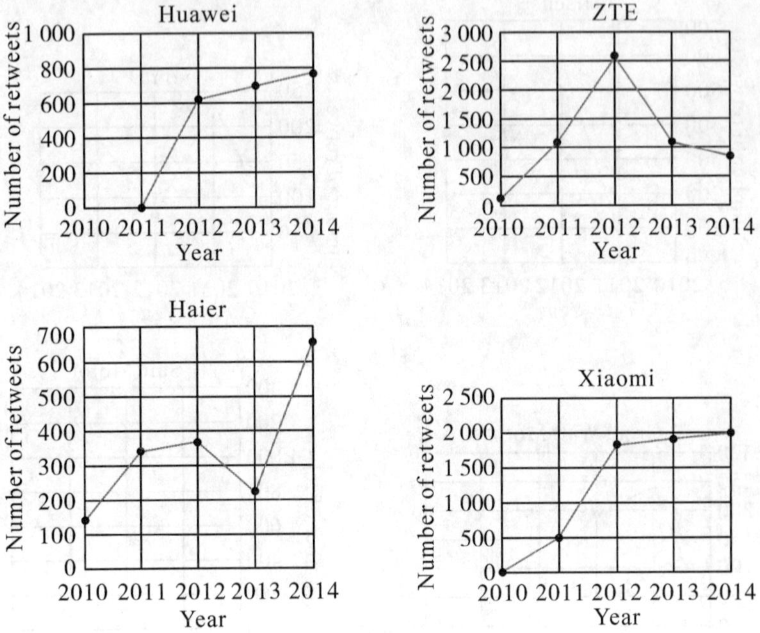

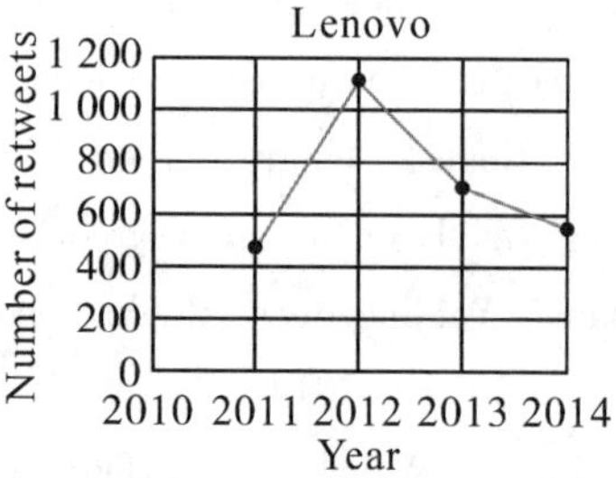
Lenovo
Number of retweets
1 200
1 000
800
600
400
200
0
2010 2011 2012 2013 2014
Year

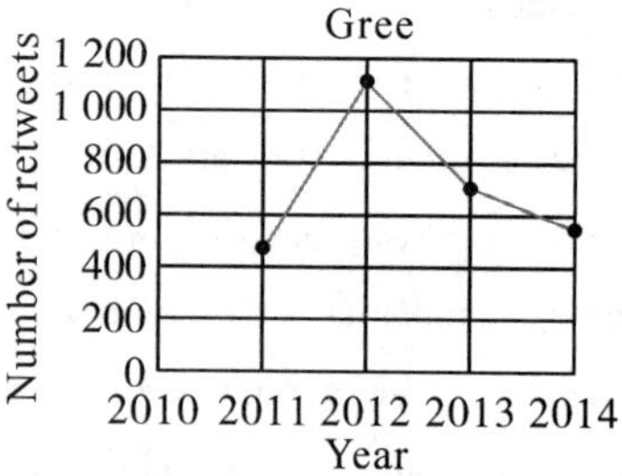
Gree
Number of retweets
1 200
1 000
800
600
400
200
0
2010 2011 2012 2013 2014
Year

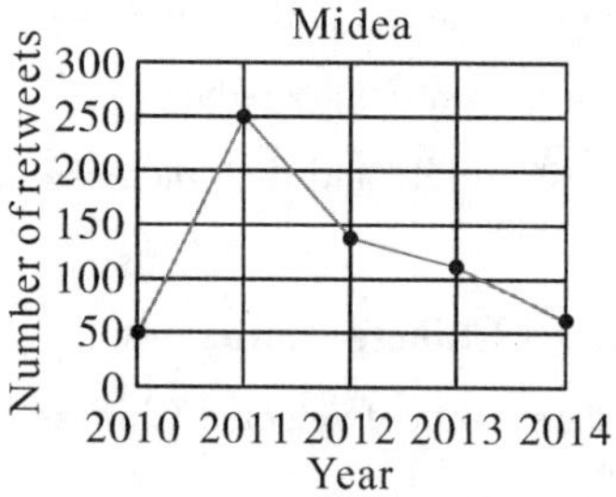
Midea
Number of retweets
300
250
200
150
100
50
0
2010 2011 2012 2013 2014
Year

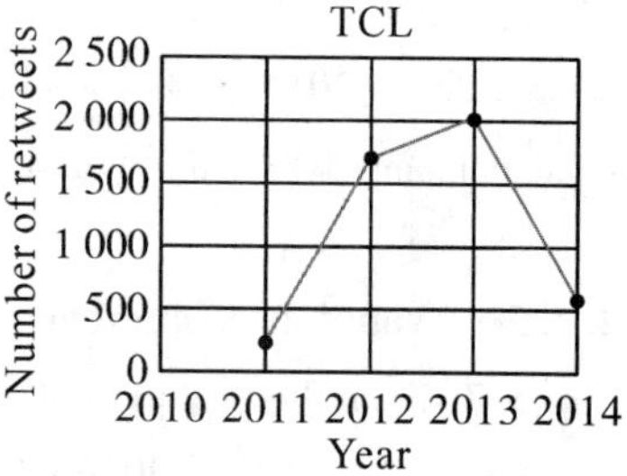
TCL
Number of retweets
2 500
2 000
1 500
1 000
500
0
2010 2011 2012 2013 2014
Year

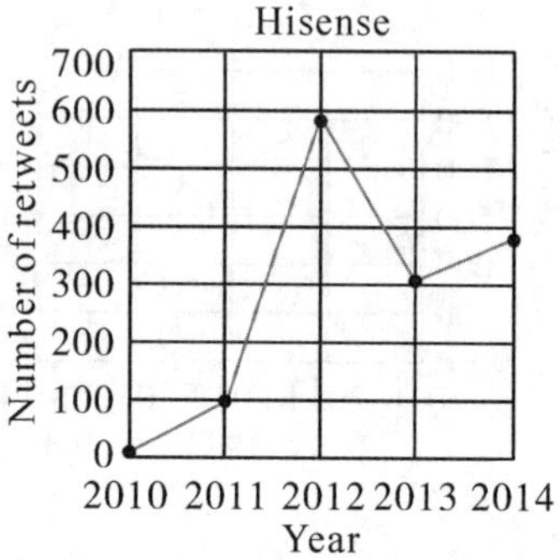
Hisense
Number of retweets
700
600
500
400
300
200
100
0
2010 2011 2012 2013 2014
Year

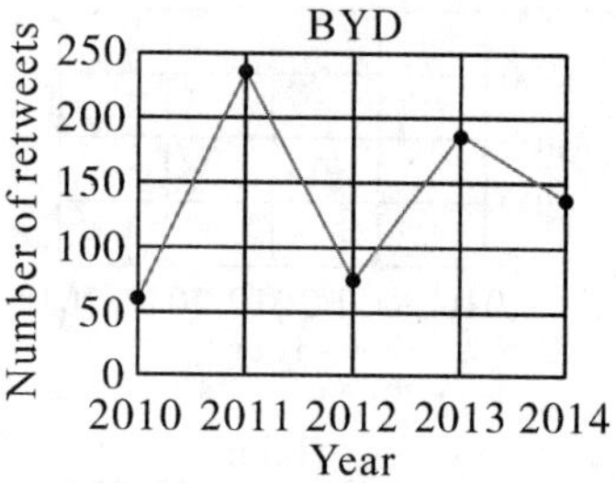
BYD
Number of retweets
250
200
150
100
50
0
2010 2011 2012 2013 2014
Year

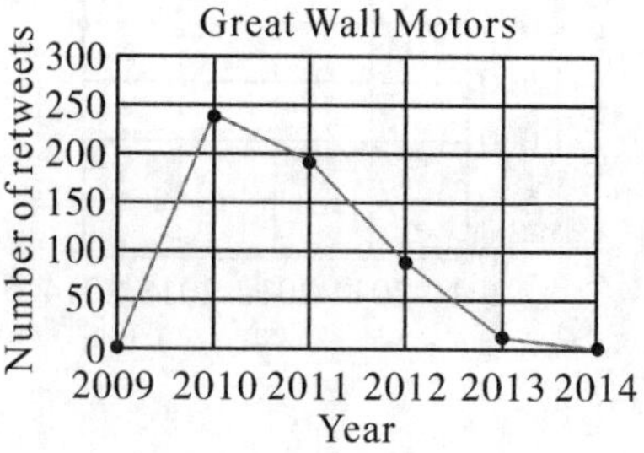
Great Wall Motors
Number of retweets
300
250
200
150
100
50
0
2009 2010 2011 2012 2013 2014
Year

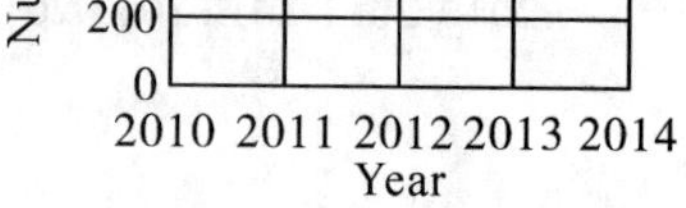
Saic Motor
Number of retweets
1 400
1 200
1 000
800
600
400
200
0
2010 2011 2012 2013 2014
Year

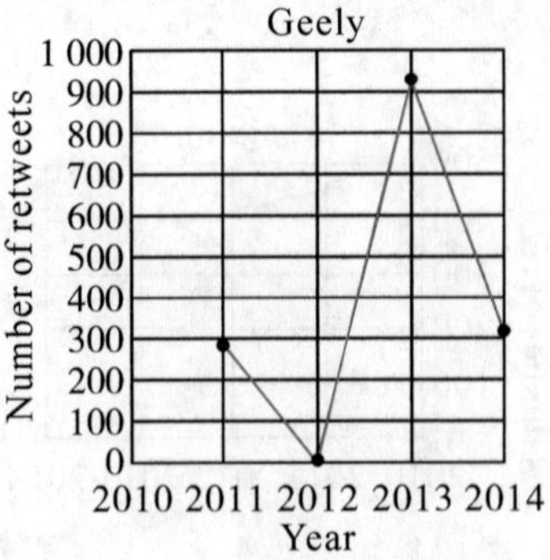
Geely
Number of retweets
1 000
900
800
700
600
500
400
300
200
100
0
2010 2011 2012 2013 2014
Year

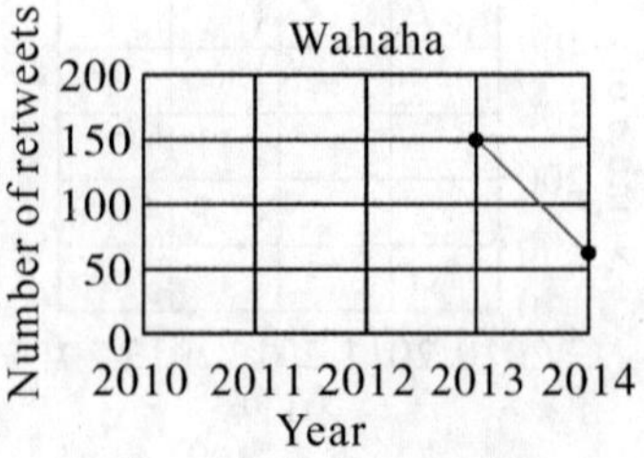
Wahaha
Number of retweets
200
150
100
50
0
2010 2011 2012 2013 2014
Year

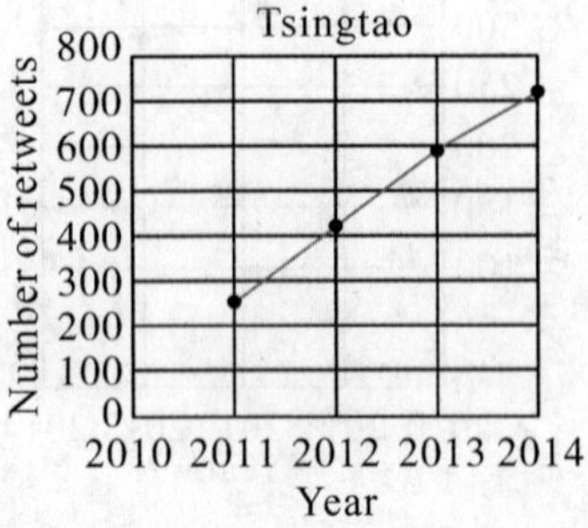
Tsingtao
Number of retweets
800
700
600
500
400
300
200
100
0
2010 2011 2012 2013 2014
Year

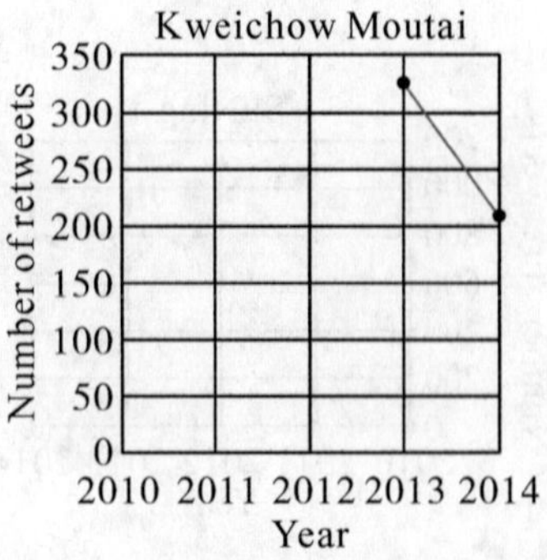
Kweichow Moutai
Number of retweets
350
300
250
200
150
100
50
0
2010 2011 2012 2013 2014
Year

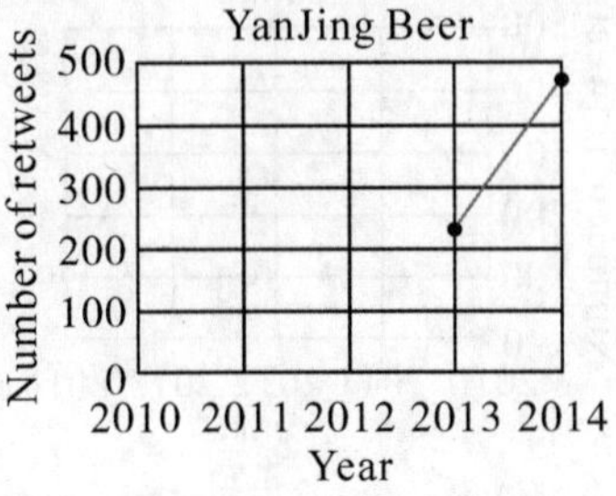
YanJing Beer
Number of retweets
500
400
300
200
100
0
2010 2011 2012 2013 2014
Year

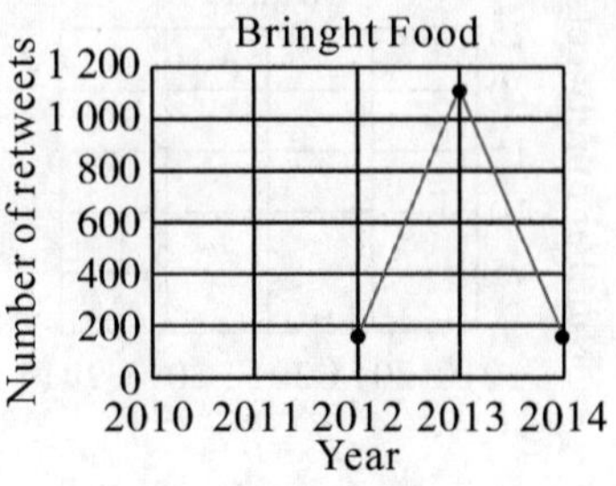
Bringht Food
Number of retweets
1 200
1 000
800
600
400
200
0
2010 2011 2012 2013 2014
Year

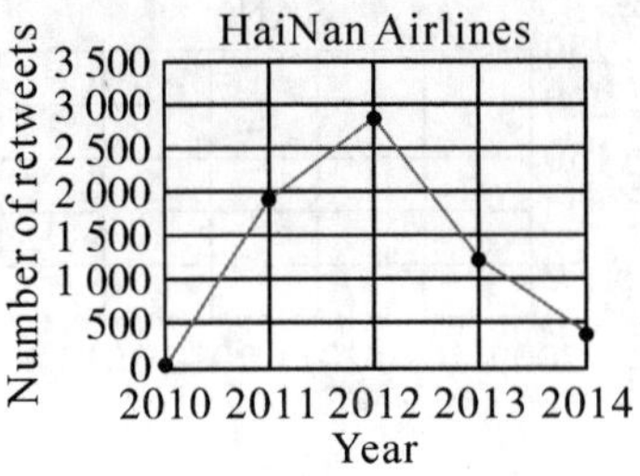
HaiNan Airlines
Number of retweets
3 500
3 000
2 500
2 000
1 500
1 000
500
0
2010 2011 2012 2013 2014
Year

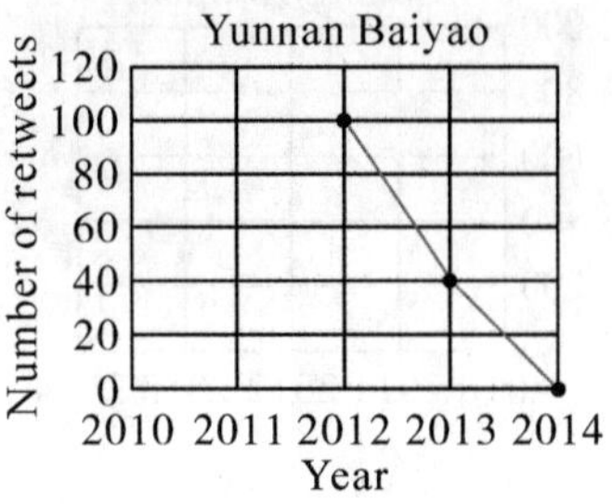
Yunnan Baiyao
Number of retweets
120
100
80
60
40
20
0
2010 2011 2012 2013 2014
Year

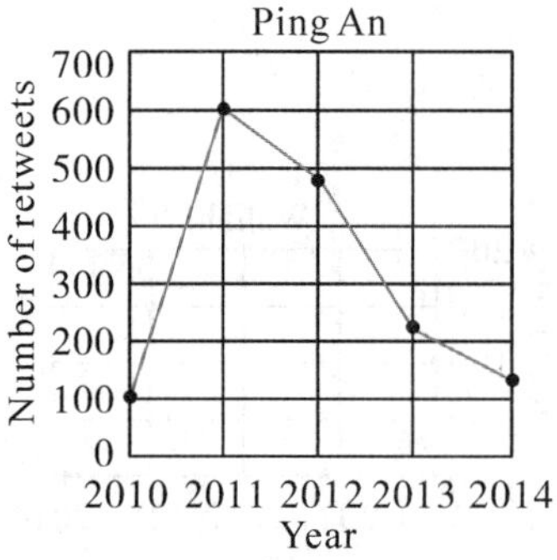
Ping An
Number of retweets
700
600
500
400
300
200
100
0
2010 2011 2012 2013 2014
Year

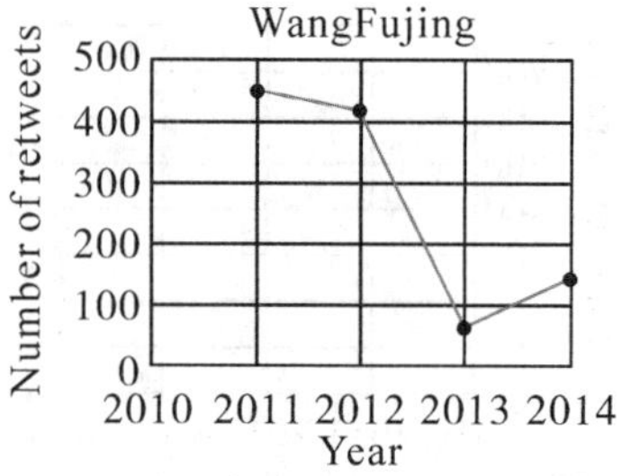
WangFujing
Number of retweets
500
400
300
200
100
0
2010 2011 2012 2013 2014
Year

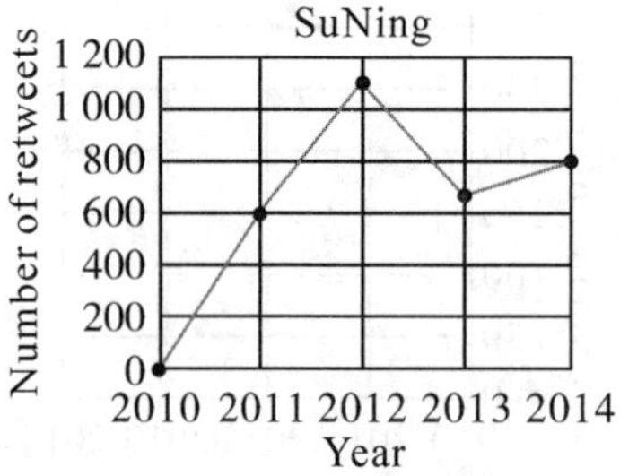
SuNing
Number of retweets
1 200
1 000
800
600
400
200
0
2010 2011 2012 2013 2014
Year

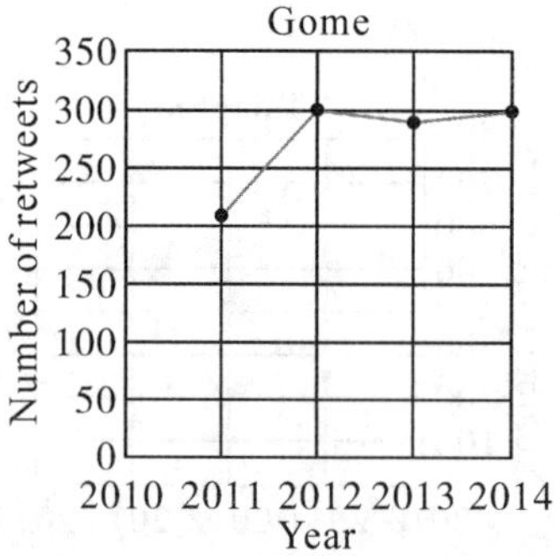
Gome
Number of retweets
350
300
250
200
150
100
50
0
2010 2011 2012 2013 2014
Year

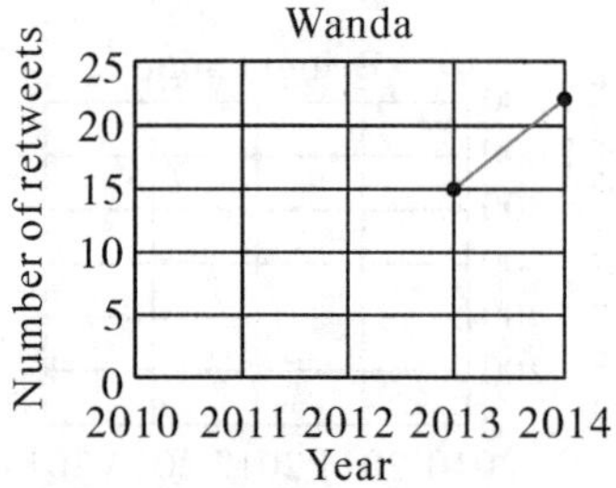
Wanda
Number of retweets
25
20
15
10
5
0
2010 2011 2012 2013 2014
Year

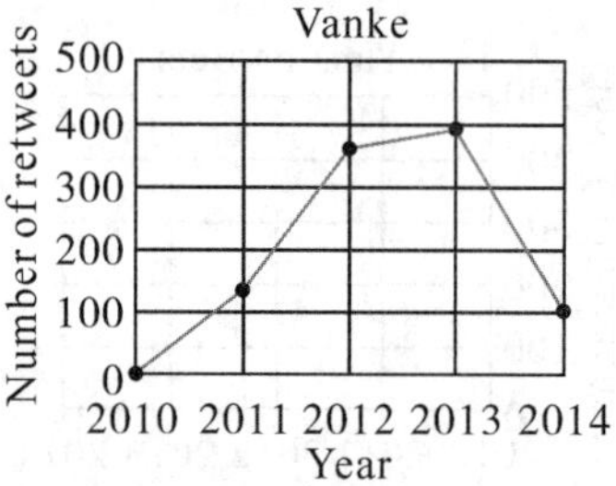
Vanke
Number of retweets
500
400
300
200
100
0
2010 2011 2012 2013 2014
Year

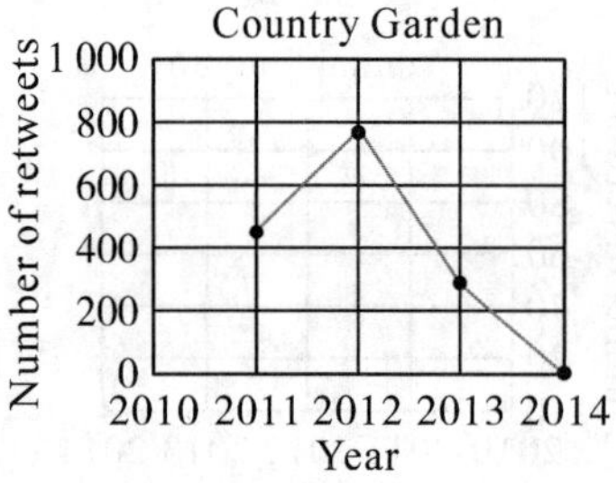
Country Garden
Number of retweets
1 000
800
600
400
200
0
2010 2011 2012 2013 2014
Year

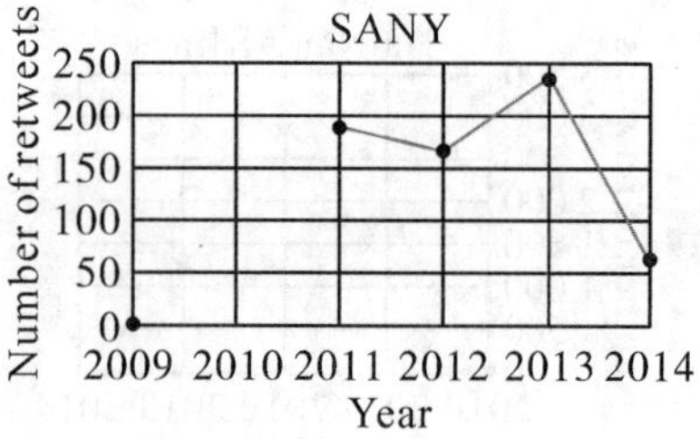
SANY
Number of retweets
250
200
150
100
50
0
2009 2010 2011 2012 2013 2014
Year

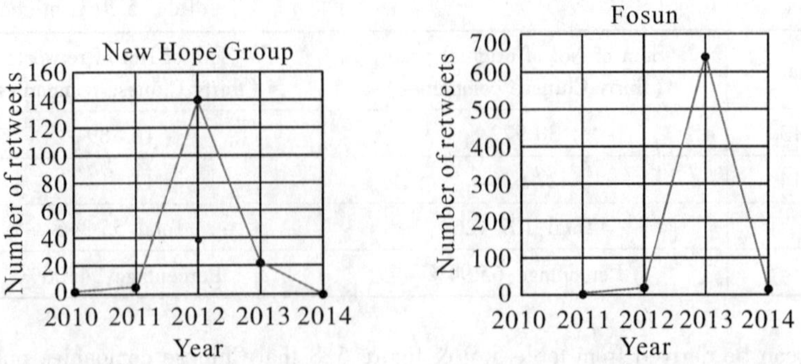

Figure 5.7 The evolution of number of retweets (Chinese companies)

Similarly, there is not a general tendency **with respect to the evolution of number of retweets** from 2009 to 2014 (referred to figure 5.7). However, **a decreasing tendency in most of Chinese companies (total 20) is detected from 2013 to 2014.**

For thirteen companies (ZTE, Lenovo, Gree, Midea, TCL, Great Wall Motors, Bright Food, HaiNan Airlines, Ping An, Vanke, Country Garden, New Hope Group, Fosun), this number increases initially and then decreases.

For five companies (Huawei, Xiaomi, Tsingtao, YanJing Beer, Wanda), this number keeps increasing from 2009 to 2014.

For eleven companies (Haier, Hisense, BYD, Saic Motor, Geely, Wahaha, Kweichow Moutai, Yunnan Baiyao, SuNing, Gome, SANY), the tendency of this number from 2009 to 2014 is of type of tooth-wise or continuous reduction.

For one company WangFujing, this number decreases initially and then increases slightly.

The sum of no. of original posts & no. of retweets of Chinese companies from 2009 to 2014 can be summarized in table 5.9.

Table 5.9 Evolution of sum of No. of original posts & No. of retweets of Chinese companies

Year	Sum of No. of original posts (thirty Chinese companies)	Sum of No. of retweets (thirty Chinese companies)
2009	106	0
2010	2 716	936
2011	14 223	9 125
2012	31 473	18 382

Table 5. 9(Continued)

Year	Sum of No. of original posts (thirty Chinese companies)	Sum of No. of retweets (thirty Chinese companies)
2013	30 972	16 889
2014	27 636	11 014
	Total:107 126	Total:55 346
	Percentage:65.94%	Percentage:34. 06%

it can be derived from table 5. 9 & figure 5. 8 that **Chinese companies published more original posts (65.94%) than retweets (34. 06%) from 2009 to 2014.** In addition, the microblogging activities of Chinese companies increased very slowly from 2009 to 2010, then grew rapidly from 2010 to 2012, and afterwards decreased slightly from 2012 to 2014. This tendency conforms generally to the evolution of usage rate of microblog in China as shown in table 5. 8 and figure 5. 5 with very little difference.

It can be found that Chinese companies published more content than Western companies in both original content and retweets during the same period by comparing table 5. 7 with table 5. 9. In addition, **both Western companies and Chinese companies published more original posts than retweets from 2009 to 2014.**

Next, the relevant research has been conducted in line with specific observation period. Before setting the observation period, KPIs including quantitative and qualitative indicators were identified and described in section 4. 2. 2. 3. Then a series of research tasks combined with the corresponding indicators such as data collection, content analysis, and data transforming were assumed.

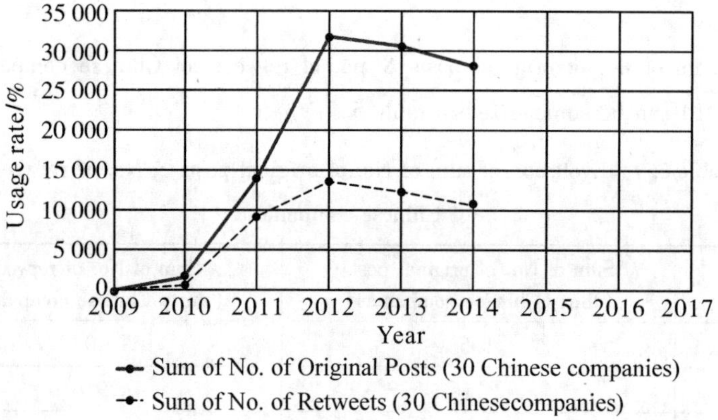

Figure 5. 8 Evolution of sum of No. of original posts & No. of retweets of Chinese companies

5.3 Establishment of the systematic measurement and classification framework

In order to measure all selected companies' social media performance on Sina Weibo platform, a systematic measurement and evaluation framework has been established. This framework initially has involved two dimensional analyses, namely, the level of activity and the level of interaction. In this research, the level of activity is to evaluate whether a company is active or not on a specific social media platform (the detailed explanation, referred to section 5.3.4.1). On the other hand, the level of interaction is to measure the degree of engagement between a company and its users (the detailed explanation, referred to section 5.3.4.2).

Taking into account the measurement of these two dimensional analyses, some indicators should be extracted from Sina Weibo channel. In this sense, KPIs concept has been applied in Sina Weibo case study.

In view of the characteristics of Sina Weibo, it is not fully open for a third party to obtain the complete data of the official account of a company, based on which the corresponding KPIs are identified.

In this research, both quantitative indicators and qualitative indicators were identified. As mentioned previously, quantitative indicators are presented as number, whereas qualitative indicators cannot be expressed in digital form but other formats such as text and picture.

Table 5.10 summarizes the identification of key performance indicators of Sina Weibo platform which has been presented in chapter 4.

In Sina Weibo case, through a four-week observation period, data regarding quantitative and qualitative KPIs were collected so as to make subsequent in-depth analysis.

Table 5. 10 Identification of Sina Weibo key performance indicators

Sina Weibo Key Performance Indicators			
Quantitative indicators		Qualitative indicators	
Change of follower number	Number of followers increased or decreased per week	Top-one post which has been retweeted the most	Three factors have been considered to study the content features of all top-one posts: (1) The best day to publish it: identification of the best day to publish it within a week; (2) The format: pictures, text, video, etc.; (3) Content relevance: is the content of top-one post related to any info about the company?
Change of following number	Number of following increased or decreased per week	Top-one post which has got the most comments	
Number of posts	Number of posts published per week	Top-one post which has got the most likes	
Sum of retweets	Number of times all posts have been retweeted in one week	—	
Sum of comments	Number of times all posts have been commented in one week	—	
Sum of likes	Number of times all posts have been liked in one week	—	

5. 3. 1 KPIs Data collection, processing & database creation

According to the established quantitative KPIs, number of posts, sum of retweets, comments and likes of all posts per week have been recorded and obtained. In addition, chapter 4 has described how to collect the KPIs data. The following part will present the collected first-hand data of Western and Chinese companies during the observation period.

5. 3. 1. 1 Data collection

The collected data during the observation period comprises qualitative and quantitative information. The original primary data collected from Sina Weibo enterprise accounts for Western and Chinese companies. **Quantitative data will be presented in two tables, namely, table 5. 11 and table 5. 12.** Table 5. 11 presents the details of collected data for thirty Western companies during the observation period.

Table 5.11 Data collection based on KPIs for Western companies

KPI	1st week	2nd week	3rd week	4th week
Company: Apple Industry: Computers				
Change of follower number	+7 691 (869 098/876 789)	+9 352 (876 789/886 141)	+5 548 (886 141/891 689)	+10 005 (891 689/901 694)
Change of following number	0 (441/441)	0 (441/441)	0 (441/441)	+1 (441/442)
Number of posts	77	158	79	68
Sum of retweets	311	773	282	266
Sum of comments	174	443	188	194
Sum of likes	723	1 322	760	799
Company: Starbucks Industry: Food Services				
Change of follower number	+1 403 (1 236 858/1 238 261)	+950 (1 238 261/1 239 211)	+1 030 (1 239 211/1 240 241)	+871 (1 240 241/1 241 112)
Change of following number	−1 (752/751)	0 (751/751)	0 (751/751)	0 (751/751)
Number of posts	15	12	14	14
Sum of retweets	2 699	829	1 132	1 335
Sum of comments	1 822	586	665	1 321
Sum of likes	2 794	1 882	2 077	2 932
Company: McDonald's Industry: Food Services				
Change of follower number	+67 042 (539 984/607 026)	+2 628 (607 026/609 654)	+448 (609 654/610 102)	+4 693 (610 102/614 795)
Change of following number	+3 (52/55)	+2 (55/57)	+3 (57/60)	+2 (60/62)
Number of posts	33	34	48	35
Sum of retweets	22 568	8 676	12 519	7 125
Sum of comments	9 408	3 648	5 468	3 978
Sum of likes	30 837	8 487	8 565	5 375
Company: Coca-Cola Industry: Beverages				
Change of follower number	−27 (62 038/62 011)	+45 (62 011/62 056)	−29 (62 056/62 027)	−57 (62 027/61 970)
Change of following number	0 (113/113)	0 (113/113)	+1 (113/114)	0 (114/114)
Number of posts	9	8	9	5
Sum of retweets	62	147	27	37
Sum of comments	33	33	30	23
Sum of likes	85	86	66	43
Company: Walt Disney Industry: Entertainment				
Change of follower number	+61 (215 572/215 633)	−112 (215 633/215 521)	−230 (215 521/215 291)	−217 (215 291/215 074)
Change of following number	0 (96/96)	0 (96/96)	+1 (96/97)	0 (97/97)
Number of posts	12	10	13	11
Sum of retweets	268	358	419	382
Sum of comments	88	55	70	69
Sum of likes	381	354	408	425

Table 5.11(Continued)

KPI	1st week	2nd week	3rd week	4th week
Company: FedEx Industry: Delivery				
Change of follower number	−392 (90 538/90 146)	−99 (90 146/90 047)	−699 (90 047/89 348)	+216 (89 348/89 564)
Change of following number	0 (109/109)	0 (109/109)	0 (109/109)	−2 (109/107)
Number of posts	6	4	8	5
Sum of retweets	11	3	10	5
Sum of comments	18	12	13	18
Sum of likes	15	5	36	16
Company: UPS Industry: Delivery				
Change of follower number	+10 (14 278/14 288)	−11 (14 288/14 277)	+5 (14 277/14 282)	+67 (14 282/14 349)
Change of following number	0 (78/78)	0 (78/78)	0 (78/78)	0 (78/78)
Number of posts	3	4	3	3
Sum of retweets	5	1	2	330
Sum of comments	2	0	7	133
Sum of likes	18	9	5	30
Company: General Electric Industry: Electronics				
Change of follower number	+12 (83 925/83 937)	+1 (83 937/83 938)	−20 (83 938/83 918)	−41 (83 918/83 877)
Change of following number	0 (989/989)	0 (989/989)	0 (989/989)	0 (989/989)
Number of posts	0	0	0	2
Sum of retweets	0	0	0	5
Sum of comments	0	0	0	2
Sum of likes	0	0	0	7
Company: American Express Industry: Consumer Credit Card and Related Services				
Change of follower number	−44 (103 054/103 010)	−95 (103 010/102 915)	−249 (102 915/102 666)	−54 (102 666/102 612)
Change of following number	−8 (246/238)	−4 (238/234)	0 (234/234)	0 (234/234)
Number of posts	0	29	28	29
Sum of retweets	0	13	16	30
Sum of comments	0	13	25	42
Sum of likes	0	25	26	61
Company: Nike Industry: Apparel				
Change of follower number	+3 545 (398 048/401 593)	+3 034 (401 593/404 627)	+2 821 (404 627/407 448)	+10 973 (407 448/418 421)
Change of following number	0 (104/104)	0 (104/104)	0 (104/104)	0 (104/104)
Number of posts	1	1	0	1
Sum of retweets	83	39	0	91
Sum of comments	28	24	0	22
Sum of likes	458	281	0	334

Table 5. 11(Continued)

KPI	1st week	2nd week	3rd week	4th week
Company:BMW Industry:Motor Vehicles				
Change of follower number	+817 (936 415/937 232)	+51 (937 232/937 283)	+2 112 (937 283/939 395)	+3 247 (939 395/942 642)
Change of following number	+1 (573/574)	0 (574/574)	+1 (574/575)	0 (575/575)
Number of posts	14	14	20	1
Sum of retweets	2 791	2 434	3 742	210
Sum of comments	1 366	792	1 121	54
Sum of likes	620	436	1 419	37
Company:Volkswagen Industry:Motor Vehicles				
Change of follower number	+60 301 (946 613/1 006 914)	+46 169 (1 006 914/1 053 083)	+31 110 (1 053 083/1 084 193)	+22 358 (1 084 193/1 106 551)
Change of following number	0 (171/171)	0 (171/171)	0 (171/171)	0 (171/171)
Number of posts	17	19	16	14
Sum of retweets	5 797	5 518	4 668	4 196
Sum of comments	4 117	3 930	3 573	3 427
Sum of likes	746	704	645	559
Company:Procter & Gamble Industry:Soaps and Cosmetics				
Change of follower number	-126 (153 633/153 507)	+18 275 (153 507/171 782)	+25 236 (171 782/197 018)	+14 393 (197 018/211 411)
Change of following number	0 (93/93)	0 (93/93)	+1 (93/94)	0 (94/94)
Number of posts	17	16	15	13
Sum of retweets	22	14	23	7
Sum of comments	31	19	20	6
Sum of likes	53	44	53	45
Company:IBM Industry:Information Technology Services				
Change of follower number	-31 (130 449/130 418)	-89 (130 418/130 329)	-27 (130 329/130 302)	+30 (130 302/130 332)
Change of following number	0 (1 572/ 1 572)	+2 (1 572/1 574)	+2 (1 574/1 576)	+1 (1 576/1 577)
Number of posts	5	9	5	3
Sum of retweets	4	20	19	15
Sum of comments	3	4	8	4
Sum of likes	4	17	13	7
Company:Accenture Industry:Information Technology Services				
Change of follower number	+27 (35 259/35 286)	+17 (35 286/35 303)	+26 (35 303/35 329)	+31 (35 329/35 360)
Change of following number	0 (90/90)	0 (90/90)	0 (90/90)	0 (90/90)
Number of posts	10	9	8	10
Sum of retweets	38	36	32	32
Sum of comments	8	9	11	10
Sum of likes	19	10	22	10

Table 5. 11(Continued)

KPI	1st week	2nd week	3rd week	4th week
Company: Johnson & Johnson Industry: Pharmaceuticals				
Change of follower number	-45 (47 857/47 812)	-45 (47 812/47 767)	-58 (47 767/47 709)	-63 (47 709/47 646)
Change of following number	0 (200/200)	0 (200/200)	0 (200/200)	0 (200/200)
Number of posts	0	0	0	0
Sum of retweets	0	0	0	0
Sum of comments	0	0	0	0
Sum of likes	0	0	0	0
Company: 3M Industry: Medical Products and Equipment				
Change of follower number	-139 (233 632/233 493)	-138 (233 493/233 355)	-208 (233 355/233 147)	+476 (233 147/233 623)
Change of following number	0 (289/289)	0 (289/289)	+1 (289/290)	0 (290/290)
Number of posts	6	5	4	10
Sum of retweets	895	35	36	257
Sum of comments	158	38	32	90
Sum of likes	23	11	10	123
Company: Microsoft Industry: Computer Software				
Change of follower number	+853 (168 462/169 315)	+252 (169 315/169 567)	+448 (169 567/170 015)	+624 (170 015/170 639)
Change of following number	0 (128/128)	0 (128/128)	+1 (128/129)	+2 (129/131)
Number of posts	21	14	14	22
Sum of retweets	911	495	22 909	17 452
Sum of comments	808	611	12 314	9 613
Sum of likes	1 058	530	1 596	1 328
Company: Boeing Industry: Aerospace and Defense				
Change of follower number	+76 (132 196/132 272)	+288 (132 272/132 560)	+259 (132 560/132 819)	+124 (132 819/132 943)
Change of following number	+1 (206/207)	0 (207/207)	0 (207/207)	+4(207/211)
Number of posts	9	8	23	10
Sum of retweets	666	668	755	399
Sum of comments	217	185	259	126
Sum of likes	321	333	767	406
Company: Exxon Mobil Industry: Petroleum Refining				
Change of follower number	+21 (9 045/9 066)	-1 (9 066/9 065)	-59 (9 065/9 006)	+98 (9 006/9 104)
Change of following number	0(21/21)	0 (21/21)	0 (21/21)	+1 (21/22)
Number of posts	0	0	0	0
Sum of retweets	0	0	0	0
Sum of comments	0	0	0	0
Sum of likes	0	0	0	0

Table 5. 11(Continued)

KPI	1st week	2nd week	3rd week	4th week
Company: Wal-Mart Stores Industry: General Merchandisers				
Change of follower number	+247 (436 806/437 053)	−792 (437 053/436 261)	+73 (436 261/436 334)	−5 (436 334/436 329)
Change of following number	0(71/71)	0(71/71)	0(71/71)	0(71/71)
Number of posts	43	22	42	41
Sum of retweets	67	50	68	54
Sum of comments	54	211	56	51
Sum of likes	136	107	167	116
Company: Nestlé S.A. Industry: Consumer Food Products				
Change of follower number	+482 (672 369/672 851)	−1 048 (672 851/671 803)	−2 424 (671 803/669 379)	+3 486 (669 379/672 865)
Change of following number	0 (229/229)	0 (229/229)	0 (229/229)	0 (229/229)
Number of posts	7	9	6	4
Sum of retweets	708	740	15 231	489
Sum of comments	111	210	2 474	109
Sum of likes	480	472	407	358
Company: Unilever Industry: Consumer Food Products				
Change of follower number	−31 (54 806/54 775)	+15 (54 775/54 790)	−131 (54 790/54 659)	−121 (54 659/54 538)
Change of following number	0 (155/155)	0 (155/155)	0 (155/155)	0 (155/155)
Number of posts	3	6	20	2
Sum of retweets	342	14	2 823	6
Sum of comments	180	3	1 544	2
Sum of likes	393	20	64	4
Company: PepsiCo Industry: Consumer Food Products				
Change of follower number	−27 (277 513/277 486)	−8 (277 486/277 478)	−344 (277 478/277 134)	−256 (277 134/276 878)
Change of following number	0 (108/108)	+1 (108/109)	+1 (109/110)	0 (110/110)
Number of posts	10	5	7	4
Sum of retweets	7 011	7 260	857	6 974
Sum of comments	3 509	1 387	493	1 203
Sum of likes	2 237	2 754	609	3 883
Company: Caterpillar Industry: Construction and Farm Machinery				
Change of follower number	+53 (61 710/61 763)	+18 (61 763/61 781)	−100 (61 781/61 681)	−18 (61 681/61 663)
Change of following number	0 (245/245)	0 (245/245)	0 (245/245)	0 (245/245)
Number of posts	1	0	2	0
Sum of retweets	0	0	23	0
Sum of comments	2	0	22	0
Sum of likes	13	0	5	0

Table 5. 11(Continued)

KPI	1st week	2nd week	3rd week	4th week
Company:Deere Industry:Construction and Farm Machinery				
Change of follower number	+5 (3 945/ 3 950)	-3 (3 950/3 947)	-3 (3 947/3 944)	+7 (3 944/3 951)
Change of following number	0 (67/67)	0 (67/67)	0 (67/67)	0 (67/67)
Number of posts	1	0	0	0
Sum of retweets	0	0	0	0
Sum of comments	0	0	0	0
Sum of likes	1	0	0	0
Company:Marriott International Industry:Hotel/Casinos/resorts				
Change of follower number	-134 (223 794/223 660)	-383 (223 660/223 277)	+98 (223 277/223 375)	-263 (223 375/223 112)
Change of following number	0 (63/63)	0 (63/63)	0 (63/63)	0 (63/63)
Number of posts	16	12	9	6
Sum of retweets	31	8	6	8
Sum of comments	48	16	20	10
Sum of likes	21	16	18	22
Company:DuPont Industry:Chemicals				
Change of follower number	+18 (15 574/15 592)	-8 (15 592/15 584)	-17 (15 584/15 567)	+13 (15 567/15 580)
Change of following number	0 (175/175)	0 (175/175)	0 (175/175)	0 (175/175)
Number of posts	4	1	6	3
Sum of retweets	48	1	18	4
Sum of comments	16	1	7	2
Sum of likes	20	1	21	13
Company:Intel Industry:Semiconductors				
Change of follower number	+219 (839 788/840 007)	-647 (840 007/839 360)	-2 017 (839 360/837 343)	+2 192 (837 343/839 535)
Change of following number	0 (410/410)	0 (410/410)	0 (410/410)	0 (410/410)
Number of posts	27	20	24	21
Sum of retweets	555	317	1 017	440
Sum of comments	508	536	882	733
Sum of likes	465	357	401	476
Company:Cisco System Industry:Network and other Communication equipment				
Change of follower number	-5 (10 844/10 839)	-9 (10 839/10 830)	-7 (10 830/10 823)	-1 (10 823/10 822)
Change of following number	0 (108/108)	0 (108/108)	0 (108/108)	0 (108/108)
Number of posts	0	0	0	0
Sum of retweets	0	0	0	0
Sum of comments	0	0	0	0
Sum of likes	0	0	0	0

Similarly, table 5.12 presents the collected first-hand data for thirty Chinese companies during the observation period. Based on the collected data from table 5.11 and table 5.12, the corresponding data processing such as data categorizing, coding, and transforming can be conducted. And then the structured database can be set up.

Table 5.12 Data collection based on KPIs for Chinese companies

KPI	1st week	2nd week	3rd week	4th week
Company: Huawei Industry: Telecom manufacturing and services				
Change of follower number	+27 (1 945 466 / 1 945 493)	−785 (1 945 493 / 1 944 708)	−122 (1 944 708/1 944 586)	−650 (1 944 586/1 943 936)
Change of following number	0 (149/149)	0 (149/149)	0 (149/149)	0 (149/149)
Number of posts	26	30	39	22
Sum of retweets	139	264	282	312
Sum of comments	129	159	177	176
Sum of likes	504	581	905	593
Company: ZTE Industry: Telecom manufacturing and services				
Change of follower number	+9 456 (979 009/988 465)	+68 (988 465/988 533)	−164 (988 533/988 369)	+543 (988 369/988 912)
Change of following number	+2 (555/557)	0 (557/557)	+1 (557/558)	0 (558/558)
Number of posts	14	22	19	13
Sum of retweets	13 866	291	97	58
Sum of comments	617	218	135	116
Sum of likes	390	1 003	474	322
Company: Haier Industry: Electronics/Electrical Appliances				
Change of follower number	+633 (140 529/141 162)	−1 030 (141 162/140 132)	−4 467 (140 132/135 665)	+12 002 (135 665/147 667)
Change of following number	+1 (455/456)	0 (456/456)	+1 (456/457)	0 (457/457)
Number of posts	26	21	21	22
Sum of retweets	6 356	9 736	13 251	6 161
Sum of comments	1 246	823	2 629	1 066
Sum of likes	2 179	1 539	1 390	2 195
Company: Xiaomi Industry: Electronics/Electrical Appliances				
Change of follower number	+87 045 (4 144 313 / 4 231 358)	−1 947 (4 231 358/4 229 411)	−1 770 (4 229 411/4 227 641)	−1 702 (4 227 641/4 225 939)
Change of following number	+3 (798/801)	+2 (801/803)	+1 (803/804)	+1 (804/805)
Number of posts	49	54	45	40
Sum of retweets	28 061	100 968	27 774	8 556
Sum of comments	12 666	23 610	7 707	6 690
Sum of likes	15 877	20 890	10 880	15 363

Table 5. 12 (Continued)

KPI	1st week	2nd week	3rd week	4th week
Company: Lenovo Industry: Electronics/Electrical Appliances				
Change of follower number	+16 452 (1 712 837/1 729 289)	+9 727 (1 729 289/1 739 016)	+15 474 (1 739 016/1 754 490)	+18 617 (1 754 490/1 773 107)
Change of following number	+3 (1 445/1 448)	+1 (1 448/1 449)	+1 (1 449/1 450)	+1 (1 450/1 451)
Number of posts	39	45	40	27
Sum of retweets	43 464	34 082	23 498	7 972
Sum of comments	17 606	14 332	11 301	6 743
Sum of likes	4 110	4 554	5 675	3 042
Company: Gree Industry: Electronics/Electrical Appliances				
Change of follower number	+115 (229 419/229 534)	+162 (229 534/229 696)	−133 (229 696/229 563)	+675 (229 563/230 238)
Change of following number	0 (309/309)	−1 (309/308)	+1 (308/309)	−1 (309/308)
Number of posts	21	23	21	15
Sum of retweets	44	91	46	28
Sum of comments	107	170	185	166
Sum of likes	78	107	112	56
Company: Midea Industry: Electronics/Electrical Appliances				
Change of follower number	+64 (460 105/460 169)	−447 (460 169/459 722)	−1 634 (459 722/458 088)	+1 453 (458 088/459 541)
Change of following number	0 (243 /243)	+2 (243/245)	0 (245/245)	0 (245/245)
Number of posts	1	7	2	1
Sum of retweets	4	2 126	2 502	16
Sum of comments	5	668	1 007	13
Sum of likes	20	110	12	21
Company: TCL Industry: Electronics/Electrical Appliances				
Change of follower number	−1 707 (2 160 193/2 158 486)	−1 825 (2 158 486/2 156 661)	+5 443 (2 156 661/2 162 104)	+9 466 (2 162 104/2 171 570)
Change of following number	0 (362/362)	0 (362/362)	0 (362/362)	0 (362/362)
Number of posts	47	40	44	43
Sum of retweets	197	2 358	1 598	3 206
Sum of comments	91	587	594	499
Sum of likes	114	126	131	144
Company: Hisense Industry: Electronics/Electrical Appliances				
Change of follower number	−107 (987 769/987 662)	−637 (987 662/987 025)	+27 (987 025/987 052)	+3 768 (987 052/990 820)
Change of following number	0 (119/119)	+1 (119/120)	+3 (120/123)	0 (123/123)
Number of posts	10	16	10	10
Sum of retweets	2 475	1 497	2 055	5 384
Sum of comments	569	374	577	2 743
Sum of likes	419	398	388	2 319

Table 5. 12(Continued)

KPI	1st week	2nd week	3rd week	4th week
Company: BYD Industry: Motor Vehicles/Motor Vehicles Parts				
Change of follower number	+6 005 (1 154 966/1 160 971)	+1 936 (1 160 971/1 162 907)	−892 (1 162 907/1 162 015)	−1 233 (1 162 015/1 160 782)
Change of following number	+3 (648/651)	0(651/651)	+2 (651/653)	+2 (653/655)
Number of posts	44	19	23	13
Sum of retweets	54 531	5 425	4 082	639
Sum of comments	21 307	1 214	867	301
Sum of likes	3 980	650	775	417
Company: Great Wall Motors Industry: Motor Vehicles/Motor Vehicles Parts				
Change of follower number	+288 (90 749/91 037)	+144 (91 037/91 181)	+64 (91 181/91 245)	+83 (91 245/91 328)
Change of following number	0 (194/194)	0 (194/194)	+1 (194/195)	0 (195/195)
Number of posts	7	3	7	8
Sum of retweets	476	294	330	559
Sum of comments	165	47	99	125
Sum of likes	135	61	83	99
Company: Saic Motor Industry: Motor Vehicles/Motor Vehicles Parts				
Change of follower number	+10 (400 829/400 839)	−287 (400 839/400 552)	−330 (400 552/400 222)	+221 (400 222/400 443)
Change of following number	0 (655/655)	0 (655/655)	0 (655/655)	+1 (655/656)
Number of posts	29	26	32	26
Sum of retweets	331	222	205	150
Sum of comments	280	232	204	142
Sum of likes	133	67	34	25
Company: Geely Industry: Motor Vehicles/Motor Vehicles Parts				
Change of follower number	+65 (73 370/73 435)	−160 (73 435/73 275)	−311 (73 275/72 964)	+1 023 (72 964/73 987)
Change of following number	0 (1 231/1 231)	0 (1 231/1 231)	0 (1 231/1 231)	+3 (1 231/1 234)
Number of posts	19	38	35	28
Sum of retweets	44	136	133	301
Sum of comments	17	98	76	85
Sum of likes	71	107	102	109
Company: Wahaha Industry: Food/Beverage				
Change of follower number	+89 (75 815/75 904)	+169 (75 904/76 073)	−176 (76 073/75 897)	+12 286 (75 897/88 183)
Change of following number	−3 (372/369)	−1 (369/368)	+2 (368/370)	+2 (370/372)
Number of posts	15	10	13	12
Sum of retweets	198	18	780	15 966
Sum of comments	80	37	486	7 967
Sum of likes	220	49	131	388

Table 5. 12(Continued)

KPI	1st week	2nd week	3rd week	4th week
Company: Tsingtao Industry: Food/Beverage				
Change of follower number	−320 (290 769/290 449)	−367 (290 449/290 082)	−202 (290 082/289 880)	+503 (289 880/290 383)
Change of following number	+1 (282/283)	0 (283/283)	0 (283/283)	0 (283/283)
Number of posts	4	3	4	3
Sum of retweets	4	6	6	1
Sum of comments	1	11	7	3
Sum of likes	9	8	12	3
Company: Kweichow Moutai Industry: Food/Beverage				
Change of follower number	−151 (531 386/531 235)	−980 (531 235/530 255)	−516 (530 255/529 739)	+1 242 (529 739/530 981)
Change of following number	0 (370/370)	0 (370/370)	0 (370/370)	+1 (370/371)
Number of posts	34	41	43	37
Sum of retweets	2 240	1 735	1 377	1 122
Sum of comments	1 689	1 390	1 194	976
Sum of likes	343	337	344	252
Company: YanJing Beer Industry: Food/Beverage				
Change of follower number	−105 (52 997/52 892)	−124 (52 892/52 768)	+44 (52 768/52 812)	+25 (52 812/52 837)
Change of following number	0 (162/162)	0 (162/162)	0 (162/162)	0 (162/162)
Number of posts	7	4	4	1
Sum of retweets	9	2	2	0
Sum of comments	10	5	3	0
Sum of likes	14	5	3	1
Company: Bright Food Industry: Food/Beverage				
Change of follower number	−31 (11 590/11 559)	−18 (11 559/11 541)	−10 (11 541/11 531)	+4 (11 531/11 535)
Change of following number	0 (376/376)	0 (376/376)	0 (376/376)	0 (376/376)
Number of posts	29	27	26	23
Sum of retweets	12	10	21	14
Sum of comments	1	1	3	6
Sum of likes	13	10	11	7
Company: HaiNan Airlines Industry: Airlines				
Change of follower number	+270 (1 650 225/1 650 495)	−573 (1 650 495/1 649 922)	+2 668 (1 649 922/1 652 590)	+4 820 (1 652 590/1 657 410)
Change of following number	+1 (834/835)	0 (835/835)	+5 (835/840)	0 (840/840)
Number of posts	51	46	86	45
Sum of retweets	765	502	1 826	872
Sum of comments	495	422	1 572	998
Sum of likes	732	623	1 429	719

Table 5. 12(Continued)

KPI	1st week	2nd week	3rd week	4th week
Company: Yunnan Baiyao Industry: Pharmaceuticals				
Change of follower number	+16 (7 707/7 723)	+12 (7 723/7 735)	+10 (7 735/7 745)	+19 (7 745/7 764)
Change of following number	0 (63/63)	0 (63 /63)	0 (63/63)	0 (63/63)
Number of posts	0	0	0	1
Sum of retweets	0	0	0	3
Sum of comments	0	0	0	0
Sum of likes	0	0	0	0
Company: Ping An Industry: Insurance				
Change of follower number	−1 845 (1 971 263/1 969 418)	−1 610 (1 969 418/1 967 808)	−1 273 (1 967 808/1 966 535)	−1 850 (1 966 535/1 964 685)
Change of following number	0 (358/358)	0 (358/358)	0 (358/358)	0 (358/358)
Number of posts	29	31	28	32
Sum of retweets	1 118	936	20 365	1 148
Sum of comments	196	85	2 593	117
Sum of likes	714	556	690	613
Company: WangFujing Industry: Wholesale/Retail/Distribution				
Change of follower number	−8 (2 774/2 766)	−4 (2 766/2 762)	−2 (2 762/2 760)	−1 (2 760/2 759)
Change of following number	0 (311/311)	0 (311/311)	0 (311/311)	0 (311/311)
Number of posts	0	0	0	0
Sum of retweets	0	0	0	0
Sum of comments	0	0	0	0
Sum of likes	0	0	0	0
Company: SuNing Industry: Wholesale/Retail/Distribution				
Change of follower number	−9 788 (5 859 688/5 849 900)	−5 260 (5 849 900/5 844 640)	−4 861 (5 844 640/5 839 779)	−5 530 (5 839 779/5 834 249)
Change of following number	0 (668/668)	0 (668/668)	+1 (668/669)	+1 (669/670)
Number of posts	53	52	48	39
Sum of retweets	966	739	1 838	633
Sum of comments	833	709	1 158	585
Sum of likes	694	456	477	419
Company: Gome Industry: Wholesale/Retail/Distribution				
Change of follower number	−1 100 (6 908 561/6 907 461)	−6 604 (6 907 461/6 900 857)	−4 439 (6 900 857/6 896 418)	+53 417 (6 896 418/6 949 835)
Change of following number	+2 (149/151)	−1 (151/150)	0 (150/150)	0 (150/150)
Number of posts	49	48	59	47
Sum of retweets	5 854	3 428	147 368	13 159
Sum of comments	1 649	1 361	2 013	6 195
Sum of likes	206	187	226	367

Table 5. 12(Continued)

KPI	1st week	2nd week	3rd week	4th week
Company:Wanda Industry:Real Estate				
Change of follower number	+2 614 (1 210 385/1 212 999)	+6 418 (1 212 999/1 219 417)	+17 228 (1 219 417/1 236 645)	+6 854 (1 236 645/1 243 499)
Change of following number	0 (1 030/1 030)	0 (1 030/1 030)	0 (1 030/1 030)	+1 (1 030/1 031)
Number of posts	12	10	10	6
Sum of retweets	1 484	1 343	968	810
Sum of comments	491	434	319	291
Sum of likes	305	193	293	528
Company:Vanke Industry:Real Estate				
Change of follower number	+34 (46 244/46 278)	−6 (46 278/46 272)	+22 (46 272/46 294)	+5 (46 294/46 299)
Change of following number	0 (745/745)	0 (745/745)	0 (745/745)	+1 (745/746)
Number of posts	0	6	0	0
Sum of retweets	0	23	0	0
Sum of comments	0	8	0	0
Sum of likes	0	8	0	0
Company:Country Garden Industry:Real Estate				
Change of follower number	−3 (17 207/17 204)	−39 (17 204/17 165)	−9 (17 165/17 156)	+86 (17 156/17 242)
Change of following number	0 (832/832)	0 (832/832)	0 (832/832)	0 (832/832)
Number of posts	0	0	0	2
Sum of retweets	0	0	0	1
Sum of comments	0	0	0	0
Sum of likes	0	0	0	1
Company:SANY Industry:Manufacturing				
Change of follower number	+12 (26 221/26 233)	−2 (26 233/26 231)	−26 (26 231/26 205)	−6 (26 205/26 199)
Change of following number	0 (110/110)	0 (110/110)	(110/110)	−2 (110/108)
Number of posts	0	0	0	0
Sum of retweets	0	0	0	0
Sum of comments	0	0	0	0
Sum of likes	0	0	0	0
Company:New Hope Group Industry:Diversification				
Change of follower number	−3 (7 192/7 189)	−3 (7 189/7 186)	−1 (7 186/7 185)	−10 (7 185/7 175)
Change of following number	0 (37/37)	0 (37/37)	0 (37/37)	0 (37/37)
Number of posts	0	0	0	0
Sum of retweets	0	0	0	0
Sum of comments	0	0	0	0
Sum of likes	0	0	0	0

Table 5. 12(Continued)

KPI	1st week	2nd week	3rd week	4th week
Company: Fosun Industry: Diversification				
Change of follower number	+43 (8 825/8 868)	+17 (8 868/8 885)	+36 (8 885/8 921)	+42 (8 921/8 963)
Change of following number	0 (539/539)	0 (539/539)	0 (539/539)	+1 (539/540)
Number of posts	2	2	0	8
Sum of retweets	4	21	0	31
Sum of comments	2	5	0	14
Sum of likes	4	8	0	28

5. 3. 1. 2 Data processing

Data processing work involves mainly two tasks (data categorizing and coding, data transforming) which is dedicated to facilitate the creation of structured database.

(1) Data categorizing and coding

The data has been categorized and coded as listed in table 5. 13.

Table 5. 13 List of data category and coding in Sina Weibo case study

No.	Abbreviation	Description	Coding/Data type
1	–	Country region	Western: 0 Chinese: 1
2	–	Industry (19 types)	As per table 4. 6
3	–	Date of first post	Date type
4	–	Annual number of original posts	Number type
5	–	Annual number of tweets	Number type
6	SumP	Sum of posts	Number type
7	SumR	Sum of retweets	Number type
8	SumC	Sum of comments	Number type
9	AveP	Average of posts	Number type
10	AveR	Average of retweets	Number type
11	AveC	Average of comments	Number type
12	F1	Measurement of the level of interaction	Number type
13	F2	Normalization of F1	Number type

Table 5. 13 (Continued)

No.	Abbreviation	Description	Coding/Data type
14	Text + Picture + Video + Link	Format of top-one post	String type
15	Text + Video + Link	Format of top-one post	String type
16	Text + Video	Format of top-one post	String type
17	Text + Picture + Video	Format of top-one post	String type
18	Text + GIF	Format of top-one post	String type
19	Text + Picture + Link	Format of top-one post	String type
20	Text + Picture	Format of top-one post	String type
21	Text	Format of top-one post	String type
22	Text + Link	Format of top-one post	String type

These categories and codes will be adopted to create the relevant database.

(2) Data transforming

In order to assess the level of interaction, i.e., the engagement on Sina Weibo, the total number of interactions with posts should be considered such as retweets, comments, and likes in this research. Engagement is a very important metric to inform the proportion of users who are actually participating in conversation and how effective the relevant campaigns are.

Under the purpose to measure the level of interaction on Sina Weibo channel per company in this research, a comprehensive consideration was made in line with the available first-hand data; a mathematical factor integrating the KPIs was set up in order to evaluate the level of interaction of companies and expressed as the following formula:

$$F1 = (AveR + AveC + AveL) / AveP$$

where AveR, AveC and AveL are the average of retweets, comments & likes per week; and AveP is the average of posts per week.

There is a four-week observation period. Each important average number can be calculated for each company. **The formula is built based on the impact of Sina Weibo marketing, i.e., the number of interactions (average number of retweets, comments, and likes) on the basis of average number of posts.**

This formula of F1 is dedicated to exploring the engagement between the company and the users, i.e., the level of interaction. **F1 is based on the average value. The magnitude of factor F1 is normally diverse. By following the method described in section 4. 4, the F1 data can be normalized to F2,** which varies between 0 and 1, where "0" denotes the minimum level of interaction among all selected samples and "1" represents the maximum level of interaction among all selected samples.

Therefore, Chinese and Western enterprises' engagement with their fans on Sina Weibo platform can be evaluated and classified on the basis of F2 as explained below:

F2 = normalized F1 = the level of interaction

After normalization of F1, F1 is converted to F2. Table 5. 14 shows the data of F1 and F2 for high reputation Western and Chinese companies.

Table 5. 14 Results of F1 & F2 for Western & Chinese companies

No.	Western company name	F1	F2	No.	Chinese company name	F1	F2
1	Apple	16. 3	0. 011 1	1	Huawei	36. 1	0. 024 3
2	Starbucks	365. 0	0. 248 6	2	ZTE	258. 6	0. 174 2
3	McDonald's	844. 4	0. 575 1	3	Haier	539. 7	0. 363 6
4	Coca-Cola	21. 7	0. 014 8	4	Xiaomi	1 484. 3	1. 000 0
5	Walt Disney	71. 2	0. 048 5	5	Lenovo	1 168. 1	0. 787 0
6	FedEx	7. 0	0. 004 8	6	Gree	14.9	0. 010 0
7	UPS	41. 7	0. 028 4	7	Midea	591. 3	0. 398 4
8	General Electric	7. 0	0. 004 8	8	TCL	55. 4	0. 037 3
9	American Express	2.9	0. 002 0	9	Hisense	417. 3	0. 281 2
10	Nike	453. 3	0. 308 7	10	BYD	951. 4	0. 641 0
11	BMW	306. 6	0. 208 8	11	Great Wall Motors	98.9	0. 066 6
12	Volkswagen	573.9	0. 390 9	12	Saic Motor	17.9	0. 012 1
13	Procter & Gamble	5. 5	0. 003 8	13	Geely	10. 7	0. 007 2
14	IBM	5. 4	0. 003 7	14	Wahaha	526. 4	0. 354 7
15	Accenture	6. 4	0. 004 4	15	Tsingtao	5. 1	0. 003 4

Table 5. 14(Continued)

No.	Western company name	F1	F2	No.	Chinese company name	F1	F2
16	Johnson & Johnson	0. 0	0. 000 0	16	Kweichow Moutai	83.9	0. 056 5
17	3M	68. 3	0. 046 5	17	YanJing Beer	3. 4	0. 002 3
18	Microsoft	980. 6	0. 667 9	18	Bright Food	1. 0	0. 000 7
19	Boeing	102. 0	0. 069 5	19	HaiNan Airlines	48. 0	0. 032 4
20	Exxon Mobil	0. 0	0. 000 0	20	Yunnan Baiyao	3. 0	0. 002 0
21	Wal-Mart Stores	7. 7	0. 005 2	21	Ping An	242.8	0. 163 6
22	Nestlé S.A.	838. 0	0. 570 8	22	WangFujing	0. 0	0. 000 0
23	Unilever	174. 0	0. 118 5	23	SuNing	49. 5	0. 033 4
24	PepsiCo	1 468. 3	1. 000 0	24	Gome	896. 6	0. 604 1
25	Caterpillar	21. 7	0. 014 8	25	Wanda	196. 3	0. 132 2
26	Deere	1. 0	0. 000 7	26	Vanke	6. 5	0. 004 4
27	Marriott International	5. 2	0. 003 5	27	Country Garden	1. 0	0. 000 7
28	DuPont	10.9	0. 007 4	28	SANY	0. 0	0. 000 0
29	Intel	72. 7	0. 049 5	29	New Hope Group	0. 0	0. 000 0
30	Cisco System	0. 0	0. 000 0	30	Fosun	9.8	0. 006 6
—	Max	1 468. 3	1. 000 0	—	Max	1 484. 3	1. 000 0
—	Min	0. 0	0. 000 0	—	Min	0. 0	0. 000 0

5. 3. 1. 3 Database creation

The method stated in section 4. 4 was followed to create the database. Table 5. 15 and table 5. 16 show the excel format database in which the quantitative data was recorded and organized for both Western and Chinese companies.

Table 5.15 Summary of database based on Western companies' Sina Weibo accounts

No.	Company name	Cou-ntry	Indu-stry	Industry detail	The date of first post	Number of original posts vs. Number of retweets						Sum of posts (SumP)	Sum of retweets (SumR)	Sum of comments (SumC)	Sum of likes (SumL)	Average of posts per week (AveP)	Average of retweets per week (AveR)	Average of comments per week (AveC)	Average of likes per week (AveL)	F1	F2
						2009	2010	2011	2012	2013	2014										
1	Apple	0	2	Computers	14/12/2010	–	67vs.15	4 230vs.523	4 026vs.488	4 655vs.305	5 073vs.183	382	1 632	999	3 604	95.50	408.00	249.75	901.00	16.32	0.011 1
2	Starbucks	0	1	Food Services	14/05/2010	–	470vs.272	827vs.390	1 118vs.170	1 226vs.303	853vs.96	55	5 995	4 394	9 685	13.75	1 498.75	1 098.50	2 421.25	364.98	0.248 6
3	McDonald's	0	1	Food Services	08/04/2011	–	–	174vs.45	637vs.131	687vs.122	718vs.198	150	50 888	22 502	53 264	37.50	12 722.00	5 625.50	13 316.00	844.36	0.575 0
4	Coca-Cola	0	1	Beverages	11/10/2010	–	83vs.70	602vs.751	1 041vs.252	1 446vs.345	1 044vs.143	31	273	119	280	7.75	68.25	29.75	70.00	21.68	0.014 8
5	Walt Disney	0	3	Entertainment	25/11/2010	–	3vs.13	164vs.144	596vs.624	1 044vs.227	804vs.164	46	1 427	282	1 568	11.50	356.75	70.50	392.00	71.24	0.048 5
6	FedEx	0	4	Delivery	05/07/2010	–	57vs.7	161vs.41	82vs.52	218vs.350	321vs.246	23	29	61	72	5.75	7.25	15.25	18.00	7.04	0.004 8
7	UPS	0	4	Delivery	20/09/2010	–	115vs.2	66vs.5	59vs.32	68vs.19	118vs.30	13	338	142	62	3.25	84.50	35.50	15.50	41.69	0.028 4
8	General Electric	0	5	Electronics	xx/12/2010	–	–	340vs.273	360vs.329	304vs.298	293vs.93	2	5	2	7	0.50	1.25	0.50	1.75	7.00	0.004 8
9	American Express	0	6	Consumer credit card and Related Service	27/04/2012	–	–	–	1 486vs.294	2 062vs.156	1 852vs.32	86	59	80	112	21.50	14.75	20.00	28.00	2.92	0.002 0
10	Nike	0	8	Apparel	06/07/2011	–	–	441vs.366	215vs.243	84vs.12	31vs.11	3	213	74	1 073	0.75	53.25	18.50	268.25	453.33	0.308 7
11	BMW	0	9	Motor Vehicles	23/02/2010	–	488vs.163	689vs.202	1 357vs.286	958vs.63	986vs.55	49	9 177	3 333	2 512	12.25	2 294.25	833.25	628.00	306.57	0.208 8
12	Volkswagen	0	9	Motor Vehicles	05/11/2012	–			221vs.38	1 116vs.143	1 023vs.55	66	20 179	15 047	2 654	16.50	5 044.75	3 761.75	663.50	573.94	0.390 9
13	Procter & Gamble	0	10	Soaps & Cosmetics	22/06/2010	–	164vs.70	422vs.341	741vs.481	861vs.338	770vs.330	61	66	76	195	15.25	16.50	19.00	48.75	5.52	0.003 8
14	IBM	0	2	Information Technology Services	31/01/2011	–	–	367vs.449	1 030vs.1 261	1 301vs.1 309	821vs.313	22	58	19	41	5.50	14.50	4.75	10.25	5.36	0.003 7
15	Accenture	0	2	Information Technology Services	09/07/2012	–	–	–	270vs.54	392vs.206	311vs.265	37	138	38	61	9.25	34.50	9.50	15.25	6.41	0.004 4
16	Johnson & Johnson	0	11	Pharmaceuticals	27/08/2012	–	–	–	287vs.52	390vs.304	183vs.29	0	0	0	0	0.00	0.00	0.00	0.00	0.00	0.000 0
17	3M	0	11	Medical Products and Equipment	18/03/2011	–	–	738vs.392	2 124vs.523	1 801vs.236	888vs.53	25	1 223	318	167	6.25	305.75	79.50	41.75	68.32	0.046 5
18	Microsoft	0	2	Computer Software	23/09/2011	–	–	192vs.218	1 090vs.660	968vs.285	646vs.93	71	41 767	23 346	4 512	17.75	10 441.75	5 836.50	1 128.00	980.63	0.667 8
19	Boeing	0	12	Aerospace and Defense	23/05/2011	–	–	372vs.355	607vs.628	451vs.297	351vs.99	50	2 488	787	1 827	12.50	622.00	196.75	456.75	102.04	0.069 5
20	Exxon Mobil	0	13	Petroleum Refining	09/03/2014	–	–	–	–	–	90vs.0	0	0	0	0	0.00	0.00	0.00	0.00	0.00	0.000 0

Table 5. 15 (Continued)

No.	Company name	Cou-ntry	Indu-stry	Industry detail	The date of first post	Number of original posts vs. Number of retweets						Sum of posts (SumP)	Sum of retweets (SumR)	Sum of comments (SumC)	Sum of likes (SumL)	Average of posts per week (AveP)	Average of retweets per week (AveR)	Average of comments per week (AveC)	Average of likes per week (AveL)	F1	F2
						2009	2010	2011	2012	2013	2014										
21	Wal-Mart Stores	0	14	General Merchandisers	08/11/2012	-	-	-	58vs.90	1 408vs.368	1 627vs.214	148	239	372	526	37. 00	59. 75	93. 00	131. 50	7. 68	0. 005 2
22	Nestlé S.A.	0	1	Consumer Food Products	12/08/2011	-	-	701vs.445	1 379vs.584	1 191vs.150	983vs.14	26	17 168	2 904	1 717	6. 50	4 292. 00	726. 00	429. 25	838. 04	0. 570 7
23	Unilever	0	1	Consumer Food Products	04/01/2011	-	-	202vs.156	378vs.275	563vs.660	399vs.684	31	3 185	1 729	481	7. 75	796. 25	432. 25	120. 25	174. 03	0. 118 5
24	PepsiCo	0	1	Consumer Food Products	19/07/2010	-	58vs.10	370vs.244	660vs.185	625vs.236	151vs.35	26	22 102	6 592	9 483	6. 50	5 525. 50	1 648. 00	2 370. 75	1 468. 35	1. 000 0
25	Caterpillar	0	15	Construction and Farm Machinery	15/11/2011	-	-	Photo album	Photo album	882vs.1 082	528vs.393	3	23	24	18	0. 75	5. 75	6. 00	4. 50	21. 67	0. 014 8
26	Deere	0	15	Construction and Farm Machinery	10/04/2011	-	-	318vs.203	453vs.243	201vs.17	93vs.0	1	0	0	1	0. 25	0. 00	0. 00	0. 25	1. 00	0. 000 7
27	Marriott International	0	7	Hotel/Casino/Resorts	22/10/2012	-	-	-	114vs.16	500vs.123	510vs.168	43	53	94	77	10. 75	13. 25	23. 50	19. 25	5. 21	0. 003 5
28	DuPont	0	10	Chemicals	01/12/2009	20vs.2	44vs.34	0vs.0	207vs.165	265vs.123	220vs.93	14	71	26	55	3. 50	17. 75	6. 50	13. 75	10.86	0. 007 4
29	Intel	0	2	Semiconductors	19/03/2012	-	-	-	1 210vs.321	1 910vs.167	1 486vs.24	92	2 329	2 659	1 699	23. 00	582. 25	664. 75	424. 75	72. 68	0. 049 5
30	Cisco System	0	2	Network and other Communication Equip	04/01/2012	-	-	-	512vs.445	30vs.456	70vs.205	0	0	0	0	0. 00	0. 00	0. 00	0. 00	0. 00	0. 000 0

Table 5.16 Summary of database based on Chinese companies' Sina Weibo accounts

No.	Company name	Cou-ntry	Indu-stry	Industry detail	The date of first post	Number of original posts vs. Number of retweets						Sum of posts (SumP)	Sum of retweets (SumR)	Sum of comments (SumC)	Sum of likes (SumL)	Average of posts per week (AveP)	Average of retweets per week (AveR)	Average of comments per week (AveC)	Average of likes per week (AveL)	F1	F2
						2009	2010	2011	2012	2013	2014										
1	Huawei	1	2	Telecom manufacturing and services	28/12/2011	–	–	1vs.0	941vs.614	917vs.703	769vs.780	117	997	641	2 583	29.3	249.3	160.3	645.8	36.08	0.024 3
2	ZTE	1	2	Telecom manufacturing and services	22/12/2010	–	107vs.13	1 034vs.1 155	1 678vs.2 591	964vs.1 108	1 015vs.798	68	14 312	1 086	2 189	17.0	3 578.0	271.5	547.3	258.63	0.174 2
3	Haier	1	5	Electronics/Electrical Appliances	13/04/2010	–	303vs.145	1 426vs.340	2 251vs.364	745vs.209	719vs.648	90	35 504	5 764	7 303	22.5	8 876.0	1 441.0	1 825.8	539.68	0.363 6
4	Xiaomi	1	5	Electronics/Electrical Appliances	19/07/2010	–	49vs.10	573vs.507	1 454vs.1 845	1 423vs.1 880	1 100vs.1 998	188	165 359	50 673	63 010	47.0	41 339.8	12 668.3	15 752.5	1 484.27	1.000 0
5	Lenovo	1	5	Electronics/Electrical Appliances	15/07/2011	–	–	618vs.477	2 927vs.1 117	3 196vs.691	2 922vs.539	151	109 016	49 982	17 381	37.8	27 254.0	12 495.5	4 345.3	1 168.07	0.787 0
6	Gree	1	5	Electronics/Electrical Appliances	27/09/2010	–	742vs.188	926vs.544	2 069vs.784	1 264vs.1 001	316vs.222	80	209	628	353	20.0	52.3	157.0	88.3	14.88	0.010 0
7	Midea	1	5	Electronics/Electrical Appliances	11/05/2010	–	66vs.53	740vs.249	1 629vs.140	1 449vs.120	1 385vs.67	11	4 648	1 693	163	2.8	1 162.0	423.3	40.8	591.27	0.398 4
8	TCL	1	5	Electronics/Electrical Appliances	10/06/2011	–	–	668vs.267	1 965vs.1 699	1 626vs.2 032	1 457vs.631	174	7 359	1 771	515	43.5	1 839.8	442.8	128.8	55.43	0.037 3
9	Hisense	1	5	Electronics/Electrical Appliances	29/10/2010	–	44vs.25	225vs.105	1 354vs.580	1 184vs.302	903vs.370	46	11 411	4 263	3 524	11.5	2 852.8	1 065.8	881.0	417.35	0.281 2
10	BYD	1	9	Motor Vehicles/Motor Vehicles Parts	24/05/2010	–	494vs.67	431vs.237	166vs.74	482vs.188	1 090vs.131	99	64 677	23 689	5 822	24.8	16 169.3	5 922.3	1 455.5	951.39	0.641 0
11	Great Wall Motors	1	9	Motor Vehicles/Motor Vehicles Parts	06/11/2009	79vs.0	340vs.240	90vs.191	142vs.92	83vs.13	125vs.0	25	1 659	436	378	6.3	414.8	109.0	94.5	98.92	0.066 6
12	Saic Motor	1	9	Motor Vehicles/Motor Vehicles Parts	17/04/2012	–	–	–	1 040vs.1 179	1 384vs.1 075	924vs.782	113	908	858	259	28.3	227.0	214.5	64.8	17.92	0.012 1
13	Geely	1	9	Motor Vehicles/Motor Vehicles Parts	21/06/2011	–	–	138vs.274	332vs.0	390vs.930	1 060vs.330	120	614	276	389	30.0	153.5	69.0	97.3	10.66	0.007 2
14	Wahaha	1	1	Food/Beverage	02/05/2013	–	–	–	–	168vs.155	63vs.66	50	16 962	8 570	788	12.5	4 240.5	2 142.5	197.0	526.40	0.354 7
15	Tsingtao	1	1	Food/Beverage	26/01/2011	–	–	605vs.267	2 161vs.442	1 511vs.583	1 712vs.735	14	17	22	32	3.5	4.3	5.5	8.0	5.07	0.003 4

Table 5. 16 (Continued)

No.	Company name	Cou-ntry	Indu-stry	Industry detail	The date of first post	Number of original posts vs. Number of retweets						Sum of posts (SumP)	Sum of retweets (SumR)	Sum of comments (SumC)	Sum of likes (SumL)	Average of posts per week (AveP)	Average of retweets per week (AveR)	Average of comments per week (AveC)	Average of likes per week (AveL)	F1	F2
						2009	2010	2011	2012	2013	2014										
16	Kweichow Moutai	1	1	Food/Beverage	19/01/2013	-	-	-	-	1 038vs.330	1 460vs.214	155	6 474	5 249	1 276	38.8	1 618. 5	1 312. 3	319. 0	83.86	0. 056 5
17	YanJing Beer	1	1	Food/Beverage	11/04/2013	-	-	-	-	272vs.224	276vs.460	16	13	18	23	4. 0	3. 3	4. 5	5.8	3. 38	0. 002 3
18	Bright Food	1	1	Food/Beverage	21/06/2012	-	-	-	252vs.185	1 040vs.1 133	1 351vs.180	105	57	11	41	26. 3	14. 3	2.8	10. 3	1. 04	0. 000 7
19	HaiNan Airlines	1	16	Airlines	20/05/2010	-	154vs.74	1 951vs.1 854	2 981vs.2 861	3 220vs.1 252	1 797vs.407	228	3 965	3 487	3 503	57. 0	991. 3	871.8	875.8	48. 05	0. 032 4
20	Yunnan Baiyao	1	11	Pharmaceuticals	16/10/2012	-	-	-	59vs.100	3vs.40	1vs.1	1	3	0	0	0. 3	0.8	0. 0	0. 0	3. 00	0. 002 0
21	Ping An	1	17	Insurance	10/10/2 009	27vs.0	210vs.100	2 520vs.614	2 537vs.466	2 254vs.234	1 767vs.136	120	23 567	2 991	2 573	30. 0	5 891.8	747.8	643. 3	242. 76	0. 163 6
22	WangFujing	1	14	Wholesale/Retail/ Distribution	25/04/2011	-	-	87vs.456	156vs.435	11vs.81	25 vs. 145	0	0	0	0	0. 0	0. 0	0. 0	0. 0	0. 00	0. 000 0
23	SuNing	1	14	Wholesale/Retail/ Distribution	02/11/2010	-	116vs.21	756vs.610	1 654vs.1 087	2 330vs.692	2 500vs.830	192	4 176	3 285	2 046	48. 0	1 044. 0	821. 3	511. 5	49. 52	0. 033 4
24	Gome	1	14	Wholesale/Retail/ Distribution	07/01/2011	-	-	311vs.213	1 434vs.305	2 367vs.294	2 132vs.305	203	169 809	11 218	986	50.8	42 452. 3	2 804. 5	246. 5	896. 62	0. 604 1
25	Wanda	1	19	Real Estate	30/08/2013	-	-	-	-	95vs.15	174vs.22	38	4 605	1 535	1 319	9. 5	1 151. 3	383.8	329.8	196. 29	0. 132 2
26	Vanke	1	19	Real Estate	25/10/2010	-	5vs.0	245vs.140	243vs.357	322vs.394	331vs.88	6	23	8	8	1. 5	5.8	2. 0	2. 0	6. 50	0. 004 4
27	Country Garden	1	19	Real Estate	13/05/2011	-	-	516vs.474	1 506vs.781	710vs.312	107vs.28	2	1	0	1	0. 5	0. 3	0. 0	0. 3	1. 00	0. 000 7
28	SANY	1	15	Manufacturing	07/07/2011	-	-	346vs.140	276vs.122	116vs.232	42vs.59	0	0	0	0	0. 0	0. 0	0. 0	0. 0	0. 00	0. 000 0
29	New Hope Group	1	18	Diversification	21/04/2010	-	86vs.0	15vs.11	71vs.138	9vs.25	0vs.0	0	0	0	0	0. 0	0. 0	0. 0	0. 0	0. 00	0. 000 0
30	Fosun	1	18	Diversification	29/06/2011	-	-	1vs.0	195vs.24	399vs.641	113vs.42	12	56	21	40	3. 0	14. 0	5. 3	10. 0	9. 75	0. 006 6

5.3.2 Comparison of key indicators between companies

This section presents the general results of comparison of key indicators between Western and Chinese companies via the descriptive statistical analyses approach. Based on the primary data from all companies and the option of descriptive statistics within "Analyze" menu in SPSS software, the relevant analysis has been conducted.

Table 5.17 presents the results of descriptive statistics of the key indicators acquired based on the data collected from Sina Weibo accounts of all selected Western and Chinese companies during observation period.

Table 5.17 Comparison of key indicators between companies (Sina Weibo)

30 Western companies										
	SumP	SumR	SumC	SumL	AveP	AveR	AveC	AveL	F1	F2
Mean	51.87	6 037.50	2 867.30	3 191.77	12.97	1 509.38	716.83	797.94	215.96	0.147 1
Minimum	0	0	0	0	0.00	0.00	0.00	0.00	0.00	0.000 0
Maximum	382	50 888	23 346	53 264	95.50	12 722.00	5 836.50	13 316.00	1 468.35	1.000 0
30 Chinese companies										
	SumP	SumR	SumC	SumL	AveP	AveR	AveC	AveL	F1	F2
Mean	80.80	21 546.70	5 939.17	3 883.50	20.20	5 386.68	1 484.79	970.88	257.26	0.173 3
Minimum	0	0	0	0	0.00	0.00	0.00	0.00	0.00	0.000 0
Maximum	228	169 809	50 673	63 010	57.00	42 452.25	12 668.25	15 752.50	1 484.27	1.000 0

It can be demonstrated from table 5.17 that the magnitudes including the mean and the maximum values of total number of posts (SumP), total number of retweets (SumR), total number of comments (SumC), total number of likes (SumL), average of SumP (AveP), average of SumR (AveR), average of SumC (AveC), average of SumL (AveL). Moreover, for Chinese companies, as shown in table 5.17, the number of all items of F1 & F2 is generally greater than those for Western companies.

Next, the exploration of the distribution of industries between Western and Chinese companies will be stated. As shown in figure 5.9, fifteen industries are distributed in Western companies. 40% of them fall into Food category (total 6) and IT category (total 6) respectively.

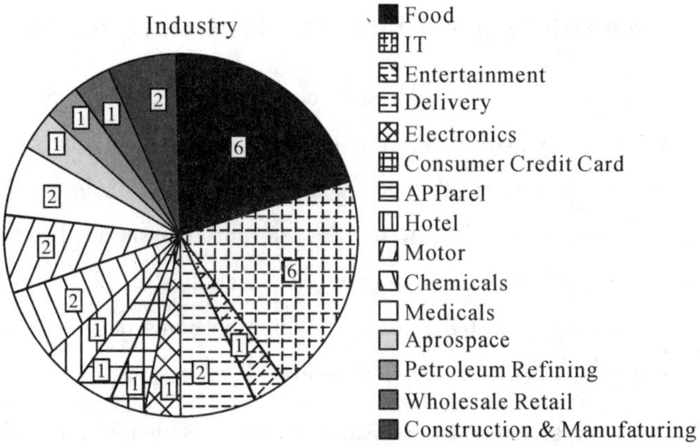

Figure 5.9 Industry distribution (Western companies)

Similarly, as shown in figure 5.10, nineteen industries are distributed in Chinese companies. 36.8% of them fall into Electronics (total 7); the second one is Food category (total 5); and the third one is Motor (total 4).

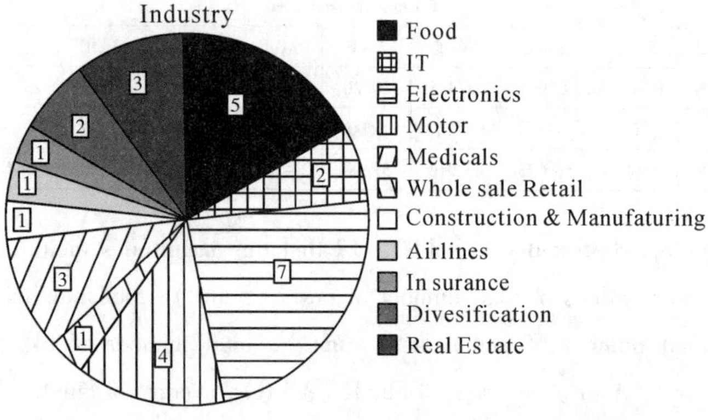

Figure 5.10 Industry distribution (Chinese companies)

Once the comparison of key indicators between companies is explained, the analysis of content features of top-one posts will be conducted in the following sections.

5.3.3 Content features of top-one posts

This section presents the results of the content features of top-one posts from all selected companies via content analysis approach. All top-one posts have been collected.

In the era of "content is king", many companies have begun to invest a lot of time and resources to do content marketing which also is one important part of microblogging marketing strategies. It is important for the companies to analyze what kind of content can get high level of interaction with their users. Normally successful posts obtain a lot of comments and likes, and are retweeted by audience many times. In this research, the three types of top posts (top-one post which has been retweeted the most; top-one post which has got the most comments; and top-one post which has got the most likes) are defined the successful content marketing.

The exact number (of retweets, comments & likes) is the rule to identify top-one post. For instance, top-one post which has got the most "likes" means the post reached the biggest number of "likes" within all posts in one week's timeline.

There are three factors to analyze the content features of these posts. They are:

①"**the best day to publish**" it which means identification of the best day to publish it within a week so as to achieve the best return;

②"**format**" (text, text + picture, text + video, etc.);

③"**content relevance**" (news, advertising, offline activity, products, services, logo, and etc.). As for the content relevance, it is of importance to detect whether the content of the post is relative to any information of company (a detailed explanation referred to section 4. 3. 3 and section 5. 3. 3. 2).

During the observation period, each company can generate up to three top posts per week, but sometimes it only had one or two top posts per week because three types (or two types) of top-one post could be the same one in an observation week.

5. 3. 3. 1 Best day to publish

How to meet the target audience on social media in the right time? Which days are the best choices to release top-one posts? These aim to let more users be able to view company's published content, and at the same time to improve participation and conversation rate. Through the data statistics, Western and Chinese companies obtained respectively one hundred seventy-four and one hundred seventy-six top-one posts during the whole observation period in this research.

Most of top-one posts from **Western companies were distributed on Thursday and Friday** (as seen in table 5. 18). Meanwhile, for **Chinese companies, most of top-one posts have been distributed on Monday, Wednesday and Friday** (as seen in table 5. 19). One point in common is that top-one posts are not suitable to be released on weekends for both Western and Chinese companies.

Table 5.18 The distribution of top-one posts (Western companies)

The distribution of top-one posts							
Monday	Tuesday	Wednesday	Thursday	Friday	Saturday	Sunday	Total
25	29	20	38	36	12	14	174

Those posts published on weekends were less lucky to become top-one posts than the posts published from Monday to Friday. Some companies published less posts on weekends than working days. Even some companies did not release anything on weekends. This also affects indirectly the audience's participation on weekends.

Table 5.19 shows the results for Chinese companies.

Table 5.19 The distribution of top-one posts (Chinese companies)

The distribution of top-one posts							
Monday	Tuesday	Wednesday	Thursday	Friday	Saturday	Sunday	Total
35	25	35	24	31	12	14	176

All top-one posts are successful ones which represent a high degree of interaction with the users. For the companies, all top-one posts are behalf of releasing important content. Therefore, **it is advisable for companies to consider "the best day" to publish the important content on Sina Weibo by avoiding weekends.**

5.3.3.2 Content relevance

It is necessary to identify whether the content of top-one post is related to any kind of information of company. As mentioned in section 4.2.2.3, **content relevance refers to any information about the company such as company news, products and services, advertising, online-offline activities, even only the appearance of company logo on the post, and so on.** If the post does not mention any information about the company, in this case, the post can be specified to have nothing to do with the company information. Figure 5.11 is an example of this type of posts.

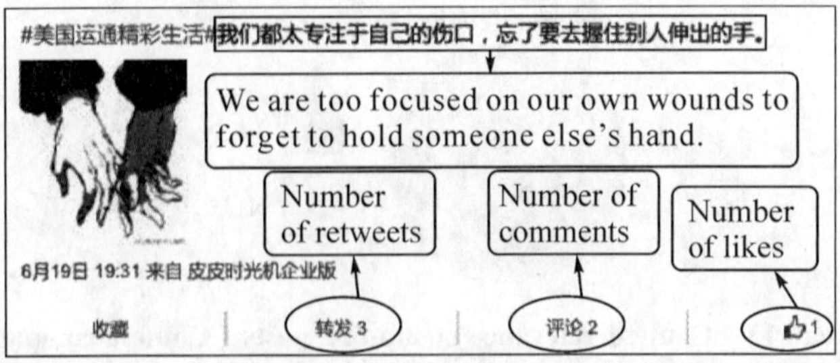

Figure 5.11 An example of top-one post from American Express's Sina Weibo account

The translation of the text content of this post is as: "*We are too focused on our own wounds to forget to hold someone else's hand.*" This post followed sequentially with number "3" "2" and "1" which denote respectively retweets, comments and likes.

This post published by American Express has been retweeted the most in the third week of the observation period in this research although this number is relatively small. Its content has nothing to do with the company's products, management, services, news, advertising, publicity, promotions and so on. So this type of post has been defined to be irrelevant to any kind of company information.

After reviewing all of top-one posts from Western companies within four weeks' timeline, the results are shown in figure 5.12.

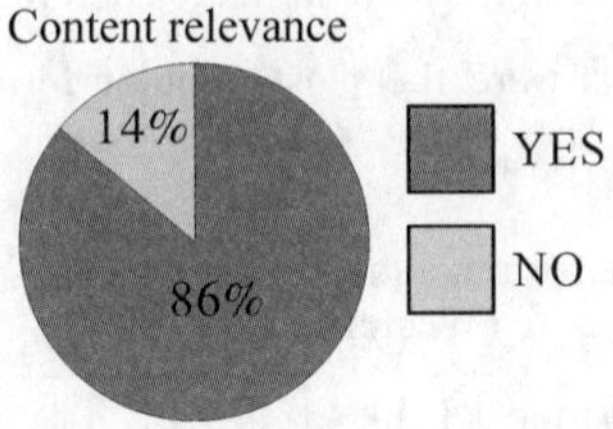

Figure 5.12 Content relevance of top-one posts (Western companies)

With respect to content relevance, for Western companies, 86% of top-one posts are related to any kind of company information. This is a high percentage implying most of top-one posts involving the information of company. From figure 5.13, it can be seen that 81% top-one posts from Chinese companies are related to any kind of company information, too.

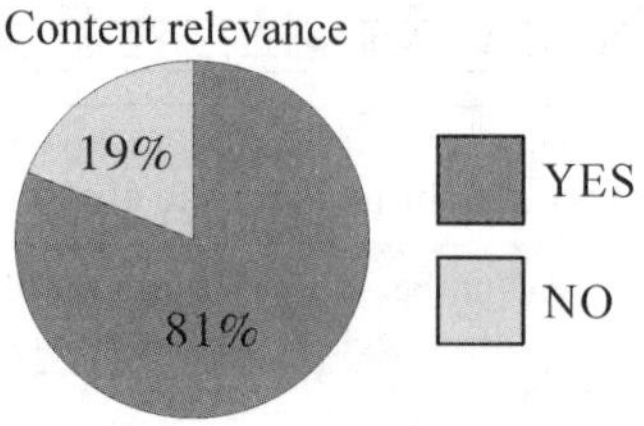

Figure 5.13 Content relevance of top-one posts (Chinese companies)

Logically, all top-one posts have received the highest number of comments or retweets or likes implying the high level of interaction with users. Moreover, high proportion of their content involves information of company. That is to say, **both Chinese and Western companies have done well in content marketing.**

5.3.3.3 The format

It can be seen from figure 5.14 that one hundred and twenty-six top-one posts from Western companies used "text plus picture" format and thirty-seven ones with "text plus picture plus link" format. **Text is the basic format that is integrated with other formats to generate new formats. Meanwhile, the use of link is also quite popular because its advantage is to help publishers release more details with a link in the limited layout.** However, video was used very little in view of the fact that there were only eight top-one posts which involved video format. Therefore, "text plus picture" and "text plus picture plus link" were the most popular format among one hundred and seventy-four Western top-one posts.

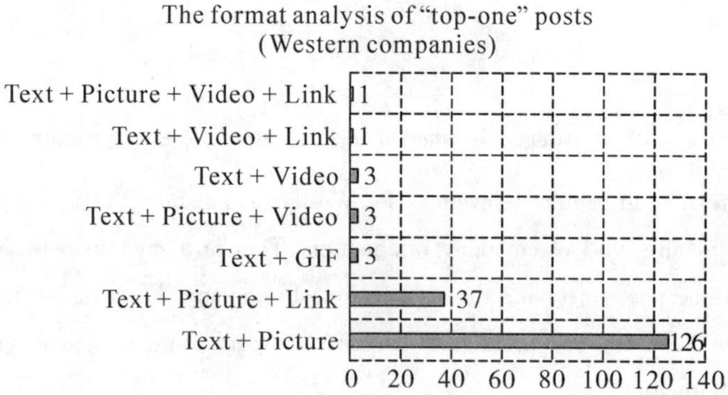

Figure 5.14 Format analysis of top-one posts (Western companies)

As can be seen in figure 5.15, one hundred and eighteen top-one posts from Chinese companies adopted "text plus picture" format and forty-two ones with "text plus picture plus link" format.

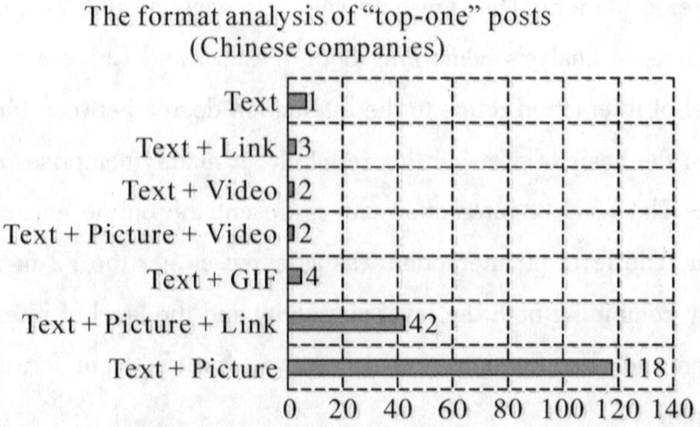

Figure 5.15 Format analysis of top-one posts (Chinese companies)

Similar results can be acquired. "Text plus picture" and "text plus picture plus link" have been the most used and popular formats among one hundred and seventy-six top-one posts from Chinese companies. Apart from these two formats, the use of link is far more than the use of video. Only four top-one Chinese posts involved video format, whereas the number of use of link was forty-five. This is the same result as obtained for the Western companies. Besides this, another unexpected phenomenon was that there were five top-one posts where only text format was utilized.

According to the format analysis of all top-one posts from Western and Chinese companies, **the formats of "text plus picture" and "text plus picture plus link" were the preferred ones used in theses top-one posts** by comparisons with other formats. To some extent, this reflects the fact that it is an era of reading pictures for the audience. However, an "unexpected" result has been found based on the video format analysis described. Only eight of one hundred seventy-four Western top-one posts and four of one hundred seventy-six Chinese top-one posts have involved video format, which indicates **the low usage rate of video format by all selected companies during the observation period.**

5.3.4 The results of cluster analysis

This section presents the cluster analysis for both Western and Chinese companies. It is necessary to point out that the cluster analysis has been conducted respectively on the following two factors: ①the level of activity; ②the level of interaction.

Firstly, **the level of activity was firstly evaluated in terms of the total number of**

posts during the observation period. It can explore whether these companies keep posting on Sina Weibo platform. The threshold values to evaluate the level of activity were set via comprehensive analysis combining both Western and Chinese companies. Secondly, **the level of interaction refers to the interaction degree between the company and the audience on the basis of posts.** In this research, **it mainly comprises retweets, comments and likes.** The level of interaction can represent the online engagement on Sina Weibo platform. **The level of interaction was assessed as per the F2 factor.**

Finally, **by combining both the level of activity and the level of interaction, a synthetic evaluation and classification system has been built** and put forward in forms of tables and graphics.

5.3.4.1 Evaluation of the level of activity

The level of activity has been represented directly by the total number of posts, i.e., sum of posts. Table 5.20 and figure 5.16 present the data of sum of posts of Western companies extracted from table 5.15. It is clear to see that the number "51.9" is denoted as MeanPO (the mean value of SumPO) published on the Western companies' Sina Weibo enterprise accounts.

Table 5.20 Sum of posts of Western companies during observation period

No.	Company name	SumP
1	Apple	382
2	Starbucks	55
3	McDonald's	150
4	Coca-Cola	31
5	Walt Disney	46
6	FedEx	23
7	UPS	13
8	General Electric	2
9	American Express	86
10	Nike	3
11	BMW	49
12	Volkswagen	66
13	Procter & Gamble	61
14	IBM	22
15	Accenture	37

Table 5.20(Continued)

No.	Company name	SumP
16	Johnson & Johnson	0
17	3M	25
18	Microsoft	71
19	Boeing	50
20	Exxon Mobil	0
21	Wal-Mart Stores	148
22	Nestlé S.A.	26
23	Unilever	31
24	PepsiCo	26
25	Caterpillar	3
26	Deere	1
27	Marriott International	43
28	DuPont	14
29	Intel	92
30	Cisco System	0
—	SumPO	1 556
—	MeanPO	51.9

Note: SumPO = sum of posts of all 30 Western companies during observation period,

MeanPO = average of posts of all 30 Western companies during observation period.

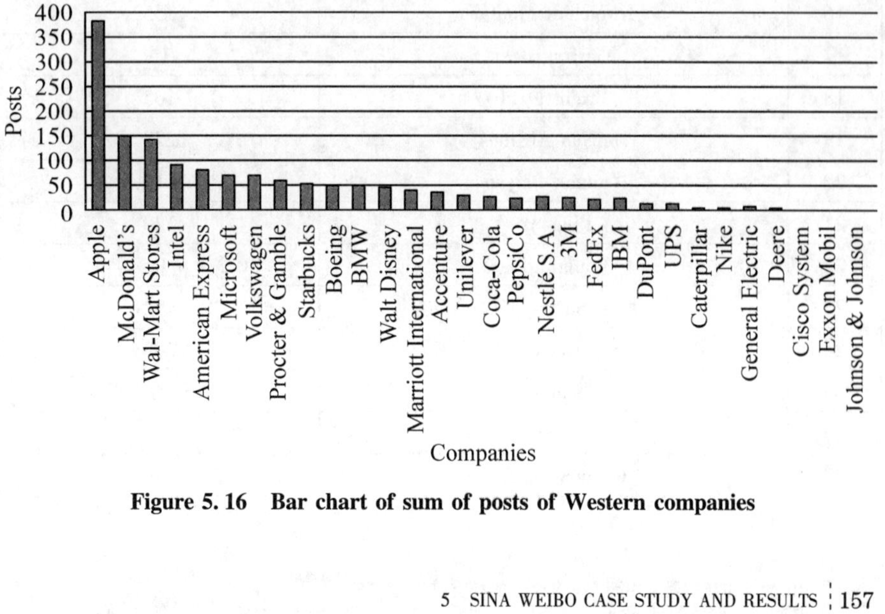

Figure 5.16 Bar chart of sum of posts of Western companies

Table 5.21 and figure 5.17 present the data of sum of posts of Chinese companies extracted from table 5.16. It is clear to see that the number "80.8" is denoted as MeanPC (the mean value of SumPC) published on the Chinese companies' Sina Weibo enterprise accounts.

Table 5.21 Sum of posts of Chinese companies during observation period

No.	Company name	SumP
1	Huawei	117
2	ZTE	68
3	Haier	90
4	Xiaomi	188
5	Lenovo	151
6	Gree	80
7	Midea	11
8	TCL	174
9	Hisense	46
10	BYD	99
11	Great Wall Motors	25
12	Saic Motor	113
13	Geely	120
14	Wahaha	50
15	Tsingtao	14
16	Kweichow Moutai	155
17	YanJing Beer	16
18	Bright Food	105
19	HaiNan Airlines	228
20	Yunnan Baiyao	1
21	Ping An	120
22	WangFujing	0
23	SuNing	192
24	Gome	203
25	Wanda	38
26	Vanke	6
27	Country Garden	2

Table 5.21 (Continued)

No.	Company name	SumP
28	SANY	0
29	New Hope Group	0
30	Fosun	12
	SumPC	2 424
	MeanPC	80.8

Note: SumPC = sum of posts of all 30 Chinese companies during observation period,

MeanPC = average of posts of all 30 Chinese companies during observation period.

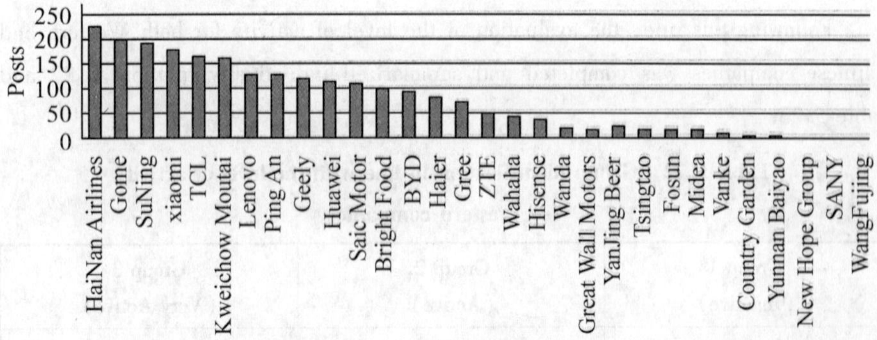

Figure 5.17 Bar chart of sum of posts of Chinese companies

It can be deducted from table 5.20 and table 5.21 that the sum of posts of seven Western companies does not exceed three and that of six Chinese companies is not greater than six. These companies can be considered as inactive because the average of posts per week does not reach two. Therefore, a reasonable threshold value to classify the level of activity as "Inactive" can be taken as eight in this research. However, it has been pointed out that this value depends on the samples selection in the case study and should be determined accordingly by make a preliminary comprehensive exploration of all the sample data.

Another generally used threshold value to denote the level of activity in statistical analysis is the Mean value, i.e., MeanPO & MeanPC in this research.

In this case study, the following rule was adopted generally to evaluate the level of activity:

(1) **Inactive** (Group 1): if **the total number of posts** released by the company dur-

ing the entire observation period **is not greater than eight.**

(2) **Active** (Group 2): if **the total number of posts** released by the company during the entire observation period **is more than eight but does not exceed the mean value** (MeanPO for Western companies and MeanPC for Chinese companies).

(3) **Very active** (Group 3): if **the total number of posts** released by the company during the entire observation period **is greater than the mean value** (MeanPO for Western companies and MeanPC for Chinese companies).

Again, this rule has been set up based on the data from the selected samples in this case study and it may vary or be updated if different samples are chosen or extra cases are added into the existing database.

Following this rule, the evaluation of the level of activity for both Western and Chinese companies was completed and summarized individually in table 5.22 and table 5.23.

Table 5.22 Group identification in line with the level of activity for Western companies

Group 1 (Inactive)	Group 2 (Active)	Group 3 (Very Active)
General Electric	Coca-Cola	Apple
Nike	Walt Disney	American Express
Caterpillar	FedEx	Volkswagen
Deere	UPS	Procter & Gamble
Johnson & Johnson	BMW	Wal-Mart Stores
Exxon Mobil	IBM	Intel
Cisco System	Accenture	McDonald's
	3M	Microsoft
	Boeing	Starbucks
	Unilever	
	Marriott International	
	Dupont	
	Nestlé S.A.	
	PepsiCo	

Table 5.23 Group identification in line with the level of activity for Chinese companies

Group 1 (Inactive)	Group 2 (Active)	Group 3 (Very Active)
Yunnan Baiyao	ZTE	Huawei
Vanke	Gree	Haier
Country Garden	Midea	Xiaomi
WangFujing	Hisense	Lenovo
SANY	Great Wall Motors	TCL
New Hope Group	Wahaha	BYD
	Tsingtao	Saic Motor
	YanJing Beer	Geely
	Wanda	Kweichow Moutai
	Fosun	Bright Food
		HaiNan Airlines
		Ping An
		SuNing
		Gome

By combing table 5.22 and table 5.23, the sixty companies can be divided into three groups accordingly as follows:

(1) **Inactive** (Group 1): SumP $\leqslant$ 8

Western companies (7): General Electric, Nike, Caterpillar, Deere, Johnson & Johnson, Exxon Mobil, Cisco System.

Chinese companies (6): Yunnan Baiyao, Vanke, Country Garden, WangFujing, SANY, New Hope Group.

(2) **Active** (Group 2): 8<SumP $\leqslant$ MeanPO/MeanPC

Western companies (14): Coca-Cola, Walt Disney, FedEx, UPS, BMW, IBM, Accenture, 3M, Boeing, Unilever, Marriott International, Dupont, Nestlé S.A., PepsiCo.

Chinese companies (10): ZTE, Gree, Midea, Hisense, Great Wall Motors, Wahaha, Tsingtao, YanJing Beer, Wanda, Fosun.

(3) **Very active** (Group 3): SumP>MeanPO/MeanPC

Western companies (9): Apple, American Express, Volkswagen, Procter &

Gamble, Wal-Mart Stores, Intel, McDonald's, Microsoft, Starbucks.

Chinese companies (14): Huawei, Haier, Xiaomi, Lenovo, TCL, BYD, Saic Motor, Geely, Kweichow Moutai, Bright Food, HaiNan Airlines, Ping An, SuNing, Gome.

As indicated in the three groups described above, **the number of companies (total 13) assigned to the inactive group is the smallest by comparison with those within active group (total 24) and very active group (total 23)**. In addition, similar number of companies has been found for active group and very active group, i.e., twenty-four companies in group 2 and twenty-three companies in group 3.

Meanwhile, it is noticeable that there are **more Chinese companies than Western companies in the very active group, implying that in general Chinese companies worked harder on posting on Sina Weibo** channel during the observation period.

5.3.4.2 Evaluation of the level of interaction

A mathematical formula was set up to measure the level of interaction by integrating the relevant key performance indicators. **A detailed explanation of this formula has been made in the section 5.3.1, namely, data transforming**. The level of interaction was first directly associated with F1. However, in order to eliminate the effect of magnitude and establish a relatively consistent evaluation and classification system, F2 was used finally to classify the sixty companies as a form of assessment of the level of interaction. Cluster analysis via SPSS software was adopted to realize the classification in line with F2.

The data of F1 & F2 for Western and Chinese companies is shown in table 5.14 from the section 5.3.1, namely, data transforming. Based on these data, SPSS was utilized to perform the cluster analyses to classify Western and Chinese companies respectively as per the value of F2 so as to assess the level of interaction.

The results for thirty Western companies are shown in figure 5.18 via SPSS analysis.

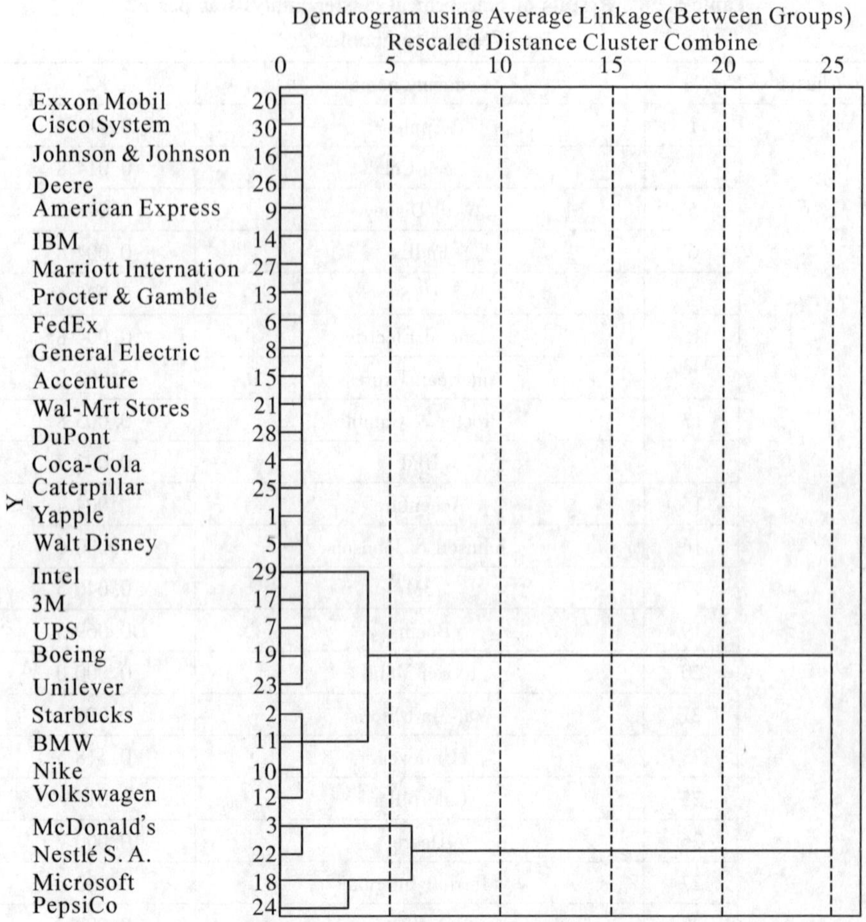

Figure 5. 18 Dendrogram of hierarchical cluster analysis as per F2 for Western companies

According to the dendrogram seen in figure 5. 18, four groups can be identified and four degrees of the level of interaction also can be summarized in table 5. 24.

As shown in table 5. 24, the four grouping ranges for Western companies can be summarized as: ① $0.0 \leqslant F2 \leqslant 0.2$; ② $0.2 < F2 \leqslant 0.4$; ③ $0.4 < F2 \leqslant 0.6$; ④ $0.6 < F2 \leqslant 1.0$.

Table 5.24 Results of hierarchical cluster analysis as per F2 for Western companies

Cluster	No.	Company name	F2
1	1	Apple	0.011 1
	4	Coca-Cola	0.014 8
	5	Walt Disney	0.048 5
	6	FedEx	0.004 8
	7	UPS	0.028 4
	8	General Electric	0.004 8
	9	American Express	0.002 0
	13	Procter & Gamble	0.003 8
	14	IBM	0.003 7
	15	Accenture	0.004 4
	16	Johnson & Johnson	0.000 0
	17	3M	0.046 5
	19	Boeing	0.069 5
	20	Exxon Mobil	0.000 0
	21	Wal-Mart Stores	0.005 2
	23	Unilever	0.118 5
	25	Caterpillar	0.014 8
	26	Deere	0.000 7
	27	Marriott Internati	0.003 5
	28	DuPont	0.007 4
	29	Intel	0.049 5
	30	Cisco System	0.000 0
2	2	Starbucks	0.248 6
	10	Nike	0.308 7
	11	BMW	0.208 8
	12	Volkswagen	0.390 9
3	3	McDonald's	0.575 0
	22	Nestlé S.A.	0.570 7
4	18	Microsoft	0.667 8
	24	PepsiCo	1.000 0

The results for Chinese companies are shown in figure 5. 19 by using the same method as the previous Western companies via SPSS software.

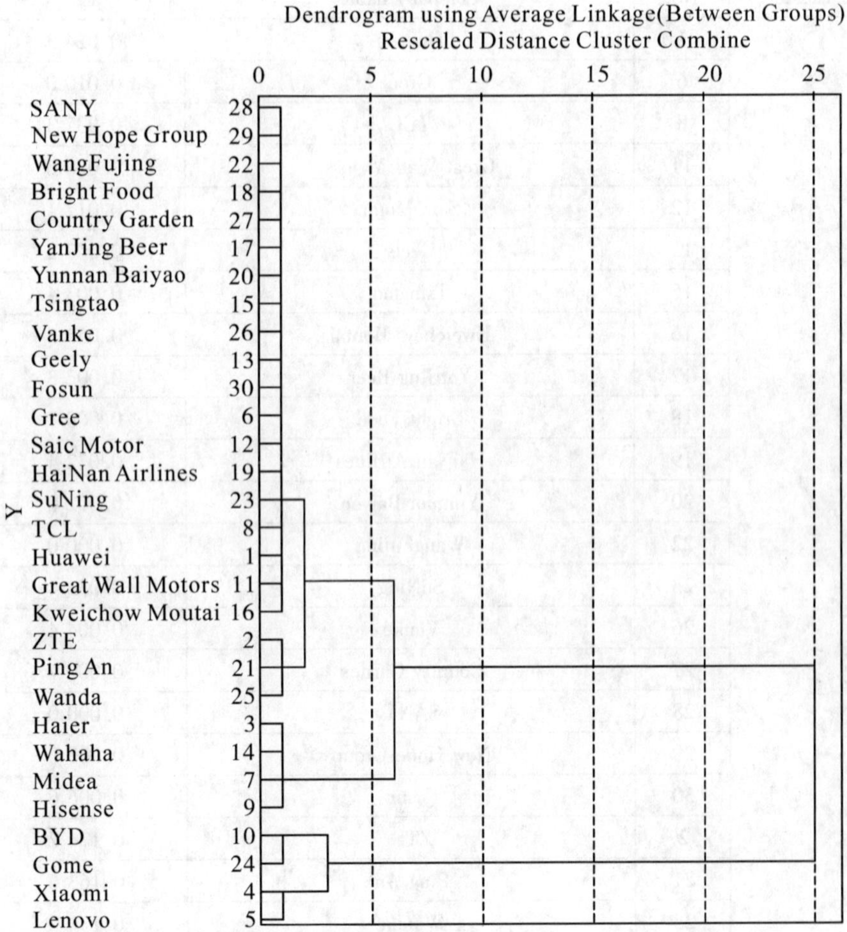

Figure 5. 19 Dendrogram of hierarchical cluster analysis as per F2 for Chinese companies

It can be found from figure 5. 19 that three groups can be identified and the corresponding results also can be summarized in table 5. 25.

Table 5. 25 Results of hierarchical cluster analysis as per F2 for Chinese companies

Cluster	No.	Company name	F2
1	1	Huawei	0. 024 3
	6	Gree	0. 010 0
	8	TCL	0. 037 3
	11	Great Wall Motors	0. 066 6
	12	Saic Motor	0. 012 1
	13	Geely	0. 007 2
	15	Tsingtao	0. 003 4
	16	Kweichow Moutai	0. 056 5
	17	YanJing Beer	0. 002 3
	18	Bright Food	0. 000 7
	19	HaiNan Airlines	0. 032 4
	20	Yunnan Baiyao	0. 002 0
	22	WangFujing	0. 000 0
	23	SuNing	0. 033 4
	26	Vanke	0. 004 4
	27	Country Garden	0. 000 7
	28	SANY	0. 000 0
	29	New Hope Group	0. 000 0
	30	Fosun	0. 006 6
	2	ZTE	0. 174 2
	21	Ping An	0. 163 6
	25	Wanda	0. 132 2
2	3	Haier	0. 363 6
	7	Midea	0. 398 4
	9	Hisense	0. 281 2
	14	Wahaha	0. 354 7
3	4	Xiaomi	0.9 000
	5	Lenovo	0. 787 0
	10	BYD	0. 641 0
	24	Gome	0. 604 1

It can be stated from table 5. 25 that Chinese companies can be divided into three clusters within 3 grouping ranges, which are: ①0. 0 ≤ F2 ≤ 0. 2; ②0. 2<F2 ≤ 0. 4; ③0. 6<F2 ≤ 1. 0. It can be seen that no companies fall into the following range: 0. 4<F2 ≤ 0. 6.

In order to maintain the same criteria to mesure the level of interaction for both Western and Chinese companies, Sina Weibo case study can adopt generally the following rule to evaluate the level of interaction and classify the companies in line with the results of table 5. 24 & table 5. 25.

(1) **Very low interaction** (Group A) **: 0. 0 ≤ F2 ≤ 0. 2.**

(2) **Low interaction** (Group B) **: 0. 2<F2 ≤ 0. 4.**

(3) **Medium interaction** (Group C) **: 0. 4<F2 ≤ 0. 6.**

(4) **High interaction** (Group D) **: 0. 6<F2 ≤ 1. 0.**

Again, these threshold values and this rule have been set up based on the data from the selected samples in this case study and it may vary or be updated if different samples are chosen or extra cases are added into the existing database.

By applying this rule, the assessment of the level of interaction for both Western and Chinese companies was done and summarized individually in table 5. 26 and table 5. 27.

Table 5. 26 Group identification in line with the level of interaction for Western companies

Group A (F2: 0. 0-0. 2) (Very low interaction)	Group B (F2: 0. 2-0. 4) (Low interaction)	Group C (F2: 0. 4-0. 6) (Medium interaction)	Group D (F2: 0. 6-1. 0) (High interaction)
Apple	Starbucks	McDonald's	Microsoft
Coca-Cola	Nike	Nestle	PepsiCo
Walt Disney	BMW		
FedEx	Volkswagen		
UPS			
General Electric			
American Express			
Procter &Gamble			
IBM			

Table 5. 26(Continued)

Group A (F2:0. 0-0. 2) (Very low interaction)	Group B (F2:0. 2-0. 4) (Low interaction)	Group C (F2:0. 4-0. 6) (Medium interaction)	Group D (F2:0. 6-1. 0) (High interaction)
Accenture			
Johnson &Johnson			
3M			
Boeing			
Exxon Mobil			
Wal-Mart Stores			
Unilever			
Caterpillar			
Deere			
Marriott International			
Dupont			
Intel			
Cisco System			

As can be seen in table 5. 26, most of Western companies are in "Group A", i.e., very low interaction. As for the medium and high level of interaction, namely, "Group C" & "Group D", there are only four companies.

For Chinese companies, there exists a similar situation to that of Western companies. It can be detected from table 5. 27 that there are only four Chinese companies falling into "Group D", i.e., high interaction. However, most of Chinese companies acquired very low interaction with their users during the observation period.

Table 5. 27 Group identification in line with the level of interaction for Chinese companies

Group A (F2:0. 0-0. 2) (Very low interaction)	Group B (F2:0. 2-0. 4) (Low interaction)	Group C (F2:0. 4-0. 6) (Medium interaction)	Group D (F2:0. 6-1. 0) (High interaction)
Huawei	Haier		Xiaomi
ZTE	Midea		Lenovo

Table 5. 27(Continued)

Group A (F2:0. 0-0. 2) (Very low interaction)	Group B (F2:0. 2-0. 4) (Low interaction)	Group C (F2:0. 4-0. 6) (Medium interaction)	Group D (F2:0. 6-1. 0) (High interaction)
Gree	Hisense		BYD
TCL	Wahaha		Gome
Geat Wall Motors			
Saic Motor			
Geely			
Tsingtao			
Kweichow Moutai			
Yanjing Beer			
Bright Food			
HaiNan Airlines			
Yunnan Baiyao			
Ping An			
WangFujing			
SuNing			
Wanda			
Vanke			
Country Garden			
SANY			
New Hope Group			
Fosun			

By combing table 5. 26 and table 5. 27, all selected companies can be divided into four groups accordingly as follows:

(1) **Very low interaction** (Group A): $0.0 \leqslant F2 \leqslant 0.2$

Western companies (22): Apple, Coca-Cola, Walt Disney, FedEx, UPS, General Electric, American Express, Procter & Gamble, IBM, Accenture, Johnson &Johnson, 3M, Boeing, Exxon Mobil, Wal-Mart Stores, Unilever, Caterpillar, Deere, Marriott International, Dupont, Intel, Cisco System.

Chinese companies (22): Huawei, ZTE, Gree, TCL, Geat Wall Motors, Saic Motor, Geely, Tsingtao, Kweichow Moutai, Yanjing Beer, Bright Food, HaiNan Airlines, Yunnan Baiyao, Ping An, WangFujing, SuNing, Wanda, Vanke, Country Garden, SANY, New Hope Group, Fosun McDonald's, Nestle.

(2) **Low interaction** (Group B): $0.2 < F2 \leqslant 0.4$

Western companies (4): Starbucks, Nike, BMW, Volkswagen.

Chinese companies (4): Haier, Midea, Hisense, Wahaha.

(3) **Medium interaction** (Group C): $0.4 < F2 \leqslant 0.6$

Western companies (2): McDonald's, Nestle.

Chinese companies (0).

(4) **High interaction** (Group D): $0.6 < F2 \leqslant 1.0$

Western companies (2): Microsoft, PepsiCo.

Chinese companies (4): Xiaomi, Lenovo, BYD, Gome.

It can be detected that twenty-two Chinese companies and twenty-two Western companies belong to very low interaction group, and eight companies fall into low interaction group.

From the perspective of effectiveness, the level of medium interaction and the level of high interaction (namely, Group C and Group D) represent relatively more favorable engagement with users on Sina Weibo channel. In this sense, **four Western companies (McDonald's, Nestle, Microsoft, PepsiCo) and four Chinese companies (Xiaomi, Lenovo, BYD, Gome) are considered as good examples in line with the level of interaction.**

5.3.4.3 Synthetic evaluation and grouping

It is necessary to integrate the level of interaction with the level of activity from the perspective of synthetic evaluation. On one side, the level of activity indicates what efforts these companies have made on Sina Weibo, i.e., the number of posts or update frequency. On the other side, the level of interaction represents how effective their efforts are, that is, the degree of engagement with users.

By integrating both two factors, the level of activity and the level of interaction, a synthetic evaluation and classification system can be established accordingly for Western and Chinese companies respectively.

For Western companies, the results of synthetic evaluation and classification have been acquired and expressed by table 5.28 & figure 5.20.

Table 5.28 Synthetic evaluation and classification for Western companies

			Level of Interaction (1) Very low interaction (Group A): $0.0 \leq F2 \leq 0.2$ (2) Low interaction (Group B): $0.2 < F2 \leq 0.4$ (3) Medium interaction (Group C): $0.4 < F2 \leq 0.6$ (4) High interaction (Group D): $0.6 < F2 \leq 1.0$			
			Very Low	Low	Medium	High
Level of Activity	(1) Inactive: $SumP \leq 8$ (2) Active: $8 < SumP \leq 51.9$ (3) Very active: $SumP > 51.9$	Inactive	General Electric Caterpillar Deere Johnson & Johnson Exxon Mobil Cisco System	Nike		
		Active	Coca-Cola Walt Disney FedEx UPS IBM Accenture 3M Boeing Unilever Marriott International Dupont	BMW	Nestlé S.A	PepsiCo
		Very Active	Apple American Express Procter & Gamble Wal-Mart Stores Intel	Starbucks Volkswagen	McDonald's	Microsoft

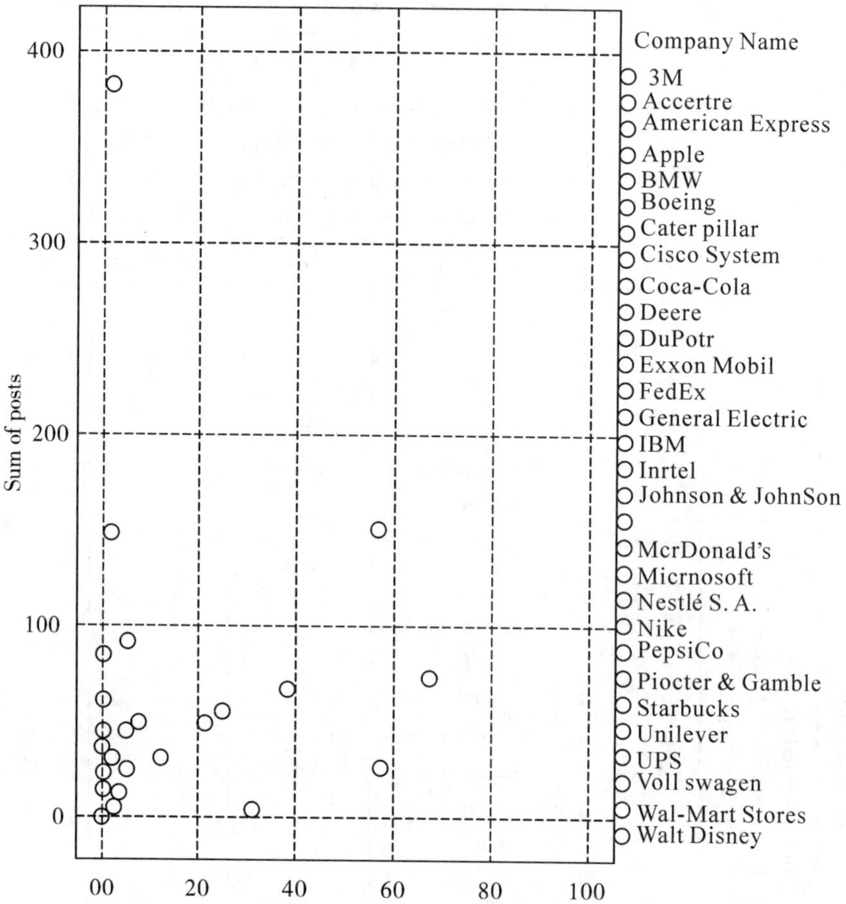

Figure 5.20 Scatter plot SumP vs. F2 for Western companies

Similarly, for Chinese companies, the results of synthetic evaluation and classification have been obtained and expressed by table 5.29 and figure 5.21.

Table 5.29 Synthetic evaluation and classification for Chinese companies

<table>
<tr><td colspan="3" rowspan="3"></td><td colspan="4">Level of Interaction</td></tr>
<tr><td colspan="4">(1) Very low interaction (Group A): $0.0 \leqslant F2 \leqslant 0.2$
(2) Low interaction (Group B): $0.2 < F2 \leqslant 0.4$
(3) Medium interaction (Group C): $0.4 < F2 \leqslant 0.6$
(4) High interaction (Group D): $0.6 < F2 \leqslant 1.0$</td></tr>
<tr><td>Very Low</td><td>Low</td><td>Medium</td><td>High</td></tr>
<tr><td rowspan="3">Level of Activity</td><td rowspan="3">(1) Inactive: $SumP \leqslant 8$
(2) Active: $8 < SumP \leqslant 80.8$
(3) Very active: $SumP > 80.8$</td><td>Inactive</td><td>Yunnan Baiyao
Vanke
Country Garden
WangFujing
SANY
New Hope Group</td><td></td><td></td><td></td></tr>
<tr><td>Active</td><td>ZTE
Gree
Great Wall Motors
Tsingtao
YanJing Beer
Wanda
Fosun</td><td>Midea
Hisense
Wahaha</td><td></td><td></td></tr>
<tr><td>Very Active</td><td>Huawei
TCL
Saic Motor
Geely
Kweichow Moutai
Bright Food
HaiNan Airlines
Ping An
SuNing</td><td>Haier</td><td></td><td>Xiaomi
Lenovo
BYD
Gome</td></tr>
</table>

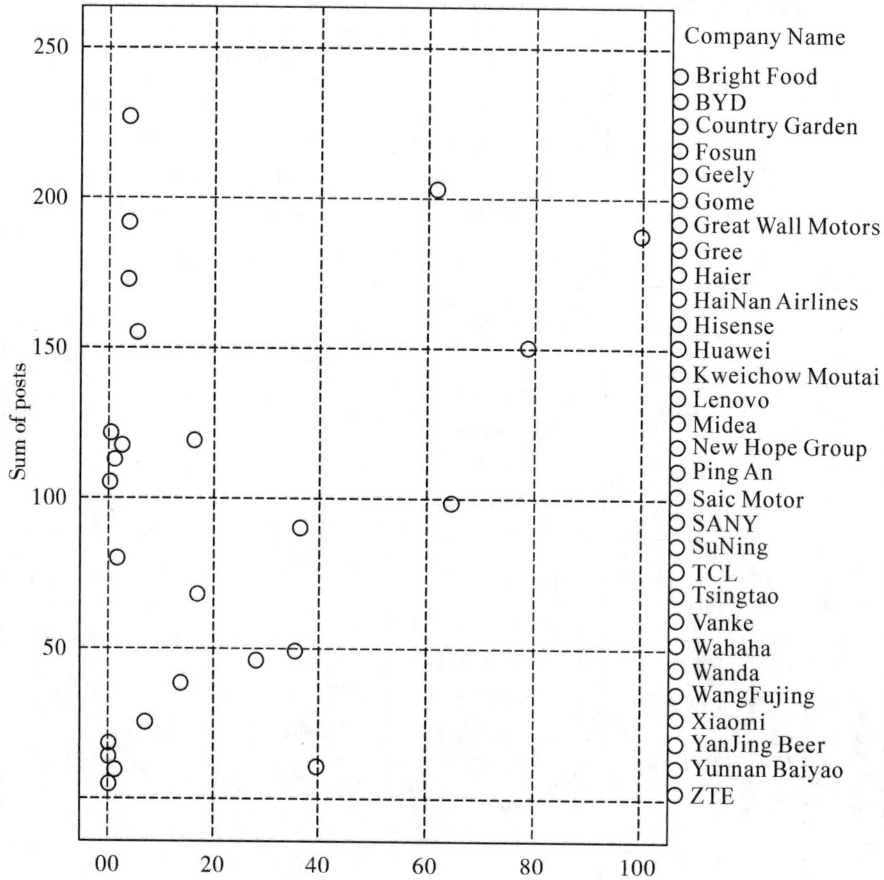

Figure 5.21 Scatter plot SumP vs. F2 for Chinese companies

By combining table 5.28 and table 5.29, the results of synthetic evaluation and classification for all selected companies have been presented as twelve groups given below:

Group S1: Inactive & very low interaction

Western companies (6): General Electric, Caterpillar, Deere, Johnson & Johnson, Exxon Mobil, Cisco System.

Chinese companies (6): Yunnan Baiyao, Vanke, Country Garden, WangFujing, SANY, New Hope Group.

Group S2: Inactive & low interaction

Western companies (1): Nike.

Chinese companies (0).

Group S3: Inactive & medium interaction

Western companies (0).

Chinese companies (0).

Group S4: Inactive & high interaction

Western companies (0).

Chinese companies (0).

Group S5: Active & very low interaction

Western companies (11): Coca-Cola, Walt Disney, FedEx, UPS, IBM, Accenture, 3M, Boeing, Unilever, Marriott International, Dupont.

Chinese companies (7): ZTE, Gree, Great Wall Motors, Tsingtao, YanJing Beer, Wanda, Fosun.

Group S6: Active & low interaction

Western companies (1): BMW.

Chinese companies (3): Midea, Hisense, Wahaha.

Group S7: Active & medium interaction

Western companies (1): Nestlé S.A.

Chinese companies (0).

Group S8: Active & high interaction

Western companies (1): PepsiCo.

Chinese companies (0).

Group S9: Very active & very low interaction

Western companies (5): Apple, American Express, Procter & Gamble, Wal-Mart Stores, Intel.

Chinese companies (9): Huawei, TCL, Saic Motor, Geely, Kweichow Moutai, Bright Food, HaiNan Airlines, Ping An, SuNing.

Group S10: Very active & low interaction

Western companies (2): Starbucks, Volkswagen.

Chinese companies (1): Haier.

Group S11: Very active & medium interaction

Western companies (1): McDonald's.

Chinese companies (0).

Group S12: Very active & high interaction

Western companies (1): Microsoft.

Chinese companies (4): Xiaomi, Lenovo, BYD, Gome.

5.3.4.4 Five models and classification

From group S1 to group S12, each group represents a different state based on the results of integrating the level of interaction and the level of activity. Through a further comprehensive analysis on the basis of the twelve groups, **five models characterized by the overall performance of companies on Sina Weibo have been developed and described below.** Table 5.30 shows the five models with the corresponding groups.

Table 5.30 Five models with the corresponding groups

Names	Groups	Overall performances
The lazy model	S1, S2	Inactive & very low or low interaction
The special model	S3, S4	Inactive & medium or high interaction
The moderate model	S5, S6	Active & very low or low interaction
The ideal model	S7, S8, S11, S12	Active & medium or high interaction, Very active & medium or high interaction
The unbalanced model	S9, S10	Very active & very low or low interaction

(1) The lazy model

This model denotes the worst performance in both the level of activity and the level of interaction and refers to Group S1 and S2. These companies were inactive on Sina Weibo. Or, in other words, they were "lazy" because they released very little content during the observation timeline. Moreover, the engagement between these companies and their users were low. Totally thirteen companies are located into the range of the lazy model.

(2) The special model

A phenomenon is that none of sixty companies fall into Group S3 and Group S4, which can be represented by the special model. This model represents those companies that have made good achievement on Sina Weibo platform although they did not make too much effort during the observation period.

(3) The moderate model

The moderate model refers to those companies in Group S5 and Group S6. In Group S5, eleven Western companies and seven Chinese companies were active with very low interaction. The reasons for this could be that their efforts were not enough, i.e., they did not pay too much attention on posting or updating, or the methods adopted by these companies might be unsuitable leading to the very low engagement with their users. Companies in Group S6 have the same situation as those of group S5, although the level of interaction of the former is slightly higher than the latter.

(4) The ideal model

Companies in the ideal model are good examples. As for many digital market managers, they are satisfied when they acquire a significant return on investment on social media marketing. This indicates that the audiences have actively participated in conversation and activities well organized with efforts by them.

In this research, the following groups belong to the ideal model: Group S7 (active & medium interaction); Group S8 (active & high interaction); Group S11 (very active & medium interaction); Group S12 (very active & high interaction).

There are totally four Western companies and four Chinese companies in this list, namely, Nestlé S. A, PepsiCo, McDonald's, Microsoft, Xiaomi, Lenovo, BYD, Gome. It is necessary to note that four Chinese companies are in the group S12, i.e., very active with high engagement, whereas, four Western companies are in Group S7, S8, S11, and S12 respectively.

(5) The unbalanced model

The unbalanced model denotes the companies which are very active intending to run a successful and effective social media campaign on Sina Weibo platform but the outcome is poor. Or, in other words, they have paid much attention on this channel by keeping posting or updating constantly. Normally they have published more posts on Sina Weibo than other companies. However, they got very poor feedback from the audience during the observation period. As for this type of companies, it is highly advisable to adjust their social media strategies by thinking on how to improve the engagement degree with their users.

Unfortunately, in this research, according to the groups of S9 & S10, seven Western companies and ten Chinese companies have fallen into this unbalanced model. It shall be time for them to take actions to change the situation.

After presenting the results of Sina Weibo case study, the authors proceed to present WeChat case study and its results in chapter 6.

6 WECHAT CASE STUDY AND RESULTS

This chapter presents WeChat case study and its results with the purpose to measure all selected companies' social media performance on WeChat platform. Specifically, the results refer to the following aspects:

- interface & menu analysis as per country region;
- interface & menu analysis as per industries;
- a systematic measurement and classification framework built to measure all companies' performance on WeChat channel, i.e., the results of the analysis of push notification marketing of WeChat official accounts.

In addition, the corresponding approaches such as KPIs concept, information architecture, descriptive statistical analysis, and cluster analysis have been applied in WeChat case study.

Since WeChat platform is defferent from Sina Weibo channel, new research approach has been adopted in WeChat case study; meanwhile some methods applied in Sina Weibo case study have also been used in WeChat case.

The following context shall be clarified regarding WeChat platform, WeChat official account and the relevant data and information which can be acquired by researchers:

(1) Most companies haven't got very rich experience in utilizing WeChat platform to benefit their business in view of the fact that WeChat was born in 2011. For many enterprises, WeChat is a quite new social media platform. In addition, commercial advertising cannot be released in WeChat moments until January of 2015.

(2) Few data can be obtained by the third party or by any fan of an official account. Taking the post as an example, only the number of "reading" "like" and

"top comments" (up to the top 100 comments) can be acquired.

(3) Some basic data cannot be obtained, e.g., the number of followers, change of fan number, number of retweets and etc. Only the administrator of an official WeChat account can know these numbers.

(4) Normally each official WeChat account has a special interface and unique menu settings consistent with their products or service.

(5) Due to the differences between the subscription account and the service account (referred to section 3.3.1), the practice of broadcasting push notifications on both types of accounts is different.

Therefore, in consideration of these statements, the analysis of performance of WeChat marketing of all selected reputation companies can be conducted following up two research lines on the basis of obtained data and information. **The first line is to analyze the interface and menu of all selected companies' WeChat official accounts.** And **the second line is to analyze these companies' push notification marketing integrating the relevant data so as to measure their performance on WeChat during the observation period.** It is necessary to point out that the systematic measurement framework built on Sina Weibo case study is adopted in the analysis of push notification marketing of WeChat case study.

In WeChat case study, it is important to note that companies are divided initially according to the analysis type and objective.

In WeChat official accounts' interface & menu analysis, two initial divisions were used:

(1) Two groups: thirty Western companies as one group & thirty Chinese companies as another one as per country origin;

(2) Nineteen categories as per industry (seen in table 4.6).

In the analysis of push notification marketing, all companies are divided into two groups initially as per WeChat account type:

(1) Group 1: twenty-three companies with service type of WeChat official account (as shown in table 6.1).

(2) Group 2: thirty-seven companies with subscription type of WeChat official account (seen in table 6.2).

Table 6.1 Twenty-three companies with service type of Wechat official account

No.	Company	WeChat name/WeChat ID	Account type (0-Service)
1	Starbucks	星巴克中国/xingbakezhongguo	0
2	McDonald's	麦当劳/mcdonalds888	0
3	FedEx	FedEx 中国/FedEx_China	0
4	Nike	NIKE/nikejdi	0
5	Wal-Mart Stores	沃尔玛/Walmart_Hyper	0
6	PepsiCo	百事中国/BAISHIPEPSICO	0
7	Deere	约翰迪尔/JohnDeereChina	0
8	Marriott International	万豪礼赏/ marriottgroup	0
9	DuPont	杜邦特能壁纸/	0
10	Intel	英特尔中国/intel-china	0
11	Haier	海尔家电/Haier_jiadian	0
12	Xiaomi	小米手机/xmsj816	0
13	Lenovo	联想/lenovo1984	0
14	Gree	格力电器/glfwh1991	0
15	Midea	美的会员/mideafw	0
16	Hisense	海信/hisense1969	0
17	Saic Motor	上汽集团/SAIC_MOTOR_	0
18	Wahaha	娃哈哈/YourWahaha	0
19	YanJing Beer	燕京啤酒/yanjing_beer_group	0
20	HaiNan Airlines	海南航空/Hnairlines	0
21	WangFujing	王府井集团/wfjbh1955	0
22	Gome	国美在线/gome1314	0
23	Fosun	复星/fuxing_2014	0

Table 6.2 Thirty-seven companies with subscription account

No.	Company	WeChat name/WeChat ID	Account type (1-Subcription)
1	Apple	iPhone 中文网/apple4cn	1
2	Coca-Cola	可口可乐中国/coke18	1
3	Walt Disney	迪士尼中国/disney_ch	1
4	UPS	UPS 中国动态/UPS_China	1
5	General Electric	GE 中国/GEandME	1

Table 6.2(Continued)

No.	Company	WeChat name/WeChat ID	Account type (1-Subcription)
6	American Express	美国运通/AmexChina	1
7	BMW	宝马中国/BMW_Official	1
8	Volkswagen	VWLive 大众共线/dzqczg	1
9	Procter & Gamble	宝洁中国/pgchina1988	1
10	IBM	IBM 中国/IBMGCG	1
11	Accenture	埃森哲中国/accenture	1
12	Johnson & Johnson	强生招聘/JNJ_recruitm	1
13	3M	3M 中国区/mmm_china	1
14	Microsoft	微软科技/mstech2014	1
15	Boeing	波音中国/boeingairpla	1
16	Exxon Mobil	埃克森美孚中国/Exx	1
17	Nestle S.A.	雀巢中国/NestleCN	1
18	Unilever	联合利华 U 关注/unile	1
19	Caterpillar	卡特皮勒中国/caterp	1
20	Cisco System	思科联天下/ciscowech	1
21	Huawei	华为/huaweicorp	1
22	ZTE	中兴通讯/ZTEInChina	1
23	TCL	TCL 铁粉社区/tcltiefen	1
24	BYD	比亚迪汽车/byd-auto	1
25	Great Wall Motors	长城汽车/greatwallmot	1
26	Geely	吉利控股集团/	1
27	Tsingtao	青岛啤酒/Tsingtao_Sin	1
28	Kweichow Moutai	国酒茅台/maotaiguojiu	1
29	Bright Food	光明食品集团/bright	1
30	Yunnan Baiyao	云南白药/newbaiyao	1
31	Ping An	中国平安/zhongguoping	1
32	SuNing	苏宁/suning365	1
33	Wanda	万达集团/guojiwanda	1
34	Vanke	万科周刊/vankeweekly	1
35	Country Garden	碧桂园/bgydream	1
36	SANY	三一重工/sanyibox	1
37	New Hope Group	新希望集团/newhopewi	1

It is necessary to point out that the analysis of WeChat push notification marketing is based on the two preliminary groups (seen in **table 6.1 and table 6.2**) because there is a significant difference between these two types of official WeChat accounts described in section 3.3.1. Moreover, table 6.3 indicates the distribution of all selected companies as per WeChat account type and country region. It can be shown that slight difference exists in the number of companies as per country region for both subscription account and service account.

Table 6.3 Distribution of companies as per WeChat account type and country region

Subscription accounts		Service accounts	
No. of Western companies	20	No. of Western companies	10
No. of Chinese companies	17	No. of Chinese companies	13
Total number	37	Total number	23

Once the two research lines have been addressed, the first research line is presented in the next section.

6.1 Interface & menu analysis of WeChat official accounts

This section presents the interface & menu analysis of WeChat official accounts and its results. Information architecture principles have been adopted to conduct the analysis. And the analysis process included observation period setting, data collection, labeling process, and so on.

As shown in figure 6.1, the interface of an official account contains of many elements such as company logo, WeChat name, WeChat ID, introduction of this account, account owner, "receive messages" "sticky on top" and "view history". When followers click the largest green button "Enter Official Account", they enter directly the official account and can carry out the corresponding operation in line with their needs.

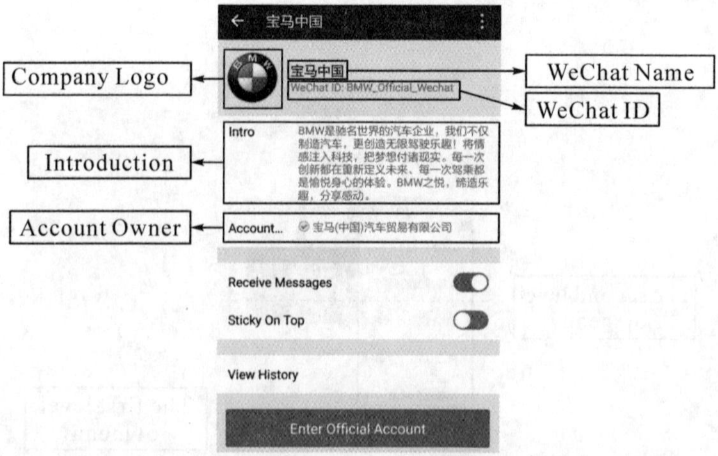

Figure 6.1　The first level of interface display (Example: BMW)

After entering the official account, the new interface, i.e., the second level of interface displays as seen in figure 6.2 (taking the company "Caterpillar" as an example). The new interface mainly includes two parts: posts and menu. Normally the menu contains two levels: the first level of menu and the second level of menu.

Figure 6.2　The second level of interface display (Example: Caterpillar)

As shown in figure 6.3, clicking on the small triangle which locates in the right corner of the first level of the menu is about to display the second level of menu.

Figure 6.3　Two levels of menu display (Example: BMW)

The menu settings reflect what functions the company wants to realize through running its WeChat official account. What's more, according to the company's needs, the menu can also be updated from time to time.

6.1.1　Observation criteria and data collection

As mentioned before, the menus of these companies' WeChat official accounts are not always the same. So the results may vary dpending on different periods set up for the analysis of these accounts' menus. In this research, **the observation period for interface & menu analysis of sixty high reputation companies' WeChat official accounts was from October 21st 2016 to November 4th 2016.** At the same time, all data can be obtained in accordance with the labeling process which is stated in the next part during the observation timeline. Besides, another observation work shall also be considered: identification of companies which would like to update their WeChat official accounts' menus in a short time, e.g., one month. According to this idea, another observation period has been set for this specific task. Therefore, this specific observation period was built for one month: from October 21st of 2016 to November 21st of 2016.

6.1.2　Labeling process

In this research, the menus of all official WeChat accounts have been analyzed via information architecture principles. Firstly, the contents of all menus were organized into categories. Specifically, the menu of each WeChat official account was reviewd and summarized into different main categories during the observation period. Secondly, each category was analyzed and divided further into several subcategories. Finally, according to the previous framework, information structure has been built with label codes.

The six main categories with label codes are presented as:

C1 — information: different type of information pvovided by the company.

C2 — service: any kind of service supported by the company.

C3 — activities: referring to those activities organized by the company.

C4 — recruitment: indicating whether the recruitment function has been set by the company.

C5 — interactive community: denoting whether the interactive community has been created by the company so as to communicate with followers (as well as communication between fans).

C6 — link to Sina Weibo: indicating whether the company's WeChat official account has been linked to its Sina Weibo account.

It is necessary to note that there are totally forty subcategories. Specifically, C1 — information, includes fourteen subcategories, namely, from C101 to C114; C2 — service, contains twenty-one subcategories, i. e., from C201 to C221; C3 — activities, comprises five subcategories, i.e., from C301 to C305. Table 6. 4 shows the details of labeling codes about all categories and subcategories.

Table 6. 4 Category and subcategory list of WeChat accounts' interface & menu analysis

Label codes	Description		
C1	Category: Information		
	Subcategory	Applied	Not applied
C101	History of company	1	0
C102	Company's main founders/leadership	1	0
C103	Products	1	0
C104	Brand	1	0
C105	Offer notice	1	0
C106	News	1	0
C107	Apps	1	0
C108	Contact Info.	1	0
C109	Cases Info.	1	0

Table 6. 4(Continued)

C110	Survey & report	1	0
C111	Cooperation Info.	1	0
C112	Company profile	1	0
C113	After-sales service	1	0
C114	Award winner list	1	0
C2	Category: Service		
	Subcategory	Applied	Not applied
C201	New product promotion	1	0
C202	Online tutorials	1	0
C203	Offers	1	0
C204	Ordering/booking	1	0
C205	Chains-seeking	1	0
C206	Track shipments	1	0
C207	Ship online	1	0
C208	Price inquiry	1	0
C209	Users' account management	1	0
C210	Feedback & questions	1	0
C211	Online shopping	1	0
C212	Customer attention	1	0
C213	Online game	1	0
C214	Location-based map	1	0
C215	Membership card management	1	0
C216	Membership registration	1	0
C217	Order tracking	1	0
C218	Anti-counterfeiting check	1	0
C219	Product recycling	1	0
C220	Redeem points	1	0
C221	Self-service solution	1	0
C3	Category: Activities		
	Subcategory	Applied	Not applied
C301	Contests	1	0
C302	Sales campaign	1	0
C303	Offline activities	1	0
C304	Award-winning activities	1	0
C305	Daily check-in	1	0

Table 6. 4(Continued)

C4	Category: Recruitment	Applied	Not applied
		1	0
C5	Category: Interactive community	Applied	Not applied
		1	0
C6	Category: Link to Sina Weibo	Applied	Not applied
		1	0

Besides the labeling procedure, some other basic information coding (shown in table 6. 5) is also necessary to create a clearly structured database for the interface & menu analysis.

Table 6. 5 Extra basic information coding for interface & menu analysis

No.	Category	Coding
1	Country region	Western: 0 Chinese: 1
2	Industry (19 types)	As per table 4. 6
3	Account type	Subscription: 1 Service: 0
4	Verification type	By Weibo 0 By Tencent 1 Not verified: 2
5	Updated	Yes: 1 No: 0

6. 1. 3 Database creation

After the work mentioned above such as data collection, labeling, and coding, the relevant database was created as shown in table 6. 6 and table 6. 7. It is necessary to clarify that table 6. 6 shows the database based on the following categories: C1, C3, C4, C5, and C6. Table 6. 7 presents the database based on the category C2. The reason for establishing two databases is due to the fact that C2 has big number of subcategories.

Table 6.6 Summary of database (Part1: C1, C3, C4, C5 & C6) based on 60 companies' WeChat accounts for interface & menu analysis

No.	Company name	WeChat name/ID	Country region	Industry	Account type	Verific-ation type	C101	C102	C103	C104	C105	C106	C107	C108	C109	C110	C111	C112	C113	C114	C301	C302	C303	C304	C305	C4	C5	C6	Upda-ted
1	Apple	iPhone 中文网/apple4cn	0	2	1	0	0	0	1	1	0	1	1	0	0	0	0	0	0	0	0	0	0	0	0	0	1	0	0
2	Starbucks	星巴克中国/xingbakezhongguo	0	1	0	1	1	0	1	1	0	1	1	0	0	0	0	0	0	0	0	0	0	0	0	0	0	0	1
3	McDonald's	麦当劳/mcdonalds888	0	1	0	1	0	0	0	0	0	0	0	0	0	0	0	0	0	0	0	1	0	0	0	0	0	0	0
4	Coca-Cola	可口可乐中国/coke1886	0	1	1	1	1	0	1	1	0	0	0	0	0	0	0	0	0	0	1	0	0	0	0	1	0	0	0
5	Walt Disney	迪士尼中国/disney_china	0	3	1	1	1	1	1	1	1	1	0	0	0	0	0	0	0	0	0	0	1	0	0	1	0	0	0
6	FedEx	FedEx 中国/FedEx_China	0	4	0	1	0	0	0	0	1	1	0	1	1	0	0	0	0	0	0	0	0	0	0	1	0	0	0
7	UPS	UPS 中国动态/UPS_China_News	0	4	1	2	1	0	1	1	0	1	0	1	1	1	1	0	0	0	0	0	0	0	0	0	0	0	0
8	General Electric	GE 中国/GEandME	0	5	1	1	1	1	1	1	0	0	0	0	0	0	0	0	0	0	0	0	0	0	0	1	0	0	0
9	American Express	美国运通/AmexChina	0	6	1	1	1	0	1	1	1	0	0	0	0	0	0	0	0	0	0	0	0	0	0	0	0	0	0
10	Nike	NIKE/nikejdi	0	8	0	1	0	0	1	1	0	1	1	0	0	0	0	0	0	0	0	0	1	0	0	0	0	0	1
11	BMW	宝马中国/BMW_Official_Wechat	0	9	1	1	0	0	1	1	0	0	0	0	0	0	0	0	0	0	0	1	1	0	0	0	0	0	0
12	Volkswagen	VWLive 大众共线/dzqczg	0	9	1	1	0	0	1	1	0	0	0	0	0	0	0	0	0	0	0	0	0	0	0	0	0	0	1
13	Procter & Gamble	宝洁中国/pgchina1988	0	10	1	1	0	0	0	0	0	0	0	0	0	0	0	0	0	0	0	0	0	0	0	0	0	0	1
14	IBM	IBM 中国/IBMGCG	0	2	1	1	0	0	1	1	0	1	0	0	0	0	0	0	0	0	1	0	0	0	0	0	0	0	0
15	Accenture	埃森哲中国/accenture_china	0	2	1	1	0	0	1	1	0	1	0	1	1	1	0	1	0	0	1	0	1	0	0	0	0	0	0
16	Johnson & Johnson	强生招聘/JNJ_recruitment	0	11	1	2	0	0	0	0	0	1	0	0	0	0	0	0	0	0	0	0	0	0	0	1	0	0	0
17	3M	3M 中国区/mmm_china	0	11	1	0	1	0	1	1	0	1	0	1	0	0	0	0	0	0	0	0	0	0	0	0	0	0	0
18	Microsoft	微软科技/mstech2014	0	2	1	1	0	0	1	1	0	1	0	1	1	0	0	0	0	0	0	0	0	0	0	0	0	0	1
19	Boeing	波音中国/boeingairplanes	0	12	1	1	1	1	1	0	0	1	0	0	0	0	0	0	0	0	0	0	0	0	0	0	0	0	1
20	Exxon Mobil	埃克森美孚中国/ExxonMobil-China	0	13	1	1	0	0	0	0	0	1	0	0	0	1	0	1	0	0	0	0	0	0	0	0	0	0	0
21	Wal-Mart Stores	沃尔玛/Walmart_Hyper	0	14	0	1	0	0	1	0	1	1	1	0	0	0	0	0	0	0	0	0	0	0	0	0	0	0	0

Table 6.6 (Continued)

No.	Company name	WeChat name/ID	Country region	Industry	Account type	Verification type	C101	C102	C103	C104	C105	C106	C107	C108	C109	C110	C111	C112	C113	C114	C301	C302	C303	C304	C305	C4	C5	C6	Updated
22	Nestle S.A.	雀巢中国/NestleCN	0	1	1	1	1	1	1	1	0	0	0	1	0	0	0	0	0	0	0	0	0	0	0	0	0	0	0
23	Unilever	联合利华 U 关注/unileverofficial	0	1	1	1	0	0	1	0	0	1	0	0	0	1	0	0	0	0	0	0	1	0	0	0	0	0	1
24	PepsiCo	百事中国/BAISHIPEPSICO	0	1	0	1	0	0	1	1	0	0	1	0	0	0	0	0	0	0	0	0	0	1	0	0	1	0	1
25	Caterpillar	卡特皮勒中国/caterpillarinchina	0	15	1	1	1	0	1	1	0	1	0	1	0	0	0	1	0	0	0	0	0	0	0	0	0	0	1
26	Deere	约翰迪尔/JohnDeereChina	0	15	0	1	1	0	1	0	0	1	0	1	0	0	0	1	0	0	1	0	0	0	0	0	0	0	1
27	Marriott International	万豪礼赏/ marriottgroup	0	7	0	1	0	0	0	0	0	0	1	0	0	0	0	0	0	0	0	1	0	0	0	0	0	0	0
28	DuPont	杜邦特能壁纸/	0	10	0	1	0	0	1	1	0	1	0	0	0	0	0	0	0	1	1	0	0	0	0	0	0	0	0
29	Intel	英特尔中国/intel-china	0	2	0	1	0	0	1	0	0	1	0	0	0	0	0	0	0	0	0	0	0	1	1	0	0	0	1
30	Cisco System	思科联天下/ciscowechat	0	2	1	1	0	0	1	1	0	1	0	1	0	1	0	1	0	0	0	0	0	0	0	0	0	0	0
31	Huawei	华为/huaweicorp	1	2	1	1	0	0	1	0	0	0	0	0	1	0	1	0	1	0	0	0	0	0	0	0	0	0	0
32	ZTE	中兴通讯/ZTEInChina	1	2	1	1	0	0	1	0	0	0	0	0	0	0	0	1	0	0	0	0	0	0	0	1	0	0	0
33	Haier	海尔家电/Haier_jiadian	1	5	0	1	0	0	0	0	0	0	0	0	0	0	0	0	0	0	0	0	0	0	0	0	1	0	0
34	Xiaomi	小米手机/xmsj816	1	5	0	1	0	0	1	0	0	0	0	0	0	0	0	0	1	0	0	0	0	0	0	0	0	0	1
35	Lenovo	联想/lenovo1984	1	5	0	1	0	0	1	1	0	1	0	0	0	0	0	0	1	1	0	0	0	1	0	0	1	0	0
36	Gree	格力电器/glfwh1991	1	5	0	1	1	1	1	1	0	0	1	0	0	0	0	1	0	0	0	0	0	0	0	0	0	0	0
37	Midea	美的会员/mideafw	1	5	0	1	0	0	0	0	1	0	0	0	0	0	0	0	1	0	0	1	0	1	1	0	1	0	0
38	TCL	TCL 铁粉社区/tcltiefen	1	5	1	1	0	1	1	0	0	0	0	0	0	0	0	0	0	0	0	0	0	1	1	0	1	0	1
39	Hisense	海信/hisense1969	1	5	0	1	0	0	0	0	0	1	0	0	0	0	0	0	0	0	0	0	0	0	1	0	0	0	0
40	BYD	比亚迪汽车/byd-auto	1	9	1	1	0	0	1	1	0	1	0	0	0	0	0	0	0	0	0	0	0	0	0	0	1	0	0
41	Great Wall Motors	长城汽车/greatwallmotor	1	9	1	1	0	0	1	0	0	0	1	0	0	0	0	0	0	0	0	0	0	0	0	0	1	0	0
42	Saic Motor	上汽集团/SAIC_MOTOR_	1	9	0	1	0	0	1	1	0	1	0	0	0	0	0	1	0	0	1	0	1	1	0	0	0	0	0
43	Geely	吉利控股集团/	1	9	1	1	0	0	1	0	0	1	0	0	0	0	0	0	1	0	0	0	1	0	0	0	0	1	0
44	Wahaha	娃哈哈/YourWahaha	1	1	0	1	0	1	1	0	0	1	0	0	0	0	0	0	0	0	0	0	1	1	0	0	0	0	0

Table 6.6 (Continued)

No.	Company name	WeChat name/ID	Country region	Industry	Account type	Verific-ation type	C101	C102	C103	C104	C105	C106	C107	C108	C109	C110	C111	C112	C113	C114	C301	C302	C303	C304	C305	C4	C5	C6	Upda-ted
45	Tsingtao	青岛啤酒/Tsingtao_Since1903	1	1	1	1	0	0	0	0	0	1	0	0	0	0	0	0	0	0	0	0	1	1	0	0	0	0	0
46	Kweichow Moutai	国酒茅台/maotaiguojiu	1	1	1	1	0	0	1	1	0	1	0	0	0	0	0	1	0	0	0	0	1	0	0	0	0	0	0
47	YanJing Beer	燕京啤酒/yanjing_beer_group	1	1	0	1	0	1	1	1	0	1	0	0	0	0	0	1	0	0	0	0	0	0	0	0	0	1	0
48	Bright Food	光明食品集团/brightfoodgroup	1	1	1	1	0	0	1	1	0	1	0	1	0	0	0	1	0	0	0	0	0	0	0	0	0	1	0
49	HaiNan Airlines	海南航空/Hnairlines	1	16	0	1	0	0	0	0	1	1	0	0	0	0	0	0	0	0	0	0	0	0	0	0	0	0	0
50	Yunnan Baiyao	云南白药/newbaiyao	1	11	1	1	0	0	0	0	0	0	0	1	0	0	0	1	0	0	0	0	0	0	0	1	1	0	0
51	Ping An	中国平安/zhongguopingan_95511	1	17	1	1	0	0	1	0	0	1	0	0	0	1	0	1	0	1	0	0	1	0	0	0	0	0	0
52	WangFujing	王府井集团/wfjbh1955	1	14	0	1	0	0	1	0	0	0	0	0	0	0	0	1	0	1	0	1	0	0	0	0	1	0	0
53	SuNing	苏宁/suning265	1	14	1	0	0	0	0	0	1	0	1	0	0	0	0	0	0	0	0	1	0	0	0	0	0	0	0
54	Gome	国美在线/gome1314	1	14	0	1	0	0	1	0	0	0	1	0	0	0	0	0	0	0	0	1	0	0	0	0	0	0	0
55	Wanda	万达集团/guojiwanda	1	19	1	1	0	0	1	1	0	0	0	0	0	0	0	0	0	0	1	0	0	0	0	0	0	0	1
56	Vanke	万科周刊/vankeweekly	1	19	1	1	0	1	1	1	0	1	0	0	0	0	0	0	0	0	0	0	1	0	0	1	0	0	0
57	Country Garden	碧桂园/bgydream	1	19	1	1	0	1	1	1	0	1	0	0	0	0	0	0	0	0	0	0	1	0	0	0	0	0	0
58	SANY	三一重工/sanyibox	1	15	1	1	0	0	1	0	0	0	0	0	1	0	0	0	0	0	0	0	0	0	0	0	0	0	1
59	New Hope Group	新希望集团/newhopewindows	1	18	1	1	0	0	1	1	0	1	0	1	0	0	0	1	0	0	0	0	0	0	0	1	0	0	0
60	Fosun	复星/fuxing_2014	1	18	0	1	0	1	1	1	0	1	0	0	0	0	0	1	0	0	0	1	0	0	0	1	0	0	0

Table 6.7 Summary of database（Part 2：C2）based on 60 companies' WeChat accounts for interface & menu analysis

No.	Company Name	WeChat Name/ID	Country Region	Industry	Account Type	Verific-ation Type	C201	C202	C203	C204	C205	C206	C207	C208	C209	C210	C211	C212	C213	C214	C215	C216	C217	C218	C219	C220	C221
1	Apple	iPhone 中文网/apple4cn	0	2	1	0	0	1	0	0	0	0	0	0	0	0	0	0	0	0	0	0	0	0	0	0	0
2	Starbucks	星巴克中国/xingbakezhongguo	0	1	0	1	1	0	0	0	1	0	0	0	0	0	0	0	0	0	0	0	0	0	0	0	0
3	McDonald's	麦当劳/mcdonalds888	0	1	0	1	0	0	1	1	1	0	0	0	0	0	0	0	0	0	0	0	0	0	0	0	0
4	Coca-Cola	可口可乐中国/coke1886	0	1	1	1	0	0	0	0	0	0	0	0	0	0	0	0	0	0	0	0	0	0	0	0	0
5	Walt Disney	迪士尼中国/disney_china	0	3	1	1	0	0	0	0	0	0	0	0	0	0	0	0	0	0	0	0	0	0	0	0	0
6	FedEx	FedEx 中国/FedEx_China	0	4	0	1	0	0	0	0	0	1	1	1	1	1	0	0	0	0	0	0	0	0	0	0	0
7	UPS	UPS 中国动态/UPS_China_News	0	4	1	2	0	0	0	0	0	0	0	0	0	0	0	0	0	0	0	0	0	0	0	0	0
8	General Electric	GE 中国/GEandME	0	5	1	1	0	0	0	0	0	0	0	0	0	1	0	0	0	0	0	0	0	0	0	0	0
9	American Express	美国运通/AmexChina	0	6	1	1	0	0	0	0	0	0	0	0	0	1	0	0	0	0	0	0	0	0	0	0	0
10	Nike	NIKE/nikejdi	0	8	0	1	1	0	1	0	0	0	0	0	1	0	1	1	0	0	0	0	0	0	0	0	0
11	BMW	宝马中国/BMW_Official_Wechat	0	9	1	1	0	0	0	0	0	0	0	1	0	0	0	0	0	0	0	0	0	0	0	0	0
12	Volkswagen	VWLive 大众共线/dzqczg	0	9	1	1	0	0	0	0	0	0	0	0	0	0	0	0	0	0	0	0	0	0	0	0	0
13	Procter & Gamble	宝洁中国/pgchina1988	0	10	1	1	0	0	0	0	0	0	0	0	0	0	0	0	0	0	0	0	0	0	0	0	0
14	IBM	IBM 中国/IBMGCG	0	2	1	1	0	0	0	0	0	0	0	0	0	0	0	0	0	0	0	0	0	0	0	0	0
15	Accenture	埃森哲中国/accenture_china	0	2	1	1	0	0	0	0	0	0	0	0	0	0	0	0	0	0	0	0	0	0	0	0	0
16	Johnson & Johnson	强生招聘/JNJ_recruitment	0	11	1	2	0	0	0	0	0	0	0	0	0	0	0	0	0	0	0	0	0	0	0	0	0
17	3M	3M 中国区/mmm_china	0	11	1	0	0	1	0	0	0	0	0	0	0	0	1	0	0	0	0	0	0	0	0	0	0
18	Microsoft	微软科技/mstech2014	0	2	1	1	0	0	0	0	0	0	0	0	0	0	1	0	0	0	0	0	0	0	0	0	0
19	Boeing	波音中国/boeingairplanes	0	12	1	1	0	0	0	0	0	0	0	0	0	0	0	0	0	0	0	0	0	0	0	0	0
20	Exxon Mobil	埃克森美孚中国/ExxonMobil-China	0	13	1	1	0	0	0	0	0	0	0	0	0	0	0	0	0	0	0	0	0	0	0	0	0

Table 6.7 (Continued)

No.	Company Name	WeChat Name/ID	Country Region	Industry	Account Type	Verification Type	C201	C202	C203	C204	C205	C206	C207	C208	C209	C210	C211	C212	C213	C214	C215	C216	C217	C218	C219	C220	C221
21	Wal-Mart Stores	沃尔玛/Walmart_Hyper	0	14	0	1	0	0	0	0	1	0	0	0	1	1	0	0	0	0	0	0	0	0	0	0	0
22	Nestle S.A.	雀巢中国/NestleCN	0	1	1	1	0	0	0	0	0	0	0	0	0	1	0	0	1	0	0	0	0	0	0	0	0
23	Unilever	联合利华 U 关注/ unileverofficial	0	1	1	1	0	0	0	0	0	0	0	0	0	0	0	0	0	0	0	0	0	0	0	0	0
24	PepsiCo	百事中国/BAISHIPEPSICO	0	1	0	1	0	0	1	1	0	0	0	0	0	0	0	0	0	0	0	0	0	0	0	0	0
25	Caterpillar	卡特皮勒中国/ caterpillarinchina	0	15	1	1	0	0	0	0	0	0	0	0	0	0	0	0	0	0	0	0	0	0	0	0	0
26	Deere	约翰迪尔/JohnDeereChina	0	15	0	1	0	0	0	0	0	0	0	0	0	0	0	0	0	0	0	0	0	0	0	0	0
27	Marriott International	万豪礼赏/ marriottgroup	0	7	0	1	0	0	0	1	0	0	0	0	1	1	1	0	0	1	0	0	0	0	0	0	0
28	DuPont	杜邦特能壁纸/	0	10	0	1	1	0	0	0	0	0	0	0	0	0	0	0	0	0	0	0	0	0	0	0	0
29	Intel	英特尔中国/intel-china	0	2	0	1	0	0	0	0	0	0	0	0	0	0	1	1	0	0	0	0	0	1	0	0	0
30	Cisco System	思科联天下/ciscowechat	0	2	1	1	0	0	0	0	0	0	0	0	0	0	0	0	0	0	0	0	0	0	0	0	1
31	Huawei	华为/huaweicorp	1	2	1	1	0	0	0	0	0	0	0	0	0	0	1	0	0	0	0	0	0	0	0	0	0
32	ZTE	中兴通讯/ZTEInChina	1	2	1	1	1	0	0	0	0	0	0	0	0	0	1	0	0	0	0	0	0	0	0	0	0
33	Haier	海尔家电/Haier_jiadian	1	5	0	1	0	0	0	1	0	0	0	0	0	0	1	0	0	0	1	1	0	0	0	0	1
34	Xiaomi	小米手机/xmsj816	1	5	0	1	0	0	0	0	0	0	0	0	0	0	1	0	0	0	0	0	1	1	0	0	0
35	Lenovo	联想/lenovo1984	1	5	0	1	0	0	0	0	0	0	0	0	0	0	1	0	0	0	0	0	0	0	0	0	0
36	Gree	格力电器/glfwh1991	1	5	0	1	0	0	0	1	0	0	0	0	1	0	1	0	0	0	0	0	0	0	1	0	0
37	Midea	美的会员/mideafw	1	5	0	1	0	0	0	0	0	0	0	0	1	0	1	1	0	0	0	0	0	0	0	0	0
38	TCL	TCL 铁粉社区/tcltiefen	1	5	1	1	0	0	0	0	0	0	0	0	0	0	1	0	0	0	0	0	0	0	0	1	0
39	Hisense	海信/hisense1969	1	5	0	1	0	0	0	0	0	0	0	0	0	0	1	0	0	0	1	0	0	0	0	1	0
40	BYD	比亚迪汽车/byd-auto	1	9	1	1	0	0	0	1	0	0	0	0	0	0	0	0	0	0	0	0	0	0	0	0	0
41	Great Wall Motors	长城汽车/greatwallmotor	1	9	1	1	0	0	0	1	0	0	0	0	0	0	0	1	0	0	0	0	0	0	0	0	0

Table 6.7 (Continued)

No.	Company Name	WeChat Name/ID	Country Region	Industry	Account Type	Verification Type	C201	C202	C203	C204	C205	C206	C207	C208	C209	C210	C211	C212	C213	C214	C215	C216	C217	C218	C219	C220	C221
42	Saic Motor	上汽集团/SAIC_MOTOR_	1	9	0	1	0	0	0	0	0	0	0	0	0	0	0	1	0	0	0	0	0	0	0	1	0
43	Geely	吉利控股集团/	1	9	1	1	0	0	0	0	0	0	0	0	0	0	1	0	0	0	0	0	0	0	0	0	0
44	Wahaha	娃哈哈/YourWahaha	1	1	0	1	0	0	0	0	0	0	0	0	0	0	0	0	0	0	0	0	0	0	0	0	0
45	Tsingtao	青岛啤酒/Tsingtao_Since1903	1	1	1	1	0	0	0	0	0	0	0	0	0	0	1	0	1	0	0	0	0	0	0	0	0
46	Kweichow Moutai	国酒茅台/maotaiguojiu	1	1	1	1	0	0	0	0	0	0	0	0	0	1	1	0	0	0	0	0	0	0	0	0	0
47	YanJing Beer	燕京啤酒/yanjing_beer_group	1	1	0	1	0	0	0	0	0	0	0	0	0	0	1	0	0	0	0	0	0	0	0	0	0
48	Bright Food	光明食品集团/brightfoodgroup	1	1	1	1	1	0	0	0	0	0	0	0	0	0	1	0	0	0	0	0	0	0	0	0	0
49	HaiNan Airlines	海南航空/Hnairlines	1	16	0	1	0	0	0	1	0	0	0	0	0	1	0	0	0	0	0	1	0	0	0	1	1
50	Yunnan Baiyao	云南白药/newbaiyao	1	11	1	1	0	0	0	0	0	0	0	0	0	0	1	0	0	0	0	0	0	0	0	0	0
51	Ping An	中国平安/zhongguopingan_95511	1	17	1	1	0	0	0	0	0	0	0	0	0	0	0	0	0	0	0	0	0	0	0	0	0
52	WangFujing	王府井集团/wfjbh1955	1	14	0	1	0	0	1	0	0	0	0	0	0	0	1	1	0	0	1	0	0	0	0	0	0
53	SuNing	苏宁/suning265	1	14	1	0	0	0	1	0	1	0	0	0	1	0	1	0	0	0	0	0	0	0	0	0	0
54	Gome	国美在线/gome1314	1	14	0	1	0	0	1	0	0	0	0	0	1	0	1	1	0	0	0	1	0	0	0	0	0
55	Wanda	万达集团/guojiwanda	1	19	1	1	0	0	0	0	0	0	0	0	0	0	0	0	0	0	0	0	0	0	0	0	0
56	Vanke	万科周刊/vankeweekly	1	19	1	1	0	0	1	0	0	0	0	1	0	0	0	1	0	0	0	0	0	0	0	0	0
57	Country Garden	碧桂园/bgydream	1	19	1	1	0	0	0	0	0	0	0	0	0	0	0	0	0	0	0	0	0	0	0	0	0
58	SANY	三一重工/sanyibox	1	15	1	1	0	0	1	0	0	0	0	0	0	0	1	1	0	0	0	0	0	0	0	0	0
59	New Hope Group	新希望集团/newhopewindows	1	18	1	1	0	0	0	0	0	0	0	0	0	0	0	0	0	0	0	0	0	0	0	0	0
60	Fosun	复星/fuxing_2014	1	18	0	1	0	0	1	0	0	0	0	0	0	0	1	0	1	0	0	0	0	0	0	0	0

6.1.4 The results of interface & menu analysis

According to the collected data (seen in table 6.6 and table 6.7), **the interface & menu analysis** of all selected WeChat official accounts mainly **was performed from two angles: country region and industry sector.**

6.1.4.1 Interface & menu analysis as per country region

All the interface & menu analysis results as per country region are shown in table 6.8 to table 6.11. Specifically, the overall results of interface & menu analysis as per Country Region are summarized in table 6.8. Meanwhile, table 6.9, table 6.10 and table 6.11 present the results of comparison of each category between Western and Chinese companies.

In general, it has been found from table 6.8 that the top five subcategories are: C103 – products, C106 – news, C104 – brand, C211 – online shopping, C112 – company profile, which have been adopted the most by all selected companies. In particular, **three types of information, namely, C103 – products, C106 – news, and C104 – brand were all companies' favorites** because the total number of companies involving these three types of information **in their WeChat official accounts' menu setting** were forty-seven, thirty-six and thirty-one respectively during the observation period.

Besides the overall findings, it is important to explore their respective results of Western and Chinese companies individually. Firstly, the results of interface & menu analysis for Western companies are indicated in table 6.9, table 6.10 and table 6.11. The following findings can be extracted:

(1) Favorite subcategory ranking of "C1 – information" category: ① products; ② news; ③ brand; ④ history of company; ⑤ contact information.

(2) Favorite subcategory ranking of "C2 – service" category: ① feedback & questions; ② online shopping; ③ users' account management.

(3) Favorite subcategory ranking of "C3 – activities" category: ① contests; ② offline activities; ③ sales campaign.

Table 6.8 Summary of results of interface & menu analysis as per Country Region

Country Region	C101	C102	C103	C104	C105	C106	C107	C108	C109	C110	C111	C112	C113	C114	C201	C202	C203	C204	C205	C206	C207	C208	C209	C210	C211	C212	C213	C214	C215	C216	C217	C218	C219	C220	C221	C301	C302	C303	C304	C305	C4	C5	C6	Updated
30 Western companies	11	4	24	19	4	20	6	9	4	5	1	5	0	1	3	2	3	3	3	1	1	2	4	6	5	2	1	1	0	0	0	1	0	0	1	5	3	5	2	1	5	2	0	11
30 Chinese companies	1	7	23	12	3	16	4	3	2	1	1	11	5	3	2	0	6	5	1	0	0	1	4	2	20	7	2	0	3	3	1	1	1	4	2	2	5	8	6	3	5	8	3	4
60 companies	12	11	47	31	7	36	10	12	6	6	2	16	5	4	5	2	9	8	4	1	1	3	8	8	25	9	3	1	3	3	1	2	1	4	3	7	8	13	8	4	10	10	3	15

Table 6.9 Results of comparison of C1 between Western and Chinese companies

	C1: Information												
Western companies	Products	News	Brand	History of company	Contact info.	Apps	Company profile	Survey & report	Company's main founders/leadership	Offer notice	Cases info.	Award winner list	Cooperation info.	After-sales service
	C103	C106	C104	C101	C108	C107	C112	C110	C102	C105	C109	C114	C111	C113
	24	20	19	11	9	6	5	5	4	4	4	1	1	0
Chinese companies	Products	News	Brand	Company profile	Company's main founders/leadership	After-sales service	Apps	Offer notice	Award winner list	Contact info.	Cases info.	Survey & report	Cooperation info.	History of company
	C103	C106	C104	C112	C102	C113	C107	C105	C114	C108	C109	C110	C111	C101
	23	16	12	11	7	5	4	3	3	3	2	1	1	1

Table 6.10 Results of comparison of C2 between Western and Chinese companies

	C2: Services																				
Western companies	Feedback & questions	Online shopping	Users' account management	Ordering/ Booking	Chains-seeking	New product promotion	Offers	Customer Attention	Price inquiry	Online tutorials	Track shipments	Ship online	Online game	Location-based map	Anti-counterfeiting check	Self-service	Redeem points	Membership card management	Membership registration	Order tracking	Product recycling
	C210	C211	C209	C204	C205	C201	C203	C212	C208	C202	C206	C207	C213	C214	C218	C221	C220	C215	C216	C217	C219
	6	5	4	3	3	3	3	2	2	2	1	1	1	1	1	1	0	0	0	0	0
Chinese companies	Online shopping	Customer Attention	Offers	Ordering/ Booking	Users' account management	Redeem points	Membership card management	Membership registration	New product promotion	Online game	Feedback & questions	Self-service	Anti-counterfeiting check	Product recycling	Price inquiry	Chains-seeking	Order tracking	Track shipments	Ship online	Online tutorials	Location-based map
	C211	C212	C203	C204	C209	C220	C215	C216	C201	C211	C210	C221	C218	C219	C208	C205	C217	C206	C207	C202	C214
	20	7	6	5	4	4	3	3	2	2	2	2	1	1	1	1	1	0	0	0	0

Table 6.11 Results of comparison of C3, C4, C5, C6 & UPDATED between Western and Chinese companies

	C3: Activities					C4: Recruitment	C5: Interactive community	C6: Link to Sina Weibo	Updated Within one month
Western companies	Contests	Offline activities	Sales campaign	Award-winning activities	Daily check-in	Recruitment	Interactive community	Link to Sina Weibo	-
	C301	C303	C302	C304	C305	C4	C5	C6	Updated
	5	5	3	2	1	5	2	0	11
Chinese companies	Offline activities	Award-winning activities	Sales campaign	Daily check-in	Contests	Recruitment	Interactive community	Link to Sina Weibo	-
	C303	C304	C302	C305	C301	C4	C5	C6	Updated
	8	6	5	3	2	5	8	3	4

Secondly, according to table 6.9, table 6.10 and table 6.11, the results of interface & menu analysis for thirty Chinese companies can be obtained; the following findings have been explored:

(1) Favorite subcategory ranking of "C1: information" category: ① products; ② news; ③ brand; ④ company profile; ⑤ company's main founders/leadership.

(2) Favorite subcategory ranking of "C2: service" category: ① online shopping; ② customer; attention ③ offers.

(3) Favorite subcategory ranking of "C3: activities" category: ① offline activities; ② award-winning activities; ③ sales campaign.

Finally, some differences are demonstrated through general comparisons between Chinese and Western enterprises:

(1) **More Chinese companies** (total 5) **paid attention to after-sales service information** on their WeChat official accounts' menus setting **by comparison with Western companies** (total 0).

(2) Much more Chinese companies (total 20) recognized the importance of online shopping service compared with Western companies (total 5). This also implies that **Chinese companies highlighted more profit-related services such as online shopping** service to promote their products or services.

(3) More **Chinese companies** (total 8) **were dedicated to the construction of interactive community** than Western companies (total 2). **Chinese companies preferred to provide customer attention service.** Instead, **Western companies emphasized more Q&A type service to answer questions or inquiries.**

(4) Chinese companies organized more award-winning activities than Western companies.

(5) It seems that **more Western companies** (total 11) **endeavored to adjust or optimize their WeChat official accounts' menus by updating action than Chinese companies** (total 4) did during the specific observation timeline: from October 21st to November 21st of 2016.

It is very interesting to note that Chinese companies are more concerned about the information of company's leaders than Western companies. This difference is deemed to be induced by the different Chinese and Western cultures, which can be explained well by the Hofstede's cultural dimensions theory (Hofstede et al., 2010). In line with Hofstede's 6-D model of national culture, the PDI (power distance index) of China is much higher than those of occidental countries. The higher PDI in China implies that people in Chinese societies accept more easily a hierarchical order in which everyone has a place without any further justification. Thus, it is understandable that the Chinese companies' leaders are usually highlighted with privileges and their information (leader's profile, leader's saying, etc.) is frequently incorporated into the company's publicizing platforms.

6.1.4.2 Interface & menu analysis as per industry

The industries of all selected companies have been introduced when the magazine Fortune published the list of most admired companies every year. In this research, sixty companies' industries can be integrated into nineteen categories (seen in table 4.6) via the coding process. It is necessary to note that the purpose of the integrating aims to bring those companies of similar industries into one general industry. For instance, Starbucks, McDonald's, Coca-Cola and Nestle S.A. are integrated into Food industry.

Food industry is the biggest industry in this research because there are eleven food companies among total sixty companies. Behind that, three popular industries follow by IT (total 8), Electronics (total 8), and Motor (total 6) in this research.

All the overall results of interface & menu analysis as per industry are given in table 6.12. First of all, the results of the main five industries, i.e., Food, IT, Electronics, Motor, and Wholesale are stated below.

(1) As for the eleven companies of Food industry, the following findings can be given:

Favorite subcategory ranking of "C1 – information" "C2 – service" & "C3 – activities" categories: ① products; ② news; ③ brand; ④ online shopping; ⑤ offline activities.

(2) As for the eight companies of IT industry, the following findings can be found:

Favorite subcategory ranking of "C1 – information" & "C2 – service" categories: ① products; ② news; ③ brand; ④ online shopping.

(3) As for the eight companies of Electronics industry, the following findings can be made:

• Favorite subcategory ranking of "C1 – information" "C2 – Service" & "C5 – Interactive community" categories: ① online shopping; ②products; ③ interactive community.

• 50% of electronic companies had interactive community aiming to provide a communication space not only between users, but also between the company and the user.

• It is worth to mention that online shopping is top-one subcategory because seven of eight electronic companies used this service function in their WeChat official accounts' menu setting.

(4) As for the six companies of Motor industry, the following findings can be given:

Favorite subcategory ranking of "C1 – information" & "C3 – activities" categories: ① products; ②brand; ③ news; ④ offline activities.

(5) As for the four companies of Wholesale Retail industry, the following findings can be found:

• Favorite subcategory ranking of "C1 – information", "C2 – Service" & "C3 – activities" categories: ① products; ② Apps; ③ online shopping; ④ offers; ⑤ users' accounts management.

• Companies in Wholesale Retail industry used more service account (total 3) than subscription account (only 1).

In addition to the five main industries, companies in the other two sectors, Medical & Real Estate, have used subscription accounts because they have paid too much attention to provide information to their followers.

In general, **companies in Food and IT sectors were mainly to provide information of products, news and brand, followed by providing online shopping service.**

Besides, **companies in Electronics industry** focused on **providing online shopping service, products information, and building interactive community**.

In addition, **companies in Motor industry mainly provided information of products, brand, and news**.

As for **companies in Wholesale Retail industry,** they preferred to **provide information, e.g., products & Apps and** service function such as **online shopping, offers** and **users' accounts management**.

Table 6.12 Summary of results of interface & menu analysis as per industry

Company name	Country Region	Industry	Account Type	Verification Type	C101	C102	C103	C104	C105	C106	C107	C108	C109	C110	C111	C112	C113	C114	C201	C202	C203	C204	C205	C206	C207	C208	C209	C210	C211	C212	C213	C214	C215	C216	C217	C218	C219	C220	C221	C301	C302	C303	C304	C305	C4	C5	C6	Updated
Starbucks	0	1	0	1	1	0	1	1	0	1	1	0	0	0	0	0	0	0	1	0	0	0	1	0	0	0	0	0	0	0	0	0	0	0	0	0	0	0	0	0	0	0	0	0	0	0	0	1
McDonald's	0	1	0	1	0	0	0	0	0	0	0	0	0	0	0	0	0	0	0	0	1	1	1	0	0	0	0	0	0	0	0	0	0	0	0	0	0	0	0	0	1	0	0	0	0	0	0	0
Coca-Cola	0	1	1	1	1	0	1	1	0	0	0	0	0	0	0	0	0	0	0	0	0	0	0	0	0	0	0	0	0	0	0	0	0	0	0	0	0	0	0	1	0	0	0	0	1	0	0	0
Nestle S.A.	0	1	1	1	1	1	1	1	0	0	0	1	0	0	0	0	0	0	0	0	0	0	0	0	0	0	0	1	0	0	1	0	0	0	0	0	0	0	0	0	0	0	0	0	0	0	0	0
Unilever	0	1	1	1	0	0	1	0	0	1	0	0	0	1	0	0	0	0	0	0	0	0	0	0	0	0	0	0	0	0	0	0	0	0	0	0	0	0	0	0	0	1	0	0	0	0	0	1
PepsiCo	0	1	0	1	0	0	1	1	0	0	1	0	0	0	0	0	0	0	0	0	1	1	0	0	0	0	0	0	0	0	0	0	0	0	0	0	0	0	0	0	0	0	1	0	0	1	0	1
Wahaha	1	1	0	1	0	1	1	0	0	1	0	0	0	0	0	0	0	0	0	0	0	0	0	0	0	0	0	0	0	0	0	0	0	0	0	0	0	0	0	0	0	1	1	0	0	0	0	0
Tsingtao	1	1	1	1	0	0	0	0	0	1	0	0	0	0	0	0	0	0	0	0	0	0	0	0	0	0	0	0	1	0	1	0	0	0	0	0	0	0	0	0	0	1	1	0	0	0	0	0
Kweichow Moutai	1	1	1	1	0	0	1	1	0	1	0	0	0	0	0	1	0	0	0	0	0	0	0	0	0	0	0	1	1	0	0	0	0	0	0	0	0	0	0	0	0	1	0	0	0	0	0	0
YanJing Beer	1	1	0	1	0	1	1	1	0	1	0	0	0	0	0	1	0	0	0	0	0	0	0	0	0	0	0	0	1	0	0	0	0	0	0	0	0	0	0	0	0	0	0	0	0	0	1	0
Bright Food	1	1	1	1	0	0	1	1	0	1	0	1	0	0	0	1	0	0	1	0	0	0	0	0	0	0	0	0	1	0	0	0	0	0	0	0	0	0	0	0	0	0	0	0	0	0	1	0
Sum1			6	11	3	3	9	7	0	7	2	2	0	1	0	3	0	0	2	0	2	2	2	0	0	0	0	2	4	0	2	0	0	0	0	0	0	0	0	1	1	4	3	0	1	1	2	3
Apple	0	2	1	0	0	0	1	1	0	1	1	0	0	0	0	0	0	0	0	1	0	0	0	0	0	0	0	0	0	0	0	0	0	0	0	0	0	0	0	0	0	0	0	0	0	1	0	0
IBM	0	2	1	1	0	0	1	1	0	1	0	0	0	0	0	0	0	0	0	0	0	0	0	0	0	0	0	0	0	0	0	0	0	0	0	0	0	0	0	1	0	0	0	0	0	0	0	0
Accenture	0	2	1	1	0	0	1	1	0	1	0	1	1	1	0	1	0	0	0	0	0	0	0	0	0	0	0	0	0	0	0	0	0	0	0	0	0	0	0	1	0	1	0	0	0	0	0	0
Microsoft	0	2	1	1	0	0	1	1	0	1	0	1	1	0	0	0	0	0	0	0	0	0	0	0	0	0	0	0	1	0	0	0	0	0	0	0	0	0	0	0	0	0	0	0	0	0	0	1
Intel	0	2	0	1	0	0	1	0	0	1	0	0	0	0	0	0	0	0	0	0	0	0	0	0	0	0	0	0	1	1	0	0	0	0	0	1	0	0	0	0	0	0	1	1	0	0	0	1
Cisco System	0	2	1	1	0	0	1	1	0	1	0	1	0	1	0	1	0	0	0	0	0	0	0	0	0	0	0	0	0	0	0	0	0	0	0	0	0	0	1	0	0	0	0	0	0	0	0	0
Huawei	1	2	1	1	0	0	1	0	0	0	0	0	1	0	1	0	1	0	0	0	0	0	0	0	0	0	0	0	1	0	0	0	0	0	0	0	0	0	0	0	0	0	0	0	0	0	0	0
ZTE	1	2	1	1	0	0	1	0	0	0	0	0	0	0	0	1	0	0	1	0	0	0	0	0	0	0	0	0	1	0	0	0	0	0	0	0	0	0	0	0	0	0	0	0	1	0	0	0
Sum2			7	7	0	0	8	5	0	6	1	3	3	2	1	3	1	0	1	1	0	0	0	0	0	0	0	0	4	1	0	0	0	0	0	1	0	0	1	2	0	1	1	1	1	1	0	2
Walt Disney	0	3	1	1	1	1	1	1	1	1	0	0	0	0	0	0	0	0	0	0	0	0	0	0	0	0	0	0	0	0	0	0	0	0	0	0	0	0	0	0	0	1	0	0	1	0	0	0
Sum3			1	1	1	1	1	1	1	1	0	0	0	0	0	0	0	0	0	0	0	0	0	0	0	0	0	0	0	0	0	0	0	0	0	0	0	0	0	0	0	1	0	0	1	0	0	0
FedEx	0	4	0	1	0	0	0	0	1	1	0	1	1	0	0	0	0	0	0	0	0	0	0	1	1	1	1	1	0	0	0	0	0	0	0	0	0	0	0	0	0	0	0	0	1	0	0	0
UPS	0	4	1	2	1	0	1	1	0	1	0	1	1	1	1	0	0	0	0	0	0	0	0	0	0	0	0	0	0	0	0	0	0	0	0	0	0	0	0	0	0	0	0	0	0	0	0	0
Sum4			1	3	1	0	1	1	1	2	0	2	2	1	1	0	0	0	0	0	0	0	0	1	1	1	1	1	0	0	0	0	0	0	0	0	0	0	0	0	0	0	0	0	1	0	0	0

Table 6.12 (Continued)

Company name	Country Region	Industry	Account Type	Verification Type	C101	C102	C103	C104	C105	C106	C107	C108	C109	C110	C111	C112	C113	C114	C201	C202	C203	C204	C205	C206	C207	C208	C209	C210	C211	C212	C213	C214	C215	C216	C217	C218	C219	C220	C221	C301	C302	C303	C304	C305	C4	C5	C6	Updated
General Electric	0	5	1	1	1	1	1	1	0	0	0	0	0	0	0	0	0	0	0	0	0	0	0	0	0	0	0	1	0	0	0	0	0	0	0	0	0	0	0	0	0	0	0	0	1	0	0	0
Haier	1	5	0	1	0	0	0	0	0	0	0	0	0	0	0	0	0	0	0	0	0	1	0	0	0	0	0	0	1	0	0	0	1	1	0	0	0	0	1	0	0	0	0	0	0	1	0	0
Xiaomi	1	5	0	1	0	0	1	0	0	0	0	0	0	0	0	0	1	0	0	0	0	0	0	0	0	0	0	0	1	0	0	0	0	0	1	1	0	0	0	0	0	0	0	0	0	0	0	1
Lenovo	1	5	0	1	0	0	1	1	0	1	0	0	0	0	0	0	1	1	0	0	0	0	0	0	0	0	0	0	1	0	0	0	0	0	0	0	0	0	0	0	0	0	1	0	0	1	0	0
Gree	1	5	0	1	1	1	1	1	0	0	1	0	0	0	0	1	0	0	0	0	0	1	0	0	0	0	1	0	1	0	0	0	0	0	0	0	1	0	0	0	0	0	0	0	0	0	0	0
Midea	1	5	0	1	0	0	0	0	1	0	0	0	0	0	0	0	1	0	0	0	0	0	0	0	0	0	1	0	1	1	0	0	0	0	0	0	0	0	0	0	1	0	1	1	0	1	0	0
TCL	1	5	1	1	0	1	1	0	0	0	0	0	0	0	0	0	0	0	0	0	0	0	0	0	0	0	0	0	1	0	0	0	0	0	0	0	0	1	0	0	0	0	1	1	0	1	0	1
Hisense	1	5	0	1	0	0	0	0	0	1	0	0	0	0	0	0	0	0	0	0	0	0	0	0	0	0	0	0	1	0	0	0	1	0	0	0	0	1	0	0	0	0	0	1	0	0	0	0
Sum5			2	8	2	3	5	3	1	2	1	0	0	0	0	1	3	1	0	0	0	2	0	0	0	0	2	1	7	1	0	0	2	1	1	1	1	2	1	0	1	0	3	3	1	4	0	2
American Express	0	6	1	1	1	0	1	1	1	0	0	0	0	0	0	0	0	0	0	0	0	0	0	0	0	0	0	1	0	0	0	0	0	0	0	0	0	0	0	0	0	0	0	0	0	0	0	0
Sum6			1	1	1	0	1	1	1	0	0	0	0	0	0	0	0	0	0	0	0	0	0	0	0	0	0	1	0	0	0	0	0	0	0	0	0	0	0	0	0	0	0	0	0	0	0	0
Marriott International	0	7	0	1	0	0	0	0	0	0	1	0	0	0	0	0	0	0	0	0	0	1	0	0	0	0	1	1	1	0	0	1	0	0	0	0	0	0	0	0	1	0	0	0	0	0	0	0
Sum7			0	1	0	0	0	0	0	0	1	0	0	0	0	0	0	0	0	0	0	1	0	0	0	0	1	1	1	0	0	1	0	0	0	0	0	0	0	0	1	0	0	0	0	0	0	0
Nike	0	8	0	1	0	0	1	1	0	1	1	0	0	0	0	0	0	0	1	0	1	0	0	0	0	0	1	0	1	1	0	0	0	0	0	0	0	0	0	0	0	1	0	0	0	0	0	1
Sum8			0	1	0	0	1	1	0	1	1	0	0	0	0	0	0	0	1	0	1	0	0	0	0	0	1	0	1	1	0	0	0	0	0	0	0	0	0	0	0	1	0	0	0	0	0	1
BMW	0	9	1	1	0	0	1	1	0	0	0	0	0	0	0	0	0	0	0	0	0	0	0	0	0	1	0	0	0	0	0	0	0	0	0	0	0	0	0	0	1	1	0	0	0	0	0	0
Volkswagen	0	9	1	1	0	0	1	1	0	0	0	0	0	0	0	0	0	0	0	0	0	0	0	0	0	0	0	0	0	0	0	0	0	0	0	0	0	0	0	0	0	0	0	0	0	0	0	1
BYD	1	9	1	1	0	0	1	1	0	1	0	0	0	0	0	0	0	0	0	0	0	1	0	0	0	0	0	0	0	0	0	0	0	0	0	0	0	0	0	0	0	0	0	0	0	1	0	0
Great Wall Motors	1	9	1	1	0	0	1	0	0	0	1	0	0	0	0	0	0	0	0	0	0	1	0	0	0	0	0	0	0	1	0	0	0	0	0	0	0	0	0	0	0	0	0	0	0	1	0	0
Saic Motor	1	9	0	1	0	0	1	1	0	1	0	0	0	0	0	1	0	0	0	0	0	0	0	0	0	0	0	0	0	1	0	0	0	0	0	0	0	1	0	1	0	1	1	0	0	0	0	0
Geely	1	9	1	1	0	0	1	0	0	1	0	0	0	0	0	0	1	0	0	0	0	0	0	0	0	0	0	0	1	0	0	0	0	0	0	0	0	0	0	0	0	1	0	0	0	1	0	0
Sum9			5	6	0	0	6	4	0	3	1	0	0	0	0	1	1	0	0	0	0	2	0	0	0	1	0	0	1	2	0	0	0	0	0	0	0	1	0	1	1	3	1	0	0	2	1	1
Procter & Gamble	0	10	1	1	0	0	0	0	0	0	0	0	0	0	0	0	0	0	0	0	0	0	0	0	0	0	0	0	0	0	0	0	0	0	0	0	0	0	0	0	0	0	0	0	0	0	0	1
DuPont	0	10	0	1	0	0	1	1	0	1	0	0	0	0	0	0	0	1	1	0	0	0	0	0	0	0	0	0	0	0	0	0	0	0	0	0	0	0	0	1	0	0	0	0	0	0	0	0
Sum10			1	2	0	0	1	1	0	1	0	0	0	0	0	0	0	1	1	0	0	0	0	0	0	0	0	0	0	0	0	0	0	0	0	0	0	0	0	1	0	0	0	0	0	0	0	1

Table 6.12 (Continued)

Company name	Country Region	Industry	Account Type	Verification Type	C101	C102	C103	C104	C105	C106	C107	C108	C109	C110	C111	C112	C113	C114	C201	C202	C203	C204	C205	C206	C207	C208	C209	C210	C211	C212	C213	C214	C215	C216	C217	C218	C219	C220	C221	C301	C302	C303	C304	C305	C4	C5	C6	Updated
Johnson & Johnson	0	11	1	2	0	0	0	0	0	1	0	0	0	0	0	0	0	0	0	0	0	0	0	0	0	0	0	0	0	0	0	0	0	0	0	0	0	0	0	0	0	0	0	0	1	0	0	0
3M	0	11	1	0	1	0	1	1	0	1	0	1	0	0	0	0	0	0	0	1	0	0	0	0	0	0	0	0	1	0	0	0	0	0	0	0	0	0	0	0	0	0	0	0	0	0	0	0
Yunnan Baiyao	1	11	1	1	0	0	0	0	0	0	0	1	0	0	0	1	0	0	0	0	0	0	0	0	0	0	0	0	1	0	0	0	0	0	0	0	0	0	0	0	0	0	0	0	1	1	0	0
Sum11			3	3	1	0	1	1	0	2	0	2	0	0	0	1	0	0	0	1	0	0	0	0	0	0	0	0	2	0	0	0	0	0	0	0	0	0	0	0	0	0	0	0	2	1	0	0
Boeing	0	12	1	1	1	1	1	0	0	1	0	0	0	0	0	0	0	0	0	0	0	0	0	0	0	0	0	0	0	0	0	0	0	0	0	0	0	0	0	0	0	0	0	0	0	0	0	1
Sum12			1	1	1	1	1	0	0	1	0	0	0	0	0	0	0	0	0	0	0	0	0	0	0	0	0	0	0	0	0	0	0	0	0	0	0	0	0	0	0	0	0	0	0	0	0	1
Exxon Mobil	0	13	1	1	0	0	0	0	0	1	0	0	0	1	0	1	0	0	0	0	0	0	0	0	0	0	0	0	0	0	0	0	0	0	0	0	0	0	0	0	0	0	0	0	0	0	0	0
Sum13			1	1	0	0	0	0	0	1	0	0	0	1	0	1	0	0	0	0	0	0	0	0	0	0	0	0	0	0	0	0	0	0	0	0	0	0	0	0	0	0	0	0	0	0	0	0
Wal-Mart Stores	0	14	0	1	0	0	1	0	1	1	1	0	0	0	0	0	0	0	0	0	0	0	1	0	0	0	1	1	0	0	0	0	0	0	0	0	0	0	0	0	0	0	0	0	0	0	0	0
WangFujing	1	14	0	1	0	0	1	0	0	0	0	0	0	0	0	1	0	1	0	0	1	0	0	0	0	0	0	0	1	1	0	0	1	0	0	0	0	0	0	0	1	0	0	0	0	1	0	0
SuNing	1	14	1	0	0	0	0	0	1	0	1	0	0	0	0	0	0	0	0	0	1	0	1	0	0	0	1	0	1	0	0	0	0	0	0	0	0	0	0	0	1	0	0	0	0	0	0	0
Gome	1	14	0	1	0	0	1	0	0	0	1	0	0	0	0	0	0	0	0	0	1	0	0	0	0	0	1	0	1	1	0	0	0	1	0	0	0	0	0	0	1	0	0	0	0	0	0	0
Sum14			1	3	0	0	3	0	2	1	3	0	0	0	0	1	0	1	0	0	3	0	2	0	0	0	3	1	3	2	0	0	1	1	0	0	0	0	0	0	3	0	0	0	0	1	0	0
Caterpillar	0	15	1	1	1	0	1	1	0	1	0	1	0	0	0	1	0	0	0	0	0	0	0	0	0	0	0	0	0	0	0	0	0	0	0	0	0	0	0	0	0	0	0	0	0	0	0	1
Deere	0	15	0	1	1	0	1	0	0	1	0	1	0	0	0	1	0	0	0	0	0	0	0	0	0	0	0	0	0	0	0	0	0	0	0	0	0	0	0	1	0	0	0	0	0	0	0	1
SANY	1	15	1	1	0	0	1	0	0	0	0	0	1	0	0	0	0	0	0	0	1	0	0	0	0	0	0	0	1	1	0	0	0	0	0	0	0	0	0	0	0	0	0	0	0	0	0	1
Sum15			2	3	2	0	3	1	0	2	0	2	1	0	0	2	0	0	0	0	1	0	0	0	0	0	0	0	1	1	0	0	0	0	0	0	0	0	0	1	0	0	0	0	0	0	0	3
HaiNan Airlines	1	16	0	1	0	0	0	0	1	1	0	0	0	0	0	0	0	0	0	0	0	1	0	0	0	0	0	1	0	0	0	0	0	1	0	0	0	1	1	0	0	0	0	0	0	0	0	0
Sum16			0	1	0	0	0	0	1	1	0	0	0	0	0	0	0	0	0	0	0	1	0	0	0	0	0	1	0	0	0	0	0	1	0	0	0	1	1	0	0	0	0	0	0	0	0	0
Ping An	1	17	1	1	0	0	1	0	0	1	0	0	0	1	0	1	0	1	0	0	0	0	0	0	0	0	0	0	0	0	0	0	0	0	0	0	0	0	0	0	0	1	0	0	0	0	0	0
Sum17			1	1	0	0	1	0	0	1	0	0	0	1	0	1	0	1	0	0	0	0	0	0	0	0	0	0	0	0	0	0	0	0	0	0	0	0	0	0	0	1	0	0	0	0	0	0
New Hope Group	1	18	1	1	0	0	1	1	0	1	0	1	0	0	0	1	0	0	0	0	0	0	0	0	0	0	0	0	0	0	0	0	0	0	0	0	0	0	0	0	0	0	0	0	1	0	0	0
Fosun	1	18	0	1	0	1	1	1	0	1	0	0	0	0	0	1	0	0	0	0	1	0	0	0	0	0	0	0	1	0	1	0	0	0	0	0	0	0	0	0	1	0	0	0	1	0	0	0
Sum18			1	2	0	1	2	2	0	2	0	1	0	0	0	2	0	0	0	0	1	0	0	0	0	0	0	0	1	0	1	0	0	0	0	0	0	0	0	0	1	0	0	0	2	0	0	0
Wanda	1	19	1	1	0	0	1	1	0	0	0	0	0	0	0	0	0	0	0	0	0	0	0	0	0	0	0	0	0	0	0	0	0	0	0	0	0	0	0	1	0	0	0	0	0	0	0	1
Vanke	1	19	1	1	0	1	1	1	0	1	0	0	0	0	0	0	0	0	0	0	1	0	0	0	0	1	0	0	0	1	0	0	0	0	0	0	0	0	0	0	0	1	0	0	1	0	0	0
Country Garden	1	19	1	1	0	1	1	1	0	1	0	0	0	0	0	0	0	0	0	0	0	0	0	0	0	0	0	0	0	0	0	0	0	0	0	0	0	0	0	0	0	1	0	0	0	0	0	0
Sum19			3	3	0	2	3	3	0	2	0	0	0	0	0	0	0	0	0	0	1	0	0	0	0	1	0	0	0	1	0	0	0	0	0	0	0	0	0	1	0	2	0	0	1	0	0	1

Except the overall findings, the comparative results of interface & menu analysis as per industry between Western and Chinese companies can be addressed from table 6.13 as follows:

(1) Six Western companies in Food industry provided information focusing on products, brands, history of company, and service function emphasizing on ordering/booking, chains-seeking, offers.

In particular, McDonald's used service account with strong service functions such as ordering/booking, chains-seeking, and offers.

Chinese companies in Food industry provided information focusing on news, products, brands, company profile. Four of five Chinese companies used online shopping function; three of them organized offline activities; two of them used WeChat platform linked to Sina Weibo.

(2) Western companies in IT industry used more subscription accounts (total 5) than service account (only 1). They provided information focusing on products, news, brands, and contact information. Only two (Microsoft and Intel) of them used online shopping service function.

Two Chinese companies in IT industry provided products information and online shopping service.

(3) Only one Western company (GE) in Electronic industry used subscription account so as to focus on information providing scheme and only used feedback & questions service function.

Whereas all seven Chinese electronic companies provided online shopping service; four of them created interactive community so as to communicate with their users; and most of them did not pay attention to provide information.

(4) Companies in Motor vehicles preferred subscription account (total 5) more than service account (only 1). Western companies focused on providing product and brand information. Chinese companies provided news and products information. Moreover, Chinese companies provided more service function than Western companies.

(5) All three companies in Medicals industry registered only subscription accounts. Western companies provided more information about company than Chinese company did. Both Chinese and Western companies in Medicals industry used online shopping and recruitment. However, only the Chinese company created interactive community.

(6) As for the industry of Construction & manufacturing, the unique Chinese company (Sany) provided more service function such as online shopping. The two Western companies focused on providing information.

(7) Companies in Wholesale Retail industry preferred service account. They provided information about products, offer notice and Apps. Three Chinese companies provided service such as online shopping & offers, and sales campaign activities; two of them used customer attention and users' account management.

(8) One company Boeing in Aerospace sector used subscription account so as to provide information about company and product. One company HaiNan Airlines in Airline industry used service account and provided more service function.

Generally speaking, some similarities and differences of WeChat official accounts' menu setting have been existed between Western and Chinese companies in the similar industry during the observation period. **Western companies in Food sector focused on providing information**; whereas **Chinese companies focused on online shopping.** As for **companies in IT, Motor vehicles, and Medicals sectors, both Western and Chinese companies preferred subscription accounts.** According to the samples of this research, only one **Western company in Electronic industry used feedback & questions service.** However, **Chinese electronic companies provided online shopping service and created interactive community**. As for some other industries, it is difficult to draw the results of the comparison between Chinese and Western companies in line with the number of samples are small.

Table 6.13 Comparative results of interface & menu analysis as per industry between Western and Chinese companies

Company name	Country region	Industry	Account type	Verification type	C101	C102	C103	C104	C105	C106	C107	C108	C109	C110	C111	C112	C113	C114	C201	C202	C203	C204	C205	C206	C207	C208	C209	C210	C211	C212	C213	C214	C215	C216	C217	C218	C219	C220	C221	C301	C302	C303	C304	C305	C4	C5	C6	Updated
Starbucks	0	1	0	1	1	0	1	1	0	1	1	0	0	0	0	0	0	0	1	0	0	0	1	0	0	0	0	0	0	0	0	0	0	0	0	0	0	0	0	0	0	0	0	0	0	0	0	1
McDonald's	0	1	0	1	0	0	0	0	0	0	0	0	0	0	0	0	0	0	0	0	1	1	1	0	0	0	0	0	0	0	0	0	0	0	0	0	0	0	0	0	1	0	0	0	0	0	0	0
Coca-Cola	0	1	1	1	1	0	1	1	0	0	0	0	0	0	0	0	0	0	0	0	0	0	0	0	0	0	0	0	0	0	0	0	0	0	0	0	0	0	0	1	0	0	0	0	1	0	0	0
Nestle S.A.	0	1	1	1	1	1	1	1	0	0	0	1	0	0	0	0	0	0	0	0	0	0	0	0	0	0	0	1	0	0	1	0	0	0	0	0	0	0	0	0	0	0	0	0	0	0	0	0
Unilever	0	1	1	1	0	0	1	0	0	1	0	0	0	1	0	0	0	0	0	0	0	0	0	0	0	0	0	0	0	0	0	0	0	0	0	0	0	0	0	0	0	1	0	0	0	0	0	1
PepsiCo	0	1	0	1	0	0	1	1	0	0	1	0	0	0	0	0	0	0	0	0	1	1	0	0	0	0	0	0	0	0	0	0	0	0	0	0	0	0	0	0	0	0	1	0	0	1	0	1
Sum1O			3	6	3	1	5	4	0	2	2	1	0	1	0	0	0	0	1	0	2	2	2	0	0	0	0	1	0	0	1	0	0	0	0	0	0	0	0	1	1	1	1	0	1	1	0	3
Wahaha	1	1	0	1	0	1	1	0	0	1	0	0	0	0	0	0	0	0	0	0	0	0	0	0	0	0	0	0	0	0	0	0	0	0	0	0	0	0	0	0	0	1	1	0	0	0	0	0
Tsingtao	1	1	1	1	0	0	0	0	0	1	0	0	0	0	0	0	0	0	0	0	0	0	0	0	0	0	0	0	1	0	1	0	0	0	0	0	0	0	0	0	0	1	1	0	0	0	0	0
Kweichow Moutai	1	1	1	1	0	0	1	1	0	1	0	0	0	0	0	1	0	0	0	0	0	0	0	0	0	0	0	1	1	0	0	0	0	0	0	0	0	0	0	0	0	1	0	0	0	0	0	0
YanJing Beer	1	1	0	1	0	1	1	1	0	1	0	0	0	0	0	1	0	0	0	0	0	0	0	0	0	0	0	0	1	0	0	0	0	0	0	0	0	0	0	0	0	0	0	0	0	0	1	0
Bright Food	1	1	1	1	0	0	1	1	0	1	0	1	0	0	0	1	0	0	1	0	0	0	0	0	0	0	0	0	1	0	0	0	0	0	0	0	0	0	0	0	0	0	0	0	0	0	1	0
Sum1C			3	5	0	2	4	3	0	5	0	1	0	0	0	3	0	0	1	0	0	0	0	0	0	0	0	1	4	0	1	0	0	0	0	0	0	0	0	0	0	3	2	0	0	0	2	0
Apple	0	2	1	0	0	0	1	1	0	1	1	0	0	0	0	0	0	0	0	1	0	0	0	0	0	0	0	0	0	0	0	0	0	0	0	0	0	0	0	0	0	0	0	0	0	1	0	0
IBM	0	2	1	1	0	0	1	1	0	1	0	0	0	0	0	0	0	0	0	0	0	0	0	0	0	0	0	0	0	0	0	0	0	0	0	0	0	0	0	1	0	0	0	0	0	0	0	0
Accenture	0	2	1	1	0	0	1	1	0	1	0	1	1	1	0	1	0	0	0	0	0	0	0	0	0	0	0	0	0	0	0	0	0	0	0	0	0	0	0	1	0	1	0	0	0	0	0	0
Microsoft	0	2	1	1	0	0	1	1	0	1	0	1	1	0	0	0	0	0	0	0	0	0	0	0	0	0	0	0	1	0	0	0	0	0	0	0	0	0	0	0	0	0	0	0	0	0	0	1
Intel	0	2	0	1	0	0	1	0	0	1	0	0	0	0	0	0	0	0	0	0	0	0	0	0	0	0	0	0	1	1	0	0	0	0	0	1	0	0	0	0	0	0	1	1	0	0	0	1
Cisco System	0	2	1	1	0	0	1	1	0	1	0	1	0	1	0	1	0	0	0	0	0	0	0	0	0	0	0	0	0	0	0	0	0	0	0	0	0	0	1	0	0	0	0	0	0	0	0	0
Sum2O			5	5	0	0	6	5	0	6	1	3	2	2	0	2	0	0	0	1	0	0	0	0	0	0	0	0	2	1	0	0	0	0	0	1	0	0	1	2	0	1	1	1	0	1	0	2
Huawei	1	2	1	1	0	0	1	0	0	0	0	0	1	0	1	0	1	0	0	0	0	0	0	0	0	0	0	0	1	0	0	0	0	0	0	0	0	0	0	0	0	0	0	0	0	0	0	0
ZTE	1	2	1	1	0	0	1	0	0	0	0	0	0	0	0	1	0	0	1	0	0	0	0	0	0	0	0	0	1	0	0	0	0	0	0	0	0	0	0	0	0	0	0	0	1	0	0	0
Sum2C			2	2	0	0	2	0	0	0	0	0	1	0	1	1	1	0	1	0	0	0	0	0	0	0	0	0	2	0	0	0	0	0	0	0	0	0	0	0	0	0	0	0	1	0	0	0
Walt Disney	0	3	1	1	1	1	1	1	1	1	0	0	0	0	0	0	0	0	0	0	0	0	0	0	0	0	0	0	0	0	0	0	0	0	0	0	0	0	0	0	0	1	0	0	1	0	0	0
Sum3O			1	1	1	1	1	1	1	1	0	0	0	0	0	0	0	0	0	0	0	0	0	0	0	0	0	0	0	0	0	0	0	0	0	0	0	0	0	0	0	1	0	0	1	0	0	0

Table 6. 13 (Continued)

Company name	Country region	Industry	Account type	Verifi-cation type	C101	C102	C103	C104	C105	C106	C107	C108	C109	C110	C111	C112	C113	C114	C201	C202	C203	C204	C205	C206	C207	C208	C209	C210	C211	C212	C213	C214	C215	C216	C217	C218	C219	C220	C221	C301	C302	C303	C304	C305	C4	C5	C6	Upd-ated
FedEx	0	4	0	1	0	0	0	0	1	1	0	1	1	0	0	0	0	0	0	0	0	0	0	1	1	1	1	1	0	0	0	0	0	0	0	0	0	0	0	0	0	0	0	0	1	0	0	0
UPS	0	4	1	2	1	0	1	1	0	1	0	1	1	1	1	0	0	0	0	0	0	0	0	0	0	0	0	0	0	0	0	0	0	0	0	0	0	0	0	0	0	0	0	0	0	0	0	0
Sum4O			1	3	1	0	1	1	1	2	0	2	2	1	1	0	0	0	0	0	0	0	0	1	1	1	1	1	0	0	0	0	0	0	0	0	0	0	0	0	0	0	0	0	1	0	0	0
General Electric	0	5	1	1	1	1	1	1	0	0	0	0	0	0	0	0	0	0	0	0	0	0	0	0	0	0	0	1	0	0	0	0	0	0	0	0	0	0	0	0	0	0	0	0	1	0	0	0
Sum5O			1	1	1	1	1	1	0	0	0	0	0	0	0	0	0	0	0	0	0	0	0	0	0	0	0	1	0	0	0	0	0	0	0	0	0	0	0	0	0	0	0	0	1	0	0	0
Haier	1	5	0	1	0	0	0	0	0	0	0	0	0	0	0	0	0	0	0	0	0	1	0	0	0	0	0	0	1	0	0	0	1	1	0	0	0	0	1	0	0	0	0	0	0	1	0	0
Xiaomi	1	5	0	1	0	0	1	0	0	0	0	0	0	0	0	0	1	0	0	0	0	0	0	0	0	0	0	0	1	0	0	0	0	0	1	1	0	0	0	0	0	0	0	0	0	0	0	1
Lenovo	1	5	0	1	0	0	1	1	0	1	0	0	0	0	0	0	1	1	0	0	0	0	0	0	0	0	0	0	1	0	0	0	0	0	0	0	0	0	0	0	0	0	1	0	0	1	0	0
Gree	1	5	0	1	1	1	1	1	0	0	1	0	0	0	0	1	0	0	0	0	0	1	0	0	0	0	1	0	1	0	0	0	0	0	0	0	1	0	0	0	0	0	0	0	0	0	0	0
Midea	1	5	0	1	0	0	0	0	1	0	0	0	0	0	0	0	1	0	0	0	0	0	0	0	0	0	1	0	1	1	0	0	0	0	0	0	0	0	0	0	1	0	1	1	0	1	0	0
TCL	1	5	1	1	0	1	1	0	0	0	0	0	0	0	0	0	0	0	0	0	0	0	0	0	0	0	0	0	1	0	0	0	0	0	0	0	0	1	0	0	0	0	1	1	0	1	0	1
Hisense	1	5	0	1	0	0	0	0	0	1	0	0	0	0	0	0	0	0	0	0	0	0	0	0	0	0	0	0	1	0	0	0	1	0	0	0	0	1	0	0	0	0	0	1	0	0	0	0
Sum5C			1	7	1	2	4	2	1	2	1	0	0	0	0	1	3	1	0	0	0	2	0	0	0	0	2	0	7	1	0	0	2	1	1	1	1	2	1	0	1	0	3	3	0	4	0	2
American Express	0	6	1	1	1	0	1	1	1	0	0	0	0	0	0	0	0	0	0	0	0	0	0	0	0	0	0	1	0	0	0	0	0	0	0	0	0	0	0	0	0	0	0	0	0	0	0	0
Sum6O			1	1	1	0	1	1	1	0	0	0	0	0	0	0	0	0	0	0	0	0	0	0	0	0	0	1	0	0	0	0	0	0	0	0	0	0	0	0	0	0	0	0	0	0	0	0
Marriott International	0	7	0	1	0	0	0	0	0	0	1	0	0	0	0	0	0	0	0	0	0	1	0	0	0	0	1	1	1	0	0	1	0	0	0	0	0	0	0	0	1	0	0	0	0	0	0	0
Sum7O			0	1	0	0	0	0	0	0	1	0	0	0	0	0	0	0	0	0	0	1	0	0	0	0	1	1	1	0	0	1	0	0	0	0	0	0	0	0	1	0	0	0	0	0	0	0
Nike	0	8	0	1	0	0	1	1	0	1	1	0	0	0	0	0	0	0	1	0	1	0	0	0	0	0	1	0	1	1	0	0	0	0	0	0	0	0	0	0	0	1	0	0	0	0	0	1
Sum8O			0	1	0	0	1	1	0	1	1	0	0	0	0	0	0	0	1	0	1	0	0	0	0	0	1	0	1	1	0	0	0	0	0	0	0	0	0	0	0	1	0	0	0	0	0	1
BMW	0	9	1	1	0	0	1	1	0	0	0	0	0	0	0	0	0	0	0	0	0	0	0	0	0	1	0	0	0	0	0	0	0	0	0	0	0	0	0	0	1	1	0	0	0	0	0	0
Volkswagen	0	9	1	1	0	0	1	1	0	0	0	0	0	0	0	0	0	0	0	0	0	0	0	0	0	0	0	0	0	0	0	0	0	0	0	0	0	0	0	0	0	0	0	0	0	0	0	1
Sum9O			2	2	0	0	2	2	0	0	0	0	0	0	0	0	0	0	0	0	0	0	0	0	0	1	0	0	0	0	0	0	0	0	0	0	0	0	0	0	1	1	0	0	0	0	0	1
BYD	1	9	1	1	0	0	1	1	0	1	0	0	0	0	0	0	0	0	0	0	0	1	0	0	0	0	0	0	0	0	0	0	0	0	0	0	0	0	0	0	0	0	0	0	0	1	0	0
Great Wall Motors	1	9	1	1	0	0	1	0	0	0	1	0	0	0	0	0	0	0	0	0	0	1	0	0	0	0	0	0	0	1	0	0	0	0	0	0	0	0	0	0	0	0	0	0	0	1	0	0
Saic Motor	1	9	0	1	0	0	1	1	0	1	0	0	0	0	0	1	0	0	0	0	0	0	0	0	0	0	0	0	0	1	0	0	0	0	0	0	0	1	0	1	0	1	1	0	0	0	0	0

Table 6.13 (Continued)

Company name	Country region	Industry	Account type	Verification type	C101	C102	C103	C104	C105	C106	C107	C108	C109	C110	C111	C112	C113	C114	C201	C202	C203	C204	C205	C206	C207	C208	C209	C210	C211	C212	C213	C214	C215	C216	C217	C218	C219	C220	C221	C301	C302	C303	C304	C305	C4	C5	C6	Updated
Geely	1	9	1	1	0	0	1	0	0	1	0	0	0	0	0	0	1	0	0	0	0	0	0	0	0	0	0	0	1	0	0	0	0	0	0	0	0	0	0	0	0	1	0	0	0	0	1	0
Sum9C			3	4	0	0	4	2	0	3	1	0	0	0	0	1	1	0	0	0	0	2	0	0	0	0	0	0	1	2	0	0	0	0	0	0	0	1	0	1	0	2	1	0	0	2	1	0
Procter & Gamble	0	10	1	1	0	0	0	0	0	0	0	0	0	0	0	0	0	0	0	0	0	0	0	0	0	0	0	0	0	0	0	0	0	0	0	0	0	0	0	0	0	0	0	0	0	0	0	1
DuPont	0	10	0	1	0	0	1	1	0	1	0	0	0	0	0	0	0	1	1	0	0	0	0	0	0	0	0	0	0	0	0	0	0	0	0	0	0	0	0	1	0	0	0	0	0	0	0	0
Sum100			1	2	0	0	1	1	0	1	0	0	0	0	0	0	0	1	1	0	0	0	0	0	0	0	0	0	0	0	0	0	0	0	0	0	0	0	0	1	0	0	0	0	0	0	0	1
Johnson & Johnson	0	11	1	2	0	0	0	0	0	1	0	0	0	0	0	0	0	0	0	0	0	0	0	0	0	0	0	0	0	0	0	0	0	0	0	0	0	0	0	0	0	0	0	0	1	0	0	0
3M	0	11	1	0	1	0	1	1	0	1	0	1	0	0	0	0	0	0	0	1	0	0	0	0	0	0	0	0	1	0	0	0	0	0	0	0	0	0	0	0	0	0	0	0	0	0	0	0
Sum110			2	2	1	0	1	1	0	2	0	1	0	0	0	0	0	0	0	1	0	0	0	0	0	0	0	0	1	0	0	0	0	0	0	0	0	0	0	0	0	0	0	0	1	0	0	0
Yunnan Baiyao	1	11	1	1	0	0	0	0	0	0	0	1	0	0	0	1	0	0	0	0	0	0	0	0	0	0	0	0	1	0	0	0	0	0	0	0	0	0	0	0	0	0	0	0	1	1	0	0
Sum11C			1	1	0	0	0	0	0	0	0	1	0	0	0	1	0	0	0	0	0	0	0	0	0	0	0	0	1	0	0	0	0	0	0	0	0	0	0	0	0	0	0	0	1	1	0	0
Boeing	0	12	1	1	1	1	1	0	0	1	0	0	0	0	0	0	0	0	0	0	0	0	0	0	0	0	0	0	0	0	0	0	0	0	0	0	0	0	0	0	0	0	0	0	0	0	0	1
Sum120			1	1	1	1	1	0	0	1	0	0	0	0	0	0	0	0	0	0	0	0	0	0	0	0	0	0	0	0	0	0	0	0	0	0	0	0	0	0	0	0	0	0	0	0	0	1
Exxon Mobil	0	13	1	1	0	0	0	0	0	1	0	0	0	1	0	1	0	0	0	0	0	0	0	0	0	0	0	0	0	0	0	0	0	0	0	0	0	0	0	0	0	0	0	0	0	0	0	0
Sum130			1	1	0	0	0	0	0	1	0	0	0	1	0	1	0	0	0	0	0	0	0	0	0	0	0	0	0	0	0	0	0	0	0	0	0	0	0	0	0	0	0	0	0	0	0	0
Wal-Mart Stores	0	14	0	1	0	0	1	0	1	1	1	0	0	0	0	0	0	0	0	0	0	0	1	0	0	0	1	1	0	0	0	0	0	0	0	0	0	0	0	0	0	0	0	0	0	0	0	0
Sum140			0	1	0	0	1	0	1	1	1	0	0	0	0	0	0	0	0	0	0	0	1	0	0	0	1	1	0	0	0	0	0	0	0	0	0	0	0	0	0	0	0	0	0	0	0	
WangFujing	1	14	0	1	0	0	1	0	0	0	0	0	0	0	0	1	0	1	0	0	1	0	0	0	0	0	0	0	1	1	0	0	1	0	0	0	0	0	0	0	1	0	0	0	0	1	0	0
SuNing	1	14	1	0	0	0	0	0	1	0	1	0	0	0	0	0	0	0	0	0	1	0	1	0	0	0	1	0	1	0	0	0	0	0	0	0	0	0	0	0	1	0	0	0	0	0	0	0
Gome	1	14	0	1	0	0	1	0	0	0	1	0	0	0	0	0	0	0	0	0	1	0	0	0	0	0	1	0	1	1	0	0	0	1	0	0	0	0	0	0	1	0	0	0	0	0	0	0
Sum14C			1	2	0	0	2	0	1	0	2	0	0	0	0	1	0	1	0	0	3	0	1	0	0	0	2	0	3	2	0	0	1	1	0	0	0	0	0	0	3	0	0	0	0	1	0	0
Caterpillar	0	15	1	1	1	0	1	1	0	1	0	1	0	0	0	1	0	0	0	0	0	0	0	0	0	0	0	0	0	0	0	0	0	0	0	0	0	0	0	0	0	0	0	0	0	0	0	1
Deere	0	15	0	1	1	0	1	0	0	1	0	1	0	0	0	1	0	0	0	0	0	0	0	0	0	0	0	0	0	0	0	0	0	0	0	0	0	0	0	1	0	0	0	0	0	0	0	1
]Sum150			1	2	2	0	2	1	0	2	0	2	0	0	0	2	0	0	0	0	0	0	0	0	0	0	0	0	0	0	0	0	0	0	0	0	0	0	0	1	0	0	0	0	0	0	0	2
SANY	1	15	1	1	0	0	1	0	0	0	0	0	1	0	0	0	0	0	0	0	1	0	0	0	0	0	0	0	1	1	0	0	0	0	0	0	0	0	0	0	0	0	0	0	0	0	0	1
Sum15C			1	1	0	0	1	0	0	0	0	0	1	0	0	0	0	0	0	0	1	0	0	0	0	0	0	0	1	1	0	0	0	0	0	0	0	0	0	0	0	0	0	0	0	0	0	1

Table 6. 13 (Continued)

Company name	Country region	Industry	Account type	Verification type	C101	C102	C103	C104	C105	C106	C107	C108	C109	C110	C111	C112	C113	C114	C201	C202	C203	C204	C205	C206	C207	C208	C209	C210	C211	C212	C213	C214	C215	C216	C217	C218	C219	C220	C221	C301	C302	C303	C304	C305	C4	C5	C6	Updated
HaiNan Airlines	1	16	0	1	0	0	0	0	1	1	0	0	0	0	0	0	0	0	0	0	0	1	0	0	0	0	0	1	0	0	0	0	0	1	0	0	0	1	1	0	0	0	0	0	0	0	0	0
Sum16C			0	1	0	0	0	0	1	1	0	0	0	0	0	0	0	0	0	0	0	1	0	0	0	0	0	1	0	0	0	0	0	1	0	0	0	1	1	0	0	0	0	0	0	0	0	0
Ping An	1	17	1	1	0	0	1	0	0	1	0	0	0	1	0	1	0	1	0	0	0	0	0	0	0	0	0	0	0	0	0	0	0	0	0	0	0	0	0	0	0	1	0	0	0	0	0	0
Sum17C			1	1	0	0	1	0	0	1	0	0	0	1	0	1	0	1	0	0	0	0	0	0	0	0	0	0	0	0	0	0	0	0	0	0	0	0	0	0	0	1	0	0	0	0	0	0
New Hope Group	1	18	1	1	0	0	1	1	0	1	0	1	0	0	0	1	0	0	0	0	0	0	0	0	0	0	0	0	0	0	0	0	0	0	0	0	0	0	0	0	0	0	0	0	1	0	0	0
Fosun	1	18	0	1	0	1	1	1	0	1	0	0	0	0	0	1	0	0	0	0	1	0	0	0	0	0	0	0	1	0	1	0	0	0	0	0	0	0	0	0	1	0	0	0	1	0	0	0
Sum18C			1	2	0	1	2	2	0	2	0	1	0	0	0	2	0	0	0	0	1	0	0	0	0	0	0	0	1	0	1	0	0	0	0	0	0	0	0	0	1	0	0	0	2	0	0	0
Wanda	1	19	1	1	0	0	1	1	0	0	0	0	0	0	0	0	0	0	0	0	0	0	0	0	0	0	0	0	0	0	0	0	0	0	0	0	0	0	0	1	0	0	0	0	0	0	0	1
Vanke	1	19	1	1	0	1	1	1	0	1	0	0	0	0	0	0	0	0	0	0	1	0	0	0	0	1	0	0	0	1	0	0	0	0	0	0	0	0	0	0	0	1	0	0	1	0	0	0
Country Garden	1	19	1	1	0	1	1	1	0	1	0	0	0	0	0	0	0	0	0	0	0	0	0	0	0	0	0	0	0	0	0	0	0	0	0	0	0	0	0	0	0	1	0	0	0	0	0	0
Sum19C			3	3	0	2	3	3	0	2	0	0	0	0	0	0	0	0	0	0	1	0	0	0	0	1	0	0	0	1	0	0	0	0	0	0	0	0	0	1	0	2	0	0	1	0	0	1

6.2 Analysis of push notification marketing

This section presents the second research line of WeChat case study, i.e., analyzing all companies' push notifications marketing during the specific observation period. **It is necessary to point out that the systematic measurement and classification framework built on Sina Weibo case study is adopted in the analysis of push notification marketing of WeChat case study.** This section begins by identifying the key performance indicators and setting observation period. Afterwards, data collection & processing, database creation are conducted. Finally, the cluster analyses for two groups (companies with subscription account & companies with service account) are presented respectively. The synthetic results are also stated by combing the findings of these two groups.

The process of the identification of KPIs for WeChat has been explained in section 4.2.2.3. Table 6.14 summarizes the identification of Wechat KPIs.

Table 6.14 Identification of WeChat KPIs

KPIs	Description
Number of push notification	How many times of sending "push notifications" in one month
Number of posts	How many posts have been published in one month
Number of readings	How many times of all posts to be read in one month
Number of likes	How many times of all posts to be liked in one month
Number of top comments	How many top comments have been received for all posts in one month

In WeChat case study, one-month observation period are set for all companies which has been described in section 4.2.2.3.

6.2.1 KPIs data collection, processing & database creation

6.2.1.1 Data collection

It shall be pointed out that WeChat is used most in the form of mobile App. In this research, data collection was done primarily through mobile phones where WeChat

App has been installed. Besides, all the collected data are the first-hand information for WeChat case study.

6.2.1.2 Data processing

Data processing work involves mainly data categorizing & coding, and data transforming to facilitate the creation of structured database.

(1) Data categorizing & data coding

The data has been categorized and coded as listed in table 6.15 so as to create the database.

Table 6.15 List of data category and coding for WeChat case study

No.	Abbreviation	Description	Coding/Data type
1	Company	Company name	String type
2	WCNID	WeChat name/WeChat ID	String type
3	Account type	WeChat account type	Service: 0 Subscription: 1
4	Country	Country region	Western: 0 Chinese: 1
5	Industry	Industry	1~19 (As per table 4.6 in section 4.1.5)
6	Industry detail	Industry detail	String type
7	Monthly trend	Monthly trend of pushing notification	1. No special trend 2. Weekend no "push notification" 3. Sunday no "push notification" 4. (1) Every Saturday no "push notification"; (2) Every Friday 5 posts; Other days 4 posts. 5. Every Tuesday sending "push notification" once involving one post
8	PuN	Total No. of times of monthly sending "push notifications"	Number type
9	P	Total No. of posts published monthly	Number type
10	R	Total No. of reading of all posts in one month	Number type
11	L	Total No. of likes of all posts in one month	Number type
12	C	Total No. of top comments of all posts in one month	Number type
13	F3	F3 = (R+L+C)/P	Number type
14	F4	F4 = Normalization of F3	Number type

These categories and codes are adopted to create the relevant database.

(2) Data transforming

Just like Sina Weibo case study, **the measurement of the level of interaction on WeChat channel was conducted in the same way, i.e., the total number of interactions such as number of reading, likes, and top comments on the basis of posts should be considered.** These numbers can reflect the proportion of users who have actually participated in one campaign such as reading, comments, and other behaviors in accordance with the available data on WeChat channel.

Therefore, a mathematical formula integrating all the KPIs was set up in order to evaluate the the level of interaction for WeChat platform and expressed as the following formula:

$$F3=(R+L+C)/P$$

where R, C and L are the total numbers of reading, top comments and likes during the observation period; and P is the total number of posts during the observation period.

The formula of F3 is dedicated to exploring the interaction between the company and its users, i.e., the level of interaction on WeChat platform. **The formula is built based on the impact of WeChat marketing, i.e., the number of interactions (total number of readings, top comments, and likes) on the basis of total number of posts.**

By following the method described in section 4.4, all the F3 data can be normalized to F4, which varies between 0 and 1, where "0" denotes the minimum level of interaction among all selected samples and "1" represents the maximum level of interaction among all selected samples. Thus, the companies' engagement with the audience on WeChat platform can be evaluated and classified in line with F4 as explained below:

F4 = normalized F3 = the level of interaction

6.2.1.3 Database creation

The procedure stated in section 4.4 was followed to create the database. Table 6.16 and table 6.17 show the excel format database in which the original data was recorded and organized for all companies (thirty-seven companies with subscription account & twenty-three ones with services account).

Table 6.16 Summary of database for companies with WeChat subscription account

No.	Company	WCNID	Account type	Country	Industry	Industry detail	Monthly trend	Monthly trend detail	PuN	P	R	L	C	F3	F4
1	Apple	iPhone 中文网/apple4cn	1	0	2	Computers	4	(1) Every Saturday no "push notification" (2) Every Friday 5 posts, other days 4 posts	26	108	187 869	392	160	1 744. 64	0. 03
2	Coca-Cola	可口可乐中国/coke18	1	0	1	Beverages	2	Weekend no "push notification"	3	3	15 947	102	35	5 361. 33	0. 11
3	Walt Disney	迪士尼中国/disney_ch	1	0	3	Entertainment	3	Sunday no "push notification"	13	19	98 898	1 076	117	5 267.95	0. 11
4	UPS	UPS 中国动态/UPS_China	1	0	4	Delivery	2	Weekend no "push notification"	10	15	9 279	140	19	629. 20	0. 01
5	General Electric	GE 中国/GEandME	1	0	5	Electronics	2	Weekend no "push notification"	9	9	62 790	442	29	7 029. 00	0. 15
6	American Express	美国运通/AmexChina	1	0	6	Consumer Credit Card and Related Services	3	Sunday no "push notification"	14	17	19 884	93	0	1 175. 12	0. 02
7	BMW	宝马中国/BMW_Official	1	0	9	Motor Vehicles	1	No special trend	24	24	1 085 303	3 193	343	45 368. 29	1. 00
8	Volkswagen	VWLive 大众共线/dzqc-zg	1	0	9	Motor Vehicles	1	No special trend	25	39	301 990	1 719	97	7 789.90	0. 17
9	Procter& Gamble	宝洁中国/pgchina1988	1	0	10	Soaps & Cosmetics	2	Weekend no "push notification"	8	8	22 018	219	8	2 780. 63	0. 05
10	IBM	IBM 中国/IBMGCG	1	0	2	Information Technology Services	2	Weekend no "push notification"	17	43	96 029	1 313	190	2 268. 19	0. 04
11	Accenture	埃森哲中国/accenture	1	0	2	Information Technology Services	2	Weekend no "push notification"	9	11	19 947	130	9	1 826. 00	0. 03
12	Johnson & Johnson	强生招聘/JNJ_recruitm	1	0	11	Pharmaceuticals	1	No special trend	6	8	32 212	280	13	4 063. 13	0. 08
13	3M	3M 中国区/mmm_china	1	0	11	Medical Products and Equipment	2	Weekend no "push notification"	12	18	65 247	349	192	3 654.89	0. 07

Table 6. 16 (Continued)

No.	Company	WCNID	Account type	Country	Industry	Industry detail	Monthly trend	Monthly trend detail	PuN	P	R	L	C	F3	F4
14	Microsoft	微软科技/mstech2014	1	0	2	Computer Software	3	Sunday no "push notification"	23	46	33 273	299	6	729.96	0. 01
15	Boeing	波音中国/boeingairpla	1	0	12	Aerospace and Defense	1	No special trend	5	5	8 327	47	34	1 681. 60	0. 03
16	Exxon Mobil	埃克森美孚中国/Exx	1	0	13	Petroleum Refining	5	Every Tuesday sending "push notification" once and one post	5	4	1 953	46	0	499. 75	0. 00
17	Nestle S.A.	雀巢中国/NestleCN	1	0	1	Consumer Food Products	2	Weekend no "push notification"	13	18	8 964	160	0	506.89	0. 00
18	Unilever	联合利华 U 关注/unile	1	0	1	Consumer Food Products	2	Weekend no "push notification"	12	15	9 556	291	20	657.80	0. 01
19	Caterpillar	卡特皮勒中国/caterp	1	0	15	Construction and Farm Machinery	2	Weekend no "push notification"	18	20	36 997	347	60	1 870. 20	0. 03
20	Cisco System	思科联天下/ciscowech	1	0	2	Network and other Communication Equip	3	Sunday no "push notification"	23	34	65 722	437	51	1 947. 35	0. 04
21	Huawei	华为/huaweicorp	1	1	2	Telecom Manufacturing and Services	1	No special trend	25	62	463 719	6 154	548	7 587. 44	0. 16
22	ZTE	中兴通讯/ZTEInChina	1	1	2	Telecom Manufacturing and Services	2	Weekend no "push notification"	20	48	191 906	2 036	104	4 042. 63	0. 08
23	TCL	TCL 铁粉社区/tcltiefen	1	1	5	Electronics / Electrical Appliances	3	Sunday no "push notification"	23	31	9 332	113	109	308. 19	0. 00

Table 6.16 (Continued)

No.	Company	WCNID	Account type	Country	Industry	Industry detail	Monthly trend	Monthly trend detail	PuN	P	R	L	C	F3	F4
24	BYD	比亚迪汽车/byd-auto	1	1	9	Motor Vehicles / Motor Vehicles Parts	1	No special trend	25	50	720 615	11 089	476	14 643.60	0.32
25	Great Wall Motors	长城汽车/greatwallmot	1	1	9	Motor Vehicles / Motor Vehicles Parts	3	Sunday no "push notification"	16	33	167 146	1 997	0	5 125.55	0.11
26	Geely	吉利控股集团/	1	1	9	Motor Vehicles / Motor Vehicles Parts	1	No special trend	15	23	154 449	1 151	75	6 768.48	0.14
27	Tsingtao	青岛啤酒/Tsingtao_Sin	1	1	1	Food / Beverage	2	Weekend no "push notification"	9	10	88 707	873	59	8 963.90	0.19
28	Kweichow Moutai	国酒茅台/maotaiguojiu	1	1	1	Food / Beverage	1	No special trend	1	1	4 122	33	0	4 155.00	0.09
29	Bright Food	光明食品集团/bright	1	1	1	Food / Beverage	2	Weekend no "push notification"	22	35	14 385	163	0	415.66	0.00
30	Yunnan Baiyao	云南白药/newbaiyao	1	1	11	Pharmaceuticals	2	Weekend no "push notification"	14	31	17 037	180	3	555.48	0.01
31	Ping An	中国平安/zhongguoping	1	1	17	Insurance	1	No special trend	26	39	543 910	3 654	66	14 041.79	0.30
32	SuNing	苏宁/suning365	1	1	14	Wholesale / Retail / Distribution	1	No special trend	21	84	45 231	511	315	548.30	0.01
33	Wanda	万达集团/guojiwanda	1	1	19	Real Estate	1	No special trend	25	54	1 070 110	5 437	434	19 925.57	0.44
34	Vanke	万科周刊/vankeweekly	1	1	19	Real Estate	3	Saturday no "push notification"	14	20	138 411	977	103	6 974.55	0.15
35	Country Garden	碧桂园/bgydream	1	1	19	Real Estate	1	No special trend	25	60	340 746	3 410	139	5 738.25	0.12
36	SANY	三一重工/sanyibox	1	1	15	Manufacturing	3	Sunday no "push notification"	23	29	148 843	772	250	5 167.76	0.11
37	New Hope Group	新希望集团/newhopewi	1	1	18	Diversification	1	No special trend	4	4	11 128	83	0	2 802.75	0.06

Table 6.17 Summary of database for companies with WeChat service account

No.	Company	WCNID	Account Type	Country	Industry	Industry Detail	Monthly Trend	Monthly Trend Detail	PuN	P	R	L	C	F3	F4
1	Starbucks	星巴克中国/xingbakezhongguo	0	0	1	Food Services	2	Weekend no "push notification"	4	22	1 869 539	12 165	251	85 543. 41	0.84
2	McDonald's	麦当劳/mcdonalds888	0	0	1	Food Services	3	Sunday no "push notification"	4	15	1 309 345	9 399	65	87 920. 60	0.86
3	FedEx	FedEx 中国/FedEx_China	0	0	4	Delivery	2	Weekend no "push notification"	4	5	13 616	96	0	2 742. 40	0. 03
4	Nike	NIKE/nikejdi	0	0	8	Apparel	1	No special trend	2	6	391 680	1 544	47	65 545. 17	0. 64
5	Wal-Mart Stores	沃尔玛/Walmart_Hyper	0	0	14	General Merchandisers	2	Weekend no "push notification"	4	20	1 398 907	3 030	241	70 108.90	0. 69
6	PepsiCo	百事中国/BAISHIPEPSICO	0	0	1	Consumer Food Products	1	No special trend	2	2	27 544	353	44	13 970. 50	0. 14
7	Deere	约翰迪尔/JohnDeereChina	0	0	15	Construction and Farm Machinery	2	Weekend no "push notification"	3	4	18 891	154	0	4 761. 25	0. 05
8	Marriott International	万豪礼赏/ marriottgroup	0	0	7	Hotel / Casino / Resorts	2	Weekend no "push notification"	4	11	31 658	115	8	2 889. 18	0. 03
9	DuPont	杜邦特能壁纸/	0	0	10	Chemicals	1	No special trend	3	3	4 268	36	3	1 435. 67	0. 01
10	Intel	英特尔中国/intel-china	0	0	2	Semiconductors	3	Sunday no "push notification"	4	24	931 890	1 041	243	38 882. 25	0. 38
11	Haier	海尔家电/Haier_jiadian	0	1	5	Electronics / Electrical Appliances	2	Weekend no "push notification"	2	4	53 661	756	19	13 609. 00	0. 13
12	Xiaomi	小米手机/xmsj816	0	1	5	Electronics / Electrical Appliances	1	No special trend	1	3	300 000	5 917	47	101 988. 00	1. 00
13	Lenovo	联想/lenovo1984	0	1	5	Electronics / Electrical Appliances	2	Weekend no "push notification"	4	14	97 627	635	175	7 031. 21	0. 07

Table 6. 17 (Continued)

No.	Company	WCNID	Account Type	Country	Industry	Industry Detail	Monthly Trend	Monthly Trend Detail	PuN	P	R	L	C	F3	F4
14	Gree	格力电器/glfwh1991	0	1	5	Electronics / Electrical Appliances	2	Weekend no "push notification"	3	7	116 278	828	0	16 729. 43	0. 16
15	Midea	美的会员/mideafw	0	1	5	Electronics / Electrical Appliances	2	Weekend no "push notification"	4	14	804 311	690	0	57 500. 07	0. 56
16	Hisense	海信/hisense1969	0	1	5	Electronics / Electrical Appliances	1	No special trend	0	0	0	0	0	0. 00	0. 00
17	Saic Motor	上汽集团/SAIC_ MOTOR_	0	1	9	Motor Vehicles / Motor Vehicles Parts	3	Sunday no "push notification"	3	4	45 472	168	13	11 413. 25	0. 11
18	Wahaha	娃哈哈/YourWahaha	0	1	1	Food / Beverage	2	Weekend no "push notification"	4	19	959 152	4 289	197	50 717. 79	0. 50
19	YanJing Beer	燕京啤酒/yanjing_beer _group	0	1	1	Food / Beverage	1	No special trend	1	3	4 821	64	1	1 628. 67	0. 02
20	HaiNan Airlines	海南航空/Hnairlines	0	1	16	Airlines	2	Weekend no "push notification"	4	20	216 680	448	0	10 856. 40	0. 11
21	WangFujing	王府井集团/wfjbh1955	0	1	14	Wholesale / Retail / Distribution	2	Weekend no "push notification"	4	18	107 011	324	112	5 969. 28	0. 06
22	Gome	国美在线/gome1314	0	1	14	Wholesale / Retail / Distribution	2	Weekend no "push notification"	4	3	5 728	8	0	1 912. 00	0. 02
23	Fosun	复星/fuxing_2014	0	1	18	Diversification	3	Sunday no "push notification"	4	16	56 045	321	18	3 524. 00	0. 03

6.2.2 The results of descriptive statistical analysis of key indicators

This part presents the basic data exploration through descriptive statistical analysis by using SPSS software for thirty-seven companies using subscription account and twenty-three companies with service account. It is necessary to note that the code "PuN" means the number of sending push notification in one month and other codes have been explained in table 6.15 in line with data categorizing & data coding.

6.2.2.1 Descriptive statistical analysis for 37 companies with subscription account

Table 6.18 presents the basic statistics results of key indicators for companies with subscription account. It can be drawn that one company only pushed feeds once to their subscribers in one month, whereas another company sent push notification twenty-sixth times to their followers. The results indicate the different level of activity between companies.

Table 6.18 Basic statistics results for companies with WeChat subscription account

Indicator		Country region	Monthly trend	PuN	P	R	L	C	F3	F4
N	Valid	37	37	37	37	37	37	37	37	37
	Missing	0	0	0	0	0	0	0	0	0
Mean		0.46	2.00	15.76	29.14	170 594.65	1 343.46	109.84	5 530.18	0.12
Minimum		0	1	1	1	1 953	33	0	308.19	00
Maximum		1	5	26	108	1 085 303	11 089	548	45 368.29	1.00
Sum		17	74	583	1 078	6 312 002	49 708	4 064	204 616.72	4.28

In order to explore the monthly trend of broadcasting push notification among all companies, i.e., finding out which days are the best choices to send push notification within a week, five trends were summarized by authors by reviewing their push notification behavior in one month. It is necessary to note that "weekend no push notification" as shown in table 6.19 means the company did not send push notification on Saturday & Sunday; "Sunday no push notification" means the company did not push feeds to its subscribers on Sunday; as for "every Saturday no push notification" + "every Friday 5 posts, other days 4 posts", only one company Apple adopted this trend; as for "every Tuesday sending push notification once involving one post", only one company Exxon Mobil adopted this trend. The overall results are shown in table 6.19. It can be found that fourteen of thirty-seven companies did not send push notification to their subscribers on weekends (Saturday + Sunday). Moreover, eight of them did not push feeds to their followers on Sunday. Therefore, **the weekends should be avoided to push feeds to their subscribers.**

Table 6.19 Frequency table: Monthly Trend (Subscription account)

Monthly trend detail		Frequency	Percent /%	Valid percent/%	Cumulative Percent/%
Valid	No special trend	13	35.1	35.1	35.1
	Weekend no "push notification"	14	37.8	37.8	73.0
	Sunday no "push notification"	8	21.6	21.6	94.6
	(1) Every Saturday no "push notification" (2) Every Friday 5 posts, other days 4 posts	1	2.7	2.7	97.3
	Every Tuesday sending "push notification" once involving one post	1	2.7	2.7	100.0
	Total	37	100.0	100.0	—

Next, the basic statistics results of PuN, R, L, C for all companies with WeChat subscription account are presented in the following bar charts. With respect to the number of push notification, the company can push thirty times in one month in line with the feature of subscription account. It can be seen from the figure 6.4; nineteen of them have pushed more than or equal to fifteen times. Or, in other words, **almost half of the companies with subscription account have sent push notification once every two days.**

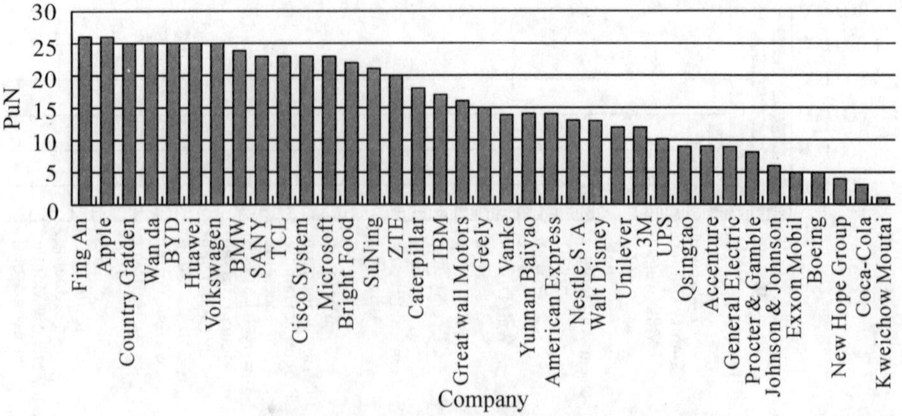

Figure 6. 4　PuN (subscription account)

With respect to the number of posts, as shown in Figure 6. 5, one curve formed by this bar chat, the first half of the curve shows the companies with a lot of publication, the latter part of the curve presents the companies with less published content. Moreover, there is a certain correlation between the number of push notification and the number of posts. **That is to say that the companies have sent push notification more times to their followers. Correspondingly, the number of posts is big, too.**

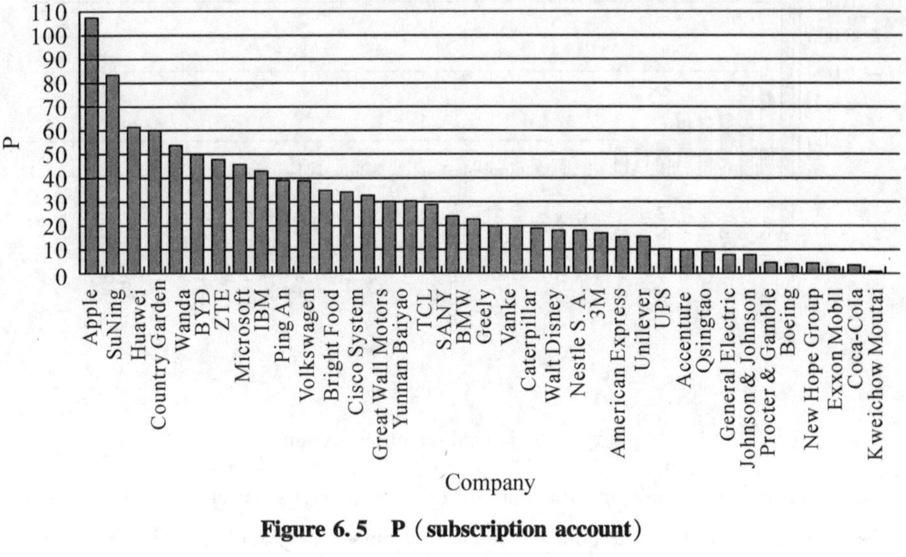

Figure 6. 5　P (subscription account)

As for the number of reading, it can be stated from Figure 6. 6 that only few companies have got the big number of reading. In addition, some companies with a lot of posts did not obtain the big number of reading, e.g., the companies Apple & SuNing.

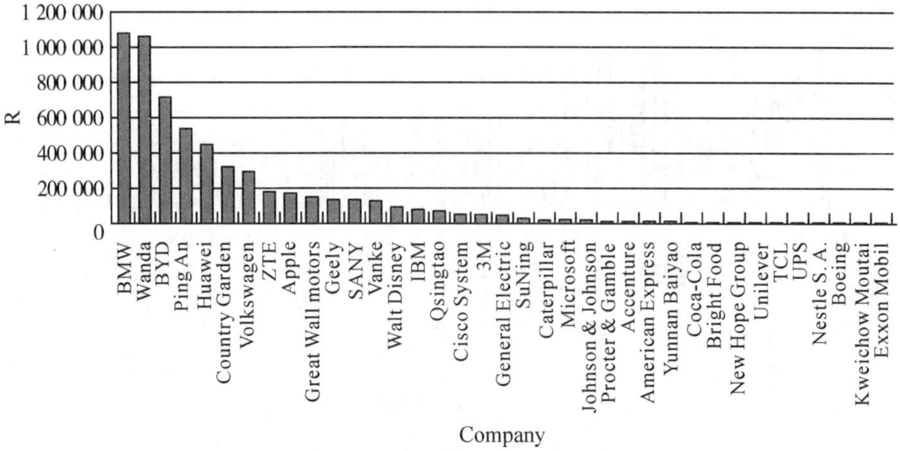

Figure 6.6　R (subscription account)

With respect to the number of likes, as shown in figure 6.7, a certain correlation exists between the number of reading and the number of likes. It can be found that **companies with big number of reading normally have acquired big number of likes, too.**

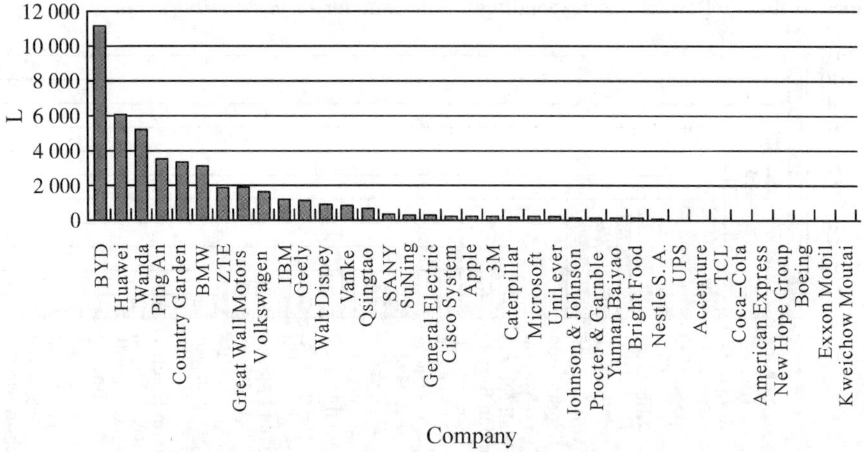

Figure 6.7　L (subscription account)

Meanwhile, by analyzing the number of top comments as shown in figure 6.8, there exist two different directions. One is that **some companies with big number of likes have acquired the big number of top comments; whereas** another direction is that **some companies with small number of likes have also obtained the big number of top comments,** e.g., companies SuNing & SANY.

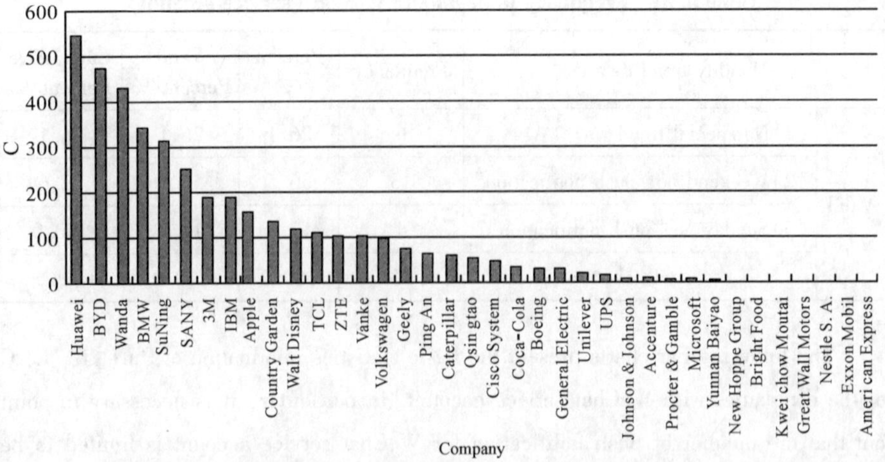

Figure 6. 8 C (subscription account)

6. 2. 2. 2 Descriptive statistical analysis for 23 companies with service account

Similarly, the basic statistics results of key indicators for companies with service account are summarized in table 6. 20. It can be found that one of them did not broadcast anything to its followers in one-month observation period. Thus this has led to the number of posts, reading, likes and top comments is "zero". Therefore, in this research, this company was inactive during the observation timeline.

Table 6. 20 Basic statistics results for companies with WeChat service account

Indicator		Country region	Monthly trend	PuN	P	R	L	C	F3	F4
N	Valid	23	23	23	23	23	23	23	23	23
	Missing	0	0	0	0	0	0	0	0	0
Mean		0. 57	1.91	3. 13	10. 30	381 048.87	1 842. 65	64. 52	28 551. 24	0. 28
Range		1	2	4	24	1 869 539	12 165	251	101 988. 00	1. 00
Minimum		0	1	0	0	0	0	0	0. 00	0. 00
Maximum		1	3	4	24	1 869 539	12 165	251	101 988. 00	1. 00

As shown in table 6. 21, thirteen of twenty-three companies did not send push notifications to their followers on weekends (Saturday + Sunday). Furthermore, four of them did not broadcast messages to their fans on Sunday. Therefore, **companies with service account preferred to avoid the weekends to broadcast push notification to their followers.**

Table 6.21 Frequency table: monthly trend (service account)

Monthly trend detail		Frequency	Percent /%	Valid Percent/%	Cumulative Percent/%
Valid	(1) No special trend	6	26.1	26.1	26.1
	(2) Weekend no "push notification"	13	56.5	56.5	82.6
	(3) Sunday no "push notification"	4	17.4	17.4	100.0
	Total	23	100.0	100.0	

The following bar charts present the basic statistics information of PuN, R, L, C of the companies with WeChat service account. In particular, it is necessary to point out that the number of push notification for WeChat service account is limited to be four in line with its feature, i.e., the maximum number of push notification is four in one month. It can be stated from figure 6.9 that **thirteen companies have sent push notification four times; four companies with three times; three companies with two times; two companies with once; and one company with "zero" push notification.**

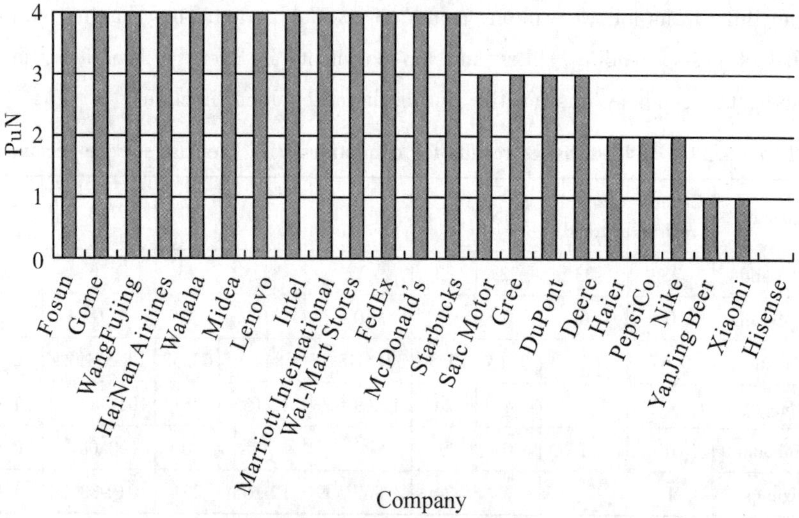

Figure 6.9 PuN (service account)

Regarding to the number of posts, it can be addressed from figure 6.10 that the number of posts for most of companies is related to their number of push notification, i.e., **big number of push notification can result in big number of posts. However, there are some exceptions, e.g., companies Gome & Dupont.**

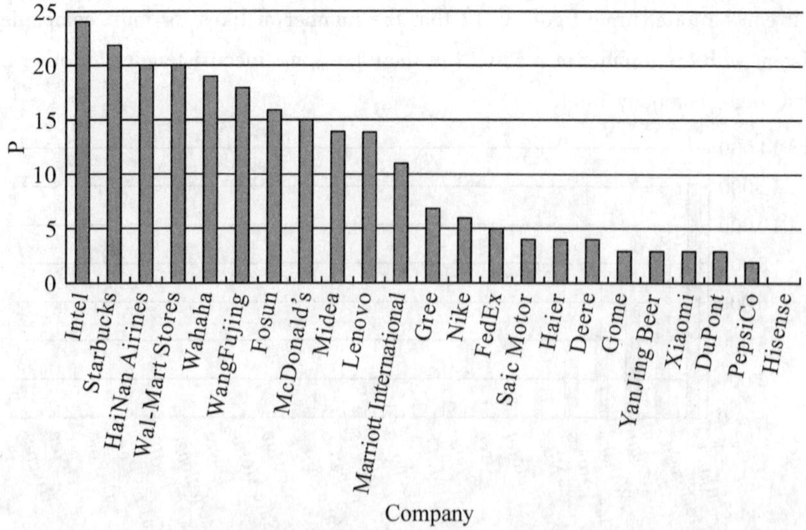

Figure 6.10 P (service account)

With respect to the number of reading, it can be drawn from figure 6.11 that there exists a certain correlation between the number of posts and the number of reading for **some companies.** For example, companies Starbucks & Wal-Mart Stores **have got a big number of readings based on their big number of posts. Nevertheless, other companies have obtained the opposite results, i.e., big number of posts does not lead to big number of reading,** e.g., companies WangFujing & Fosun.

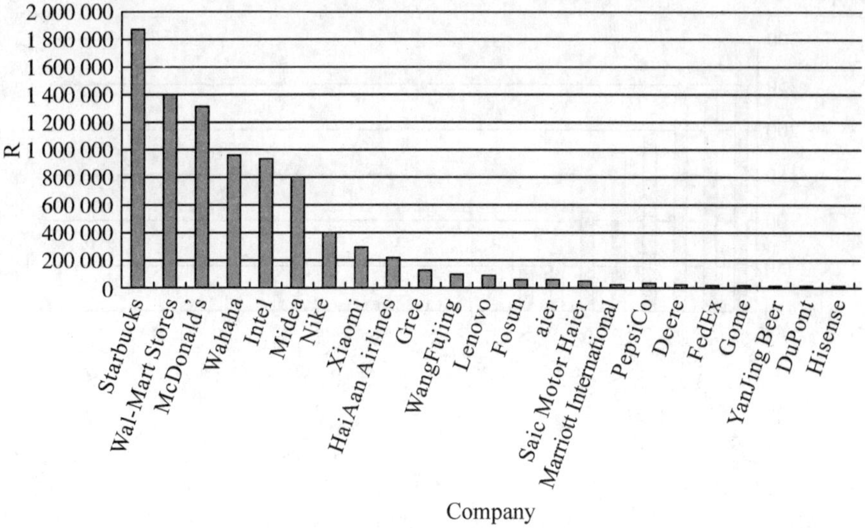

Figure 6.11 R (service account)

It can be found from figure 6. 12 that **the number of likes for most companies is consistent with the number of reading.** But there are some inconsistencies for other companies, e.g., company Intel.

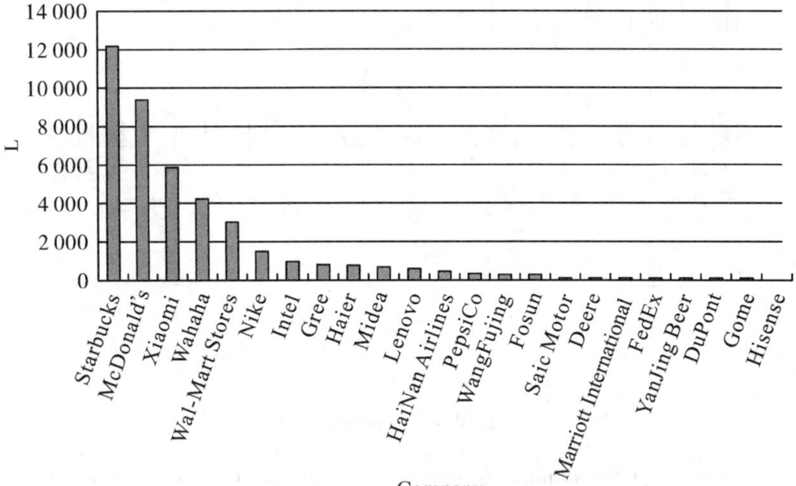

Figure 6. 12　L (service account)

As for the number of top comments, as shown in figure 6. 13, **some companies have acquired a lot of top comments based on their big number of likes. However, other companies have also obtained lots of top comments without big number of likes**, e.g., companies Lenovo & WangFujing.

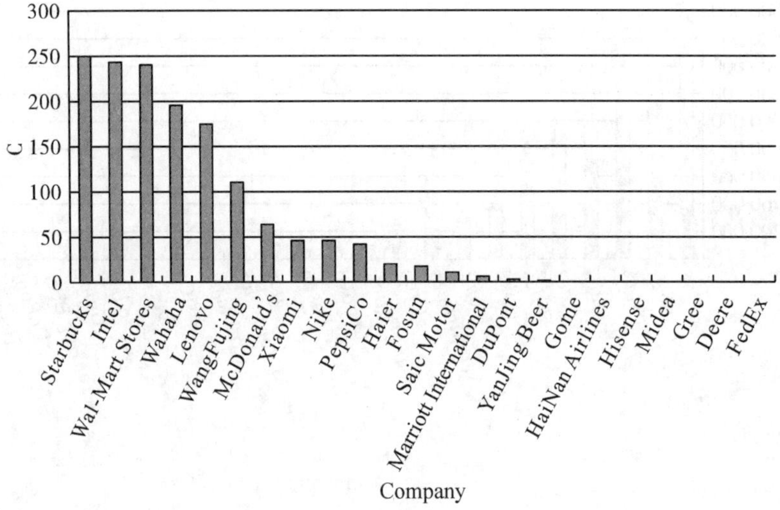

Figure 6. 13　C (service account)

Once the descriptive statistical analysis of KPIs for all companies has been explained, the cluster analysis is discussed in the next section.

6.2.3 The results of cluster analysis

This section presents the cluster analysis process and its results for companies with service account & companies with subscription account respectively.

The cluster analysis for WeChat case study has been adopted the similar approach used in Sina Weibo case study. Specifically, the cluster analysis process includes the evaluation of the level of activity and the level of interaction. Afterwards, synthetic evaluation and grouping are conducted by combining these two factors. Next, the cluster analysis for companies with service account is presented firstly in the next section.

6.2.3.1 Cluster analysis (service account)

This section presents the process and results of cluster analysis for companies with service account.

(1) Evaluation of the level of activity (service account)

As mentioned in section 3.3.1, the number of push notification is a core factor to distinguish subscription accounts from service accounts. During the observation period, the degree of activity of a company can be reflected by frequency of push notification. For any company, higher frequency of push notification, higher level of activity should be considered. So, **in WeChat case study, the level of activity was measured through PuN.**

The level of activity for WeChat case study was designed into three levels, i.e., inactive, active and very active, as the same as Sina Weibo case study. Table 6.22 summarizes the number of push notification of the companies with service account.

Table 6.22 Number of push notification of companies with service account

No.	Company	PuN
1	Starbucks	4
2	McDonald's	4
3	FedEx	4
4	Nike	2
5	Wal-Mart Stores	4

Table 6.22(Continued)

No.	Company	PuN
6	PepsiCo	2
7	Deere	3
8	Marriott International	4
9	DuPont	3
10	Intel	4
11	Haier	2
12	Xiaomi	1
13	Lenovo	4
14	Gree	3
15	Midea	4
16	Hisense	0
17	Saic Motor	3
18	Wahaha	4
19	YanJing Beer	1
20	HaiNan Airlines	4
21	WangFujing	4
22	Gome	4
23	Fosun	4
	SumPuN_Serv	72
	MeanPuN_Serv	3.1

Note: SumPuN_Serv = sum of number of push notifications of 23 companies with service account, MeanPuN_Serv = average of number of push notifications of 23 companies with service account.

By taking into account the limit of the number of push notification for service account (maximum four) in this research, manual grouping analysis as per PuN for the companies with service account was made and the results are given in table 6.23.

Table 6.23 Manual grouping as per PuN for companies with service account

Cluster	No.	Company	PuN
1	16	Hisense	0
	12	Xiaomi	1
	19	YanJing Beer	1

Table 6.23(Continued)

Cluster	No.	Company	PuN
2	4	Nike	2
	6	PepsiCo	2
	11	Haier	2
	7	Deere	3
	9	DuPont	3
	14	Gree	3
	17	Saic Motor	3
3	1	Starbucks	4
	2	McDonald's	4
	3	FedEx	4
	5	Wal-Mart Stores	4
	8	Marriott International	4
	10	Intel	4
	13	Lenovo	4
	15	Midea	4
	18	Wahaha	4
	20	HaiNan Airlines	4
	21	WangFujing	4
	22	Gome	4
	23	Fosun	4

From a practical point of view, for these twenty-three companies, three groups are classified as per the following rule:

① Inactive: PuN = [0, 1].

② Active: PuN = [2, 3].

③ Very active: PuN = [4].

The company with service account can be identified as inactive if it only sent push notification to its users once or less within a month. Nevertheless, one company can be identified as active if it broadcasted push notification twice or three times during the observation period. Moreover, one company can be identified very active if it used the maximum number of push notification, i.e., four.

The results of the companies with service account assigned to the corresponding groups are shown below:

① **Inactive**: PuN = [0, 1]

Western companies (0).

Chinese companies (3): Hisense, Xiaomi, YanJing Beer.

② **Active**: PuN = [2, 3]

Western companies (4): Nike, PepsiCo, Deere, DuPont.

Chinese companies (3): Haier, Gree, Saic Motor.

③ **Very active**: PuN = [4]

Western companies (6): Starbucks, McDonald's, FedEx, Wal-Mart Stores, Marriott International, Intel.

Chinese companies (7): Lenovo, Midea, Wahaha, HaiNan Airlines, WangFujing. Gome, Fosun.

It is necessary to note that the numerical difference of "number of push notification" for companies with service account is quite small considering the numerical range is [0, 4].

(2) Evaluation of the level of interaction (service account)

The core factors F3 & F4 for measuring the level of interaction which has been explained in detail in section 6.2.1, namely, *Data transforming*. The hierarchical cluster analysis for the companies with service account was performed via SPSS software in line with the value of F4. The results are shown in figure 6.14.

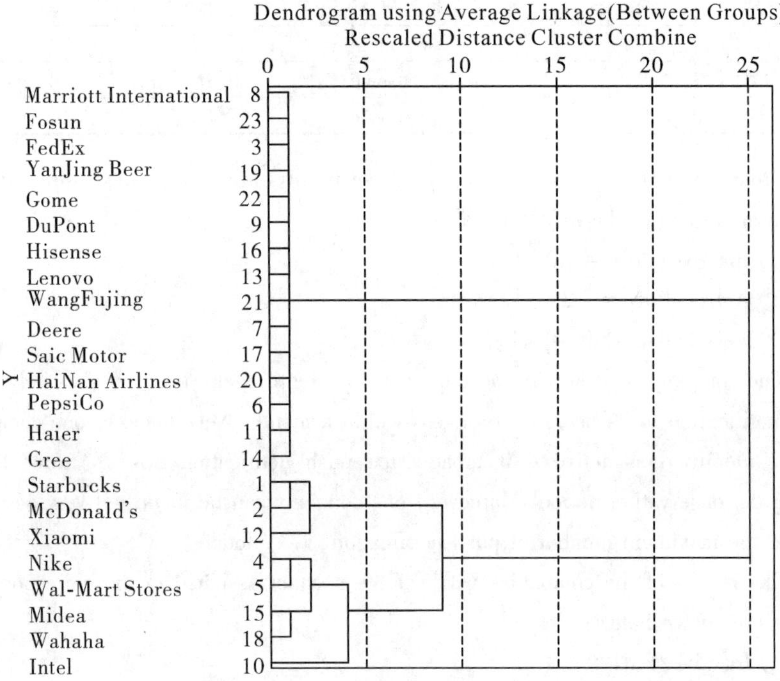

Figure 6.14 Dendrogram of hierarchical cluster analysis as per F4 for companies with service account

According to the dendrogram seen in figure 6.14, four groups can be identified and four degrees of the level of interaction can also be summarized as the same as the Sina Weibo case study, i.e., very low level of interaction, low level of interaction, medium level of interaction and high level of interaction. The four groups are presented in table 6.24.

Table 6.24 Results of hierarchical cluster analysis as per F4 for companies with service account

Cluster	No.	Company	F3	F4
1	3	FedEx	2 742.40	0.03
	6	PepsiCo	13 970.50	0.14
	7	Deere	4 761.25	0.05
	8	Marriott International	2 889.18	0.03
	9	DuPont	1 435.67	0.01
	11	Haier	13 609.00	0.13
	13	Lenovo	7 031.21	0.07
	14	Gree	16 729.43	0.16
	16	Hisense	0.00	0.00
	17	Saic Motor	11 413.25	0.11
	19	YanJing Beer	1 628.67	0.02
	20	HaiNan Airlines	10 856.40	0.11
	21	WangFujing	5 969.28	0.06
	22	Gome	1 912.00	0.02
	23	Fosun	3 524.00	0.03
2	10	Intel	38 882.25	0.38
3	4	Nike	65 545.17	0.64
	5	Wal-Mart Stores	70 108.90	0.69
	15	Midea	57 500.07	0.56
	18	Wahaha	50 717.79	0.50
4	1	Starbucks	85 543.41	0.84
	2	McDonald's	87 920.60	0.86
	12	Xiaomi	101 988.00	1.00

According to the value of F4 as shown in table 6.24, the grouping ranges for companies with service account can be summarized as: ① $0.0 \leqslant F4 \leqslant 0.2$; ② $0.2 < F4 \leqslant 0.45$; ③ $0.45 < F4 \leqslant 0.7$; ④ $0.7 < F4 \leqslant 1.0$.

Specifically, the classification rule for companies with service account is described as given below:

① Very low interaction 0. 0 ≤ F4 ≤ 0. 2.

② Low interaction: 0. 2<F4 ≤ 0. 45.

③ Medium interaction: 0. 45<F4 ≤ 0. 7.

④ High interaction: 0. 7<F4 ≤ 1. 0.

By applying this rule, the results of the companies assigned to the corresponding groups are given below.

①Very low interaction: 0. 0 ≤ F4 ≤ 0. 2.

Western companies (5): FedEx, PepsiCo, Deere, Marriott International, DuPont.

Chinese companies (10): Haier, Lenovo, Gree, Hisense, Saic Motor, YanJing Beer, HaiNan Airlines, WangFujing, Gome, Fosun.

②Low interaction: 0. 2<F4 ≤ 0. 45.

Western companies (1): Intel.

Chinese companies (0).

③Medium interaction: 0. 45<F4 ≤ 0. 7.

Western companies (2): Nike, Wal-Mart Stores.

Chinese companies (2): Midea, Wahaha.

④High interaction: 0. 7<F4 ≤ 1. 0.

Western companies (2): Starbucks, McDonald's.

Chinese companies (1): Xiaomi.

It can be seen that **totally seven of twenty-three companies with service accounts have achieved medium or high interaction with their users on WeChat** channel during the observation period.

(3) Synthetic evaluation and grouping (service account)

After integrating the two factors, "the level of activity" and "the level of interaction", a synthetic evaluation and grouping can be built for the companies with service account and expressed by table 6. 25 & figure 6. 15.

Table 6. 25 Synthetic evaluation and classification for companies with service account

			Level of Interaction (1) Very low interaction: 0. 0 ≤ F4 ≤ 0. 2 (2) Low interaction: 0. 2 < F4 ≤ 0. 45 (3) Medium interaction: 0. 45 < F4 ≤ 0. 7 (4) High interaction: 0. 7 < F4 ≤ 1. 0			
			Very low	Low	Medium	High
Level of Activity	(1) Inactive:PuN=[0,1] (2) Active:PuN=[2,3] (3) Very active:PuN=[4]	Inactive	Hisense YanJing Beer			Xiaomi
		Active	PepsiCo Haier Deere DuPont Gree Saic Motor		Nike	
		Very Active	FedEx Marriott International Lenovo HaiNan Airlines WangFujing Gome Fosun	Intel	Wal-Mart Stores Midea Wahaha	Starbucks McDonald's

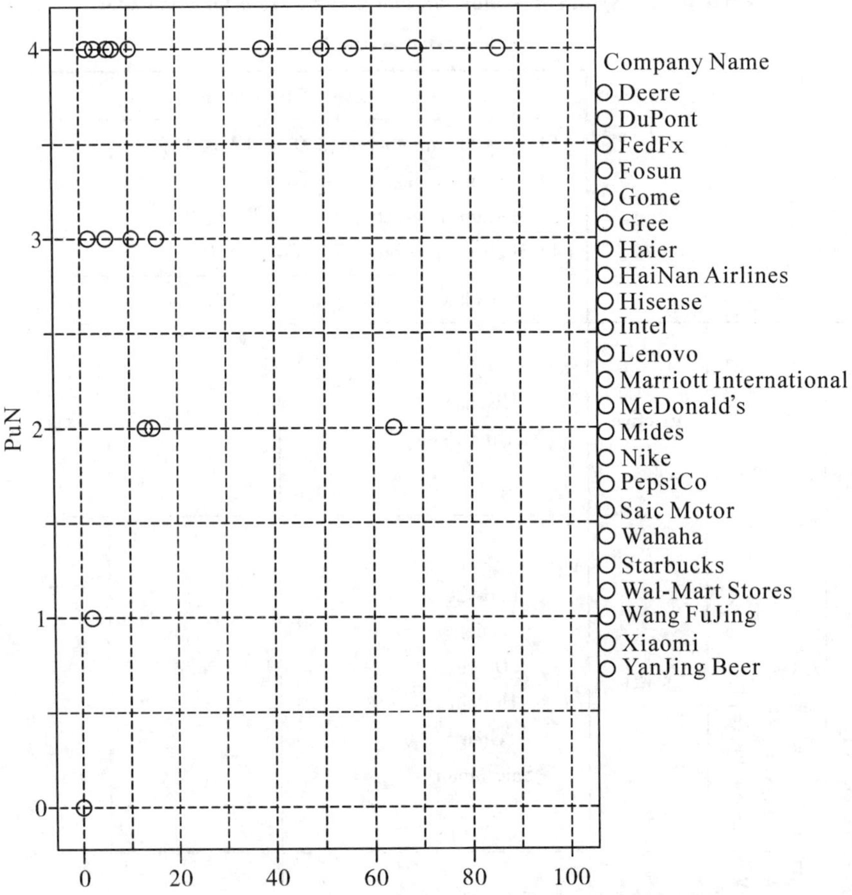

Figure 6.15 Scatter plot PuN vs. F4 for companies with service account

According to table 6.25, all companies can be divided into the following 12 groups.

Group C1: Inactive & very low interaction.

Western companies (0).

Chinese companies (2): Hisense, YanJing Beer.

Group C2: Inactive & low interaction.

Western companies (0).

Chinese companies (0).

Group C3: Inactive & medium interaction

Western companies (0).

Chinese companies (0).

Group C4: Inactive & high interaction.

Western companies (0).

Chinese companies (1): Xiaomi.

Group C5: Active & very low interaction.

Western companies (3): PepsiCo, Deere, DuPont.

Chinese companies (3): Haier, Gree, Saic Motor.

Group C6: Active & low interaction.

Western companies (0).

Chinese companies (0).

Group C7: Active & medium interaction.

Western companies (1): Nike.

Chinese companies (0).

Group C8: Active & high interaction.

Western companies (0).

Chinese companies (0).

Group C9: Very active & very low interaction.

Western companies (2): FedEx, Marriott International.

Chinese companies (5): Lenovo, HaiNan Airlines, WangFujing, Gome, Fosun.

Group C10: Very active & low interaction.

Western companies (1): Intel.

Chinese companies (0).

Group C11: Very active & medium interaction.

Western companies (1): Wal-Mart Stores.

Chinese companies (2): Midea, Wahaha.

Group C12: Very active & high interaction.

Western companies (2): Starbucks, McDonald's.

Chinese companies (0).

Once the cluster analysis for companies with service account has been completed, the same work for companies with subscription account is conducted in a similar way.

6.2.3.2 Cluster analysis (subscription account)

This section presents the process and results of cluster analysis of companies with subscription account.

(1) Evaluation of the level of activity (subscription account)

The evaluation of the level of activity for companies with subscription account was conducted in the same way as service account. Also, the level of activity was measured through PuN (the number of push notification). Table 6. 26 summarizes the number of push notifications of companies with subscription account.

Table 6. 26 Number of push notifications of companies with subscription account

No.	Company	PuN
1	Apple	26
2	Coca-Cola	3
3	Walt Disney	13
4	UPS	10
5	General Electric	9
6	American Express	14
7	BMW	24
8	Volkswagen	25
9	Procter & Gamble	8
10	IBM	17
11	Accenture	9
12	Johnson & Johnson	6
13	3M	12
14	Microsoft	23
15	Boeing	5
16	Exxon Mobil	5
17	Nestle S.A.	13
18	Unilever	12
19	Caterpillar	18
20	Cisco System	23
21	Huawei	25
22	ZTE	20

Table 6. 26(Continued)

No.	Company	PuN
23	TCL	23
24	BYD	25
25	Great Wall Motors	16
26	Geely	15
27	Tsingtao	9
28	Kweichow Moutai	1
29	Bright Food	22
30	Yunnan Baiyao	14
31	Ping An	26
32	SuNing	21
33	Wanda	25
34	Vanke	14
35	Country Garden	25
36	SANY	23
37	New Hope Group	4
	SumPuN_Subs	583
	MeanPuN_Subs	15.8

Note: SumPuN_Subs = sum of number of push notification of 37 companies with subscription account,
MeanPuN_Subs = average of number of push notification of 37 companies with subscription account.

Based on the data, Hierarchical cluster analysis as per PuN for companies with subscription account was performed by SPSS software and the results are given in figure 6. 16.

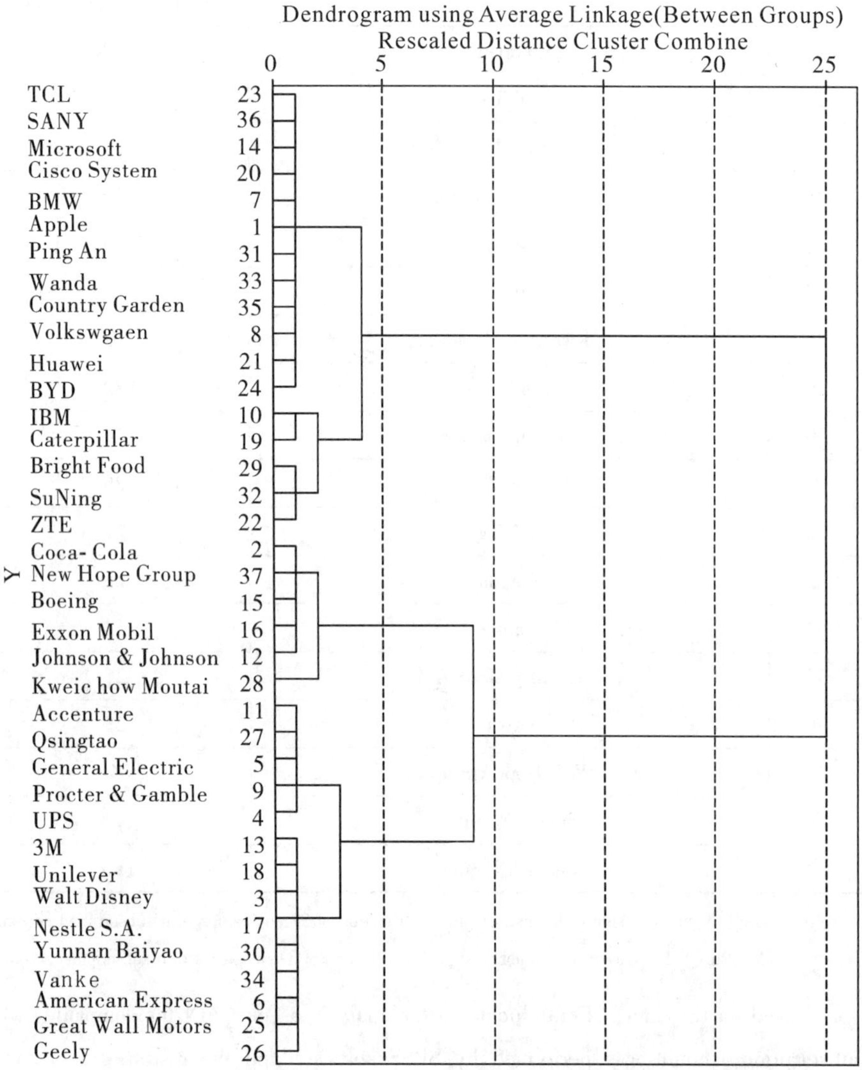

Figure 6. 16 Dendrogram of hierarchical cluster analysis as per PuN for companies with subscription account

In order to obtain three degrees of the level of activity as the same as companies with service account, it can be stated from figure 6. 16 that three grouping results can be summarized in table 6. 27.

Table 6.27 Results of hierarchical cluster analysis as per PuN for companies with subscription account

Cluster	No.	Company	PuN
1	2	Coca-Cola	3
	12	Johnson & Johnson	6
	15	Boeing	5
	16	Exxon Mobil	5
	28	Kweichow Moutai	1
	37	New Hope Group	4
2	3	Walt Disney	13
	6	American Express	14
	13	3M	12
	17	Nestle S.A.	13
	18	Unilever	12
	25	Great Wall Motors	16
	26	Geely	15
	30	Yunnan Baiyao	14
	34	Vanke	14
	4	UPS	10
	5	General Electric	9
	9	Procter & Gamble	8
	11	Accenture	9
	27	Tsingtao	9
3	1	Apple	26
	7	BMW	24
	8	Volkswagen	25
	14	Microsoft	23
	20	Cisco System	23
	21	Huawei	25
	23	TCL	23
	24	BYD	25
	31	Ping An	26
	33	Wanda	25
	35	Country Garden	25
	36	SANY	23
	10	IBM	17
	19	Caterpillar	18
	22	ZTE	20
	29	Bright Food	22
	32	SuNing	21

The results of the three groups are automatically obtained by SPSS analysis as shown in table 6. 27 and sorted by the company order of database table 6. 16. According to table 6. 27, the criteria of the level of activity can be summarized for the companies with subscription account as follows:

①Inactive: PuN ≤ 6.

②Active: 6< PuN ≤ 16①.

③Very active: PuN >16.

The grouping results and the relevant threshold values are dependent on the samples and may vary once different samples are chosen or extra cases are added into the existing database.

In line with table 6. 27, the results of companies with subscription account assigned to the corresponding groups are given below:

①Inactive: PuN ≤ 6.

Western companies (4): Coca-Cola, Johnson & Johnson, Boeing, Exxon Mobil.

Chinese companies (2): Kweichow Moutai, New Hope Group.

②Active: 6< PuN ≤ 16.

Western companies (9): Walt Disney, American Express, 3M, Nestle S. A., Unilever, UPS, General Electric, Procter & Gamble, Accenture.

Chinese companies (5): Great Wall Motors, Geely, Yunnan Baiyao, Vanke, Tsingtao.

③Very active: PuN >16.

Western companies (7): Apple, BMW, Volkswagen, Microsoft, Cisco System, IBM, Caterpillar.

Chinese companies (10): Huawei, TCL, BYD, Ping An, Wanda, Country Garden, SANY, ZTE, Bright Food, SuNing.

It can be seen that **fifteen of seventeen Chinese companies fall into active and very active groups.** This demonstrates that in general **Chinese companies with subscription accounts behaved more actively than Western companies.**

The evaluation of the level of interaction for companies with subscription account is presented in the following part.

(2) Evaluation of the level of interaction (subscription account)

The evaluation of the level of interaction for subscription account is applied the

---

① The number "16" ≈ MeanPuN_Subs (15.8).

same method as that used in service account. Thus, hierarchical cluster analysis as per F4 for companies with subscription account was carried out via SPSS software and the results have been acquired and expressed by figure 6. 17.

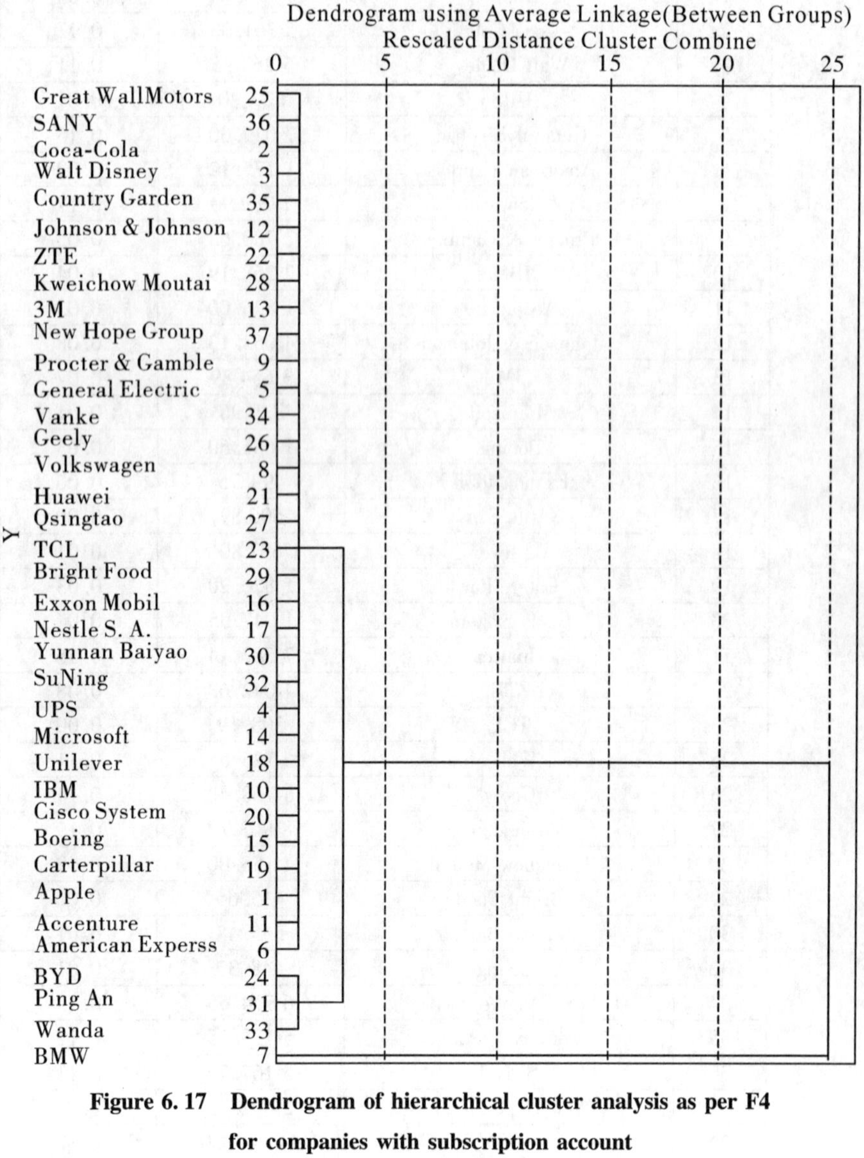

Figure 6. 17 Dendrogram of hierarchical cluster analysis as per F4 for companies with subscription account

According to figure 6. 17, it can be seen that three groups can be obtained and summarized in table 6. 28.

Table 6.28 Results of hierarchical cluster analysis as per F4 for companies with subscription account

Cluster	No.	Company	F3	F4
1	1	Apple	1 744.64	0.03
	2	Coca-Cola	5 361.33	0.11
	3	Walt Disney	5 267.95	0.11
	4	UPS	629.20	0.01
	5	General Electric	7 029.00	0.15
	6	American Express	1 175.12	0.02
	8	Volkswagen	7 789.90	0.17
	9	Procter & Gamble	2 780.63	0.05
	10	IBM	2 268.19	0.04
	11	Accenture	1 826.00	0.03
	12	Johnson & Johnson	4 063.13	0.08
	13	3M	3 654.89	0.07
	14	Microsoft	729.96	0.01
	15	Boeing	1 681.60	0.03
	16	Exxon Mobil	499.75	0.00
	17	Nestle S.A.	506.89	0.00
	18	Unilever	657.80	0.01
	19	Caterpillar	1 870.20	0.03
	20	Cisco System	1 947.35	0.04
	21	Huawei	7 587.44	0.16
	22	ZTE	4 042.63	0.08
	23	TCL	308.19	0.00
	25	Great Wall Motors	5 125.55	0.11
	26	Geely	6 768.48	0.14
	27	Tsingtao	8 963.90	0.19
	28	Kweichow Moutai	4 155.00	0.09
	29	Bright Food	415.66	0.00
	30	Yunnan Baiyao	555.48	0.01
	32	SuNing	548.30	0.01
	34	Vanke	6 974.55	0.15
	35	Country Garden	5 738.25	0.12
	36	SANY	5 167.76	0.11
	37	New Hope Group	2 802.75	0.06
2	24	BYD	14 643.60	0.32
	31	Ping An	14 041.79	0.30
	33	Wanda	19 925.57	0.44
3	7	BMW	45 368.29	1.00

In order to maintain the same grouping criteria as the service account, i.e., the following classification rule is adopted for subscription account:

①Very low interaction 0. 0 ⩽ F4 ⩽ 0. 2.

②Low interaction: 0. 2<F4 ⩽ 0. 45.

③Medium interaction: 0. 45<F4 ⩽ 0. 7.

④High interaction: 0. 7<F4 ⩽ 1. 0.

In line with Table 6. 28, it can be drawn that there is no companies listing in the group of medium interaction. The results of companies assigned to the corresponding groups are presented blow:

①Vey low interaction: 0. 0 ⩽ F4 ⩽ 0. 2.

Western companies (19): Apple, Coca-Cola, Walt Disney, UPS, General Electric, American Express, Volkswagen, Procter & Gamble, IBM, Accenture, Johnson & Johnson, 3M, Microsoft, Boeing, Exxon Mobil, Nestle S. A., Unilever, Caterpillar, Cisco System.

Chinese companies (14): Huawei, ZTE, TCL, Great Wall Motors, Geely, Tsingtao, Kweichow Moutai, Bright Food, Yunnan Baiyao, SuNing, Vanke, Country Garden, SANY, New Hope Group.

②Low interaction: 0. 2<F4 ⩽ 0. 45.

Western companies (0).

Chinese companies (3): BYD, Ping An, Wanda.

③Medium interaction: 0. 45<F4 ⩽ 0. 7.

Western companies (0).

Chinese companies (0).

④High interaction: 0. 7<F4 ⩽ 1. 0.

Western companies (1): BMW.

Chinese companies (0).

According to the grouping results, it can be noted that thirty-three of thirty-seven companies with subscription accounts had very low interaction with their followers. Only one company (BMW) acquired very high interaction with its users on WeChat platform during the observation period. **It can be detected that the overall results of the level of interaction for service account are better than that of subscription account** by comparing the results of both types of WeChat official accounts.

(3) Synthetic evaluation and grouping (subscription account)

By combination "the level of activity" and "the level of interaction", a synthetic assessment and grouping can be established accordingly for the thirty-seven companies with subscription account and stated by table 6. 29 & figure 6. 18.

Table 6. 29 Synthetic evaluation and classification for companies with subscription account

			Level of Interaction (1) Very low interaction: 0. 0 ≤ F4 ≤ 0. 2 (2) Low interaction: 0. 2 < F4 ≤ 0. 45 (3) Medium interaction: 0. 45 < F4 ≤ 0. 7 (4) High interaction: 0. 7 < F4 ≤ 1. 0			
			Very low	Low	Medium	High
Level of Activity	(1) Inactive: PuN ≤6 (2) Active: 6 < PuN ≤16 (3) Very active: PuN > 16	Inactive	Coca-Cola Johnson & Johnson Boeing Exxon Mobil Kweichow Moutai New Hope Group			
		Active	Walt Disney American Express 3M Nestle S.A. Unilever Great Wall Motors Geely Yunnan Baiyao Vanke UPS General Electric Procter & Gamble Accenture Tsingtao			
		Very Active	Apple Volkswagen Microsoft Cisco System Huawei TCL Country Garden SANY IBM Caterpillar ZTE Bright Food SuNing	BYD Ping An Wanda		BMW

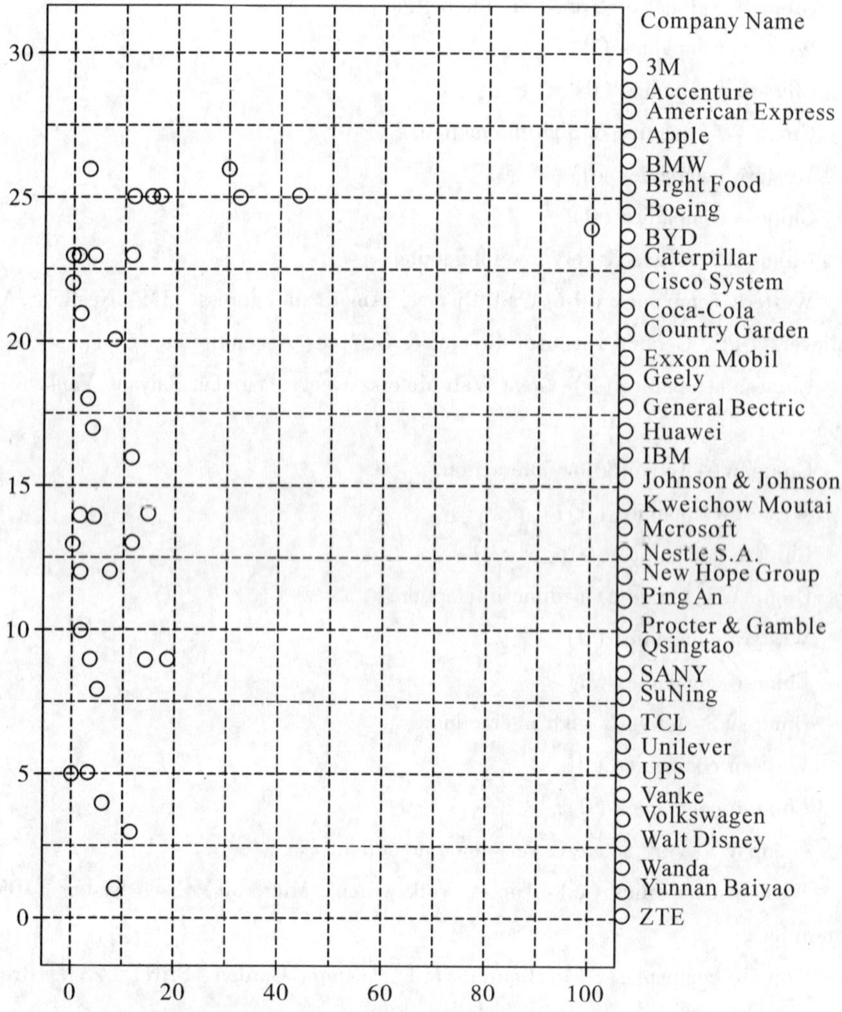

Figure 6. 18 Scatter plot PuN vs. F4 for companies with subscription account

According to table 6. 29, the synthetic evaluation results are represented by the following 12 groups.

Group W1: Inactive & very low interaction.

Western companies (4): Coca-Cola, Johnson & Johnson, Boeing, Exxon Mobil.

Chinese companies (2): Kweichow Moutai, New Hope Group.

Group W2: Inactive & low interaction.

Western companies (0).

Chinese companies (0).

Group W3: Inactive & medium interaction.

Western companies (0).

Chinese companies (0).

Group W4: Inactive & high interaction.

Western companies (0).

Chinese companies (0).

Group W5: Active & very low interaction.

Western companies (9): Walt Disney, American Express, 3M, Nestle S.A., Unilever, UPS, General Electric, Procter & Gamble, Accenture.

Chinese companies (5): Great Wall Motors, Geely, Yunnan Baiyao, Vanke, Tsingtao.

Group W6: Active & low interaction.

Western companies (0).

Chinese companies (0).

Group W7: Active & medium interaction.

Western companies (0).

Chinese companies (0).

Group W8: Active & high interaction.

Western companies (0).

Chinese companies (0).

Group W9: Very active & very low interaction.

Western companies (6): Apple, Volkswagen, Microsoft, Cisco System, IBM, Caterpillar.

Chinese companies (7): Huawei, TCL, Country Garden, SANY, ZTE, Bright Food, SuNing.

Group W10: Very active & low interaction.

Western companies (0).

Chinese companies (3): BYD, Ping An, Wanda.

Group W11: Very active & medium interaction.

Western companies (0).

Chinese companies (0).

Group W12: Very active & high interaction.

Western companies (1): BMW.

Chinese companies (0).

6.2.3.3 Five models and classification

Similarly as stated in Sina Weibo case study, seen in section 5.3.4.4, the final twenty-four groups of WeChat case study, namely, "C1-C12" and "W1-W12", each of which can be matched to different group in line with the criteria described in the table 5.30.

(1) The lazy model

In WeChat case study, four groups (W1, W2, C1 and C2) belong to this model due to their worst performance in both the level of activity and the level of interaction. There are totally eight companies fall into the lazy model.

(2) The special model

This model represents those companies that have acquired good achievement on WeChat platform although they did not make too much effort. Only one company (Xiaomi) belongs to this model. Xiaomi only broadcasted push notification once to its fans during one-month observation period, but it has achieved the greatest engagement with its users.

(3) The moderate model

The moderate model refers to those companies in four groups (W5, W6, C5 and C6). For these companies, they were active on WeChat. However, the return on investment was not satisfactory during the observation timeline. These companies need to pay more attention to the improvement of engagement with their users on WeChat channel.

(4) The ideal model

In WeChat case study, the following groups belong to the ideal model, i.e., W7, W8, W11, W12, C7, C8, C11 and C12; and the corresponding companies are Midea, Wahaha, BMW, Nike, Wal-Mart Stores, Starbucks, and McDonald's. These companies were not only active or very active on WeChat platform, but also have acquired successful engagement with their fans. In general, these companies had medium or high level of interaction with their users during the observation timeline.

(5) The unbalanced model

In WeChat case study, the unbalanced model covers fifteen Chinese companies and nine Western companies from the following four groups: W9, W10, C9 and C10. These companies have made a lot of efforts and had the intention to run effective WeChat marketing. However, the outcome was not satisfied due to the very low or low engagement with their followers.

7 DISCUSSION AND CONCLUSIONS

7.1 Discussion

This section mainly discusses the results obtained in the previous chapters. In line with cross-case analysis, two research purposes will be achieved by analyzing and comparing the results of both case studies. One purpose is to identify which companies are the most successful representatives among all selected companies on both Sina Weibo and WeChat platforms. Another purpose is to explore the key factor for successful social media performance through analyzing the most successful companies on both selected platforms.

7.1.1 Identification of the most successful representatives

Sina Weibo and WeChat are the most important and popular tools for local Chinese and Western companies. As for the sixty high reputation companies, some practical findings can be addressed via cross-case analysis based on the five-model evaluation framework and their performances on these two channels.

From the perspective of evolution, the five-model assessment framework has a gradual evolutionary process. Taking five models as a "biological chain", then the lazy model is at the lowest end of the "biological chain", the moderate model is just a little better than the lazy model, but still at its low end. The unbalanced model is in the middle of this chain because it has the potential to transform into high-end. After that, the special model and the ideal model are at the high end of this hypothetical "biological chain". Generally speaking, the evolutionary process of this biological chain is described below:

The lazy model (low-end) — the moderate model (low-end) — the unbalanced model (middle) — the special model (high-end) — the ideal model (high-end).

Table 7. 1 presents the results of cross-platform analysis based on five models and describes the overall comparison between the findings of Sina Weibo case and those of WeChat case for all selected high reputation companies. The results are described below.

Firstly, in line with the five-model evaluation framework, no distinct difference has been noted between the Chinese companies' performances and those of the Western companies on both Sina Weibo and WeChat platforms. Moreover, the detailed explanation is given below.

On one side, the lazy model & the moderate model are at the low-end of all models. And respectively, thirty-five companies on Sina Weibo channel and twenty-eight enterprises on WeChat platform are at the low-end of this chain.

On another side, the special model and the ideal model locate at the high-end of all models. Eight companies on Sina Weibo platform and eight enterprises on WeChat channel are at the high-end of this chain.

The unbalanced model is in the middle of this chain because it has the potentiality to enter into the high-end of it. Seventeen companies on Sina Weibo platform and twenty-four enterprises on WeChat channel are in the middle of five-model chain. This implies both the intention and the big opportunities for these companies to take appropriate measures to enhance their performances on Sina Weibo and WeChat platforms so as to get into the high-end of this chain.

Table 7.1 Results of cross-platform analysis based on the five models (example: sina Weibo & WeChat)

Model	Comparison			
The lazy model	Sina Weibo		WeChat	
	S1, S2		W1, W2, C1, C2	
	Chinese companies (6)	Yunnan Baiyao, Vanke, Country Garden, WangFujing, SANY, New Hope Group	Chinese companies (4)	Kweichow Moutai, New Hope Group, Hisense, YanJing Beer
	Western companies (7)	General Electric, Caterpillar, Deere, Johnson & Johnson, Exxon Mobil, Cisco System, Nike	Western companies (4)	Coca-Cola, Johnson & Johnson, Boeing, Exxon Mobil
The moderate model	Sina Weibo		WeChat	
	S5, S6		W5, W6, C5, C6	
	Chinese companies (10)	ZTE, Gree, Great Wall Motors, Tsingtao, YanJing Beer, Wanda, Fosun, Midea, Hisense, Wahaha	Chinese companies (8)	Great Wall Motors, Geely, Yunnan Baiyao, Vanke, Qsingtao, Haier, Gree, Saic Motor
	Western companies (12)	Coca-Cola, Walt Disney, FedEx, UPS, IBM, Accenture, 3M, Boeing, Unilever, Marriott International, Dupont, BMW	Western companies (12)	Walt Disney, American Express, 3M, Nestle S. A., Unilever, UPS, General Electric, Procter & Gamble, Accenture, PepsiCo, Deere, DuPont
The unbalanced model	Sina Weibo		WeChat	
	S9, S10		W9, W10, C9, C10	
	Chinese companies (10)	Huawei, TCL, Saic Motor, Geely, Kweichow Moutai, Bright Food, Hainan Airlines, Piang An, SuNing, Haier	Chinese companies (15)	Huawei, TCL, Country Garden, SANY, ZTE, Bright Food, SuNing, BYD, Ping An, Wanda, Lenovo, HaiNan Airlines, WangFujing, Gome, Fosun
	Western companies (7)	Apple, American Express, Procter & Gamble, Wal-Mart Stores, Intel, Starbucks, Volkswagen	Western companies (9)	Apple, Volkswagen, Microsoft, Cisco System, IBM, Caterpillar, FedEx, Marriott International, Intel
The special model	Sina Weibo		WeChat	
	S3, S4		W3, W4, C3, C4	
	Chinese companies		Chinese Companies (1)	Xiaomi
	Western companies		Western companies	
The ideal model	Sina Weibo		WeChat	
	S7, S8, S11, S12		W7, W8, W11, W12 C7, C8, C11, C12	
	Chinese companies (4)	Xiaomi, Lenovo, BYD, Gome	Chinese companies (2)	Midea, Wahaha
	Western companies (4)	Nestlé S.A, PepsiCo, McDonald's, Microsoft	Western companies (5)	BMW, Nike, Wal-Mart Stores, Starbucks, McDonald's

Secondly, those companies falling in the same model on both Sina Weibo and WeChat platforms have been identified. It is of significance to find out the representative companies in a generalized way based on five models. The results are shown in figure 7. 1.

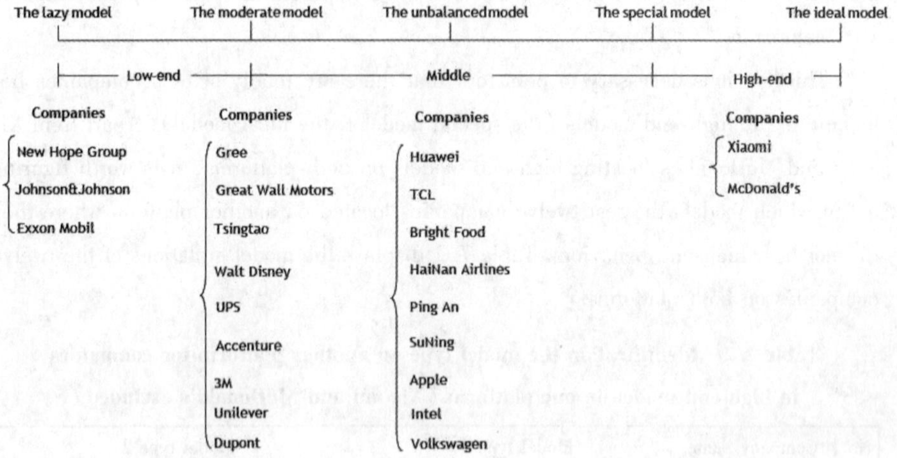

Figure 7. 1 Identifications of companies through five models on both platforms

As indicated in figure 7. 1, **three companies (New Hope Group, Johnson & Johnson, and Exxon Mobil)** are at the lowest-end of the five-model because they have acquired the worst performances on both Sina Weibo and WeChat platforms during the observation period. Or, in other words, they **have been identified as the most failed representative companies of this research.**

In addition, nine companies (Gree, Great Wall Motors, Tsingtao, Walt Disney, UPS, Accenture, 3M, Unilever, Dupont) are also at the low-end of the five-model, but to some degree better than the lowest ones. These companies need to enhance greatly their engagement with their followers although they were active on both platforms during the observation period.

Moreover, nine companies (Huawei, TCL, Bright Food, HaiNan Airlines, Ping An, SuNing, Apple, Intel, Volkswagen) locate in the middle of the five-model, and they have a great potentiality to convert into the high-end. These companies have spent a lot of time and have made big efforts on both platforms. But the outcome was not satisfied due to the very low engagement with their followers in consideration of what they have invested. Better interaction with their fans can be acquired if suitable adjustments on their communication strategies are made.

Furthermore, in the high-end of the five-model chain, one Chinese company (Xiaomi) and one Western company (McDonald's); both of them have had very favorable performances on both Sina Weibo and WeChat platforms. Or, in other words, they have been identified as the most successful representatives among the selected sixty companies.

Thirdly, it is necessary to point out that there are totally sixteen companies belonging to the high-end models (the special model & the ideal model). Apart from Xiaomi and McDonald's locating high-end models on both platforms, it is worth figuring out at which models the rest twelve companies located on another platform where they did not bear high-end behaviors. Table 7.2 displays the model situations of the twelve companies on both platforms.

Table 7.2 Identification the model type on another platform for companies in high-end model on one platform (Xiaomi and McDonald's excluded)

No.	Company name	Model type 1	Model type 2
1	Lenovo	The ideal model on Sina Weibo	The unbalanced model on WeChat
2	BYD	The ideal model on Sina Weibo	The unbalanced model on WeChat
3	Gome	The ideal model on Sina Weibo	The unbalanced model on WeChat
4	Nestle S.A.	The ideal model on Sina Weibo	The moderate model on WeChat
5	PepsiCo	The ideal model on Sina Weibo	The moderate model on WeChat
6	Microsoft	The ideal model on Sina Weibo	The unbalanced model on WeChat
7	Midea	The ideal model on WeChat	The moderate model on Sina Weibo
8	Wahaha	The ideal model on WeChat	The moderate model on Sina Weibo
9	BMW	The ideal model on WeChat	The moderate model on Sina Weibo
10	Nike	The ideal model on WeChat	The lazy model on Sina Weibo
11	Wal-Mart Stores	The ideal model on WeChat	The unbalanced model on Sina Weibo
12	Starbucks	The ideal model on WeChat	The unbalanced model on Sina Weibo

It can be seen from table 7.2 that except Nike, the rest eleven companies locate in moderate or unbalanced model on another platform. This also indicates that there exist big chances for these companies to dig out the reasons why they were not as successful on one platform as they did on another platform. By taking the right remedial measures accordingly, they can enhance their performances on the platform where they failed and then convert into the high-end model on this exact platform.

Generally speaking, **Xiaomi and McDonald's have been identified as the most successful representatives among all selected companies on both Sina Weibo and WeChat platforms.**Next, it is necessary to explore why these two companies have obtained the successful social media performance on both platforms.

7.1.2 Exploration of key factor for social media success on both platforms

As Xiaomi and McDonald's have been identified as the most successful representatives on both Sina Weibo and WeChat platforms among the selected sixty companies, it will be meaningful to find out the key factor accounting for the success of these two companies. For this purpose, it is necessary to explore what kind of content so that they have acquired such a high interaction with their followers. Therefore, further exploration of all top-one posts on Sina Weibo and push notifications on WeChat from Xiaomi and McDonald's during the observation period has been carried out.

On one hand, all top-one posts published by Xiaomi and McDonald's during four weeks' observation period have been analyzed so as to figure out the key factor of successful social media performance on both platforms.

Firstly, as for all top-one posts from Xiaomi on Sina Weibo Channel, this exploration is described below.

Figure 7.2 shows top-one posts from Xiaomi during the first week on sina weibo. Respectively, the one which has been retweeted the most; the one which has got the most comments and the one which has got the most likes. The first post stated those users who retweeted this post and signed up for this event would have the opportunity to win a Xiaomi mobile phone (total number of prize is 100). This post has got the biggest number of retweeting (5 448) during the first week's observation. The second post raised a question (What are the three components of the Internet era in your opinion?) with "surprise" notice to attract their fans' feedback. The third post mentioned, "*Raise your hand if you have more than two Xiaomi products*" trying to arouse the real Xiaomi fans to purchase more Xiaomi products.

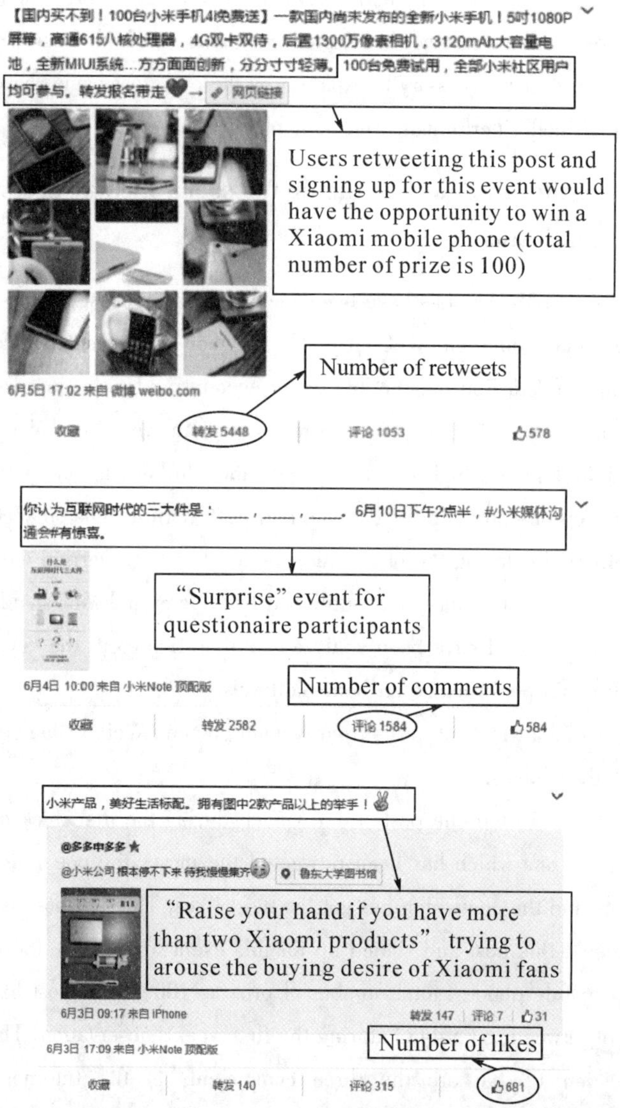

Figure 7.2 Top-one posts during the first week on Sina Weibo (Xiaomi)

Figure 7.3 explained that the users would have the chance to win a Xiaomi router if they retweeted it. This post has been the same one for three types of top-one posts during the second week's observation. Or, in other words, it has been retweeted the most, commented the most, and liked the most by users in the second week's timeline.

Figure 7.3 Top-one post during the second week on Sina Weibo (Xiaomi)

In figure 7.4, the first post was not only top-one post which has been retweeted the most, but also the top-one post which has got the most comments. The first post stated that those followers who retweeted this post would have the chance to win a lamp. The second post presented the high evaluations of a Xiaomi product from external media with photos and videos to attract Xiaomi fans which have got the most likes within the third week's timeline.

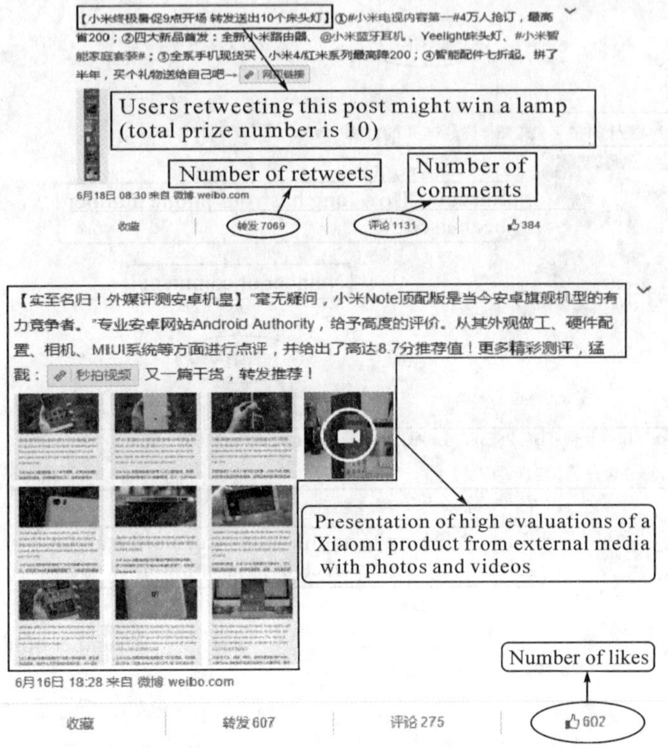

Figure 7.4 Top-one posts during the third week on Sina Weibo (Xiaomi)

Figure 7. 5 presents three posts which have been most retweeted, commented, and liked respectively during the fourth week's observation. The first post provided the pictures of spine movements which could favor the health of their users who were office staff. The second post was a survey: "*How long has your phone number been used?*" The third one was also a survey aiming to explore which telecom operators have been used by their users.

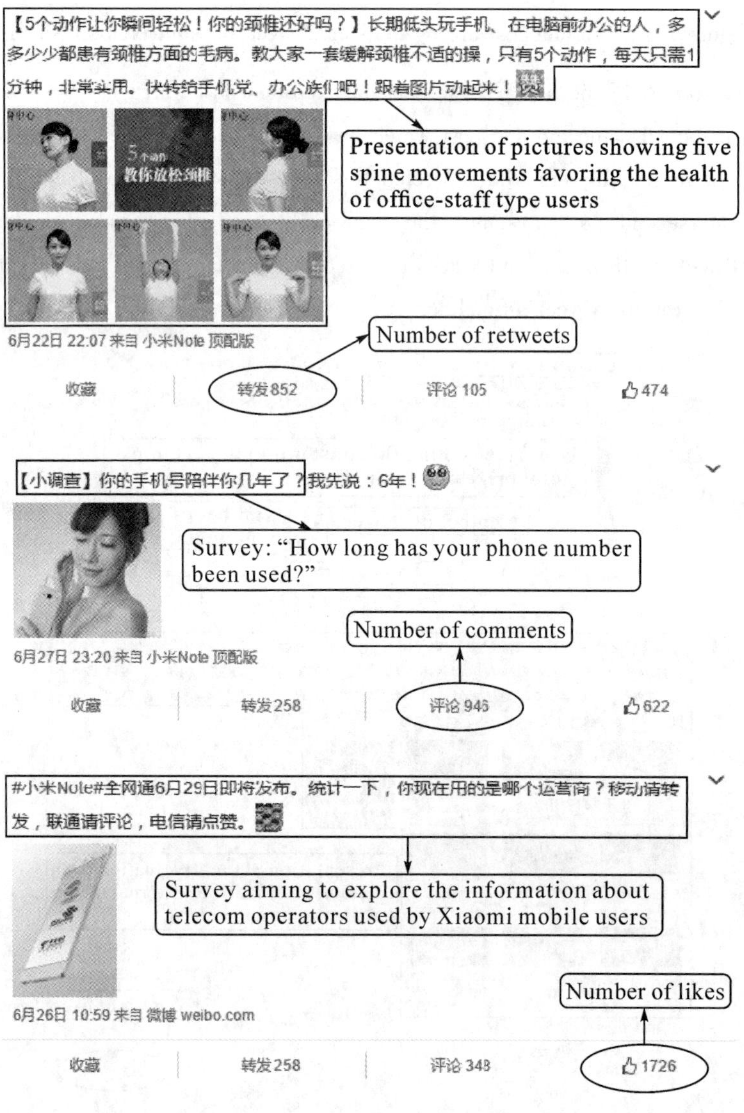

Figure 7. 5 Top-one posts during the fourth week on Sina Weibo (Xiaomi)

Secondly, the study on all top-one posts of McDonald's on Sina Weibo is presented below.

As shown in figure 7.6, the first post has been retweeted the most during the first week's observation. The second post has got the most comments and likes. The first top-one post mentioned that the users would have the opportunity to win a value of ¥20 meal coupon (total prize number is 10) if they retweeted this post. The second top-one post instructed users how to obtain a McDonald's coffee coupon in order to test a new Sina Weibo function.

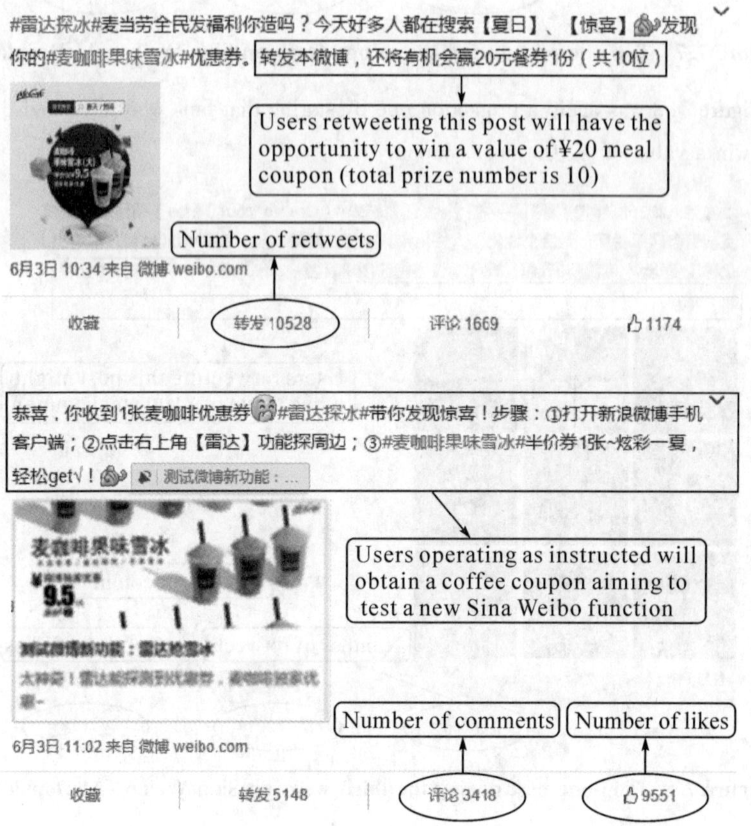

Figure 7.6 Top-one posts during the first week on Sina Weibo (McDonald's)

Figure 7.7 shows the top-one post released by McDonald's during the second week's observation. This post was published to call users to retweet this post so as to refuel students who would attend high school entrance exam. These young students are usually fans of McDonald's. This post has obtained the biggest number of retweets, comments and likes.

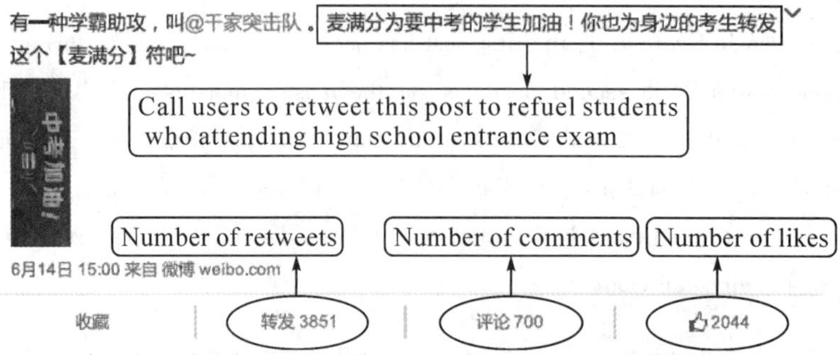

Figure 7.7　Top-one post during the second week on Sina Weibo (McDonald's)

Figure 7.8 was again a promotion one by stating that fans who retweeted this post might win a value of ¥100 meal coupon.

Figure 7.8　Top-one post during the third week on Sina Weibo (McDonald's)

As seen in figure 7.9, the top-one post in the fourth week from McDonald's on Sina Weibo commented that a self-service food ordering machine had been added to one McDonald's restaurant and promoted a value of ¥100 meal coupon to award those users who retweeted this post.

Figure 7.9 Top-one post during the fourth week on Sina Weibo (McDonald's)

After analyzing all top-one posts of Xiaomi and McDonald's, it is clear that at least half of them focused on providing some benefit to their users via participating in an event. Or, in other words, creating users' benefit-oriented content is the key factor for successful social media marketing on Sina Weibo channel.

On the other hand, the feeds which have been pushed to their followers by Xiaomi and McDonald's on WeChat platform have been also analyzed so as to explore the core factor of high engagement of these two companies.

According to figure 7.10, three posts were intergrated together to push to their users at one time by Xiaomi during one-month observation period. The first post was a product promotion with discount within the specified period. The second post was related with production information by presenting a new Xiaomi product and technology with celebrities' effect. The content of the third one was that their fans might win a Xiaomi mobile phone by participating in the relevant activity.

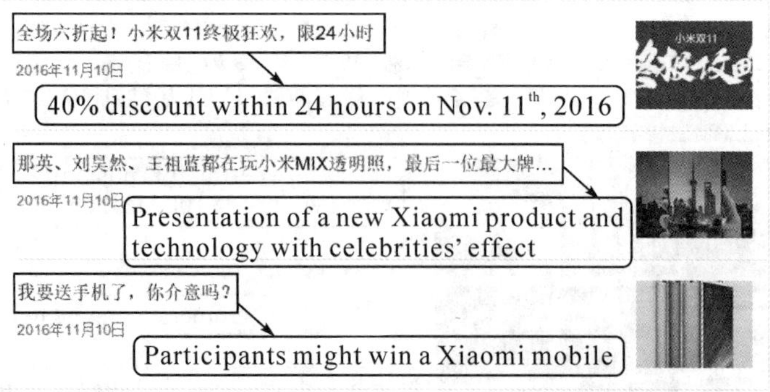

Figure 7.10　One-time push notification during the observation period (Xiaomi)

As indicated in figure 7.11, four posts were integrated into one time's push notification by McDonald's on WeChat channel. The first post introduced an economical menu in order to help their fans to order menus in the most cost-effective way. The second post was a product promotion with McDonald's VIP card combining Hello Kitty logo. The third post was also a product promotion within a specified period. The fourth one reminded the youths to submit a CV serving as a recruitment plan.

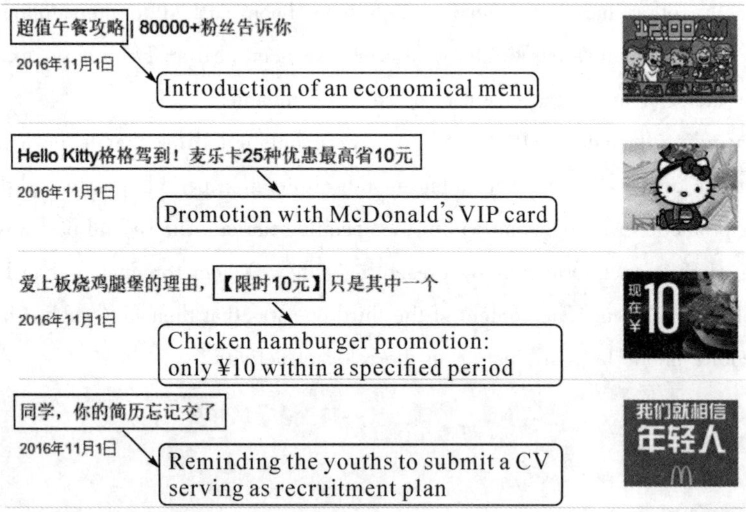

Figure 7.11　One-time push notification during the observation period (McDonald's)

After analyzing the feeds released by Xiaomi and McDonald's on WeChat application, the finding can be drawn that most of them were related to users' benefit such as product discount, coupon, and money saving.

In all, through all these analyses on top-one posts of Xiaomi and McDonald's on Sina Weibo and their feeds on WeChat during the observation period, it can be noted that most of these top-one posts on Sina Weibo and those feeds pushed on WeChat focused on providing awards, promotions or other types of benefits to their users by participating in an event. Therefore, **creating users' benefit-oriented content has been identified to be the key factor to achieve successful social media performance on both Sina Weibo and WeChat platforms.**

7.2 Conclusions

This research aims to explore and evaluate big high reputation companies' social media performances in the context of Chinese digital marketing. For this purpose, four research questions were put forward and the corresponding solution strategies were devised.

In the first place, the context of Chinese social media including its historical roots and the relevant social media platforms has been introduced and analyzed.

On one hand, in general, its overall social media landscape is very different from its Western counterparts. Chinese digital customers' profiles are described in line with their Internet behavior and habits. **Several dominant use of China's social media marketing such as the integration of social media and e-commerce, group buying, and mobile social media marketing are stated as the highlights.** Moreover, some big challenges are identified for local and multinational companies. Based on the above analysis, five main recommendations have been recommended for local and multinational companies by He & Pedraza-Jiménez (2015), which include: ① do market research and digital consumer research; ② listen to WOM (Word of Mouth); ③ identify the KOLs (Key Opinion Leaders); ④ mind the young generation; ⑤ attend social media marketing training courses.

On the other hand, the analysis of Chinese social media platforms demonstrates that Sina Weibo and WeChat are currently the two most popular and the most used social media platforms in China. This is the answer of the second research question (RQ2).

Secondly, **thirty Chinese companies and thirty Western companies have been se-**

lected carefully under certain criteria to answer the first research question (RQ1). As explained in this study, the selection of representative companies was an important preparation due to its influence on the finding of this research because different samples lead to different results. **One of the contributions of this study is that it has provided a special reference about how to select representative companies, i.e., the establishment of selection patterns.** The first step is to define some certain selection rules according to the research topics and objectives. Afterwards, the related resources such as database, magazines, and websites need to be gathered, analyzed and compared in order to determine which ones meet the best the established selection rules.

In this research, the main selection criterion is reputation, and combined with other filtering principles are set up to conduct the selection process. **The resource provider is the magazine *FORTUNE*** due to its famous and convincing publications — World's most Admired Companies and China's Most Admired Companies (released by FORTUNE CHINA) in line with its assessment rules such as social responsibility, innovation, people management, product quality, and etc., which together means corporate reputations. The referred lists in this research were published in 2014. From the two lists, companies that represented high reputation for both Western region and China had been picked out. In addition, further filtering was carried out because some companies in the lists did not match the relevant requirements to implement this study. Finally, in this way, sixty representative high reputation Chinese and Western enterprises were determined as the research objects. The selected companies cover a wide range of industries. Fifteen industries are distributed in the thirty Western companies whereas nineteen industries are encountered in the thirty Chinese companies. For Western companies, the dominating industries are Food category & IT category in view of the fact that the numbers of selected companies within these two industries are both six (the largest). For Chinese companies, the principal industries are Electronics, Food category, and Motor by considering that the numbers of selected companies in these three sectors are seven, five and four respectively. In both cases, Food category is the principal industry in common.

Thirdly, from the perspective of methodology, two cases studies in line with two Chinese social media platforms: Sina Weibo and WeChat, have been carefully designed, planned and performed. **Another contribution of this research is that a synthetic methodological procedure has been set up, formulated and adopted in two**

case studies by incorporating both qualitative and quantitative approaches such as KPIs concept, information architecture principle, content analysis and statistical method (e.g., cluster analysis). Case studies formed fundamentally the research core and other approaches were applied to analyze the cases. In general, similar methodologies and procedures have been applied to both cases. However, due to the different features of the two platforms, some specific approaches and processes have been adopted to the corresponding platform.

On one hand, in Sina Weibo case study, database was set up based on the data collected during the observation period in line with the identified KPIs. Afterwards, the database was utilized to conduct qualitative study (content analysis) in view of qualitative indicators and quantitative analyses (e.g., cluster analysis) by considering quantitative indicators.

On the other hand, in view of the fact that WeChat, as a rising star of Chinese social media landscape, is a mobile-oriented social platform, two main research lines were followed respectively in combination with their objectives. For the first research line — WeChat official accounts' interface & menu analysis, information architecture approach was adopted in line with two angles, i.e., industries & country region. Another main research line was the analysis of push notification marketing of all selected companies, in which KPIs concept and statistical analysis have been applied in a similar way as in Sina Weibo case study. The concept of integrating two main research lines gives practical guidance for the young social media channel — WeChat.

This comprehensive research methodology and procedure do not only apply to this research but also can be extended to other investigations on social medial platforms although to some degree they are tailor-made for specific cases. At least, this study provides a certain philosophy to formulate research methodology under similar conditions.

Fourthly, **a systematic measurement and classification framework has been established via a three-stage procedure: ① initial two dimensional analyses (the level of activity and the level of interaction); ② synthetic cluster analysis (12 groups); ③ the generation of five models and the corresponding classification.** The building of this framework is in response to the third research question (RQ3).

At the first stage, two critical factors — the level of activity & the level of interaction have been defined and evaluated separately via cluster analysis. On one side, the former factor is an indicator about companies' participation on the social media platforms, i.e., whether a company is active or not. It can measure what efforts companies have made such as the updating frequency, the number of posts, and the times of pushing feeds. On the other side, the latter one denotes the degree of engagement with their users, and the percentage of users actually participating in the conversation. It can assess to which degree of effectiveness companies have reached after all efforts they made. According to the results of grouping analysis, the level of activity was classified into three degrees — inactive, active, and very active; and the level of interaction was grouped into four degrees — very low interaction, low interaction, medium interaction, and high interaction for both Sina Weibo and WeChat platforms. In order to define the classification rules, it is necessary to consider together the characteristics of the selected platform and the available data and indicators. At the same time, it needs to be pointed out that the classification rules are set up as per the division threshold values, which are dependent on case selection and sample data. That is to say, the rules and the classification results may vary or be updated if different cases or samples are chosen or extra sample data are added into the existing database.

At the second stage, synthetic cluster analysis in combination with the level of activity (3 degrees) and the level of interaction (4 degrees) yields 12 ($=3\times4$) groups. Each group represents a certain state of companies' behaviors on social media platforms.

At the third stage, in consideration of the closeness of the twelve groups, **five models have been generalized and summarized, which are: ① the lazy model; ② the special model; ③ the moderate model; ④ the ideal model; ⑤ the unbalanced model.**

The lazy model, as the name implies, refers to the lowest level of activity and level of interaction among all models.

The moderate model is to some extent better than the lazy model. Corporations in this model are active on social media channels, but with poor effectiveness due to very low or low level of interaction with their users. Two reasons could explain this performance: ① few attention paid to updating or posting; ② unsuitable ways to engagement with their users.

The special model, its particularity lies in the point that quite good return on investment in social media marketing is acquired although not too much effort has been made. The emergence of this type of model might depend on the special social media platform & its account features, or whether there is a distinct relative magnitude difference in "the level of activity". After analyzing the companies within the special model for both Sina Weibo and WeChat case studies, one finding was demonstrated that this phenomenon occurs only when the relative difference in "the level of activity" is very small. For instance, Xiaomi using WeChat service account, has obtained very successful engagement with its followers although it was inactive (only pushed once notification during the observation period). Noticeably, the range of the number of push notification in WeChat service account is limited to be [0, 4].

The ideal model coincides with a famous proverb, "*no pain no gain*". Companies in this model are active or very active on a specific social media platform; meanwhile they have achieved medium or high interaction with their users. These companies have made a certain amount of efforts and have acquired a very satisfactory return from the perspective of ROI.

Companies in the unbalanced model have the desire to run effective and significant social media campaigns and usually they have made a lot of efforts such as keeping updating, posting constantly, and so on. However, the outcome is not as expected and inconsistent with the efforts they have made due to the very low engagement with their followers. The advice for the companies in this model is to revise their social media strategies so as to figure out effective ways to improve the engagement degree.

It is worth pointing out that **one of the highlights of this research is the identification of two companies (Xiaomi & McDonald's)** at the high-end of five models. In this sense, **they were considered as the most successful representatives among all selected sixty companies.** Whereas, **three companies (New Hope Group, Johnson & Johnson, and Exxon Mobil)** at the lowest-end of the five-model and **were detected the most failed representative companies** of this research. And all these answered the fourth research question (RQ4).

Especially, after analyzing the top-one posts of Xiaomi and McDonald's on Sina Weibo and their posts on WeChat during the observation timeline, it can be noted that most of these top-one posts on Sina Weibo and those posts on WeChat focused on providing awards, promotions or other types of benefits to their users by participating in an event. This strategy enabled these two companies to achieve very high interaction with their followers. Thus, **benefit-oriented content is deemed to be the key factor to achieve successful social media marketing on the two Chinese social media platforms.**

Fifthly, this research has revealed some common or similar findings related with the selected Chinese and Western companies in line with their performances on selected social media platforms.

(1) In general, **Western companies preferred to build closer relationships with companies of Western origin inside the selected sixty companies' social community on Sina Weibo platform. And Chinese companies had the same preference**, i.e., to establish closer connections with Chinese companies.

(2) The booming of Sina Weibo marketing for both Chinese and Western companies has occurred from 2010 to 2012.

(3) Both Chinese companies and Western companies published more original posts than retweets on Sina Weibo platform. In addition, **releasing the important content on Friday can be a good choice** for all companies whereas **it is advisable to avoid publishing important posts at weekends.**

(4) "Text plus picture" and "text plus picture plus link" were the most favorite formats by Western and Chinese companies **on Sina Weibo channel.**

(5) Both Chinese and Western companies focused on providing information about products, news, and brand while configuring the interface & menu of their WeChat official accounts.

(6) Most of Western and Chinese companies did not send push notifications to their users at weekends via WeChat platform.

Sixthly, some differences in the overall social media performances of Chinese and Western companies on both platforms have also been explored.

(1) In a general sense, **thirty high reputation Chinese companies behaved better than thirty high reputation Western companies on Sina Weibo.** The former has obtained a higher degree of activity and interaction than the latter during the observation timeline. In addition, Chinese companies were more active than Western ones from the perspective of history of the usage of Sina Weibo because Chinese companies have released more contents, i.e., tweets than Western enterprises from 2009 to 2014.

(2) The favorite days for Western companies to publish important content on Sina Weibo were Thursday and Friday. Whereas, for Chinese companies, the favorable days were Monday, Wednesday and Friday.

(3) The results of interface & menu analyses of WeChat official accounts indicated that Chinese companies focused mainly on providing company profile, after-sales service information & company leaders' information whereas Western ones put

more emphases on the history of company & contact information.

(4) **Chinese companies preferred to make profit by providing online shopping service on WeChat platform** by comparison with Western companies. However, **Western companies paid more attentions to user's feedback & questions.**

(5) Chinese companies organized more award-winning activities and behaved more actively in interactive community to interact with their users on WeChat platform than Western companies did.

(6) **More Western companies updated the interfaces & menus** of their WeChat official accounts so as to adjust or optimize it **within one-month observation timeline than Chinese companies** have done.

Seventhly, five main industries (Food, IT, Electronics, Motor & Wholesale), have been distributed in the selected sixty companies although there are totally nineteen sectors. From the viewpoint of industry difference, some interesting findings have been found as follows:

(1) The analysis on the mutual fans between companies demonstrated that **companies preferred to follow companies from their own or similar industries on Sina Weibo platform.**

(2) Companies in Electronics and Wholesale industries used more service accounts on WeChat platform. However, corporations in IT, Motor, Medical, Construction and Manufacturing, Real Estate sectors preferred to use subscription account. No special preference has been observed for companies in Food sector in view of the fact that almost half of them utilized subscription accounts and the other half adopted service accounts.

(3) **Companies in Electronics and Wholesale industries paid much more attention to online shopping function on WeChat** channel than those ones in other sectors. Moreover, **companies in Electronics industry engaged more with their users via the interactive community than companies in other sectors.** In addition, companies in Wholesale sector provided more apps download function for their users than companies of other industries.

(4) Companies in Food, IT, and Motor sectors focused on providing the following main information: products, news, and brand.

7.3 Innovation points

Some main innovation points of this research lie in that it presents a study from the following specific points of view:

(1) Focusing on Chinese digital market and the most popular Chinese social media channels;

(2) Selecting sixty enterprises in a general, semi-macro-scale and comparative sense:

①high reputation and leader in each sector;

②both domestic Chinese companies (30) and Western ones (30);

③covering a wide range of industries.

(3) Adopting a comprehensive research methodology framework by combining and integrating different types of methodologies including qualitative and quantitative approaches such as case studies, grounded theory, KPIs concept, information architecture, content analysis, and statistical analysis.

(4) Classifying the level of activity and the level of interaction based on KPIs identification.

(5) Establishing a systematic measurement and classification framework to evaluate enterprises' performances on social media platforms.

As a matter of fact, most of existing researches in this field are relevant to Western social platforms such as Facebook, Twitter, Instagram, LinkedIn, YouTube, Pinterest and etc., and not sufficient researches focusing on Chinese social medial channels have been conducted.

Moreover, a great number of previous studies are of micro scale, focusing on just one or several companies, or only one social platform, or only one industry, etc. For example, some researches involved few companies in line with one specific social media platform so as to carry out and compare the differences of performances of all selected companies on this unique platform.

Whereas, to some degree, this study made a semi-macro-scale study by covering a number of companies from different regions (Chinese & Western), a wide range of industries, and more than one popular Chinese social media channels. Therefore, the scope of this research is wider involving more companies, countries and industries.

This research is dedicated to give more referential instructions or recommendations for mainly big and high reputation companies in Chinese digital market. In particular, this research puts forward a systematic measurement and classification framework to evaluate companies' performances on Chinese social media platforms in order to help penetrate the Chinese market with a lot of potentiality. Although this measurement criterion is tailor-made for the most popular social media applications in China, it raises a train of thought and may be extended to other relevant social media studies.

From the perspective of practicality, this research tries to set up some kind of guidance for both Chinese and Western companies that would like to run significant and effective social media campaigns in China.

7.4 Further work

During the research process, some limitations of this research have been detected and thus lead to new research directions in the future.

At first, findings and conclusions of this research are generally suitable for large-scale and high-reputation companies, but these results may not be applicable for small and medium-sized enterprises. However, the research procedure and framework can be adopted to make some similar analyses on other types of companies.

In addition, it is necessary to point out that, in Sina Weibo case study, thirty Chinese companies have been taken into account as an independent group and another group formed by the thirty Western companies. The motivation for establishing two groups was to compare the results of both within-group and across-group. An interesting direction for further research is to integrate Western and Chinese companies into one group. Hence the clustering criteria will be different and thus lead to different findings and results. Besides, the number of followers has not been adopted in Sina Weibo case study because it has not been identified as an indicator to conduct the two dimensional analyses, although the change of follower number has been collected in this research. Another interesting direction for further research could be conducting some analysis by combining with the number of fans.

Moreover, as mentioned in this research, some data about the companies' Sina

Weibo and WeChat marketing cannot be obtained by the third party. Cooperation with some of these companies might be resorted to obtain more data, e.g., the revenue in Chinese market during the observation period and the cost to run campaigns. With these extra data, it will be interesting to study the relationships among efforts, cost, reach, engagement and the revenue.

What's more, the industry distribution in these sixty companies is quite diverse (19 industries) and some sectors consist of one company or two companies. For example, only one company (Walt Disney) belongs to Entertainment industry; only one company (Boeing) belongs to Aerospace sector; only one company (Ping An) belongs to Insurance industry; only one company (Exxon Mobil) belongs to Petroleum Refining sector, and etc. It cannot conduct a comparative study while one industry concludes only one company. In addition, the industry's dispersion has led to fragmented results of industry-based analysis.

In the future, some extensions in company number or in the observation period could be made to enrich the database so that more generalized findings might be revealed.

Also, analyzing the differences in social media performances from intercultural communication perspective between Chinese and Western enterprises by applying Hofstede's national/organizational culture dimension theory (Hofstede et al., 2010) could also be an attractive research direction.

Finally, in view of the fact that in recent years more and more Chinese companies have been trying to extend their business in Western countries, another practical research direction can be investigating social media performances of Chinese and Western companies in line with Western popular social media tools such as Facebook and Twitter.

References

BERELSON, BERNARD, 1952. Content analysis in communications research [M]. New York: Free Press.

GLASER B, STRAUSS A L, 1967. The discovery of grounded theory [M]. Chicago: Aldine.

HOLSTI O R, 1969. Content analysis for the social sciences and humanities [M]. Upper Saddle River: Addison-Wesley.

REIN M, SCHON D, 1977. Problem setting in policy research [M] // WEISS C. Using social policy research in public policy-making. Lexington, MA: D. C. Heath.

KASSARJIAN H H, 1977. Content analysis in consumer research [J]. Journal of Consumer Research (4): 8-18.

BERRY L L, 1983. Relationship marketing [M] // BERRY L L, SHOSTACK G L, UPAH G. Emerging perspectives on service marketing. Chicago: AMA: 25-28.

GUMMESSON E, 1983. A new concept of marketing [R]. Grenoble: the 1983 EMAC Annual Conference.

YIN R K, 1984. Case study research: design and methods [M]. Beverly Hills: Sage Publications.

WRIGHT C R, 1986. Mass communication: a sociological perspective [M]. New York: Random House.

STRAUSS A, 1987. Qualitative analysis for social scientists [M]. New York: Cambridge University Press.

GHERARDI S, TURNER B A, 1987. Real men don't collect soft data [D]. Trento: University of Trento.

BERNARD H R, 1988. Research methods in cultural anthropology [M]. Newbury

Park, CA: Sage.
CARNEY T F, 1990. Collaborative inquiry methodology [R]. Windsor: University of Windsor, Division for Instructional Development.
FITZ-GIBBON C T, 1990. Performance indicators: a BERA dialogue [M]. Clevedon, Avon: Multi-lingual Matters.
FOMBRUN C, SHANLEY M, 1990. What's in a name? reputation building and corporate strategy [J]. Academy of Management Journal, 33 (2): 233-258.
STRAUSS A, CORBIN J, 1990. Basics of qualitative research: grounded theory procedures and techniques [M]. Newbury Park, CA: Sage.
GRNROOS C, 1991. The marketing strategy continuum: towards a marketing concept for the 1990s [J]. Management Decision, 29 (1): 7-13.
CUTLER B D, JAVALGI R G, 1992. A cross-cultural analysis of visual components of print advertising: The United States and European community [J]. Journal of Advertising Research, 32 (1): 71-80.
YOON E, GUFFEY H J, KIJEWSKI V, 1993. The effects of information and company reputation on intentions to buy a business service [J]. Journal of Business Research, 27 (3): 215-228.
GRNROOS C, 1994. From marketing mix to relationship marketing: towards a paradigm shift in marketing [J]. Management Decision, 32 (2): 4-20.
MILES M B, HUBERMAN A M, 1994. Qualitative data analysis: an expanded sourcebook [M]. Thousand Oaks: Sage.
ALBERS-MILLER N D, GELB B D, 1996. Business advertising appeals as a mirror of cultural dimensions: a study of eleven countries [J]. Journal of Advertising, 25 (4): 57-70.
RAFAELIL S, SUDWEEKS F, 1997. Net interactivity [J]. Journal of Computer Mediated Communication, 2 (4): 23.
HUSSEY J, HUSSEY R, 1997. Business research: a practical guide for undergraduate and post-graduate students [M]. London: MacMillan Press Ltd.
POWELL R R, 1997. Basic research methods for librarians [M]. 3rd ed. Greenwich: Ablex Publishing Corporation.
ROBSON W, 1997. Strategic management and information systems: an integrated approach [M]. 2nd ed. London: Financial Times Professional Limited.
NEUMAN W, 1997. Social research methods: qualitative and quantitative approa-

ches [M]. Needham Heights, MA: Allyn & Bacon.
TELLIS W M, 1997. Introduction to case study [J]. The Qualitative Report, 3 (2): 35.
WURMAN R S, 1997. Information Architects [R]. New York: Graphis Inc.
KOHN L T, 1997. Methods in case study analysis [R]. Birmingham: The Center for Studying Health System Change.
FOMBRUN C, VAN RIEL C, 1997. The reputational landscape: a convergence of research and practice [J]. Corporate Reputation Review, 1 (1/2): 1-16.
FRY H, KETTERIDGE S, MARSHALL S, 1999. A handbook for teaching and learning in higher education [M]. Glasgow: Kogan Page.
JU-PAK K H, 1999. Content dimensions of web advertising: a cross-national comparison [J]. International Journal of Advertising, 18 (2): 207-231.
CHARMAZ K, 2000. Grounded theory: objectivist and constructivist methods [M]// DENZIN N K, LINCOLN Y S. Handbook of qualitative research. 2nd ed. Thousand Oaks: Sage: 509-535.
BARAN S J, 2002. Introduction to mass communication [M]. 2nd ed. New York: McGraw Hill.
BRYANT A, 2002. Re-grounding grounded theory [J]. Journal of Information Technology Theory and Application (4): 25-42.
PATTON M Q, 2002. Qualitative Research and Evaluation Methods [M]. 3rd ed. Thousand Oaks: Sage.
BORGATTI S P, EVERETT M G, FREEMAN L C, 2002. UCINET for windows: software for social network analysis [M]. Harvard, MA: Analytic Technologies.
YIN R K, 2002. Case study research: design and methods [M]. Thousand Oaks: Sage.
YIN R K, 2003. Case study research: design and methods [M]. 3rd ed. London: Sage.
MCNAY H, 2003. Information architecture-visual displays [R]. Orlando: Professional Communication Conference.
KITCHEN P J, LAURENCE A, 2003. Corporate reputation: an eight-country analysis [J]. Corporate Reputation Review, 6 (2): 103-117.
COX R F, ISSA R R A, AHRENS D, 2003. Management's perception of key performance indicators for construction [J]. Journal of Construction Engineering and

Management, 129 (2): 142-151.

DELLAROCAS C, 2003. The digitalization of word of mouth: Promise and challenges of online feedback mechanisms [J]. Management Science, 49 (10): 1407-1424.

HENNIG-THURAU T, GWINNER K P, WALSH G, et al., 2004. Electronic word-of-mouth via consumer-opinion platforms: what motivates consumers to articulate themselves on the internet? [J]. Journal of Interactive Marketing, 18 (1): 38-52.

KRIPPENDORFF K, 2004. Content analysis: an introduction to its methodology [M]. 2nd ed. Thousand Oaks: Sage.

AHN T, RYU S, HAN I, 2004. The impact of the online and offline features on the user acceptance of Internet shopping malls [J]. Electronic Commerce Research and Applications (3): 405-420.

ROMESBURG H C, 2004. Cluster analysis for researchers [M]. North Carolina: Lulu.

SINGH N, BAACK D W, 2004. Web site adaptation: a cross cultural comparison of US and Mexican web sites [J]. Journal of Computer-Mediated Communication, 9 (4): 1.

HOX J J, BOEIJE H R, 2005. Data collection, primary vs. secondary [M] // KIMBERLY KEMPF-LEONARD. Encyclopedia of social measurement. Elsevier: Amsterdam: 593-599.

GRAHAM P, 2005. Web 2.0 [EB/OL]. http://www.paulgraham.com/web20.html, 11-01.

MACNAMARA J, 2005. Media content analysis: its uses, benefits and Best Practice Methodology [J]. Asia Pacific Public Relations Journal, 6 (1): 1-34.

CHARMAZ K, 2006. Constructing grounded theory: a practical guide through qualitative analysis [M]. London: Sage.

BARNETT M, JERMIER J, LAFFERTY B, 2006. Corporate reputation: the definitional landscape [J]. Corporate Reputation Review, 9 (1): 26-38.

GRASSEL E, SCHIRMER B, 2006. The use of volunteers to support family careers of dementia patients: results of a prospective longitudinal study investigating expectations towards and experience with training and professional support [J]. Zeitschrift Fur Gerontologie Und Geriatrie, 39 (3): 217-226.

JIA W T, DING Y W, 2006. Brief introduction of IA in China [J]. Library Work and Research (4): 10.

MANN B L, 2006. Case study research and online learning: Types, typologies and thesis research [M] // BRUCE L MANN. Selected styles in web-based educational research. Hershey: Information Science Publishing: 70-79.

MANN B L, 2006. An intrinsic quantitative case study of WebCT developers [M] // BRUCE L MANN. Selected styles in web-based educational research. Hershey: Information Science Publishing: 80-89.

GRAHAM M E, BANSAL P, 2007. Consumers' willingness to pay for corporate reputation: the context of airline companies [J]. Corporate Reputation Review, 10 (3): 189-200.

ABONYI J, FEIL B, 2007. Cluster analysis for data mining and system identification [M]. Boston, MA: Birkhauser Basel.

FOMBRUN C J, 2007. List of lists: a compilation of international corporate reputation ratings [J]. Corporate Reputation Review, 10 (2): 144-153.

ZAINAL Z, 2007. Case study as a research method [D]. Johor Bahru: Universiti Teknologi Malaysia.

YANG D J, WU J M, 2007. Review and Prospect of Relationship Marketing: a Citation Analysis [J]. Contemporary Management Research, 3 (3): 267-284.

SMITH T, COYLE J R, LIGHTFOOT E, et al., 2007. Reconsidering models of influence: the relationship between consumer social networks and word-of-mouth effectiveness [J]. Journal of Advertising Research, 47 (4): 87-397.

MAYFIELD A, 2008. What is social media: an e-book from iCrossing [EB/OL]. http://www.icrossing.co.uk/fileadmin/uploads/eBooks/What_is_Social_Media_iCrossing_ebook.pdf, 03-07.

ANDERSON J Q, RAINIE L, 2008. The future of the internet III. Pew Research Internet Project [EB/OL]. http://www.pewinternet.org/files/old-media//Files/Reports/2008/PIP_FutureInternet3.pdf, 03-25.

CHARMAZ K, 2008. Constructionism and the grounded theory method [M] // HOLSTEIN J A, GUBRIUM J F. Handbook of constructionist research. New York: The Guilford Press: 397-412.

DRURY G, 2008. Opinion piece: social media: should marketers engage and how can it be done effectively? [J]. Journal of Direct, Data and Digital Marketing Practice, 9 (3): 274-277.

MA H, YANG H, LYU M R, et al., 2008. Mining social networks using heat diffusion processes for marketing candidates selection [R]. New York: Proceedings of the 17th ACM conference on information and knowledge management.

KAARIO K, PELTOLA T, Tiedon hallinta tietointensiivisissä yrityksissä – kenen on valta ja vastuu? [M]. Jyvskyl: Docendo Finland Oy.

RESMINI A, ROSATI L, 2009. The semantic environment: heuristics for a cross-context human-information interaction model [M] // DUBOIS et al. The engineering of mixed reality systems. London: Springer.

WALSH G, MITCHELL V W, JACKSON P R, et al., 2009. Examining the antecedents and consequences of corporate reputation: a customer perspective [J]. British Journal of Management, 20 (2): 187–203.

BHARGAVA B, 2009. Manifesto for the content curator: the next big social media job of the future [EB/OL]. http://www.rohitbhargava.com/2009/09/manifesto-for-the-content-curator-the-next-big-social-media-job-of-the-future.html,09-30.

CHARMAZ K, 2009. Shifting the grounds: constructivist grounded theory methods [M] // MORSE J M, STERN P N, CORBIN J, et al. Developing grounded theory: The second generation. Walnut Creek: Left Coast Press: 127–154.

CRESWELL J W, 2009. Research design. qualitative, quantitative and mixed methods approach [M]. London: Sage.

TRUSOV M, BUCKLIN R E, PAUWELS K, 2009. Effects of word-of-mouth versus traditional marketing: findings from an internet social networking site [J]. Journal of Marketing, 73 (5): 90–102.

YIN R K, 2009. Doing case study research [M]. 4th ed. Thousand Oaks: Sage.

HOFSTEDE G, HOFSTEDE G J, MINKOV M, 2010. Cultures and organizations: software of the mind [M]. 3rd ed. New York: McGraw-Hill.

LIANG J, 2010. Taobao sells 205 Benzes within 35 hours [EB/OL]. http://english.peopledaily.com.cn/90001/90776/90882/7139958.html,09-14.

CNN, 2010. Taobao sells 205 Benzes in just over three hours [EB/OL]. http://travel.cnn.com/shanghai/shop/taobao-sells-205-benzes-just-over-three-hours-653638, 09-17.

ABEDNIYA A, MAHMOUEI S S, 2010. The impact of social networking websites to facilitate the effectiveness of viral marketing [J]. International Journal of Advanced Computer Science and Applications, 1 (6): 139–146.

CULNAN M J, MCHUGH P J, ZUBILLAGA J I, 2010. How large US companies can use Twitter and other social media to gain business value [J]. MIS Quarterly Executive, 9 (4): 243-259.

KAUFFMAN R J, LAI H, HO C T, 2010. Incentive mechanisms, fairness and participation in online group-buying auctions [J]. Electronic Commerce Research and Applications, 9 (3): 249-262.

KAPLAN A M, HAENLEIN, M, 2010. Users of the world, unite! The challenges and opportunities of social media [J]. Business Horizons, 53 (1): 59-68.

KOZINETS R V, DE VALCK K, WOJNICKI A C, et al., 2010. Networked narratives: understanding word-of-mouth marketing in online communities [J]. Journal of Marketing, 74 (2): 71-89.

MORAN E, 2010. Marketing in a hyper-social world: The tribalization of business study and characteristics of successful online communities [J]. Journal of Advertising Research, 50 (3): 232-239.

PERCY W S, VISVANATHAN N, WATSON C, 2010. Relationship marketing: Strategic and tactical challenges for SMEs [J]. African Journal of Business Management, 4 (13): 2596-2603.

PARMENTER D, 2010. Key performance indicators (KPI): developing, implementing, and using winning KPI's [M]. Hoboken, NJ: John Wiley & Sons Inc.

PREZ-MONTORO GUTIRREZ M, 2010. Arquitectura de la Información en entornos web [M]. Gijón: Trea.

WALKER K, 2010. A systematic review of the corporate reputation literature: definition, measurement, and theory [J]. Corporate Reputation Review, 12 (4): 357-387.

LEEDY P, ORMROD J, 2001. Practical research: Planning and design [M]. 7th ed. Upper Saddle River, NJ: Merrill Prentice Hall.

SPENCER D, 2010. A practical guide to information architecture [M]. Penarth: Five Simple Steps.

SUGIYAMA K, ANDREE T, 2011. The Dentsu Way: Secrets of Cross Switch Marketing from the World's Most Innovative Advertising Agency [M]. McGraw-Hill Education: 77-79.

JING X, XIE J, 2011. Group buying: a new mechanism for selling through social interactions [J]. Management Science, 57 (8): 1354-1372.

YU L L, ASUR S, HUBERMAN B A, 2011. What trends in chinese social media [EB/OL]. https://papers.ssrn.com/sol3/papers.cfm? abstract_id=1888779, 07-19.

KIETZMANN J H, HERMKENS K, MCCARTHY I P, et al., 2011. Social media? get serious! understanding the functional building blocks of social media [J]. Business Horizons, 54 (3): 241-251.

GUPTA N, 2011. Forecast: social media revenue, worldwide, 2010-2015 [R]. Stamford: Gartner.

HANNA R, ROHM A, CRITTENDEN V L, 2011. We're all connected: the power of the social media ecosystem [J]. Bus Horiz, 54 (3): 265-273.

CNNIC, 2011. The 27th statistical report on internet development in China [R]. Beijing: China Internet Network Information Center.

CNNIC, 2011. The 28th statistical report on internet development in China [R]. Beijing: China Internet Network Information Center.

CHU S J, KIM Y, 2011. Determinants of consumer engagement in electronic word-of-mouth (eWOM) in social networking sites [J]. International Journal of Advertising, 30 (1): 47-75.

ASUR S, HUBERMAN B A, SZABO G, et al., 2011. Trends in social media: Persistence and decay [R]. Barcelona: the Fifth International AAAI Conference on Weblogs and Social Media: 434-437.

BARRATT M, CHOI T Y, LI M, 2011. Qualitative case studies in operations management: Trends, research outcomes, and future research implications [J]. Journal of Operations Management, 29 (4): 329-342.

CIC (CHINA INVESTMENT CORPORATION), 2011. From social media to social business, topic 1: an overview of the evolution of Chinese social media [EB/OL]. [2014-03-25]. https://www.slideshare.net/CIC_China/from-social-media-to-social-business-topic-1.

SAWANG S, 2011. Performance indicators for innovation implementation: perception vs. actual usage [J]. Asia Pacific Management Review, 16 (1): 23-29.

LANGE D, LEE P M, DAI Y, 2011. Organizational reputation: a review [J]. Journal of Management, 37 (1): 153-184.

CNNIC, 2012. The 29th statistical report on internet development in China [R]. Beijing: China Internet Network Information Center.

CNNIC, 2012. The 30th statistical report on internet development in China [R].

Beijing: China Internet Network Information Center.

KAPLAN A M, 2012. If you love something, let it go mobile: mobile marketing and mobile social media 4x4 [J]. Business Horizons, 55 (2): 129-139.

WALSH G, BARTIKOWSKI B, BEATTY S E, 2012. Impact of customer-based corporate reputation on non monetary and monetary outcomes [J]. British Journal of Management, 25 (2): 166-185.

COHEN A, DUCHAN, G, 2012. The usage characteristics of Twitter in the learning process [J]. Interdisciplinary Journal of E-Learning and Learning Objects (8): 149-163.

YU L L, ASUR S, HUBERMAN B A, 2012. Artificial inflation: the true story of trends in sina weibo [R]. Ithaca: arXiv preprint.

CHIU C, LIN D, SILVERMAN A, 2012. China's social-media boom [EB/OL]. https://s3-ap-northeast-1.amazonaws.com/mckinseychinavideos/PDF/McKinsey-Chinas-Social-Media-Boom1.pdf.

SULLIVAN J, 2012. A tale of two microblogs in China Media [J]. Culture & Society, 34 (6): 773-783.

SHEN J, 2012. Xiaomi, China's Apple success story? [EB/OL]. http://www.chinadaily.com.cn/business/2012-06/07/content_16064278.htm, 06-07.

SCHREIER M, 2012. Qualitative content analysis in practice [M]. Thousand Oaks, CA: Sage.

SCHULTZ H, BLOCK M P, SCHULTZ D E, 2013. Understanding China's digital generation: a marketer's guide to understanding young Chinese consumers [M]. Sacramento: Prosper Publishing: 101-124.

MISHRA O, 2013. Social media measurement KPI's for your brand [EB/OL]. https://www.slideshare.net/csharpdflat/social-media-measurement-kpis, 06-13.

LIU D H, CHEN S L, 2013. Advertising communication: new rules from the AIDMA, AISAS to ISMAS [J]. Advertisinc Panorama (4): 3.

MA L, 2013. Electronic word-of-mouth on microblogs: a cross-cultural content analysis of Twitter and Weibo [J]. Intercultural Communication Studies XXII (3): 18-42.

CHEN C P, 2013. Exploring personal branding on YouTube [J]. Journal of Internet Commerce (12): 332-347.

CVIJIKJ I P, SPIEGLER E D, MICHAHELLES F, 2013. Evaluation framework for social media brand presence [J]. Social Network Analysis and Mining, 3 (4):

1325-1349.

CHOW, LOW-LAI, 2013. How brands can use Sina Weibo to reach Chinese consumers. Warc. Event reports. Festival of media Asia, March [EB/OL]. http://goo.gl/Cn531E, 03-25.

DINK IN FORRESTER, 2013. Chinese enterprises face 4 challenges in social media marketing (in Chinese) [EB/OL]. http://www199it.com/archives/169264.html, 03-25.

CNNIC, 2013. The 31st statistical report on internet development in China [R]. Beijing: China Internet Network Information Center.

CNNIC, 2013. The 32nd statistical report on internet development in China [R]. Beijing: China Internet Network Information Center.

ZIGOR A, 2013. Occidente copia a China (occident copy China) [EB/OL]. http://tecnologia. elpais. com/tecnologia/2013/03/01/actualidad/1362160234_435886. html, 03-01.

CHEN Y D, 2013. Microblog marketing for business [M]. Beijing: China Machine Press.

EMARKETER, 2013. Which social networks are growing fastest worldwide? [EB/OL]. https://www. emarketer. com/Article/Which-Social-Networks-Growing-Fastest-Worldwide/1009884, 05-13.

STELZNER M A, 2013. 2013 Social media marketing industry report: how marketers are using social media to grow their businesses. Social Media Examiner [EB/OL]. http://www. socialmediaexaminer. com/SocialMediaMarketingIndustryReport2013.pdf, 06-15.

TSAI T, YANG P, WANG W, 2013. Pilot study toward realizing social effect in O2O commerce services [R]. Kyoto: 5th International Conference on Social Informatics.

WANG J, YANG Y, 2013. Blue book of social mentality: annual report on social mentality of China (2012-2013) [M]. China: Social Sciences Academic Press.

PODOBNIK V, 2013. An analysis of Facebook social media marketing key performance indicators: the case of premier league brands [R]. Zagreb: The 12th International Conference on Telecommunications, Pripuzic, Kresimir: 131-138.

XU T, 2014. Social, digital & mobile in China 2014 [EB/OL]. https://wearesocial.com/us/blog/2014/04/social-digital-mobile-china-2014/, 06-15.

LIEN C H, CAO Y, 2014. Examining WeChat users' motivations, trust, attitudes, and positive word-of-mouth: evidence from China [J]. Computers in Human Behavior (41): 104-111.

LIM J, 2014. A model of functional rules for social media in the networked news sphere [J]. Asian Journal of Communication, 24 (3): 279-294.

EU SME CENTRE, 2014. Report: online education market in China [EB/OL]. https://www.ccilc.pt/sites/default/files/eu_sme_centre_report_-_online_education_market_in_china_jul_2014.pdf, 01-15.

FERNANDEZ-PLANELLS A, FIGUERAS-MAZ M, P MPOLS C F, 2014. Communication among young people in the Spanish revolution [J]. New Media & Society, 16 (8): 1287-1308.

CNNIC, 2014. The 33rd statistical report on internet development in China [R]. Beijing: China Internet Network Information Center.

CNNIC, 2014. The 34th statistical report on internet development in China [R]. Beijing: China Internet Network Information Center.

CNNIC, 2014. The report on internet development in rural China in 2013 [R]. Beijing: China Internet Network Information Center.

CNNIC, 2014. Chinese social media users' behavior research report in 2014 [R]. Beijing: China Internet Network Information Center.

DU Y, TANG Y, 2014. Study on the development of O2O E-commerce platform of china from the perspective of offline service quality [J]. International Journal of Business and Social Science, 5 (4): 308-312.

BASKARADA S, 2014. Qualitative case study guidelines [J]. The Qualitative Report, 19 (40): 1-18.

ZHENG Z L, ZHANG Q P, WANG B, 2014. Research on model of online knowledge sharing for CoPS R&D team based on WeChat platform [R]. Singapore: International Conference on Management Science and Engineering: 891-897.

WANG Y C, XU L, LIU J Z, et al., 2014. Microblog marketing: a case study at Sina Weibo [R]. Singapore: International Conference on Management Science and Engineering: 501-506.

LEE E, 2014. 2013 China's group-buying turnover rockets 67.7% YOY to 35.88 billion yuan [EB/OL]. http://technode.com/2014/01/15/2013-group-buying-turnover-rockets-68-percent-yoy-in-china/, 01-15.

RUZZENE A, 2014. Using case studies in the social sciences: methods, inferences, purposes [D]. Rotterdam: Erasmus University Rotterdam.

SULLIVAN J, 2014. China's Weibo: is faster different? [J]. New media & society, 16 (1): 24-37.

XIA X, ZHU J, 2014. The Study of O2O Business Model Development Strategy in SMEs [J]. International Journal of Business and Social Science, 5 (9): 1.

MATHEW C, 2014. Introducing key performance indicators: perspective of higher education performance monitoring and evaluation in Nigeria [J]. Journal of Education and Practice, 5 (29): 130-135.

MIN T, 2014. Research on Wechat marketing strategy of enterprises which is based on the SICAS model [J]. International Journal of Business and Social Science, 5 (61): 213-217.

MOORE R L, 2014. Information architecture for social media: a case study on building an event backchannel with Twitter [J]. Journal of Social Media and Interactive Learning Environments, 2 (1): 21-36.

YAZAN B, 2015. Three approaches to case study methods in education: Yin, Merriam, and Stake [J]. The Qualitative Report, 20 (2): 134-152.

ZHANG P, 2015. Research on strategy of model innovation of WeChat marketing [R]. Chongqing: Joint International Mechanical, Electronic and Information Technology Conference (JIMET 2015): 474-477.

ZHANG Z, LI B, ZHAO W, et al., 2015. A study on the retweeting behaviour of marketing microblogs with high retweets in Sina Weibo [R]. Yangzhou: 2015 Third International Conference on Advanced Cloud and Big Data: 20-27.

CAYLOR B, 2015. Social media KPIs: your key performance indicators for success [EB/OL]. http://www.caylor-solutions.com/25-social-media-kpis/, 07-01.

DU Z, 2015. Research into factors affecting the attitudes of university students towards WeChat marketing based on AISAS mode [R]. DeKalb: IEEE International Conference on Electro Information Technology: 66-69.

GUILLET B D, KUCUKUSTA D, LIU L, 2015. An examination of social media marketing in China: how do the top 133 hotel brands perform on the four Chinese social media sites? [J]. Journal of Travel & Tourism Marketing, 33 (6): 783-805.

CNNIC, 2015. The 35th statistical report on internet development in China [R]. Beijing: China Internet Network Information Center.

CNNIC, 2015. The 36th statistical report on internet development in China [R]. Beijing: China Internet Network Information Center.